Ulla Kriebernegg, Roberta Maierhofe
Alive and Kicking at All Ages

The series **Aging Studies** is edited by Heike Hartung, Ulla Kriebernegg and Roberta Maierhofer.

ULLA KRIEBERNEGG, ROBERTA MAIERHOFER,
BARBARA RATZENBÖCK (EDS.)

Alive and Kicking at All Ages

Cultural Constructions of Health and Life Course Identity

[transcript]

The printing of this book was supported by the University of Graz.

Bibliographic Information published by the Deutsche Nationalbibliothek
The Deutsche Nationalbibliothek lists this publication in the Deutsche Natio-
nalbibliografie; detailed bibliographic data are available in the Internet at
http://dnb.d-nb.de

Cover concept: Kordula Röckenhaus, Bielefeld
Cover illustration: © Alex Rotas, www.alexrotasphotography.com
Typeset by Mark-Sebastian Schneider, Bielefeld
Printed by Majuskel Medienproduktion GmbH, Wetzlar
ISBN 978-3-8376-2582-0
PDF-ISBN 978-3-8394-2582-4

Content

Re-Thinking Material Realities and Cultural Representations of Age and Aging

Ulla Kriebernegg, Roberta Maierhofer, Barbara Ratzenböck

This issue of the *Aging Studies* series is devoted to the aspect of health, life expectancy, and life course identity. The title "Alive and Kicking at All Ages" might be read ambivalently, on the one hand as a forceful and self-confident assertion of strength, endurance, and energy at all ages of life, or on the other, as a mocking reinforcement of the stereotypical notion that it might be ludicrous to link old age to vitality, health, and well-being. Although – as gerontologists have pointed out time and again – illness and death cannot be linked to a specific age and living a long(er) life does not necessarily mean that these added years are determined by sickness and suffering, preconceived notions very often equate health with youth. In addition, one of the predominant discourses in the field of scientific anti-aging studies is the notion that old age itself is a disease that can be cured. Biomedical enhancement of the human lifespan, for example, has led to heated debates on what in essence it means to be human, and invites questions regarding the ethical and moral aspects of biogerontological research.

Susan Sontag makes the point that illness is *not* a metaphor and argues that "the most truthful way of regarding illness – and the healthiest way of being ill – is one most purified of, and resistant to, metaphoric thinking" (3). She admits, however, that this is not an easy task, as the way we perceive illness as metaphor is so pervasive and influential. She wants to describe "not what it is really like to emigrate to the kingdom of the ill and live there, but the punitive or sentimental fantasies concocted about that situation: not real geography, but stereotypes of national character" (3). Sontag talks about "rhetorical ownership" (181) regarding illness, and how this is "possessed, assimilated in argument and in cliché" (181-82), which determine both individual experience as well as social policy. We are sometimes seduced in accepting the detachment from meanings, as these metaphors seem "particularly liberating, even consoling" (182). Illness used as a figure or metaphor – similar to age – needs to be deconstructed. Sontag understands this well when she states, "But the metaphors cannot be distanced just by abstaining from them. They have to be exposed, criticized, belabored, used up" (182).

This is exactly what the authors of the *Aging Studies* series do. As the contributions to this volume prove, Sontag's challenge has been accepted, and the notions of health and age are discussed in terms of the literal and the metaphoric, the personal and the public, the human and the environmental. Analyzing the interplay of age and health leads to a re-evaluation of established concepts of young and old, healthy and ill in historical and disciplinary contexts. In this volume, papers analyze the cultural ambiguities of social functions both of material realities as well as cultural representations from an interdisciplinary vantage point.

Focusing on the interplay between continuity and change, presence and absence of physical and mental well-being are discussed as part of life course identities and with respect to how our notions of agency are influenced by our understanding of health and illness within a subversive deconstruction of normative age concepts. The authors of this volume offer suggestions on how negative images of old age as physical decrepitude and disease can be deconstructed by presenting interpretations of material realities and cultural representations that manage to challenge both structures and narratives of what it means to grow and be old. Thus, depictions of appreciation of life even in the oldest age as forms of "successful frailty" are being reclaimed both by the authors of this volume as well as by us reading these texts.

This volume came out of the biennial conference of the *European Association of American Studies* (EAAS) in Izmir/Turkey in the spring of 2012. The conference took place under the motto of Thomas Jefferson, who wrote in a letter to John Garland Jefferson on June 11, 1790, "Leave all the afternoon for exercise and recreation, which are as necessary as reading. I will rather say more necessary because health is worth more than learning" (EAAS). US-Americanists from different disciplines engaged in discussions on illness and health, and asked fundamental questions about the state of the nation, its history and ideology. In the context of the theme of the conference, "The Health of the Nation," health was discussed as characteristic of Americans, quoting Emerson's dictum, "the first wealth is health" (EAAS). As a founding member of the *European Network in Aging Studies*, the *Center for Inter-American Studies* (C.IAS) of the University of Graz suggested two workshops with overwhelming resonance, so that for both workshops, "The Ages of Life: Health, Life Expectancy, and the Ambiguities of Living and Aging" (Maierhofer) and "Illness and its Metaphors: Challenging Medical Discourse from a Gendered Perspective" (Domínguez Rué/Kriebernegg) two panels each were offered. Many of the participants of these workshops later submitted papers for this volume.

In March 2011, at the conference "Aging, Old Age, Memory, Aesthetics" of the University of Toronto, the *European Network in Aging Studies* was presented and an invitation was issued to attend the inaugural ENAS conference to be held in October of that year at the University of Maastricht/Netherlands, and born out of enthusiasm and the already established need for more structural collaboration the *North American Network in Aging Studies* (NANAS) was in course established. The collaborative ties were intensified, and academic collaboration is now taking place on many levels. Examples are international teaching collaborations with Stephen Katz and Leni Marshall at the summer school of the *Center for Inter-American Studies* on the topic of "Collective Identities" at Seggau Castle in the Austrian wine country in the summer of 2013, participation in grant proposals both submitted in the US and Canada as well as to various European funding institutions, and ENAS members joining the meeting of NANAS at the idyllic campus of Hiram College in Ohio. When in October 2013, the *Center for Inter-American Studies* of the University of Graz hosted Margaret Cruikshank as a Fulbright Professor and Ros Jennings, director of the Women, Ageing and Media Research Centre (WAM) and Head of the Postgraduate Research Centre (PRC) of the University of Gloucestershire, as a guest lecturer, the network in Age/Aging Studies did in no way feel virtual anymore. True to Peg Cruikshank's statement in her pivotal book *Learning to Be Old*, where she attempts "to bring together matters usually treated separately" (x), these meeting places and collaborative opportunities have provided exactly such converging of different approaches, theoretical backgrounds, and individual interests. While discussing Cruikshank's theses concerning social myths and fears about aging, sickness, and social roles during her Fulbright stay at the University of Graz, for students as well as colleagues the practical aspects of aging merged with theoretical concerns shared. This transatlantic cooperation of critical and cultural gerontologists, Age/Aging Studies scholars, and practitioners in the field aims at shaping not only academic discourse on age and aging but also political decision making.

When the European Commission declared 2012 the *European Year for Active Ageing and Solidarity between Generations* in order to raise awareness of the contribution that older people make to society, to encourage policymakers and relevant stakeholders at all levels to take action with the aim of creating better opportunities for active aging and strengthening solidarity between generations, health was one of the most important aspects mentioned in the policy papers. Employment, participation in society, and independent living were the touchstones of the goals defined by this campaign that declared active aging as a means of empowerment in order to remain in charge of our own lives as long as possible:

Worried about growing older? About your place in society when you're 60, 70 or 80? There is a lot to life after 60 – and society is coming increasingly to appreciate the contribution older people can make. That's what active aging is about – getting more out of life as you grow older, not less, whether at work, at home or in the community. And this can help not just you as an individual but society as a whole. (Europa.eu)

Fig. 1: "Meeting of the Like-Minded." Gertrud Simon, Barbara Ratzenböck, Roberta Maierhofer, Heidrun Mörtl, Peg Cruikshank, Ros Jennings, Ulla Kriebernegg at the University of Graz (Austria), October 15, 2013.

Good will and the well-meaning intentions of this campaign were underscored by the narrow definition of age as "active," thus limiting and reducing the aspect of health and well-being in terms of preconceived notions of activity. Images posted on the website supported this interpretation as old people were presented in physical mobility ignoring mental and cognitive agility. The need for interdisciplinary cooperation and activism in the political sphere becomes evident when looking at such campaigns and strategies. In order to truly achieve the aims drafted on a political level, we as scholars in the field of Age/Aging Studies believe that more research is necessary in terms of the cultural construction of age and aging. This volume intends to take the notion of positive and active aging a step further by deconstructing the aspect of health and illness in terms of life expectancy and life-course identity. It is divided into two sections: Contributions discussing material realities in terms of social, political, and cultural structures, and those dealing with representations of age and aging in terms of cultural expressions.

MATERIAL REALITIES

In her article, "Ageility Studies: The Interplay of Critical Approaches in Age Studies and Disability Studies," Leni Marshall explores the many productive intersections of Disability and Age Studies. The multiple social and emotional dimensions of aging and of disability create instructive contrasts, such as the contradictions of perceived visibility and political power or the connotations and consequences of attempted "rehabilitation." Marshall convincingly argues that conscious aging as an activist response is aging with an awareness of Age Studies and with an understanding of individual identity as adaptable, capable of remaining intact even as it changes. Conscious ageility as a new form of awareness can be achieved by combining the two fields' critical understanding of the body, both in terms of theories and praxis.

Claiming identity over the life course is Beverly Lunsford's thrust in her article "I May be Old and Sick, But I Am Still a Person." The potential bias by the general public as well as attitudes of healthcare professionals toward aging can affect healthcare provided for older adults. The *Center for Aging, Health and Humanities* established at George Washington University in 1995 addresses stereotypes of age and aging by conducting research on the creative potential of older adulthood. In 2009, a curriculum with a more person-centered approach to care of the older adult was developed in order to minimize biases toward aging. This approach encourages individualized care rather than the tendency to provide a "one size fits all" type of healthcare. Lunsford presents this person-centered approach as a means of providing safe and effective care for older adults with chronic illnesses, while supporting and respecting their quality of life. To achieve person-centered care, the humanities and creative arts are facilitators as a meaningful way to gain perspective of the older adult as a person with potential, rather than a healthcare problem to solve.

In the contribution "Health and Everyday Bodily Experiences of Old Mexican Women," Meiko Makita explores the ways in which a group of women (60-89 years of age) experience physical aspects of aging and old age. By exploring women's narratives of health, Makita focuses on embodied age and the women's tendency of equating "feeling good" with being healthy. These women experience their bodies as vulnerable to disease, distress and dysfunction, and objectify their bodies as outside of their control. As health is something owned, it is the mind that becomes the site for personal agency in terms of experience.

By focusing on the dynamics of individual differences of experiencing the speed of time passing, Elena Bendien discusses temporality as both existential as well as personal. In her article "Kwik-fit versus Varying Speeds of Aging," particular speed frames, especially in institutional care, are analyzed in terms of personal aspects of experiencing time.

In his contribution "Preemptive Biographies: Life and the Life Course in the Age of Security Administration," Rüdiger Kunow discusses recent developments in biotechnology. Neoliberal governance – so Kunow – has, especially in the United States, fundamentally changed the understanding of human life and the life course. Aging and old age are now the ultimate frontier of preemptive thinking and offer fulfillment of the ancient dream of eternal youth, if not eternal life. Biotechnical interventions increase pressure to ameliorate or altogether avoid old age. Aging and old age have for the longest part of human history been understood as fate; preemptive thinking is now turning this into a matter of choice.

Julian Wangler's article "Internalization or Social Comparison? An Empirical Investigation of the Influence of Media (Re)Presentations of Age on the Subjective Health Perception and Age Experience of Older People," focuses on media representation in the Federal Republic of Germany. Although the concept of "activating" older people by presenting positive images and avoiding negative portrayals of old age is at the heart of most political initiatives, little empirical research has so far been undertaken to establish the effect of such media campaigns on successful health communication. The question whether and to what extent media (re)presentations of the elderly can influence subjective health perception and age experience is unexpectedly answered, as the images do not have the effect intended.

At the end of this section, Elisabeth Boulot discusses the consequences of ageist positions in terms of employment and provides legal insights into job related age discrimination. In her article "Combating Age Discrimination in the Workplace. A Study of the United States' Rights-Based Response," Boulot examines whether the Age Discrimination in Employment Act passed by the Johnson administration in 1967 has managed to achieve higher employment of older workers. Boulot presents an overview of the history of ADEA, and suggests possible explanations why workers still face similar discriminatory practices despite the established legislation. By comparing the US to other discrimination legislations, Boulot raises the question whether discrimination in the work-force can be fought by a rights-based response, or whether other measures might be necessary.

CULTURAL REPRESENTATIONS

The paper "'There's a reason we're here': Performative autobiographics and age identity in performer-created intergenerational theater" co-authored by Sally Chivers, David Barnet, Jacquie Eales, and Janet Fast offers a textual analysis of archival materials of the intergenerational theater company, GeriActors & Friends (GF). Examining materials from the first decade of the theater company in relation to interviews with members of the theater company, this contribution shows how a "library of experience" can be made public in a culture determined to see older adults as physically problematic, if they are noticed at all. The article convincingly argues that progression from reflecting common experiences to a more deliberate practice of collective and collaborative auto-biography offers insight into the role of age identity in contemporary theater practice, and the potential for overtly intergenerational collaboration to result in the telling of new stories of growing old in a graying world, stories that challenge images of aging as tied only to physical decrepitude and disease, without ignoring that health is a key part of aging.

Ricca Edmondson and Eileen Fairhurst examine in their article "Images of Living and Aging: Counter-Cultural Constructions of Health and Wisdom" two calendars intended for daily use that feature older people, their activities, and how they should be seen. These calendars – one from the UK, one from Ireland – are specifically intended to impact on public perceptions of older people; in different ways, they offer creative subversions of everyday expectations about the life course and what it has to offer. Using dynamic interplays of words and images, they urge counter-cultural ways of imagining the activity, health and also the wisdom of older people. These modes of imagining accentuate pro-ductive, mutual, social and intergenerational relationships and take different forms in their different cultural contexts.

Sherryl Wilson's essay "She's Been Away: Aging, Madness and Memory" explores the ways in which television drama is able to mount a challenge to the dominate discourse that positions aging as decline and mental decrepitude. Rather, old age and madness are used as a means to mount a feminist social critique. The case study is She's Been Away, a TV drama written by Stephen Poliakoff and broadcast in the UK on BBC 1 in 1989, and centers on an elderly woman discharged from the psychiatric hospital in which she has been living for 60 years. The article argues that it is the combination of Lillian's age and her intergenerational relation with her niece-in-law that subvert the well-worn tropes and reconfigures aging as wisdom able to produce a new sense of empow-erment; the confluence of madness, old age and memory disrupts expectations and punctures the consciousness. As such, She's Been Away is both a celebration of the unruly older woman, a critique of the cultural construction of madness, and a meditation on the power of memory to produce counter-discourse.

In her article "Illness and Love in Old Age in Jonathan Franzen's The Cor-rections and Elizabeth Strout's Olive Kitteridge" Anne-Meike Dackweiler chal-lenges preconceived notions of romantic love as belonging to the young. By analyzing the nexus of romantic love, old age, and illness as paradigmatic for contemporary Anglo-American literature, Dackweiler suggests that the binary opposition of the despised sexual and respectable but asexual old is being re-placed by positive individual attitudes of the 'frail old' towards love, despite or precisely because of their illnesses.

Amelia DeFalco's essay "Uncanny Witnessing: Dementia, Narrative, and Identity in Fiction by Munro and Franzen" considers the repercussions of dementia for narrative-based models of identity. In particular, the essay examines fiction by Alice Munro and Jonathan Franzen that depicts dementia as eroding subjectivity and narrative, at the same time prompting fleeting insights into otherness that awaken caregivers to their own difference. These fictional narratives suggest that dementia may complicate assumptions about identity and selfhood, shifting attention from discrete selves to collaborative relationships. As Munro's stories, "The Bear Came Over the Mountain" and "Spelling," along with Franzen's novel, *The Corrections*, suggest, dementia's transformation of communication and identity tests human structures of meaning and being, revealing both the limits of understanding, and what lies beyond.

In her article "Shaking off Shackles: LTC Freedom in 'The Bear Came Over the Mountain' and *The Other Sister*," Patricia Life explores two Canadian texts where the protagonists' lives are interpreted to have improved after admission to long-term care institutions. Both texts counter the 20th-century narrative of the nursing home-as-horror, and instead offer new narratives of home-as-haven and aging-as-opportunity, thus contesting the aging-as-decline narrative. Selective forgetting, remembering, and refocusing facilitated by living in a new environment allow the protagonists to live to greater advantage.

Ellen Matlok-Ziemann argues in her contribution to this volume, "'Old women that will not be kept away': Undermining Ageist Discourse with Invisibility and Performance" that both William Faulkner's *Intruder in the Dust* and Eudora Welty's *The Purple Hat* offer valuable insights into how characters despite and because of their marginalization are empowered to resist ageist discourses.

Drawing on Michel Foucault, the article "Scrutinizing the 'medical glance': Bodily Decay, Disease and Death in Margaret Atwood's *The Edible Woman*," Marta Cerezo Moreno discusses Margaret Atwood's first novel as revolving around a two-level structure of surface and depth, visibility, and invisibility. The main protagonist's dream-like vision of her own bodily dissolution stands as the first of a series of recurrent images developed by the text as regards bodily decay, decomposition, disease, and death. Marian's body turns into a tangible and decomposing space subjected to a patriarchal medical glance in order to control and dominate her subjectivity.

Maricel Oró-Piqueras argues in her article with the title "Wisdom versus Frailty in Ursula Le Guin's *Voices* and Doris Lessing's 'The Reason for It'" that by managing and modeling our external appearance a body is perceived as vigorous and productive, whereas signs of aging are interpreted as signs of frailty and illness. Ursula Le Guin's novel *Voices* (2006) and Doris Lessing's short story "The Reason for It" (2003) present futuristic societies in which vigor and youth are predominant.

The final article of this volume "From Cane to Chair: Old Age and Story-telling in Juvenile Literature by Hawthorne, Goodrich, and Mogridge" by Eriko Ogihara-Schuck examines 19th century juvenile literary works by Nathaniel Hawthorne, Samuel G. Goodrich, and George Mogridge as providing a complex view of aging. Attention is particularly paid to the representations of the elderly narrators who accept aging as an ambiguous process and offer the possibility of successful frailty.

The wide scope of the articles presented in the fifth volume of the publication series of the *European Network in Aging Studies* (ENAS) is product and mission at the same time. It is only a starting point for investigation into the deconstruction of our understanding of normative human behavior. Once we stop talking about universal concepts of shaping our life courses, we will be able to overcome preconceived notions of what it means to be and grow old.

Fig. 2: "Moving ENAS Forward." Experts' Meeting at the University of Lleida (Spain), April 8-10, 2013.

REFERENCES

Cruikshank, Margaret. *Learning to Be Old.* 3rd ed. Lanham: Rowman & Little-field, 2013. Print.

European Association of American Studies (EAAS). *Conference Announcement Izmir 2012.* Web. 29 Oct. 2013.

Europa.eu. *European Year for Active Ageing and Solidarity between Generations.* About the Year. 9 Apr. 2013. Web. 29 Oct. 2013.

Sontag, Susan. *Illness as Metaphor and AIDS and Its Metaphors.* New York: Picador, 1990. Print.

Material Realities

Ageility Studies

The Interplay of Critical Approaches in Age Studies and Disability Studies

Leni Marshall

> "Society is no readier to accept crippledness than to accept death, war, sex, sweat, or wrinkles."
> ~ Nancy Mairs

Disability studies scholars consider how disability is enacted, defined, and represented; age studies scholars similarly consider age, aging, and old age. Interestingly, perhaps ironically, neither disability nor old age are ailments, per se, yet both fall under the rubric of "health" and, even when a disability is permanent, both tend to be viewed by the medical profession as conditions in need of curative remedies. Both categories also evolve over an extended stretch of time, yet each is highly likely to be rejected as a significant factor impacting one's identity.[1] In many respects, these two fields have much in common, yet there has been a dearth of critical material linking the scholarship of these two fields. Appreciating the productive advances that stem from cross-disciplinary exchange, this essay first considers arenas of overlap and divergence between disability studies and age studies, then focuses on the issue of visibility, offers a critical exploration of "rehabilitation," and finally advances a consideration of conscious ageility.

OVERLAP AND DIVERGENCE

The current lack of connection between age studies and disability studies has logical roots. When asked what old people are like, the majority of respondents

---

1 | According to Tobin Siebers, "'identity' stands for the means by which an individual 'comes to join a particular social body'" (cited in Cassuto 220).

connect aging and old age with disability and death (Barrett and Cantwell; Blunk and Williams; Gutheil, Chernesky, and Sherratt; Joyner and DeHope; Lamb, "20"; Palmore, "Three" 89). Because of these stereotypes, focusing attention on other aspects of aging-into-old-age has been critical to the development of age studies as an emerging field (Cruikshank). People hold so many negative ideas about what it means to be old that it is little wonder that disability studies scholars' knowledge of and willingness to engage with age studies has been so limited. Only a small number of researchers in either field have had enough of a deep understanding of critical analyses in both subjects to responsibly connect the two (e.g., Stone). Attempts to disentangle assumptions about senescence, mental and physical ability, illness, and death, so that people understand that disability does not equal old age and that old age does not equal disability, can be an uphill battle.

Nonetheless, each of the fields has developed analytic structures that can be useful in the other. While humanities-based age studies scholars often theorize about concepts that are not yet quantifiable with the assessment tools currently available in social and medical sciences, disability studies has been able to offer critical analyses that integrate concepts from the humanities and social sciences more thoroughly. For instance, age studies scholarship has provided critical responses to the conflation of agedness and disability (e.g., Marshall, "Changing"). Age studies has plenty to learn in return, as Sally Chivers explains: "[T]here is no need to chart a new way of thinking about aging as experienced in relation to social and cultural environments because disability studies already clearly, cogently, and consistently articulates that way of thinking" (22). She and other scholars, such as Michael Bérubé, Lennard Davis, Jane Gallop, Rüdiger Kunow, Erin Gentry Lamb, Sharon-Dale Stone, and Kathleen Woodward, are working to close the distance between disability studies and age studies.

Already, the two fields contain a notable amount of overlap. For example, age studies scholars reading Harilyn Rousso's memoir, *Don't Call Me Inspirational: A Disabled Feminist Talks Back*, will find a significant number of direct parallels in the experiences of people whose bodies are Othered by old age and those Othered by disability: the phenomenon of the stranger in one's mirror image; the separation of the self from the body, which leads to addressing the body as a separate entity from the self; even the pressure to use products such as Botox to make the body (in Rousso's case, her vocal cords) more normative. The bodily experiences of disability and of aging-into-old-age have more than enough in common for age studies' and disability studies' theories and praxis each to help the other advance.

Aging happens to each person at the same rate and is a daily, ongoing process. For some, that ongoing process happens in concert with the individual's embodied knowledge of disability. People with disabilities say that "a disabled person ages quicker than an able bodied" (Zarb and Oliver 32),[2] equating negative feelings about having a disability, especially one likely to increase over time, with agedness. Conversely, elders' prejudice against disability lead to euphemisms that emphasize a distance between the self and the disability, as well as a reluctance to use assistive devices such as wheelchairs, walkers, and hearing aids, because the stigma of being thought of as *old-enough-to-be-disabled* or just being thought of as *disabled* trump the use and safety value of those devices (Sheets 38).

As old age and disability converge in a body over time, it becomes more and more difficult to differentiate between the two. When an 80-year-old receives an artificial knee, is that person being treated for old age, because cartilage has a finite lifetime that can be shorter than the human lifespan, or is that person being treated for disability, because without a knee replacement the person would be wheelchair-bound? What if the person in question was twenty-something and had worn out knees because of a work-related responsibility or because of a sport such as long-distance cycling? This conflation of old age and disability is a large part of what has kept scholars in each of those venues from seeing the union of these areas of study as highly productive, despite the fertile ground in overlap between the two.

For aged and/or disabled human bodies, no matter how much physical therapy, medication, and effort go into it, the body will not – cannot – return to youth or non-disability. The inability to turn back time becomes a common ground for aged and disabled bodies and the ideas surrounding them. Perhaps this is the basis by which people with disabilities mark their bodies as aging more quickly: their bodies are temporally beyond a cultural norm. In this formulation, Otherness is coded as *aged-ness*. Conversely, elders may try to maintain their connection to the cultural norm of able-bodied-ness in an effort to stave off the Otherness that they code as *disability*. In discussions about "successful aging," one of the signs of so-called success is that a person is visibly old without also being visibly disabled (Chivers 21).[3] As Judith Butler suggests of lesbian bodies, aged/disabled bodies similarly lose "cultural legitimacy and, hence, [are] cast, not outside or prior to culture, but outside cultural *legitimacy*, still within culture, but culturally 'out-lawed'" (Butler 87). The disabled/aged body becomes the Other. Clearly, there is plenty of reason that aged subjects resist the added "illegitimacy" of disability, that a person with a disability would reject the extra layer of Otherness that accompanies the label of *old*, and that

---

2 | See also Sheets 38, for a discussion of the physical "premature aging" associated with disability.

3 | The concept of successful aging has been widely critiqued in age studies and beyond (e.g., Calasanti and Slevin; Cruikshank; Gullette; Katz; Stone 62; Woodward).

anyone who could pass as belonging in neither category would decide to do so.[4] In this cultural context, rejecting disability and agedness as aspects of identity is logical.

People's resistance to accepting the labels of *old*, *disabled*, or both makes sense in considerations of social standing, but the logic is flawed in its disconnection from a reality that many people share: the so-called "disability paradox." People with disabilities, on average, consistently report higher levels of quality of life than temporarily-able bodied people (Albrecht and Devlieger, "Disability Paradox"[5]); there is a corresponding rise in elders' versus younger people's quality-of-life self-reports (Carstensen; Hetherington). This phenomenon – a seemingly-logical, sometimes almost visceral resistance to accepting a change in identity *that often leads to a higher level of self-reported quality of life* – suggests that a branch of additional critical considerations of disability and age is vital for improving understanding of the paradox and to develop people's awareness of the complex situation.[6]

Moreover, although a positive experience is not guaranteed for aging and for disabilities that are acquired after birth or that change over time, those experiences create a *possibility* for learning and emotional development that does not exist for people who are young and/or temporarily able-bodied. Scholars and the general public need a better understanding of the full range of old age's and disabilities' potential effects. Accepting one's status as aged and/or disabled often is likely to have a positive impact on one's satisfaction with life.

VISIBILITY

In both disability studies and age studies, the self-acceptance of the way one's body works and looks has been theorized to be key. In age studies, accepting the aged body

can result in a *clarity* of vision that was missing in the younger self [because . . .] the losses of aging must be accompanied by what a person gains by advancing through

---

4 | Stone argues that elders' age-based marginalization may make accepting disability-based Othering easier. She offers an extended discussion of the connected stigmas of age and disability (63-65).

5 | There were multiple responses to Albrecht and Devlieger's article, including the following: Ameratunga; Atkin; Drum, Horner-Johnson, and Krahn; Jørgensen; Koch (to which Albrecht and Devlieger responded in 2000); and Ubel et al. Also of note is Moller's interesting philosophical positioning of Albrecht and Devlieger's arguments.

6 | Articles by Kielhofner and Marshall ("Through") suggest ways in which disability and age, respectively, can create the potential for psychological growth.

time: new experiences, new ideas, and long-term connections with people and events. Most adults easily could speak about positive changes that children will experience over time. As people age, they say that they know themselves better, are happier with how they shape their lives, and enjoy having more experience from which to draw. (Marshall, "Through" 69, citing Carstensen; emphasis in the original)

Disability studies borrows from queer theory, suggesting that a self-acceptance of one's disability is an extended coming out process, one that involves "taking up an identity in your own eyes and in the eyes of others, [. . . shifting] the discourse from struggle against self to struggle against the disabling society" (Swain and Cameron 74, 77):

Having come out, the disabled person no longer regards disability as a reason for self-disgust, or as something to be denied or hidden, rather as an imposed oppressive social category to be challenged and broken down. The forms this challenge takes are varied. They include direct political action and campaigning for equal opportunities to access education, employment, transport, housing, leisure facilities, and control over personal lives; research on disability issues controlled by disabled people; and the creation of alternative cultural representations of disability through the practice of Disability Arts. (Swain and Cameron 76)

The focus on the individual in the age studies passage versus the connection to collective action in the disability studies quotation is telling.

Despite the abundance of senior communities, regional groups such as the Old Women's Project, online constituencies such as the Older Wiser Lesbians, and political and communication vehicles such as AARP and American Society on Aging, there is not a broadly accepted Elder culture with which people connect, whereas a sizable number of people do identify with disability-focused alliances (e.g., Deaf culture, Crip culture).[7] The existence of an identifiable culture means that people with disabilities can work (have worked) together to exert political influence leading to change. In contrast, seniors' votes have tended

---

7 | Whether there are other disability-focused cultures or just disability communities is a topic still under debate (e.g., Mitchell and Snyder versus Pierce). Also, the presence or absence of a defining culture seems to lead to a broad divergence of responses to the possibility of a cure. For example, contrast Nancy Mairs's sympathy for the task of the doctors who treat her multiple sclerosis ("Doctors [. . .] have trouble dealing with MS patients, whose disease in its intransigence defeats their aims and mocks their skills [. . .] . I may be frustrated, maddened, depressed by the incurability of my disease, but I am not diminished by it, and they are" [20]) with the "[m]embers and proponents of Deaf culture [who] vigorously oppose implants both as a seriously invasive treatment of dubious efficacy and as a threat to Deaf culture" (Tucker).

to align more closely with other identity categories than with age (Rosenbaum). Paradoxically, the *perceived* political power of disabled people is relatively small, while there is a popular (mis)conception that elders vote as a large united bloc. Politicians and pundits alike consider the importance of "the senior vote" (e.g., Campo-Flores) in a country primed to fear the power of the "silver tsunami."[8]

People's willingness or reluctance to identify with a particular group or identity can be closely linked to their beliefs and stereotypes about that group, which is, in turn, linked to that group's social visibility. A critical consideration of the prevalence and attributes of cultural images about disability and aging yields an array of contradictions. The first of the two discussed below demonstrates that people with disabilities have a higher level of social visibility than do people of advanced age. The second of the two employs a different critical lens and the relative positions in the hierarchy get reversed.

Foundational texts in age studies and disability studies suggest diametrically opposed experiences of visibility-based-on-difference. In age studies, the difference of old age leads to invisibility, as these four representative examples demonstrate. One: in the 1980s, aged feminist activists such as Baba Copper, Barbara Macdonald, and Cynthia Rich responded to the condescension and other ageist behaviors they encountered at feminist gatherings and political actions, and the criticism they received as being selfish and "bad mothers" when they spoke up objecting to those incidents. Turning those experiences into critical explorations of Ageism and reflecting feelings of being unseen, Copper published *Over the Hill*, a book with a title suggesting a geographic invisibility; Macdonald and Rich co-authored *Look Me in the Eye*, their title a demand for greater visibility. Two: turning forty, my colleagues have rejoiced at their ability to walk by construction sites without attracting attention; at fifty they tend to fume about times when younger people, oblivious that someone else was present on a sidewalk or in a hallway, have walked into them. Three: feminist Marge Piercy wrote a poem recommending that the government employ old women as spies because nobody sees them. Four: "With the exception of disability studies and work on illness narratives, our implicit and unexamined assumption when we make reference to the body as a category of cultural criticism is that the body is a youthful healthy body," writes cultural theorist Kathleen Woodward, "[i]n academic and artistic circles [. . .] the older female body has been significant only in terms of its absence" ("Performing" 162). Woodward's article then focuses on a few of the stellar, engaged, and thought-provoking exceptions to that otherwise-absent gaze, demonstrating the positive possibilities of critical engagement with images of old age.

---

8 | A recent Google search for "silver tsunami" yielded more than 77,200 results, an EBSCO search 341.

In disability studies, the assumption is that people are staring. For example, when reality television camera crews began tracking every move of the *Push Girls* stars, each of whom uses a wheelchair, the stars reported that the presence of that constant gaze was a relatively minor change. The four women are so used to being watched they have a nickname for the phenomenon, PS, short for "people staring" (McCarthy). Kevin Conneley, an X-Games medalist who was born without legs and who prefers to use a skateboard rather than a wheelchair, reverses the gaze. An avid world traveler, wherever he goes, he photographs the people who stare at him. In their curiosity, he says, they create stories to explain why a skateboarding man with a sporadic birth defect has come to photograph them (Inskeep; Millett). For more than 20 years, Rosemarie Garland-Thomson has theorized and published about disability and disability as spectacle. She considers extended looking – attention – to be a type of social capital, that prolonged, mutual exchanges of gazes can create a "mutually vivifying visual dance" among the starers and the starees (5). The relative invisibility of agedness contrasts dramatically with the hyper-visibility of bodies with disabilities, "people who look or act in ways that contradict our expectations" (6), such as the two female professors whose photo appears in the first chapter of Garland-Thomson's book, women who she calls "practiced starees" (8). One is armless and the other one, who wears shorts, has braces and kneepads on both her legs. "When we do see the usually concealed site of disability writ boldly on others, we stare in fascinated disbelief and uneasy identification" (20). Garland-Thomson's book explores the many ways that a gaze, given or received, may encourage or stymie communication and exchange.

These scholarly analyses suggest that people with disabilities always already have greater social visibility than do people of advanced age. Indeed, cultural critic Sally Chivers asserts "that old age requires disability to be legible within an efficient capitalist society [. . . in part because] in the public imagination, disability exists separately from old age, but old age does not ever escape the stigma and restraints imposed upon disability" (8). The relative height of disability's social power may seem peculiar to some disability studies and cultural studies scholars. Tobin Siebers defines ableism as a belief that constructs disabled people as intellectually, emotionally, and aesthetically substandard; Siebers suggests that "as long as anyone, at any time, may be thought inferior based on mental and physical characteristics, disabled people will continue to be classified as people without quality" (12). Considering historical constructions of devalued people – African Americans during the time of slavery and Jews in Hitler's Europe, for example – one might fear that ableism continues to frame people with disabilities, despite their hyper-visibility, as less than human. That construction makes elders' invisibility all the more concerning. The content of Garland-Thomson's book drives this point home stunningly. In more than 200 pages of discussion about staring, the phrase *old age* appears once. In the first chapter, she offers a list of disabilities, and *old age* is one of the items, as if people's bodies had to relinquish an annual tithe, paying for each annum with the coin of physical ability (19). The term *aging* also occurs once, as one of several examples of baroque stares: "[. . .] the aging adult startled by the replication of his parent in his own face" (53), which occurs right before the beginning of a multi-page section on "Staring at Death." Is it easier to stare at death than it is to stare at old age?

Reading social visibility through the lenses of disability studies and age studies leaves little question about who is seen and who is not. Popular culture, on the other hand, offers a radically different picture. Flip through a magazine, surf television channels, drive past a forest of billboards, or host a film festival, and do a headcount. Were there more visibly aged people or more people with disabilities? And how many people were there who were both visibly aged and visibly disabled? The Bechdel test, named after graphic artist Alison Bechdel,[9] offers a simple but telling assessment of gender visibility in film. There are three parts to the question in this evaluation: (1) does the movie "have at least two [named] women in it, (2) who talk to each other, about (3) something besides a man?" Every year, I am chagrined to see how few popular movies fulfill these criteria. For a class project, my age studies literature students have to review one of that year's award-winning films; one of the assessment measures they apply in doing an age studies analysis is what they call the Marshall test: (1) does the movie have at least two named elders in it, (2) who talk to each other, about (3) something other than the younger characters? The number of critically acclaimed movies that fulfill these criteria is dismayingly small, but it has risen almost annually over the last decade. If a disability studies scholar was to adapt this test to assess the presence of people with a noticeable mental or physical disability in award-winning feature-length films, in many years, the number of films fulfilling all three criteria would be close to zero.

Another area of interest is the visibility of that body to itself, a topic that age studies and disability studies approach from very different angles. Perhaps this is because the path leading up to a visage of old age happens via roughly the same process for every individual, and because there are so many, many products available that can help people pass as younger along the way. Moreover, people who literally *buy in* with these products can use them and almost self-pass as less aged. That is, a person using youth-enizing options such as hair dye, Botox injections, or face lifts participates in the procedures occasionally, but can then almost forget that he or she actively participated in covering up evidence of advanced age.

Disabilities, on the other hand, arrive via a broader range of processes. A person may engage with disability unexpectedly (e.g., via a car accident) or

---

9 | See www.bechdeltest.com.

as more of an ongoing process over the course of multiple decades (as with post-polio syndrome). Also, the means by which a person might pass as non-disabled tend to be more temporary. Incontinence products need to be changed relatively frequently or their purpose is defeated; blood sugar levels and insulin must be attended to regularly; at the end of a meeting in which everyone has been seated, eventually one must navigate out of the room using an ambulatory aid; etc. Even if no one else sees these proceedings, the person is likely to have to interact with his or her own disabilities every day.

A person's reluctance to claim the self that is reflected in the mirror may become a symbolic resistance to the changing concept of self that can accompany advanced age and disability: "That's just the physical part. There's so much else" (Yorkston et al. 1700-01). In trying to give students who are not disabled an experience akin to disability, vocational rehabilitation instructors had sent their students on an excursion around campus or through the community with a handicap that mimics physical impairment. However, this approach has not been in use much for at least five years:

Many disability advocates have criticized programs that try to "simulate" what it is like to have different disabilities. Their concern is that such exercises often reinforce stereotypes and emphasize a "deficit" model of disability. Putting socks on our hands to simulate fine motor problems or sitting in a wheelchair for a few hours is seldom a realistic way to understand the experience of disability. (Osier 8)

That idea seems to have been adopted widely enough that the practice has fallen largely into disuse in the disability studies community.

In parallel and in about the same timeframe, some age studies scholars discontinued the use of age simulation exercises for similar reasons: because it teaches students that old age is "about" physical changes; there is no way to simulate the psychological or emotional development that happens over multiple decades (Woodward, *Telephone interview*). In a class of temporarily able-bodied students, this exercise equates advanced age with disability and suggests that the experience of aging into old age is only about *losing* – losing memory, losing friends and family to death, and losing bodily ability. Students tend to respond positively, reporting afterwards that the experience taught them a useful lesson, but one might wonder what lesson it is they are learning.

In gerontology, on the other hand, M.I.T. made headlines in January 2012 when they unveiled the AGNES (Age Gain Now Empathy System) suit, a device that MIT's Age Lab website says they designed so that people could "better understand the physical challenges associated with aging" ("AGNES"). The name of the device and the headlines announcing it have encouraged people to assume the suit has even greater power: "The Suit That Makes You Feel 75 Years Old" (Greenwood), "Aging Suit from MIT to Raise Empathy for the Elderly"

(Mandal), and "Find Out What it's Like to be Elderly" (Weber). Evidently, the headline writers had not focused on the idea that the suit was designed only to address the physical challenges. In academic discourse, such as at the 2013 conference of the Association for Gerontology in Higher Education, there were hallway debates about whether or not the lessons that students learn outweigh the drawbacks of such an experience.

In a classroom setting, it might not be possible to convey how visible signs of disability and old age change one's sense of self when "that image we see [in the mirror] is at once familiar and strange, the me and the not-me" (Garland-Thomson 53). The seemingly not-me aspects are the ones that critical scholarship in both fields suggests are useful – almost imperative – to accept. In age studies, it has been theorized that accepting the self in the seemingly-Other mirrored image can lead to greater personal and psychological development (Marshall, "Through"), but there is a general lack of quantitative research verifying this theory. Some scholarship has evolved based on Pauline Boss's ideas about ambiguous loss, but it is not as well-developed as the concepts in disability studies, where the use value of such acceptance has been measured and critiqued (e.g., Alvani, Hosseini, and Alvani; Crisp; Livneh, "Part I"; Livneh, "Part II"; and Telford, Kralik, and Koch); the foundation of those studies is Elizabeth Kübler-Ross's stages of response to death. In both fields, however, often the medical-industrial complex actively discourages acceptance, via praxis positing instead that bodies that are disabled or aged need treatment and can be "rehabilitated."

REHABILITATION

There are many groups of people that society tries to rehabilitate: alcoholics, drug addicts, convicted criminals, and people with disabilities. The success rate of rehabilitation varies widely within each of these populations. Because there are some successes in every population, people who do not "achieve rehabilitation" may be held responsible for their seeming recalcitrance and lose a significant amount of social capital. People inhabiting aged bodies and permanently disabled bodies that cannot be rehabilitated back to a level of social normativity may be viewed as failures, morally and psychologically, as well as physically.

Framing disability as a moral failure is not uncommon.[10] Julia Passanante Elman's work offers a representative example from American popular culture, focusing on television network ABC's *After School Specials* series, which a significant portion of the country's school-aged children viewed during the 1970s. In those shows, Elman explains, adolescence and immaturity were develop-

---

10 | E.g., Stone 62; Roush and Sharby 1716.

mental stages that needed to be overcome, and in many of the programs, negotiating experiences of disability, disease, and mortality paved a path to maturity
and cultural citizenship. "The *Special's* ableist approach operates by mapping
'immaturity' onto disability and 'maturity' onto rehabilitation" ("After" 261-
62). In these shows, Elman argues, disability was used as a punishment, and
characters had to become more tolerant, more self-accepting, and/or more willing to act in a culturally normative role in order to be rehabilitated. Elman also
considers "teen sick-lit" books popular in the 1980s and 1990s. Although there
were exceptions, she suggests, the majority of these books served as what one
might call "secondhand inspiration porn," in which teenagers must "overcome"
their negative responses to a friend's physical or mental differences in order to
reach maturity ("Feeling" 181).[11] With an association of joy and belonging connected to a person's ability to be psychologically rehabilitated, it is little wonder
that people consciously or unconsciously consider unrehabilitated bodies as
morally suspect.

Disability studies critiques the presumed link between the physical and
moral aspects of normality, suggesting that the medical model of disability,
which frames disability as an individual deficiency, is itself a form of oppression (e.g., Anderberg; Kielhofner[12]). People familiar with Deaf culture's equation of cochlear implants and genocide may extrapolate those ideas to gain a
basic understanding of rehabilitation's additional potential detriments to the
populations it strives to serve. In this analysis, the goals of rehabilitation are
ethically suspect, and rehabilitation is based on a power differential in which
the rehabilitee is impelled into a nonreciprocal relationship of care (Pound 197)
that reinscribes paternalistic cultural ideologies of difference (Anderberg). The
goal of medical-model rehabilitation becomes the self-sufficiency and productivity associated with an unattainably normative body (Phelan and Kinsella;
Pound); bodies that cannot reach that goal are always already failures, a framework that creates and compounds feelings of negative self-image and social
alienation. Such analyses have flourished in disability studies during the last
few decades in part because of advances in the critical theories. Developments
in the biological sciences, pharmacology, and technology also are key factors,
expanding the potential for treatment and rehabilitation, as well propagating
an ethically-questionable cultural coercion to employ those advances.

---

11 | In the 21st century, this trend may be continuing, albeit with less moralistic
simplicity, in vehicles such as graphic novels. For example, in Charles Burns' popular
Black Hole series, visible old age, physical disability, and class difference are the
manifestations of a plague that infects only teen bodies.

12 | Kielhofner's article also provides a useful general overview of disability studies'
key elements.

Similar advances influence aging processes as well. Consider, for example, professional women's virtually ubiquitous use of hair dye, as well as the responses (as seen in Bennett) to a potential "cure" for grey hair.[13] For most medical procedures, people think about the financial costs and health risks, but questions about the cultural cost are equally important. How much cultural capital does one acquire from not having grey hair? How does the *de facto* requirement for having hair of color impact people differently across the spectrum of socioeconomic diversity? And why do people think that grey hair needs to be treated? As Barbara Marshall and Stephen Katz suggest, such technologies can disrupt the traditional binary parings of function and dysfunction, and normal versus pathological development.

That is, some age-related physical changes impact aged bodies visibly in such a way that they recast the aged body as Other. When preventative or curative options become available, those visible changes become socially unacceptable, even pathological. The functionality – indeed, the performativity – of the youthful body, such as its ability to have hair of color, to be virile, or to be receptive to virility, for example, becomes the new standard of acceptability for all bodies, and "'normal' is no longer normative, but a negotiable biosocial condition" (Marshall and Katz 7-8). Taking that approach one step farther, some of the anti-aging discourse suggests that even the *risk* of deviation from the norm, "the potential for disease," is itself an illness in need of treatment (Conrad 163). Much like people with disabilities who refuse therapy or whose goals for rehabilitation do not follow the traditional model, people who decline to hide or "cure" the visible signs of aging, or whose socioeconomic circumstances make such treatment options unavailable, pay a social and psychological cost for their "choice."

These factors – resistance to the medical model of rehabilitation and ageist responses to aging, and the high valuing of normative performatives in both cases – have brought age studies and disability studies to very similar locations. Responses focus on the importance of recognizing the diversity of embodiments and experiences, considering social responses to social coercion, and critiquing medicalization and the deficit model. The refusal of one-size-fits-all solutions is key in both fields.

Disability studies calls for a distinction between disability and impairment, and individualized, person-centered analyses, particularly paying attention to each individual's goals, as in Anderberg's catalog of rehabilitative objectives: *parroting* the functioning of the temporarily able-bodied; replicating the flavor and color of that functioning, *chameleon-like*; or having a common core but looking very different, *poodle-like* (see also Kielhofner 491). Age studies schol-

---

13 | See Gullette, *Agewise*, Chapter 5, for an extended discussion of youth-enizing treatments such as hair dye and cosmetic surgery.

ars enumerate various dimensions of aging, such as Calasanti and Slevin's discussion of *chronological, functional, subjective,* and *occupational aging,* and offer multiple models of the aging process, as in Cruikshank's list: *successful aging, productive aging, aging comfortably,* and *conscious aging* (*Learning* 2-5). Engaging these concepts increases people's sensitivity to the social and emotional contexts that serve as the foundation for genuinely client-centered responses. Such treatments would focus on supporting the individual's engagement in activities that develop positive self-identity and improve the individual's perceived quality of life.

Considering those many distinctions, it may seem that responsible approaches to rehabilitation would need to be so highly individualized that they would be nearly impossible to generate, let alone fund. Both disability studies and age studies, however, are discovering a set of data-driven best practices based on two premises: first, that the "formation of identity is fundamentally relational" (Phelan and Kinsella 89; see also Basting), and second, that the principal burdens of disability and aging are the social responses (Kielhofner). In this model, the key is to create environments in which people's disabilities and advanced age are not barriers to participatory citizenship. These settings go beyond encouraging young and temporarily-able-bodied people to care about people with disabilities and people of advanced age. The goal of this model is to create opportunities for equal engagement from all, in which acts of exchange generate full social identities that recognize the "being, belonging, and becoming" of each participant (Pound 201). In both fields, scholars and activists alike call for the 21st-century equivalent of consciousness raising, emphasizing the importance of increasing everyone's awareness about often-overlooked and critically under-theorized experiences of individuality and diversity for people of advanced age and people with disabilities, as well as for the need for social change that creates more settings that are physically and participatorily accessible to all.

CONCLUSION: CONSCIOUS AGEILITY

With improved awareness of these elements comes the possibility of *conscious aging.* Conscious aging means aging with an awareness of age studies concepts and an activist response to ageism, with an understanding of one's self-identity and social identity as variable, and with an appreciation for the possibility that the self can remain whole even as it changes.[14] As a parallel, *conscious disability*

---

14 | This definition is based largely on Cruikshank's discussion of conscious aging in *Learning to Be Old,* with additional influence by Moody 47-49, Schachter-Shalomi and Miller, and http://www.consciousaging.com. This definition allows for, but does not focus on, the spiritual aspects and development some associate with conscious aging.

would be an awareness of disability studies concepts and an activist response to ableism, with an understanding of one's self-identity and social identity as variable, and with an appreciation for the possibility that the self can remain undamaged even as one's identity changes. Everyone has a stake in supporting these approaches – not just people with disabilities and people of advanced age and the people who care about them personally or professionally and the scholars and activists, but *everyone*. Those people who are able-bodied are only temporarily so, and unless death intervenes, everyone becomes old.

The virtual inevitability that each person who lives long enough will embody both disability and advanced age suggests that disability studies and age studies scholars need to do more than just engage the useful analytical concepts and praxis from the other field. Rather, there needs to be a place where the academic arenas of disability studies and age studies merge, combining their experience and their commitment to intersectional analyses. The potential of that nexus includes the prospect of establishing a critical praxis that integrates an awareness of both age studies and disability studies concepts, an activist response to the ignorant conflation and negative stereotypes of advanced age and disability, an understanding of one's self-identity and social identity as mutable, and an appreciation for the possibility that the self can develop undamaged while navigating through the conflicted yet fertile terrain of *conscious ageility*.

References

"AGNES (Age Gain Now Empathy System)." *Age Lab*. Massachusetts Institute of Technology, 2013. Web. 21 Mar. 2013.

Albrecht, Gary L., and Patrick J. Devlieger. "Disability Assumptions, Concepts And Theory: Reply To Tom Koch." *Social Science & Medicine* 50.6 (2000): 761-62. PsycINFO. Web. 18 Mar. 2013.

———. "The Disability Paradox: High Quality Of Life Against All Odds." *Social Science & Medicine* 48.8 (1999): 977-88. CINAHL Plus with Full Text. Web. 18 Mar. 2013.

Alvani, Seyed Reza, Seyed Mehrshad Parvin Hosseini, and Shokoofeh Alvani. "Living With Chronic Illnesses And Disability." *International Journal Of Business, Humanities & Technology* 2.5 (2012): 102-10. Academic Search Premier. Web. 20 Mar. 2013.

Ameratunga, Shanthi. "Disability Counts Or Does It?" *Injury Prevention* 11.3 (2005): 129-30. SPORTDiscus with Full Text. Web. 19 Mar. 2013.

Anderberg, Peter. "Making Both Ends Meet." *Disability Studies Quarterly* 25.3 (2005): n. pag. *Education Research Complete*. Web. 21 May 2013.

Anderson, Trudy. "Aging Education in Higher Education: Preparing for the 21st Century." *Educational Gerontology* 25.6 (Sept. 1999): 571-79. Print.

Atkin, Karl. "Adults With Disabilities Who Reported Excellent Or Good Quality Of Life Had Established A Balance Of Body, Mind, And Spirit [Commentary On Albrecht GL, Devlieger PJ. "The Disability Paradox: High Quality Of Life Against All Odds." *Soc Sci Med* 48.8 (Apr. 1999): 977-88]." *Evidence Based Nursing* 3.1 (2000): 31. CINAHL Plus with Full Text. Web. 18 Mar. 2013.

Barrett, Anne, and Laura Cantwell. "Drawing on Stereotypes: Using Undergraduates' Sketches of Elders as a Teaching Tool." *Educational Gerontology* 33.4 (Apr. 2007): 327-48. Print.

Basting, Anne Davis. *Forget Memory: Creating Better Lives for People with Dementia.* Baltimore: Johns Hopkins UP, 2009. Print.

Bennett, Ronni. "If Grey Hair Were 'Curable.'" *Changing Aging: Exploring Life Beyond Adulthood.* Changingaging.org. 13 May 2013. Web. 14 May 2013.

Blunk, Elizabeth, and Sue Williams. "The Effects of Curriculum on Preschool Children's Perceptions of the Elderly. *Educational Gerontology* 23.3 (Apr./May 1997): 233-41. Print.

Boss, Pauline. "The Trauma And Complicated Grief Of Ambiguous Loss." *Pastoral Psychology* 59.2 (2010): 137-45. Academic Search Complete. Web. 22 Mar. 2013.

———, ed. "Ambiguous Loss." *Family Relations* 56.2 (2007): 105-230. Education Full Text (H.W. Wilson). Web. 22 Mar. 2013.

———. "Ambiguous Loss Theory: Challenges For Scholars And Practitioners." *Family Relations* 56.2 (2007): 105-10. OmniFile Full Text Mega (H.W. Wilson). Web. 22 Mar. 2013.

———. *Ambiguous Loss: Learning to Live with Unresolved Grief.* Cambridge, MA: Harvard UP, 2000. Print.

Boss, Pauline, and Donna Carnes. "The Myth Of Closure." Family Process 51.4 (2012): 456-69. CINAHL Plus with Full Text. Web. 22 Mar. 2013.

Burns, Charles. *Black Hole.* New York: Pantheon, 2008. Print.

Butler, Judith. *Bodies that Matter.* New York: Routledge, 1993. Print.

Calasanti, Toni, and Kathleen Slevin, eds. *Age Matters: Realigning Feminist Thinking.* New York: Routledge, 2006. Print.

Campo-Flores, Arian. "Medicare Complicates the Senior Vote." *Wall Street Journal - Eastern Edition* 30 Oct. 2012: A1. MasterFILE Premier. Web. 20 Mar. 2013.

Carstensen, Laura. A Long Bright Future: An Action Plan for a Lifetime of Happiness, Health, and Financial Security. New York: Random House/Crown, 2009. Print.

Cassuto, Leonard. "Disability Studies 2.0." *American Literary History* 22.1 (13 Nov. 2009): 218-31. Print.

Chivers, Sally. *The Silvering Screen: Old Age and Disability in Cinema.* Toronto: U of Toronto P, 2011. Print.

Conrad, Peter. *The Medicalization of Society: On the Transformation of Human Conditions into Treatable Disorders*. Baltimore: John Hopkins UP, 2007. Print.

Copper, Baba. *Over the Hill: Reflections on Ageism between Women*. Freedom, CA: The Crossing Press, 1988. Print.

Crisp, Ross. "A Qualitative Study Of The Perceptions Of Individuals With Disabilities Concerning Health And Rehabilitation Professionals." *Disability & Society* 15.2 (2000): 355-67. PsycINFO. Web. 20 Mar. 2013.

Cruikshank, Margaret. *Learning to Be Old: Gender, Culture, and Aging*. Lanham, MD: Rowman and Littlefield, 2003. Print.

———. Personal conversation. June 2009.

Drum, Charles E, Willi Horner-Johnson, and Gloria L Krahn. "Self-Rated Health And Healthy Days: Examining The 'Disability Paradox.'" *Disability And Health Journal* 1.2 (2008): 71-78. MedLine. Web. 18 Mar. 2013.

Elman, Julie Passanante. "Feeling Real: Disability, Teen Sick-Lit and the Condition of Adolescence." *Journal of Literary and Cultural Disability Studies* 6.2 (July 2012):175-91. Print.

———. "*After School Special* Education: Rehabilitative Television, Teen Citizenship, and Able-Bodiedness." *Television and New Media* 11.4 (July 2010): 260-92. Print.

Garland-Thomson, Rosemarie. *Staring: How We Look*. New York: Oxford UP, 2009. Print.

Greenwood, Veronique. "The Suit That Makes You Feel 75 Years Old." *Discover Magazine's Discoblog*, 3 Jan. 2012. Web. 21 Mar. 2013.

Gutheil, Irene, Roslyn Chernesky, and Marian Sherratt. "Influencing Student Attitudes Toward Older Adults: Results of a Service-Learning Collaboration." *Educational Gerontology* 32.9 (Oct. 2006): 771-84. Print.

Hetherington, Peter. "Research Dispels Old Myths About Aging." *The Guardian*. 29 May 2012. Guardian.co.uk. Web. 4 May 2013.

Inskeep, Patty. "Connolly's World View is the Topic of Oct. 23 Lecture." *MSU News*. Montana State University, 22 Oct. 2007. Web. 21 Mar. 2013.

Isaacs, Lenora, and David Bearison. "The Development of Children's Prejudice Against the Aged." *International Journal of Aging and Human Development* 23.3 (1986): 175-94. Print.

Jørgensen, Merete. "A Disability Paradox." *Canadian Family Physician* 51 (2005): 1474. CINAHL Plus with Full Text. Web. 19 Mar. 2013.

Joyner, Mildred, and Eli DeHope. "Transforming the Curriculum Through the Intergenerational Lens." *Journal of Gerontological Social Work* 48.1/2 (2006): 127-37. Print.

Katz, Stephen. "Growing Older Without Aging? Positive Aging, Anti-Ageism, and Anti-Aging." *Generations* 25.4 (2001-2002 Winter): 27-32. Print.

Kielhofner, Gary. "Rethinking Disability and What To Do About It: Disability Studies and Its Implications for Occupational Therapy." *American Journal of Occupational Therapy* 59.5 (Sept./Oct. 2005): 487-96. Print.

Koch, Tom. "The Illusion Of Paradox: Commentary On Albrecht, G.L. and Devlieger, P. J. (1998). 'The Disability Paradox: High Quality Of Life Against All Odds.' *Social Science & Medicine* 48: 977-988." *Social Science & Medicine* 50.6 (2000): 757-59. OmniFile Full Text Mega (H.W. Wilson). Web. 18 Mar. 2013.

Lamb, Erin Gentry. "'20 is the new 65': Pedagogical Approaches to Reconciling the Future Self and the Aging Other Through Life as a Story." NWSA Convention, Cincinnati Convention Center, Cincinnati, OH. 20 June 2008.

———. Telephone interview. 17 July 2008.

Livneh, Hanoch. "Denial Of Chronic Illness And Disability: Part I. Theoretical, Functional, And Dynamic Perspectives." *Rehabilitation Counseling Bulletin* 52.4 (2009): 225-36. Professional Development Collection. Web. 20 Mar. 2013.

———. "Denial Of Chronic Illness And Disability: Part II. Research Findings, Measurement Considerations, And Clinical Aspects." *Rehabilitation Counseling Bulletin* 53.1 (2009): 44-55. Professional Development Collection. Web. 20 Mar. 2013.

Macdonald, Barbara, and Cynthia Rich. *Look Me In the Eye: Old Women, Aging, and Ageism.* Minneapolis, MN: Spinsters Ink, 1983. Print.

Mairs, Nancy. "On Being a Cripple." *Plaintext.* Tucson: Univ. of Arizona, 1986. 9-20. Print.

Mandal, Ananya. "Aging Suit from MIT to Raise Empathy for the Elderly." *News Medical,* 3 Jan. 2012. Web. 21 Mar. 2013.

Mann, William C., Catherine Llanes, Michael D. Justiss, and Machiko Tomita. "Frail Older Adults' Self-Report of Their Most Important Assistive Device." *OTJR: Occupation, Participation & Health* 24.1 (2004): 4-12. CINAHL Plus with Full Text. Web. 19 Mar. 2013.

Marshall, Barbara, and Stephen Katz. "The Embodied Life Course: Post-ageism or the Renaturalization of Gender?" *Societies* 2 (Oct. 2012): 222-34. Web. 14 Dec. 2012.

Marshall, Leni. "Through (With) the Looking Glass: Lacan and Woodward in Méconnaissance, the Mirror Stage of Old Age." *Feminist Formations* 24.2 (August 2012): 52-76. Print.

———. "Changing Bodies, Changing Minds: Constructions of Age via Doris Lessing's *The Diaries of Jane Somers.*" *Doris Lessing Studies* 24.1&2 (Summer/Fall 2004): 19-22. Print.

McCarthy, Ellen. "A Platform to Push Their Message: Reality Show Features Four Women who Consider Themselves Ambassadors for Those with Disabilities." *Guelph Mercury* (ON) 16 Jun 2012: C9. Newspaper Source Plus. Web. 21 Mar. 2013.

McGuire, Sandra, Diane Klein, and Donna Couper. "Aging Education: A National Imperative." *Educational Gerontology* 31.6 (June 2005): 443-60. Print.

Millett, Ann. "Staring Back And Forth: The Photographs Of Kevin Connolly." Disability Studies Quarterly 28.3 (2008): 12. Education Research Complete. Web. 21 Mar. 2013.

Mitchell, David, and Sharon Snyder. *Vital Signs: Crip Culture Talks Back*. Boston: Fanlight Productions, 1995. Print.

Moller, Dan. "Wealth, Disability, And Happiness." *Philosophy & Public Affairs* 39.2 (2011): 177-206. Humanities International Complete. Web. 18 Mar. 2013.

Moody, Harry R. *Aging: Concepts and Controversies*. Thousand Oaks, CA: Pine Forge Press, 2009. Print.

Osier, Jan. "Teaching Disability Awareness in the Classroom." *Teaching Inclusionary Practices for Students (TIPS)*. 23 Jan. 2004. Web. 21 Mar. 2013.

Palmore, Erdman. "Three Decades of Research on Ageism." *Generations* 29.3 (Fall 2005): 87-90. Print.

Phelan, Shannon, and Elizabeth Anne Kinsella. "Occupational Identity: Engaging Socio-Cultural Perspectives." *Journal of Occupational Science* 16.2 (July 2009): 85-91. Print.

Pierce, Barbara. "No Such Thing As Blind Culture." *National Federation of the Blind*. Nov. 2008. Web. 18 Mar. 2013.

Piercy, Marge. "I Met a Woman who Wasn't There." *NWSA Journal* 18.1 (Spring 2006): 1-2. Print.

Port, Cynthia. "No Future? Aging, Temporality, History, and Reverse Chronologies." *Occasion: Interdisciplinary Studies in the Humanities* 4 (31 May 2012). Web. 9 Aug. 2013.

Pound, Carole. "Reciprocity, Resources, and Relationships: New Discourses in Healthcare, Personal, and Social Relationships" *International Journal of Speech-Language Pathology* 13.3 (June 2011): 197-206. Print.

Rosenbaum, David E. "A New Respect for Age in Florida." *New York Times*. 21 Oct. 2000: A12. MasterFILE Premier. Web. 20 Mar. 2013.

Roush, Susan E., and Nancy Sharby. "Disability Reconsidered: The Paradox of Physical Therapy." *Physical Therapy* 91.12 (Dec. 2011): 1715-27. EBSCO. Web. 5 May 2013.

Rousso, Harilyn. *Don't Call Me Inspirational*. Philadelphia: Temple UP, 2013. Print.

Schachter-Shalomi, Zalman, and Ronald S. Miller. *From Age-ing to Sage-ing: A Profound New Vision of Growing Older*. New York: Grand Central Publishing, 1997. Print.

Sheets, Debra. "Aging with Disability: Ageism and More." *Generations* 29.3 (Fall 2005): 37-41. Print.

Siebers, Tobin. "Aesthetics and the Disqualification of Disability." *Association on Higher Education and Disability.* 18 June 2011. Web. 18 Mar. 2013.

Sparrow, Robert. "Defending Deaf Culture: The Case of Cochlear Implants." *Journal Of Political Philosophy* 13.2 (June 2005): 135-52. Academic Search Complete. 17 Mar. 2013. Web. 9 Aug. 2013.

Stone, Sharon-Dale. "Disability, Dependence, and Old Age: Problematic Constructions. *Canadian Journal on Aging* 22.1 (2003): 59-67. Print.

Swain, John, and Colin Cameron. "Unless Otherwise Stated: Discourses of Labeling and Identity in Coming Out." *Disability Discourse.* Ed. Mairian Corker and Sally French. Buckingham: Open UP, 1999. 68-78. Print.

Telford, Kerry, Debbie Kralik, and Tina Koch. "Acceptance And Denial: Implications For People Adapting To Chronic Illness: Literature Review." *Journal Of Advanced Nursing* 55.4 (2006): 457-64. Academic Search Premier. Web. 20 Mar. 2013.

Tucker, Bonnie P. "Deaf Culture, Cochlear Implants, And Elective Disability." *Hastings Center Report* 28.4 (1998): 6-14. *CINAHL Plus with Full Text.* Web. 22 Mar. 2013.

Ubel, Peter, Norbert Schwarz, George Lowenstein, and Dylan Smith. "Misimagining The Unimaginable: The Disability Paradox And Health Care Decision Making." *Health Psychology* 24 (2005): S57-S62. Family & Society Studies Worldwide. Web. 19 Mar. 2013.

Weber, Harrison. "Find Out What it's Like to be Elderly With This Suit by MIT." *TNW: The Next Web*, 2 Jan. 2012. Web. 21 Mar. 2013.

Woodward, Kathleen. "Performing Age, Performing Gender." *NWSA Journal* 18.1 (Spring 2006): 162-89. Print.

———. Telephone interview. 24 July 2008.

Yorkston, Kathryn, Kara McMullan, Ivan Moulton, and Mark Jensen. "Pathways of Change Experienced by People Aging with Disability: A Focus Group Study." *Disability and Rehabilitation* 32.20 (2010): 1697-704. Print.

Zarb, Gerry, and Mike Oliver. *Ageing with a Disability: What Do They Expect After All These Years?* London: University of Greenwich, 1993. Web. 9 Aug. 2013.

I May be Old and Sick, But I Am Still a Person

Beverly Lunsford

A classroom of young adults in a health professions course was asked what comes to mind when they think about older adults and aging. They answered, "being frail and sick," "dementia," "inability to do what one used to do." In fact, each comment held a negative view of aging and older adults. However, we have many older adults in the public eye that present a very different view of aging such as Nelson Mandela who was inaugurated President of the Republic of South Africa at the age of 76 and celebrated his 95th birthday in 2013. Queen Elizabeth II, born in 1926 and became the Queen of England in 1951, is the second longest serving monarch. Only five other British kings and queens have reigned for 50 years or more; and Elizabeth II is the oldest monarch to celebrate a Diamond Jubilee in 2012 at age 85. Another person who continues to re-emerge is the rock star Mick Jagger who turned 70 in 2013. He notes that "[p]eople have this obsession. They want you to be like you were in 1969. They want you because otherwise their youth goes with you. It's very selfish but it's understandable." So why does aging have a negative connotation, and how does that affect healthcare in particular?

Societal stereotypes about older adults and aging from US data are consistent in two main themes. Elderly people are viewed as warm (positive), as well as incompetent (negative) (Cuddy and Fiske 3). These themes cross national and cultural dimensions, as recent data show that the mixed bias is evident in other cultures (Cuddy, Fiske, Kwan, et al. 1).

A 2001 metanalysis of health care professionals' attitudes toward older adults indicated that they are viewed as difficult to understand, critical of young people's behavior, and emotionally dependent (Cooper and Coleman). The researchers also found that nurses viewed mentally intact people as their "favorites," while those with dementia were "less favorite." Nurses in long-term care tended to perceive older people more negatively in terms of mental and physical dependence. One still hears faculty and medical students discussing depression in older adults and the comment "If I were his age, I'd be depressed too" (Gelenberg 1657).

In spite of the negative attitudes, a 2013 survey of a nationally representative sample of 2,012 adults regarding public attitudes about aging, health care and personal life satisfaction (PEW, March 21 to April 8, 2013) found that Americans were generally optimistic about their own futures, including old age. Despite negative attitudes toward aging, most Americans indicated that they want to live longer than the average life expectancy in the US of 78.7 years (Murphy, Xu, and Kochanek).

The potential bias by the general public as well as attitudes of healthcare professionals toward older adults and aging can affect the healthcare provided for older adults. The Center for Aging, Health and Humanities (The Center) was established at George Washington University in 1995 to address the stereotypes of older adulthood by conducting research on the creative potential of older adulthood. In 2009, The Center faculty developed a gerontology curriculum to support a more person-centered approach to care of the older adult to minimize biases toward aging. This approach also encourages individualized care rather than the tendency to provide a "one size fits all" type of healthcare. A person-centered approach provides safe and effective care for older adults with chronic illnesses, while supporting and respecting their quality of life. To achieve person-centered care, The Center utilizes the humanities and creative arts as a meaningful way to view the older adult as a person with potential, rather than a healthcare problem to solve (Center, 2013). Consider the following poem that illustrates the potential impact of humanities to our understanding of the human experience:

"The Little Boy and the Old Man"

Said the little boy, "Sometimes I drop my spoon."
Said the little old man, "I do that too."
The little boy whispered, "I wet my pants."
"I do that too," laughed the little old man.
Said the little boy, "I often cry."
The old man nodded, "So do I."
"But worst of all," said the boy, "it seems
Grown-ups don't pay attention to me."
And he felt the warmth of the wrinkled old hand.
"I know what you mean," said the little old man. (Silverstein 92)

This chapter will discuss the effect of age, aging, and ageism in relation to the healthcare professional's approach to care for older adults, especially in the United States. Person-centered care will be discussed as a means of refocusing healthcare on the older adult as a person of value, whose quality of life should be of the utmost consideration, even in the presence of serious, chronic illness. For the purposes of this review, the section on age refers to the growing numbers and incidence of older adults in the United States and around the world. Aging refers to the challenges that older adults encounter with physical, psychological, social and spiritual results of growing older, especially in the presence of chronic illness. A recent conceptual analysis of Ageism defines it as "negative or positive stereotypes, prejudice and/or discrimination against (or to the advantage of) elderly people on the basis of their chronological age or on the basis of a perception of them as being 'old' or 'elderly'" (Iversen, Larsen, and Solem 4).

AGE

There have been dramatic changes over the past 30 years in the age distribution of older adults in America and around the world. The projection is that there will be continued and substantial changes over the next 50 years. Figure 1 illustrates the change in percentage of older adults in the United States population from 1960 in which 9% of the US population were over 65 (U.S. Census Bureau, 1960), to 2010 when this percentage grew to about 12% of the population in the United States (U.S. Census Bureau, 2012). The percentage of adults over 65 is projected to be about 18% by 2030 and almost 24% by 2050. In fact, in the United States a baby boomer (born between 1946 and 1964 when there was an unprecedented surge in the birthrate) turns 65 every eight seconds (Rand). Figure 1 illustrates the dramatic increase and projected increase in the percentage of older adults in the US.

Fig. 1. Changes in Percentage of US Population Over 65 Years of Age 1960-2050.

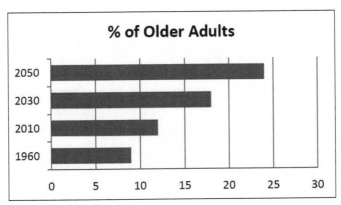

U.S. Census Bureau, *"United States Census Bureau Reports," Census 2000 Summary File 1, 2010 Census Summary File 1*; U.S. Census Bureau

Overall, there has been an increase from 10% to roughly 20% of the population in industrialized and developed countries since 1960 (WHO, *Are you ready?*). In less developed countries, approximately 5% of the population is over 65. Even though less developed countries have a smaller percentage of people over 65 and a slower pace of growth because of lower life expectancy and higher birth rates, these countries will also experience the growing percentage of older adults (U.S. Census International Population Reports, *An Aging World*). In both developed and less developed countries, the greatest rate of growth is in the world's oldest old population, e.g. those people 80 and over, which is greater than the rate of growth for 65 and over (WHO, *Are you ready?*).

Japan has the highest percentage of older adults with 22%, having recently surpassed Italy who previously held that distinction (U.S. Census International Population Reports, *An Aging World*). In the 25 years from 2002 to 2027, the 65-plus population of Poland will increase by 50%, but in China the percentage of population 65-plus will increase by 100% from seven to 14% of the total population (U.S. Census Bureau International Population Reports, *An Aging World*). There are certainly variabilities around the world, but in all countries including in Sub-Saharan Africa, the population 60-plus will increase by over 90% from 2006 to 2030 (Velkoff and Kowal).

By 2020, for the first time, there will be more people over 65 than children under 5 years of age in the US and other developed countries (U.S. Census Bureau, *An Aging World*). One of the reasons for this change is the worldwide shift in the birth and death rates from 1950 to 2010, in which the birth rate has seen a steady decline from 23.7/1000 population to 13/1000 population (Martin, et al.). There has been a more focused intent on family size so that many people, not only in the United States, but around the world are having fewer babies. Prolonged lifespans increase the percentage of older adults. Indeed older adults are living well into their 80s and 90s and even 100s and as mentioned earlier this is the fastest growing segment of the population over 65 (WHO, *Are you ready?*).

AGING

While people worldwide may celebrate the ability to live longer lives, there is also the awareness that there are many older adults who experience major health challenges that accompany aging. Historically, communicable diseases and trauma were the leading causes of death. But as environmental conditions, nutrition, and healthcare improved, noncommunicable diseases have become the predominant cause of death for older adults worldwide (Adeyi, Smith, and Robles). Figure 2 shows the percentage of persons aged 70 or older who report having selected chronic conditions, in which the major chronic health problems reported are heart disease, hypertension, stroke, cancer, diabetes, and arthritis. Figure 2 also illustrates the difference in the incidence of these diseases between 1995 and 2006, which is the most recent year with complete data for comparison (Center for Disease Control and Prevention).

Fig. 2. Percent of Older Adults with Chronic Illness.

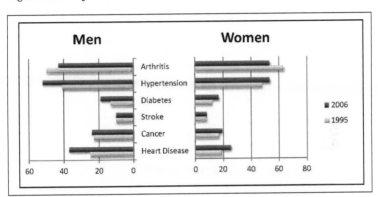

Center for Disease Control and Prevention, *Supplement on Aging & 2nd Supplement on Aging - National Health Interview Survey*

In 1995, there were 25% of men who had heart disease compared to 37% in 2006. For women, there were 19% afflicted with heart disease in 1995, compared to 26% in 2006. Hypertension also increased for both men and women, from 41% to 52% for men and from 48% to 54% for women. Stroke is the one disease that has remained about the same in that 10-year period at 8% for women and 10% for men in both 1995 and 2006. Cancer grew slightly from 23% to 24% in men, and 17% to 19% in women. Diabetes also grew from 13% to 19% for men and 12% to 17% in women. Arthritis is a disease that has decreased in incidence from 50% to 43% for men and 64% to 54% for women.

For worldwide comparison, the WHO provides the primary cause of death for older adults, rather than the incidence of chronic illness to illustrate the impact of chronic illness in older adults in the US. Globally, the primary cause of death for older adults is cardiovascular disease which accounts for 48% of deaths. Cancer is the second leading cause of death (21%). Cardiovascular disease and cancer are followed by respiratory diseases such as asthma and chronic obstructive pulmonary disease and diabetes as cause of death (WHO, *The top 10 causes of death*).

Usually, older adults do not have just one chronic condition; they may have several comorbid illnesses. In the United States, Medicare beneficiaries over 65 have more than three chronic illnesses (Anderson). These chronic illnesses can result in intermittent and progressive loss of function. Figure 3 shows the percent of increase of functional limitation from activities of daily living for older adults from 4% when there is no chronic condition to 15% with one chronic condition, 28% for two conditions, 43%, 52% and 67% respectively for three, four and five chronic conditions (Center for Disease Control and Prevention). Certainly, as the number of chronic conditions increases, there's a significant impact on the functional and/or activity capabilities of the older adult.

Fig. 3. Percent of Activity Limitation with Increasing Numbers of Chronic Illnesses.

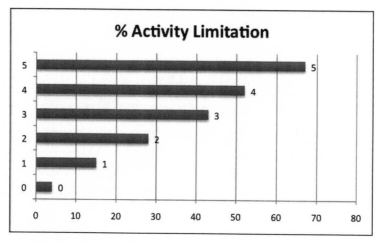

Center for Disease Control and Prevention, *Supplement on Aging & 2nd Supplement on Aging - National Health Interview Survey*

The Medicare data on the beneficiaries over 65 with three or more chronic illnesses in the United States also indicates that these older adults see more than 14 different specialists in a year's time (Anderson). They might see a primary care provider as well as specialists such as cardiologists, orthopedists, rheumatologists, infectious disease specialists, ophthalmologists, dentists, endocrinologists, and pulmonologists to address multiple conditions with many related issues/symptoms.

One would hope that the involvement of many specialists in the care of an older adult with complex chronic illness translates into really good outcomes for the older adult, but in fact, it doesn't. RAND Health developed a set of measures, Assessing Care of Vulnerable Elders (ACOVE), to assess the quality of care for vulnerable older adults (RAND). The ACOVE measures reflected the best available clinical evidence and expert opinions to guide primary care for older adults. Researchers determined that vulnerable elderly living on their own received about half of the recommended care for their conditions (Wenger, et al.). Less than one-third received recommended care for selected conditions primarily affecting older adults, i.e. impaired mobility, urinary incontinence, and impaired cognitive function.

Several themes emerge for older adults who experience increasing chronic and life threatening illnesses. Many times, the focus of healthcare professionals is on the disease and curative treatment rather than the person and his/her family and/or significant others.[1] The older adult may experience a loss of personhood when there is a major focus on sophisticated diagnosis and treatment, medications, and specialty care; while there is less attention to the concerns of the older adult about how this will affect their daily living, both short-term and long-term, and how it will affect their quality of life. Other themes include lack of attention to pain and symptom management, lack of education for the individual and family/caregivers (or lack of education in a way that they are able to understand and utilize), and lack of consistent, supportive and compassionate care. One example is that we may spend $50,000 to implant a defibrillator for an older adult who has coronary artery disease. However, when they are discharged to home, there may be no notice of whether they have the ability to get food into their home, medications filled, or transportation for a medical appointment for follow-up!

AGEISM

In addition to the themes of specific health problems that emerge with chronic illness and a health system ill-designed to meet the needs of the older adult, there are many biases or negative attitudes and behaviors toward older adults. Three biases will illustrate some of the difficulties in the healthcare of older adults with serious, chronic illness, e.g. most older adults will develop memory loss and become incompetent, most older adults are unhappy, and older adults are a drain on society's resources.

Ageism and Memory Loss in Older Adults

Older adults, in fact people of all ages are concerned about developing memory loss and Alzheimer's Disease when they get older. There is evidence indicating that the cognitive processes are slower and may be more prone to error (Glisky). However, even if performance of tasks may decline, most people perform daily routines where new learning is less critical. In fact, in areas of expertise, age-related decline is minimal until advanced ages. Even though the ability

---

1 | Family will be used in the rest of this paper; it will represent family and/or other significant persons.

to perform tasks may decrease, daily routines can become rituals, and it may become less critical to insert new information. Thus, older adults will continue to perform as well, and in areas of developed expertise the decline with age is minimal until very advanced ages. Even if an older adult feels their memory is significantly impaired, a now classic study by Baltes and Kliegl indicates that memory can improve dramatically with practice.

Although there is the prevailing belief that memory declines with age; there is also research that suggests this may be the result of cultural beliefs. Rahhal, et al. conducted a study on memory versus learning, in which instructions to read statements were given exactly the same for two groups of younger and older participants. One group of the younger and older participants respectively was asked to "remember" as many statements from the list as possible. The other groups, one younger and one older, were asked to "learn" as many statements as they could. Thus, the instructions were the same except the emphasis was different, e.g. one was on memory and the other on learning. There was a significant difference between older and younger participants who were asked what statements they "remembered;" however, there was no difference between age groups when the instructions given were in relation to "learning." This suggests that cultural beliefs may influence the older adults' ability to recall information.

Another study by Hess, et al. investigated the difference in memory among three groups of younger and older participants after they read messages about memory. Each paired group was first given messages that were either positive, neutral or negative regarding the ability of older adults to remember. The first group was given a positive news article to read about memory that indicated memory may improve with age. The second group was given a negative article indicating that memory declined with aging, and the third group was given a neutral article about the changes in memory with aging. Then participants were asked to write down as many words as they could remember from a given list. Younger participants out-performed all older groups, but the older participants who read the positive message about memory did much better than the other older participant groups. This older group of participants also used an effective memory strategy, semantic clustering, to group words for more effective recall. These findings indicate the potential for other influencing factors, e.g. for memory in older adults.

These differences and the potential bias toward older adults as people with probable loss of memory and impairment in daily living emphasize the need to assess and view each person individually. If the healthcare professional believes that memory loss is a normal part of aging, he or she may not assess for memory loss and potential cognitive impairment, even though it should be part of a routine geriatric assessment. Even when there are "red flags" that may indicate memory loss and potential cognitive impairment, the healthcare professional (and even family caregivers) may dismiss it as something that may be expected in the older adult, thus precluding the possibility of therapy for treatable and reversible memory loss. This also reinforces the stereotype mentioned earlier, which is so prevalent in societal surveys of attitudes toward older adults indicating that people believe older adults are incompetent (Cooper and Coleman).

Ageism and Mental Health

Another bias that affects the healthcare of older adults is that older people are miserable. But mental health can actually improve with age, except in the presence of organic brain disorders such as dementia and related diseases. One might think that with getting older and anxious about having less time ahead, experiencing more physical health problems and limitations, and experiencing the loss of family, friends, and functioning that older adults would be less happy. But in fact, older people have a greater sense of well-being with a greater sense of focus on what they believe is really essential (Carstensen, Mikels, and Mather 347). They may be less likely to get anxious about small stuff, and they may have greater freedom to enjoy life without the encumbrance of children in the home. Older adults may reevaluate what is really important and display a greater ability to enjoy simple pleasures.

It could help healthcare professionals to appreciate the variance in time perception between younger and older adults that may explain the higher level of well-being in older adults. Laura Carstensen, Derek Isaacowitz, and Susan Charles describe the phenomenon of older adults who have experienced many losses and adjustments to difficulties in life as the paradox of aging with the socioemotional selectivity theory (SST). In SST, the focus is on one's perceived time horizons and how that affects one's motivation. Rather than chronological age determining our sense of possibility in life, changing perceptions of time affect our outlook on what we want or can do in the time remaining. Two broad categories of goals can change in relation to one's perspective of time remaining. The first one is an unlimited perception of time with the desire to acquire information, expand horizons and seek relationships. This is common in young adults who engage in educational opportunities and develop new careers. The second perspective is a constrained perception of time, in which the individual seeks emotional satisfaction in relationships, investment in things that are deemed most important, and deepening existing relationships.

This is illustrated in comments from Sheryl Crow, a musician who developed breast cancer in 2006 at the age of 44. Prior to the discovery of her breast cancer, she probably represented the younger group of people who are more likely to have an open and unlimited perception of time. But when she was faced with breast cancer, her perception of time became more constrained. She didn't know whether she had a few months, a few years, but certainly she's no longer looking to the future as unlimited for her. One of the things she said is that it really changed her perspective of what was important to her, that she was much more intentional in the relationships that she wanted to nurture, and the music she wanted to write (WebMD).

It is not uncommon to hear people who are faced with their own mortality express a greater appreciation for living what life they have remaining, in a more meaningful and intentional way. Tsevat (196) found this phenomenon in people with HIV/AIDS who felt their lives were changed for the better when they were diagnosed with HIV/AIDS. They expressed a new sense of meaning and purpose that gave them a new perspective for whatever time remained in their life. It represents this sense of changing time perspectives from an un-limited future, to making the most of the time remaining.

This discussion indicates that older adults are not miserable because of their aging. However, it is important to recognize that older adults do expe-rience depression and it is not a normal part of aging (National Alliance on Mental Illness). Approximately 8 to 16% of older adults living in the commu-nity experience significant symptoms of depression (Blazer). Chronic illness is frequently accompanied by depression and it can result in greater pain, lower quality of life, risk of suicide, greater loss of functioning, and higher use of healthcare (Blazer; Bruce et al.; Gellis; Kang-Yi and Gellis). The problem is that depression is under-recognized and undertreated in older adults, which may be related to bias that older adults have reason to be sad.

Burden of Older Adults

One of the issues that has arisen in the United States and many other coun-tries, is a discussion of whether older people living longer is a burden on soci-ety and drain of critical resources, rather than a valuable human resource. As people work past retirement age, are they taking jobs from younger people? Politicians have raised doubts about the social support systems and pension plans that have developed over the years. Are they adequate for paying medical and living expenses for people who are living into their 90s or will they bank-rupt the younger generation who will be paying for older adults, leaving little for retirement of the younger workers?

However, there needs to be greater discussion of the resources older adults are currently providing for society, as well as how these resources may be used to meet the challenges of the future. As previously discussed, older adults have relatively good mental health with good skills for resolving problems. There is no need to sideline older adults or encourage retirement without reinvestment of those skills and resources. Many older adults provide childcare and care-giver services for family and friends. Older adults contribute through volun-teer and non-profit work which provides incredible resources. Talents of older adults could be more focused on the needs of the disadvantaged such as the AARP Experience Corps, which places older adults in disadvantaged schools (American Association of Retired Persons). In addition, many faith-based organizations deploy retired members as short and long-term volunteers in various work around the world to address human needs.

There is certainly a delicate balance for healthcare professionals in particular, when caring for an older adult who is facing a serious, chronic illness to weigh the benefits and burdens of illness for any one person and not the potential resources they may consume. While the US healthcare system may be able to offer very good diagnostic services and treatments, it may pose a significant burden for an older adult with diminished physical stamina. For instance, if treatment for a metastatic cancer will involve six months of chemotherapy that invokes a week of acute illness every two to three weeks with limited potential for cure, the older adult may view this choice very differently than a 30 year-old adult with young children (Gawande). The suffering the older adult may endure during the six months, as well as the possibility of cancer treatment itself causing life threatening illness for a frail body, may cause the older adult to forego further treatment for the cancer. They may express the sense of satisfaction that they have lived a good life and they want to live each remaining day as fully as possible, rather than be desperately ill from chemotherapy.

In providing the education and support for the older adult and his/her family to make healthcare decisions about the choices they face for treatment versus ongoing supportive care with the cancer, the healthcare professional may have difficulties if he or she feels a particular bias of diminishing and ill spent resources for older adults, that would be better focused on younger people. This also affects older adults who fear they are not being offered the same quality and quantity of care as well-to-do and/or ethnic majority populations. So they may choose to have "everything possible" to ensure they receive "good" care, in spite of the low potential for improving their condition, or extending their life.

Paradigm Change to Person-Centered Care

There needs to be a paradigm shift in the healthcare of older adults for healthcare professionals to view them as people with potential, unique individuals who are worthy of dignity and respect. Ageism that views an older adult as one who is likely to lose his/her memory, experience unhappiness as they age, become a burden to society, and essentially viewed as someone with complex health problems to solve must be supplanted with a paradigm that celebrates the wisdom and resources of the older adult as well as preserves the dignity and quality of life. To accomplish this paradigm shift, The Center advocates for a person-centered approach to the care of older adults with a focus on quality of life and creative potential of each individual. The Center encourages the use of humanities for faculty and learners to illuminate the needs and experiences of older adults and their families, as well as to foster self-reflection and construction of meaning for the healthcare professional. The humanities offer the opportunity to gain insight into the intersection of the human experience and the rapidly changing landscape of science, technology, and public policy in healthcare. This occurs through the stories exchanged and the thoughts shared in a common quest for reaching the highest potential and maximizing the quality of lives for caregivers and those who are recipients of care.

Person-centered care focuses on the abilities of older adults, as well as the physical, psychological, social and spiritual challenges they may encounter with aging. The phrase "person-centered" recognizes that at the center of care is a human being defined not solely by their status as a patient, but by the "whole person" who comes for healthcare. Person-centered care focuses on enhancing quality of life for the person and his/her family; restoring the person to the center of the healthcare environment; honoring individual preferences, values and beliefs; and encouraging relationship-building among the older adult, family, and healthcare professionals. In addition, person-centered care recognizes that healthcare professionals serve older adults in health prevention and community settings, and referring to them as "patients" connotes an ill person rather than a holistic wellness perspective.

The Person-Centered Care Model defines the role of the individual and family as the driving force in developing goals of care and implementing plans for treatment. It offers people the chance to identify and describe what is important to them, emphasizing collaboration and care that is based on continuous healing relationships, cooperation among clinicians, and strong interprofessional respect and communication (IOM, *Crossing the Quality Chasm*; *Retooling for an aging America*). Healthcare professionals who offer person-centered care have the opportunity to learn and grow with the person who is at the core of the services and can influence the systems of care to respond to the requests and desires of the individuals served. In this system, there is intentionality in being with people, a conscious awareness of building relationships and sharing our thoughts and feelings. There is attention to making the environment more personalized to the older adult's values, preferred routines, rituals and needs. In the person-centered care model, the older adult is engaged in decision-making and receives the support they need to take responsibility for their care. In addition, there is attention to the importance of respectful, coordinated and efficient transitions, especially to ensure safety, reduce suffering and/or disease exacerbation and unnecessary readmission. Person (and family)-centered care places an individual's needs, experiences, meaningful routines and social relationships at the forefront of care plans and procedures. It considers the unique experiences and perspectives of the individual and families and requires a two-way approach to information, communication and education that focuses on the individual's preferences and goals of care. American Nurses Association President Karen Daley emphasizes that the person-centered care approach considers the individual's experience and preferences for care planning, rather than clinical outcomes alone (American Nurses Association). Daley emphasizes that the needs of individuals cannot be based on the systems' definition of care priorities and health outcomes. For example, a frail older adult with diabetes and diminished appetite may choose to eat foods that are not on a diabetic diet. The health outcomes may need to be adjusted based on the needs and priorities of the older adult; and it may result in more effective care. If we can use the person-centered care approach, it will improve healthcare and reduce cost, which is consistent with the IOM reports (*Crossing the Quality Chasm; Retooling for an aging America*).

Person-centered care was introduced in the early 1980s to enable people with developmental disabilities to have a voice and self-determination in their lives (Kitwood). By the late 1990s, the concept was emerging in healthcare literature to ensure that the recipients of care were being included in the decision-making and their own values and preferences were being considered in the care plan. This concept was embraced by the Nursing Home Reform Act of 1987 (U.S. Public Health), the Artifacts of Culture Change tool (Bowman and Shoeneman) and more national organizations. Person-centered care is also one of the overreaching goals of health advocacy, creating safer medical systems, and reducing healthcare suffering and even costs.

In the field of gerontology and geriatrics, person-centered care encourages a new paradigm of the individual in their environment to enhance the way we see older adults as people who still have the potential to grow and develop, including those with Alzheimer's and other cognitive impairment. When Kitwood introduced person-centered care in terms of dementia, he was inspired by Rogerian psychotherapy with its emphasis on authentic contact and communication.

Person-centered care is consistent with a landmark consensus report issued in 2001 by the IOM. This report described the urgent need to improve the United States healthcare system, including the need for healthcare directed by the individual's and family's needs and preferences. The IOM defines patient-centered care as "healthcare that establishes a partnership among practitioners, patients, and their families (when appropriate) to ensure that decisions respect patients' wants, needs, and preferences and that patients have the education and support they need to make decisions and participate in their own care" (IOM, *Crossing the Quality Chasm*). The IOM report identifies six critical elements for patient-centered care that also appear in subsequent patient-centered care models including:

1. Care based on continuous healing relationships,
2. Care customized according to patient needs and values,
3. Patient is the source of control,
4. Knowledge is shared and information flows freely,
5. Transparency is necessary, and
6. Needs are anticipated.

(Institute of Medicine, *Crossing the Quality Chasm*)

Many organizations are trying to adopt more person-centered environments that offer residents and older adults a higher quality of living in a more home or community-like environment, rather than a sterile, more traditional institutional setting. This is based on the premise that residents and patients may be happier and healthier when they can maintain their adult rituals such as schedules (patterns) around mealtime, bathing, waking and sleeping, as well as when they are treated with dignity and respect as people, not just a disease to be treated or a resident to maintain. People who have lived with a pet all of their adult years, may want to bring their pet with them when they must move into an assisted living or long-term care environment, so organizations are trying to determine how to accommodate infectious disease regulations with personal preferences of older adults. While these adaptations in organizations may just seem to be ways to increase patient satisfaction, the evidence indicates that healthcare is safer for older adults in all settings, including long-term care and acute care, when they are respected and listened to, as well as engaged in planning and decision-making in regards to their care (IOM, *Crossing the Quality Chasm*).

Patient-centered care is also a global concern. The International Alliance of Patients' Organizations (IAPO), a global alliance representing individuals of all nationalities across all disease areas, promotes patient-centered healthcare around the world. In 2006, the IAPO issued its Declaration on Patient-Centered Healthcare, which states, "the essence of patient-centered healthcare is that the healthcare system is designed and delivered to address the healthcare needs and preferences of patients so that healthcare is appropriate and cost-effective." The IAPO established five principles of patient-centered healthcare:

1. Respect,
2. Choice and empowerment,
3. Patient involvement in health policy,
4. Access and support, and
5. Information.

(International Alliance of Patients' Organizations (IAPO), *Declaration on Patient-Centered Healthcare*)

In some respects, patient-centered care is synonymous with person-centered care. The Center advocates for the use of the term person-centered care in recognition that healthcare professionals also work with older adults in community settings in which care-recipients are not acute "patients." Therefore, it is inappropriate to refer to the older adult in a wellness program, support group, or arts activities program as a "patient." In addition, when trying to form partnerships between healthcare professionals and the older adult in acute and primary care settings, the sense of an egalitarian relationship or partnership may be enhanced by referring to and viewing the individual not in the context of a patient or illness, but as a person first. Thus, the Center adopted person-centered as a more holistic and intentional term to shape the learner's concept of the older adult as a holistic being within their environment and partner in their healthcare. The Center faculty developed six critical elements for person-centered care to guide practice (healthcare professionals) and education (faculty in geriatrics and gerontology) to improve care of older adults.

The *first core element is engagement of the older adult and his/her family* (or those of primary significance to the older adult) in a partnership to address healthcare concerns. This includes education for the older adult and family to be able to make healthcare decisions and participate in his/her care. It also includes anticipatory guidance for maintaining quality of life, as well as addressing developmental challenges and potential problems along the life trajectory. This may involve education in the use of online information and healthcare professionals need to be skilled to incorporate tools such as health coaching, motivational interviewing, decision aids, technology support, family presence in rounds, preference-sensitive decision-making, and other emerging tools to foster greater engagement by patients and their families (Peikes, et al.).

The *second is respect for the preferences, values and beliefs, including cultural attributes.* The healthcare professional needs to build a relationship to discern what gives each individual hope and the sense of quality of life. The older adult's hopes and dreams will vary based on his/her own values and beliefs. Each person has a unique sense of what gives life beauty and joy, which may also be an expression of his/her culture. When the healthcare professional utilizes the humanities to gain a better understanding of their own experiences as a healthcare provider, it reinforces the value of the humanities for understanding the human experience of the older adult, his/her family, and even the healthcare colleagues who collaborate to provide comprehensive and supportive healthcare.

A *third element is communication,* especially to create space for the individual and family to discuss medical and health concerns, as well as their fears, hopes and anxieties. Healthcare professionals can engage the older adult and family in discussions for goal setting and advanced care planning, including breaking bad news in a sensitive manner and setting, holding difficult discussions in compassionate and supportive ways, and addressing family conflicts. A basic tenet of communication with older adults and families is respect for each individual as a person. When facing life-threatening illness, people want to feel listened to, cared for, and to be known as people rather than diseases. Showing empathy, thoughtfulness, acceptance, respectfulness, and patience can help older adults feel supported as they make decisions that impact their quality of life. Another key strategy to help healthcare professionals view the older adult as someone with potential and not a healthcare problem is to engage the individual and family to discern strengths that facilitate their life journey. This involves active listening as well as encouraging the sharing of narratives and stories of the older adult to build positive relationships.

A *fourth element is recognition of the importance of comfort and supportive care* for older adults and their families. This must include the sensitivity to non-medical needs such as the need for spirituality and meaning making as well as the possibility of suffering. Holistic modalities can be employed that support well-being and focus on self-awareness and self-expression, relaxation, joy and well-being.

Another element is *attention to the coordination and integration of care* for older adults across all setting. There must be accountability by each healthcare professional to ensure safety, security, and personhood during transitions in care across settings, including home, hospital, nursing homes, rehabilitation, etc. This accountability must extend to all providers communicating the plan of care, goals of care, treatment concerns, etc. to other healthcare professionals involved in the care of any one older adult. This requires team building and interdisciplinary collaboration. It also behooves the healthcare professionals to engage in nurturing self, team members, and collaborators to enhance their resilience as caregivers.

The *final element is recognition of the importance of community outreach and involvement* for maintaining function, independence, and quality of life for older adults. There must be system supports for person-centered care. In addition, there must be societal awareness of the importance of opportunities for creative expression in the community and healthcare settings for lifelong learning for older adults, opportunities for spiritual and social engagement, and opportunities for continued growth and development.

To help teach or create practice change, the humanities offer opportunities to gain insight into the intersection of the human experience and the rapidly changing landscape of science, technology, and public policy in healthcare. This occurs through the stories we tell and hear and the thoughts we share in our common quest for reaching our highest potential and maximizing the quality of our lives and the lives of those for whom we care. This understanding of the facets of the lives of patients, families, and healthcare professionals is then reflected in a more individualized and person-centered approach to care.

When healthcare professionals and family caregivers are able to experience the power of creative arts for older adults as well as themselves, they are more able to appreciate the capacity of the older adult for growth and development as well as continued relationships and participation in community. The importance of the creative arts for older adults was demonstrated in research by the late Gene D. Cohen who conducted a multisite study with the aim of measuring the impact of professionally conducted cultural programs on the physical health, mental health, and social functioning of older adults. Cohen's study was the first controlled study to look at the impact of tapping into creative potential, as opposed to focusing only on the physical problems as a way to promote healthy aging. The study had an intervention and a control group of 150 older adults in each. The ages of the participants ranged from 65 to 103 years with an average age of 80 and 30% reflected racial and ethnic minorities.

The intervention group engaged in weekly participatory arts programs for six months and the control group continued their usual weekly activities. The outcomes indicated that the intervention group had better health than the control group as measured in fewer doctor's visits, fewer episodes of illness and less medication. They were less anxious and had a lower incidence of depression, as compared to the control group. The intervention group actually increased their other activities and social engagement. Thus, Cohen demonstrated the value of creative engagement for older adults to enhance their health and well-being.

QUALITY OF LIFE

The person-centered care approach enables healthcare professionals and organizations to transcend traditional views of older adults and disease-focused healthcare to view the older adult in the context of their family and community, e.g. the context of their quality of life, even though they are facing serious, chronic illnesses over many years. Quality of life is defined as "the individual's perception of their position in life in the context of the culture and value system where they live and in relation to their goals, expectations, standards and concerns" (World Health Organization Quality of Life Assessment). This is a complex concept that incorporates the person's physical health, psychological state, level of independence, social relationships, personal beliefs, and relationship to salient features of the environment.

The Quality of Life Model illustrated in Figure 4 provides a way to assess the impact of health and illness for every person as a unique bio-psycho-social-spiritual being who is complex in nature and who varies in their stages of growth and development. By treating each person as a unique bio-psycho-social-spiritual being, healthcare providers can help older adults to find opportunities for continued growth, development, and creative activities to enhance their ability to cope, adapt, and continue to find hope and meaning through illness and dying. By considering each quality of life dimension, healthcare professionals can individualize care and help older adults to build upon their strengths and assets to minimize the sense of loss or impairment that accompanies serious and progressive illnesses. For instance, if an older adult is losing the ability to walk or drive independently the *Quality of Life Model* below provides a framework for exploring strengths and assets within the psycho-social and spiritual dimensions. This may reveal alternate opportunities to fulfill role expectations, socialize or continue to practice spiritual activities that are important to them. One possibility is arranging for the older adult to obtain a ride with others or have spiritual community activities come to their home.

Table 1. Quality of Life Model. Adapted from City of Hope.

Physical	Psychological
Functional Ability	Anxiety
Strength/fatigues	Depression
Sleep and rest	Enjoyment/leisure
Nausea	Pain distress
Appetite	Happiness
Constipation	Fear
Pain	Cognition/attention
Social	**Spiritual**
Financial issues	Hope
Caregiver issues	Suffering
Roles and relationships	Meaning of pain
Affection/Sexual Function	Religiosity
Appearance	Transcendence

(City of Hope Pain & Palliative Care Resource Center)

Certainly, the quality of life may be severely challenged in older adults by real or threatened disability, loss of functioning, and altered family and social relationships. While one might assume that health and quality of life are complementary and overlapping, in the context of the earlier definition, quality of life is really a subjective concept based on the person's overall assessment of well-being – a composite of many personal and clinically important factors, expressed within the content of one's culture, society, and environment (Ferrell, Dow, and Grant).

Quality of life and one's sense of well-being is integrally tied to one's sense of hope and ability to continue participating in life decisions, including health-care decision-making.

Fostering hope is also an integral element in one's sense of well-being and quality of life for older adults facing serious, progressive illness. When discuss-ing diagnoses, future symptoms and management, prognosis and treatment options, it is important to communicate a balance of realism and hope (Hagerty et al. 1278). Hope can take many forms, including hope for a cure, living longer than expected, attending a special event, exploring achievable goals, being a part of everyday living with good support, care, pain and symptom manage-ment, finding meaning in life. The sense of hope for older adults may come from relationships, one's own faith and belief system, being able to maintain dignity and a sense of humor as well as finding inner peace. Healthcare pro-fessionals can enhance hope by "being there" and treating the individual as a whole person with dignity and worth. Realism involves open and honest dis-cussions about the disease prognosis, treatment options, likely complications, symptoms, and exacerbations of the disease that may occur. Then the older adult and his or her family will feel a sense of control and confidence as they journey through various aspects of the illness and they will be able to focus on other sources of hope and opportunities that may still lie ahead.

A story that captures the essence of overcoming Ageism and the realities of aging while capitalizing on the person and their resources is of The Intergen-erational School (TIS) in Cleveland, Ohio. The school was developed by Cathy Whitehouse in collaboration with her husband Peter Whitehouse, a neurosci-entist who has a practice caring for people with Alzheimer's and related demen-tias. The public charter school opened in 2000 to serve low income children from disadvantaged backgrounds in the Cleveland area. His wife is the direc-tor of the public charter school. The patients from Whitehouse's practice with mild-to-moderate neurocognitive impairments are offered the opportunity to volunteer and mentor in the charter school.

The older adults visit the school one day per week and some of their inter-ventions include engaging in singing, reading, and storytelling. Certainly, the child can read to them or they can read to the child. They also participated in environmental science, as the school is located near a watershed where they can go out and study together, explore together, both young and older adults. A study of the older adult volunteers at TIS compared them to a similar group of older adults who participated in an adult education course (George and Singer). They found a statistically significant decline in the stress levels, a decline in depression, increase in sense of usefulness, and a change in cognitive func-tioning for the older adults who volunteered at the charter school which did not occur in the control group.

The qualitative results indicated that the older adults' perceived health benefits were reduced stress and depression, a greater level of energy and sense of cognitive stimulation, increase in the sense of purpose and usefulness, and certainly increase in social relationships. While the group with neurocognitive disorders certainly had very serious, chronic illness, they were still able to engage meaningfully and in ways that enhance their health and well-being. In addition, the children in this school are testing higher than children in the other Cleveland public schools as well as the private schools. So many positive benefits are derived from this program!

Healthcare professionals and older adults and their families need to be aware of the challenges of aging and Ageism for maximizing the quality of life in older adulthood. Healthcare professionals will be more able to provide excellent medical and healthcare when they utilize an integrated geriatric and palliative care framework that includes consideration of the needs and potential of older adults as well as compassion for individuals who may be suffering from chronic illnesses. This framework assumes a person-centered approach that focuses on the individual needs of each person with sensitivity to their preferences, values, and beliefs. By consideration of the individualized goals of care for each older adult and family, the healthcare professional will be able to help the older adult achieve the highest quality of life. When healthcare professionals approach each older adult as a person of value and dignity, they are more able to see them as a person with potential rather than a healthcare problem to solve.

REFERENCES

Adeyi, Olusoji, Owen Smith, and Sylvia Robles. *Public Policy and the Challenge of Noncommunicable Diseases*. Washington, D.C.: World Bank, 2007. Print.

American Association of Retired Persons. AARP Experience Corps, 6 Dec. 2012. Web. 5 July 2013.

American Nurses Association. "Person-Centered Care what does it Actually Mean." *American Nurse* 44.6 (2012): 3. Print.

Anderson, Gerald. "Hospital and Chronic Care." Powerpoint presentation to the American Hospital Association. Princeton, NJ: Robert Wood Johnson Foundation Partnership for Solutions. 16 June 2004.

Baltes, Paul, and Reinhold Kliegl. "Further Testing Limits of Plasticity: Negative Age Differences in a Mnemonic Skill are Robust." *Developmental Psychology* 29.1 (1992): 121-25. Print.

Blazer, Dan. "Depression in late life: Review and commentary." *Journal of Gerontology. A Biological Science and Medical Science* 58 (2003): 249-65. Print.

Bowman, Carmen, and Karen Schoeneman. "Development of the Artifacts of Culture Change Tool_Report of Contract HHSM-500-2005-00076P, Quality of Life Proxy Indicators, HHSM-500-2005-00076P between the Centers for Medicare & Medicaid Services (CMS) and Edu-Catering, LLP." Centers for Medicare & Medicaid Services, 26 Apr. 2006. Web. 14 Aug. 2013.

Bruce, Martha, et al. "Major Depression in Elderly Home Health Care Patients." *American Journal of Psychiatry* 159 (2002): 1367-74. Print.

Carstensen, Laura, Derek Isaacowitz, and Susan Charles. "Taking Time Seriously: A Theory of Socioemotional Selectivity." *American Psychologist* 54.3 (1999): 165-81. Print.

———, Joseph Mikels, and Mara Mather. "Aging and the Intersection of Cognition, Motivation, and Emotion." *Handbook of the Psychology of Aging*. Ed. James Birren and K. Warner Schaie. San Diego: Elsevier, Inc., 2006. 343-62. Print.

Center for Aging, Health and Humanities. The George Washington University, 15 Aug. 2013. Web. 1 Oct. 2013.

Center for Disease Control and Prevention. *Supplement on Aging & 2nd Supplement on Aging*. Center for Disease Control and Prevention, 2006, 8 Aug. 2009. Web. 1 July 2013.

City of Hope. "Quality of Life Model: City of Hope Pain & Palliative Care Resource Center." City of Hope, 26 Sept. 2013. Web. 1 Oct. 2013.

Cohen, Gene. "Research on creativity and aging: The positive impact of the arts on health and illness." *Generations* 30.1 (2006): 7-15. Print.

Cooper, Sarah, and Peter Coleman. "Caring for the Older Person: An Exploration of Perceptions using Personal Construct Theory." *Age and Ageing* 30 (2001): 399-402. Print.

Cuddy, Amy, and Susan Fiske. "Doddering but Dear: Process, Content, and Function in Stereotyping of Older Persons." *Ageism: Stereotyping and Prejudice Against Older Persons*. Ed. Todd D. Nelson. Cambridge: Bradford Press. (2002): 3-26. Print.

———, et al. "Stereotype Content Model Across Cultures: Toward Universal Similarities and some Differences." *British Journal of Social Psychology* 48 (2009): 1-33. Print.

Ferrell, Betty, Karen Dow, and Marcia Grant. "Measurement of the Quality of Life in Cancer Survivors." *Quality of Life Research* 4.6 (1995): 523-31. Print.

Gawande, Atul. "Letting Go. What should medicine do when it can't save your life?" *The New Yorker*, 2 Aug. 2010. Web. 10 Sept. 2013.

Gelenberg, Alan. "Depression is Still Underrecognized and Undertreated." *Archives of Internal Medicine* 159.15 (1999): 1657-58. Print.

Gellis, Zvi. "Evidence-based practice in older adults with mental health disorders." *Social Work Desk Reference*. 2nd edition. Ed. Albert Roberts. New York: Oxford UP, 2010. 843-52. Print.

George, Daniel, and Mendel Singer. "Intergenerational Volunteering and Quality of Life for Persons With Mild to Moderate Dementia: Results From a

5-Month Intervention Study in the United States." *American Journal Geriatric Psychiatry* 19.4 (2011): 392-96. Print.

Glisky, Elizabeth. "Changes in Cognitive Function in Human Aging." *Brain Aging: Models, Methods, and Mechanisms.* Ed. David Riddle. Boca Raton, Fl: Taylor and Francis Group CRC Press, 2007. 4-5. Print.

Hagerty, Rebecca G., et al. "Communicating with Realism and Hope: Incurable Cancer Patients' Views on the Disclosure of Prognosis." *Journal of Clinical Oncology* 23.6 (2005): 1278-88. Print.

Hess, Thomas, et al. "The Impact of Stereotype Threat on Age Differences in Memory Performance." *Journals of Gerontology: Series B; Psychological Sciences and Social Sciences* 58B.1 (2003): 3-11. Print.

Institute of Medicine. Crossing the Quality Chasm: A New Health System for the 21st Century, Consensus Report. Washington, D.C.: Institute of Medicine, 2001. Print.

———. Retooling for an Aging America: Building the Health Care Workforce, Consensus Report. Washington, D.C.: Institute of Medicine, 2008. Print.

International Alliance of Patients' Organizations (IAPO). *Declaration on Patient-Centered Healthcare,* 2006. Web. 10 July 2013.

Iversen, Thomas, Lars Larsen, and Per E. Solem. "A Conceptual Analysis of Ageism." *Nordic Psychology* 61.3 (2009): 4-22. Print.

Jagger, Mick. *Brainy Quote.com.* Web. 5 July 2013.

Kang-Yi, C.D., and Zvi Gellis. "Systematic Review of Community-based Health Interventions on Depression For Older Adults With Heart Disease." *Aging and Mental Health* 14.1 (2010): 1-19. Print.

Kinsella, Kevin, and Wan He. "An Aging World, 2008." *U.S. Census Bureau International Population Reports,* issued June 2009. Web. 5 July 2013.

Kitwood, Tom. "On Being a Person." *Dementia Reconsidered: The Person Comes First.* Buckingham, UK: Open UP, 1997. 7-19. Print.

Martin, Joyce, et al. "Births: Final Data for 2010." *National Vital Statistics Reports 60.1.* Hyattsville, MD: National Center for Health Statistics, 2012. Print.

Murphy, Sherry, Jiaquan Xu, and Kenneth Kochanek. "Deaths: Final Data for 2010." *National Vital Statistics Report 60.4.* Hyattsville, MD: National Center for Health Statistics, 2012. Print.

National Alliance on Mental Illness. *Depression in Older Persons Fact Sheet,* Oct. 2009. Web. 28 Sept. 2013.

PEW. "Living to 120 and Beyond: Americans' Views on Aging, Medical Advances and Radical Life Extension, PEW Research Religion and Public Life Project." *PEW Research Religion and Public Life Project,* 6 Aug. 2013. Web. 5 July 2013.

Peikes, Deborah, Aparajita Zutshi, Janice Genevro, Kimberly Smith, Michael Parchman, and David Meyers. *Early Evidence on the Patient-Centered*

Medical Home. Final Report. Prepared by Mathematica Policy Research under Contract Nos. HHSA290200900019I/HHSA29032002T and HHSA290200900019I/HHSA29032005T. AHRQ Publication No. 12-0020-EF. Rockville, MD: Agency for Healthcare Research and Quality, Feb. 2012. Web. 8 Oct. 2013.

Rahhal, Tamara, Lynn Hasher, and Stanley Colcombe. "Instructional Manipulations and Age Differences in Memory: Now You See them, Now You Don't." *Psychology and Aging* 16.4 (2001): 697-706. Print.

Rand, Barry. "Where we Stand, Facing the Challenge Of Turning 65. Increased Life Expectancy, Decreased Pensions and Social Security Benefits Add to the Challenge." *AARP Bulletin* 1, Jan. 2011. Web. 5 July 2013.

RAND. Developing Quality of Care Indicators for the Vulnerable Elderly: The ACOVE Project. Rand Corporation, 2004. Web. 10 Sept. 2013.

Scholle, Sarah, Phyllis Torda, Deborah Peikes, Esther Han, and Janice Genevro. "Engaging patients and families in the medial home. Agency of Healthcare Research and Quality." *AHRQ Publications No. 10-0083-EF.* Rockville, MD: U.S. Department of Health and Human Services, 2010. Print.

Silverstein, Shel. "Little Boy and the Old Man." *A Light in the Attic.* 1st edition. New York: HarperCollins, 1981. 92. Print.

The Intergenerational School (TIS), A Community of Lifelong Learners. *tisonline.org,* 2012. Web. 5 July 2013.

Tsevat, Joel, et al. "The Will to Live among HIV-Infected Patients." *Annals of Internal Medicine* 131.3 (1999): 194-98. Print.

U.S. Census Bureau International Population Reports. *An Aging World.* U.S. Census Bureau International Population Reports 2008. Web. 10 Sept. 2013.

U.S. Census Bureau. *Census 2000 Summary File 1; 2010 Census Summary File 1.* U.S. Census Bureau, 2012. Web. 10 Sept 2013.

———. *United States Census Bureau Reports.* Table 1a (1960). Web. 10 Sept. 2013.

USA.gov. *Code of Federal Regulations.* Title 42, Chapter IV, Part 483, 1 Oct. 2002. Web. 4 Oct. 2013.

United Nations Department of Economic and Social Affairs. "World Economic and Social Survey 2007: Development in an Aging World" un.org, 2007. Web. 10 Sept 2013.

Velkoff, Victoria, and Paul Kowal. *Population Aging in Sub-Saharan Africa: Demographic Dimensions 2006. U.S. Census Bureau International Population Reports 2007.* Washington, D.C.: U.S. Dept. of Commerce, Economics and Statistics Administration, U.S. Census Bureau, 2007. Print.

Kennedy, Lauren. "Sheryl Crow's 8 Life Lessons." *WebMD,* 24 Apr. 2009. Web. 5 July 2013.

Wenger, N. S., et al. "A Controlled Trial of a Practice- Based Intervention to Improve Primary Care for Falls, Incontinence, and Dementia." *Journal of the American Geriatrics Society.* 57 (2009): 547-55. Print.

World Health Organization. "Are you ready? What you need to know about aging. World Health Day 2012- toolkit for event organizers." *World Health Organization*, 2012. Web. 10 Sept. 2013.

———. "The top 10 causes of death. Fact sheet No 310." *World Health Organization*, 2013. Web. 10 Sept. 2013.

———. "The World Health Organization Quality of Life Assessment: Position Paper from the World Health Organization." *Social Science & Medicine* 41.11 (1995): 1403-09. Print.

Health and Everyday Bodily Experiences of Old Mexican Women

Meiko Makita

> Mexican women have a very lively awareness of the body. For them, the body, woman's and man's, is a concrete, palpable reality. Not an abstraction or a function but an ambiguous magnetic force, in which pleasure and pain, fertility and death are inextricably intertwined (Paz, "Reflections" 409).

The scarcity of research currently available regarding the individual lived experiences of aging and old age in Mexico points to our lack of understanding on this subject. In this chapter, I explore the ways in which a group of old Mexican women experiences the corporeal aspects of aging and old age. I focus on exploring embodied old age, particularly the tensions and contradictions between the body, mind and society (see Csordas; Tulle). Put simply, the focus is on the lived experience of *having* and *being* an aging body. I do this through the analysis of in-depth interviews using both feminist and life course perspectives. My aim is to uncover not only how old women conceptualize experiences but also how they *feel* experiences (see Reeve et al.), the emotion derived from the lived experience. As Lyon and Barbalet (54) argue, the role of emotions is a crucial link in understanding the relationship between the body and the social world, the experience of embodied sociality, and in this case "embodied aging."

The chapter draws on my doctoral research, which consisted of an exploration of old women's subjective experiences across the life course. It involved in-depth life-story interviews with 32 women[1] aged 60 to 89 of whom 20 were living in the community (either alone or with relatives) and 12 in a nursing home in the metropolitan area of Monterrey, Mexico. I managed to include women from a wide range of social, economic, and cultural backgrounds. These differences might have impacted the findings with respect, for instance, to limiting

---

1 | Anonymity of participants is preserved by the use of pseudonyms.

their generalization across the whole population of old Mexican women. However, I was not interested in generalizing from the experience of my informants but rather in learning from their experience (Chambers 265). Moreover, in my study, I aimed for diversity rather than homogeneity, which I argue enables a further exploration of the complexities of women's aging and old age.

My informants were mostly recruited employing an opportunity sampling, a strategy that proved adequate for the nature and purpose of my study: elicit the voices of "ordinary"[2] old Mexican women. I used a biographical perspective as a method of research and analysis and focused on how my informants made sense of their lives and identities. Its emphasis on the intersection of individual lives and wider social and structural contexts made it a perfect means to explore the meanings of old age and the experience of growing old in Mexican women's lives. In fact, it is precisely such intersection that uncovers both the patterns of women's lifelong gendered and social inequalities and their sites of agency and empowerment. In this chapter, I focus on exploring old women's narratives of health: their notions of their own bodies undergoing physical changes and their strategies to manage their health and aging bodies in relation to self and others.

The chapter first takes a look at various definitions of health and disease by way of providing a brief conceptual template prior to the presentation of the empirical data. It then concentrates on the participants' various and general ideas about what "healthy" means, presenting several notions of health in terms of function, fate, absence of disease/pain, and attitude. This is then contrasted with individual accounts of health status with emphasis on the notion of "normal" health for an old person, followed by some concluding remarks.

WHAT DOES BEING "HEALTHY" MEAN?

Within contemporary sociological theory the concept of "health" by way of encoding and articulating social structures such as class, race, gender, sexuality and age has become central to the definition of *Self* and its counterpart, *Other* (Crawford, "Boundaries" 1348-49). Bio-medically, socially and morally, the "healthy self," Crawford has argued, is constructed in opposition to the "unhealthy other." For instance, the World Health Organization defines health as "a state of complete physical, mental and social wellbeing, not merely the absence of disease or infirmity" (WHO). However, as Figlio asserts, the term "health" by itself is not necessarily the opposite of disease or illness; "perfect

---

2 | I emphasise this word because I was not interested in studying solely a specific segment of the population of old women, like for instance veteran athletes, an ethnic minority, lesbians or disabled people.

health" would be the counterpart to disease (qtd. in Lupton 69). The concept of health therefore is certainly complex as it denotes more than a medical condition or the absence of illness. Moreover, official definitions of health do not allow for people's own personal definitions, which are relative, dynamic and derived from lived experiences that represent those who do not conform to the normative notion of health (Lupton 72).

Now, the concepts of disease and illness are also complex. In his article, "Disease and illness: distinctions between popular and professional ideas of sickness," Eisenberg (143) proposed to differentiate between the two terms by stating that medical practitioners *diagnose* and *treat* "diseases," which in the scientific paradigms of modern medicine are seen as abnormalities in the function or structure of body organs and systems, while "illnesses" are *experienced* and *suffered* by an individual and are also, as other authors have argued, social or symbolic pathogens or events that threaten to disrupt everyday activities, role performances and obligations upon which self-identity relies (Crawford, "Boundaries" 1356; Bury 168).

With these ideas in mind, I opted for asking my informants to describe what being healthy means to them, before asking them to reflect on their own current *health status*. I wanted to see whether their ideas or values of health, as a categorical concept, would differ from their assessment of their own health status. Certainly, I expected their accounts to be shaped by their personal experiences and day-to-day concerns and to be embedded in their socio-cultural setting – the question remained *how?*

Women's Definitions of Health

In what follows, I present the participants' general notions of what being healthy is, and their own health status perceptions with a view to uncovering how they construct their ideas about the relation between health and an aging body in the context of their everyday lives.

Most of the women defined "healthy" beyond just bio-medical or physical terms; very few focused on the absence or presence of a specific disease, illness, pain or impairment. In their descriptions of what "healthy" means to them, there was an evident sense of embodiment as most of them initially stated that "feeling good" was the very first sign of being healthy. They were certainly referring to the *emotions* derived from their bodily experiences, from what they "do" with their bodies. In this sense, it is through the body that their emotional wellbeing finds its confirmation (Crawford, "Cultural" 80). For most of these women, the state of "feeling good" constitutes the meaning and, drawing on Crawford ("Boundaries" 1348), the symbolic substance of being healthy. However, more extensive accounts or categories of *health* were evident: health as function, health as fate, health as absence of disease/pain, and health as attitude.

HEALTH AS FUNCTION

"To be healthy? Well, it's to feel good, feeling (pause) to feel you are well, that you can do things, that you are able to manage on your own" (Leonor, age 63 M[3]). As this quote shows, for the majority of the women to be healthy was equivalent to "feeling good." However, an impressively consistent theme emerged in several interviews. Many of the informants discussed the word "healthy" in terms of "being able to do your own things" and "manage on your own" as expressed by Leonor. They went on to relate health with everyday activities such as personal care, domestic chores (e.g. cleaning, cooking), caring for others, or "being able to go out on your own" as stated by Victoria (age 65 W), or engaging in social activities, which clearly reflects on issues of independence and remaining active, as it was also stressed by Maria Inés (age 85 W) and Adela (age 64 M). In this sense, the meaning of being healthy definitely expands bio-medical interpretations. Thus, feeling good is certainly not an end in itself but rather a means in order to take care of themselves.

For these women, being healthy was unmistakably explained in relation to having a physically *able body*; a body that remains functioning. Being healthy, by means of remaining functional, has a purpose: self-care and care for others, an attitude/action that one could argue is motivated by the women's cultural values and traditions (i.e. motherhood, family, feminine identity).

HEALTH AS FATE

Another understanding of "healthy" was constructed in terms of *determinism* in the sense of fate or destiny. Such understanding includes two main ideas. One is the notion that health is determined by genetic characteristics, and thus we are predetermined to have a certain health status and/or health issues. The other is the idea that health is determined by God's will, regardless of what people did or not to remain healthy or to prevent becoming ill. This construction of health as fate is important because it connects being healthy to religious beliefs on the one hand, and to biological predispositions on the other. In this latter respect, Victoria (age 65 W) was the only informant who elaborated on the notion of health as a genetic predisposition. Although she recognized that people could improve their health and quality of life by taking some pertinent

---

3 | The letters indicating marital status are explained in a table at the end of this chapter.

actions, such as eating healthily and doing physical exercise, she highlighted that these actions have a minimal impact and that it is mainly genes that determine whether one is healthy or not. Within such deterministic views, it seems there is little room for personal control and the possibility to influence one's own health status, as the emphasis is on inherent biological constraints and limitations.

The second notion of health as fate – as determined by God – offers a more self-reflective idea of one's own health and bodily experiences and certainly about one's life purposes and existence. Thus, this notion of health embodies agency, as the person actively exercises his or her beliefs and gives a religious meaning to the construct of health. Although the assessment of the relationship between religion and health has proven problematic, some research has revealed that older people are certainly more deeply involved in religion than younger people (Barna qtd. in Krause and Bastida 114). This religious involvement or spirituality is evident in the majority of the informants, thus one could argue that their religious faith is central not only to their notions of health and illness, but also an essential aspect of aging and old age.

Xóchitl (age 85 W) and Angeles (age 89 W) were the two informants that explicitly gave a religious account about the meaning of being healthy. Both of them conceptualize health according to their faith; both see health and illness indistinctively as a mandate from God.

Xóchitl: Well, it depends; being healthy depends on each person's health, right? [. . .] But I think it's also that God's will has them like that!
Researcher: Like that, how?
Xóchitl: Sick, I mean; it's definitely God's will if you are sick or not, 'cos you can take lots of vitamins and lots of everything, anything, but what God, our lord says, that's what is going to happen.
Researcher: So, no matter what you do [. . .]
Xóchitl: Well, there are many things to think about, like when I see people that have never, ever worked, well that's also something not good, but still when God says you are gonna get sick, you get sick, no matter what that person does. Because no one is going to die healthy and sane! [. . .] You shouldn't say "not me", "I'm healthy and good and this and that, so it's not going to happen."

As Xóchitl's account reveals, the understanding that God has designated a certain fate for each person, allowing things to happen, and specifically allowing a person to be healthy or sick, is built within a deep religious faith that forms part of her identity. It is through her beliefs that Xóchitl is able to explain and accept why people would get ill or unwell, and so one could argue that her understanding of health as God's will is a key management strategy she uses to cope with illness and disease. Certainly, Xóchitl's notion of health is relevant in the sense that it is consistent with the findings of some scholars that have long argued that one of the main functions of religious faith is to give people a sense of meaning and purpose in life (see Spilka et al.). Even though in her account there is no other possible explanation as to why people get sick, her brief comments of "I see people that have never, ever worked" could be regarded as another explanation for health and disease on the grounds of the benefits of keeping physically active. However, she might also be looking at "work" as an activity by which a person feels useful and serves him/herself, other people, and ultimately serves God. Since her view of health is indeed deterministic, it is also not surprising that she recognizes how vulnerable anyone is to illness and disease. As will be shown later, such awareness of vulnerability is a theme shared by many of my informants, notwithstanding their varied definitions of health and notions of their own state of health.

Previously, Angeles first gave me an account of health in terms of functional independence; however, later on she added other interesting aspects to her definition of "healthy." Although there is no mentioning of sickness in both parts of her account, the latter one clearly goes beyond the physical aspects she initially referred to: "But I also think to be healthy is (pause) well, most of the time with people's suffering and your own suffering you teach yourself to be good, to be a better person each day and understand all the people that suffer, right? So, I'm very grateful to God, because thanks to *"Diosito"* [God] I've always been all right, I've always had everything I've needed and my children look after me." Here, it seems that Angeles has a deeply embodied notion of health embedded in her religious faith, with feelings and sentiments as key aspects, especially that of "suffering." For her, to be healthy converges with her desire and/or opportunity to be a *good person*, thus for her, being "healthy" is, as Blaxter would argue, "the sign of moral wellbeing" (45). What is even more interesting is how she identifies understanding other people's suffering and her own as a means of becoming a better person, and by extension, a good Catholic. This latter aspect is relevant because it certainly evokes views of *suffering* and *pain* deeply rooted in Mexican Catholic culture, which are also closely associated with views of health, issues of care and notions of being a burden in old age.

Historically, there are several accounts of why pain and suffering are central features of Mexican culture. First, Spanish Colonization brought native people and *mestizos* into a status of subordination and domination and thus both natives and *mestizos* encountered a great deal of pain and suffering (see Rodríguez; Leon). Second, in his book *El Laberinto de la Soledad (The Labyrinth of Solitude)*, Nobel Prize winner Octavio Paz discussed at length the roles "suffering" and "solitude" play in the psyche of many Mexicans today. Paz defines solitude as "the feeling and knowledge that one is alone, alienated from the world and oneself [. . .]" ("Laberinto" 88). Furthermore, he states that solitude creates a dualism: self-awareness and a longing to escape from ourselves. He also stresses that "popular language reflects this dualism by identifying solitude with suffering [. . .]" (Paz, "Laberinto" 89). Third, several authors argue that because of the impact of Spanish colonialism and subsequent historical events (e.g. Mexican Independence, Mexican Revolution, Mexican-US relationship) many Mexicans sought relief in their religious faith, that is, Catholicism, which is particularly visible in the manifestations of faith surrounding *Our Lady of Guadalupe* (see Rodríguez; Leon; Elizondo). According to Rodríguez, the *Virgin of Guadalupe* has a role "so central to Mexican culture that any consideration of the Mexican people in general [. . .] must include reference to her" (46). This is why, the historical accounts of pain and suffering came to shape the way many Mexicans live their religion and consequently the way they deal with the difficulties or challenges they encounter: health and illness.

Thus, for Angeles to be healthy is the result of a cultural learning process; the outcome of understanding one's own and others' pain and suffering. Moreover, suffering *per se* is not as central as the learning experience that derives from it, which helps to fully understand the suffering of others, which at the same time is in line with the precepts of Catholic faith. Whilst Xóchitl's explanation of health was constructed on the grounds of God's – arbitrary – will, Angeles adds other dimensions to such an explanation: (1) her deep sense of appreciation and gratitude toward God and his purpose, and (2) the importance of her family interaction and care. The former aspect is relevant because some studies have shown that feelings of gratitude towards God are related to better physical and mental health (Krause and Bastida 118). However, the same can be argued about the effects on health of positive interpersonal relationships. As Krause and Bastida (121) contend, the potential influence of significant others emerges as a central feature in the process of dealing with [illness] and suffering. Thus, with such realization of health/suffering placing religious faith as its centerpiece, one could argue, Angeles is also revealing the strategy she uses for coping with her health problems.

Health as the Absence of Disease/Pain

As stated earlier, very few of the informants defined "healthy" by focusing on the absence or presence of disease, illness, pain or impairment. These types of accounts are in line with the biomedical discourse of health, however, they also reflect the role of emotions in the individual's experience, and since illness and pain are lived/felt in the body these are certainly embodied accounts. Amalia (age 67 W), Raquel (age 81 W), Guadalupe (age 82 W) and Norma (age 86 NM) shared this view of health.

"Well, to me [healthy] means to be a little more comfortable, the less diseases one has the better one feels!" (Guadalupe). Guadalupe defines "being healthy" as the counterpart to having a disease: The fewer diseases, the healthier a person is. This account, however, also reveals another definition of health, that is, a definition of health grounded in the everyday "social-emotional experience" (Crawford, "Cultural" 85). Thus, being healthy is not only valued upon the absence or presence of a disease but in terms of *being comfortable*. To Guadalupe both the cause and purpose of being healthy is to *feel* comfortable. Amalia's account of health takes on a similar line: "[Healthy] is to feel that your body is not giving you any signals of pain, or that something is bothering you. It's having enough energy to do things, without making a huge effort and without feeling that your body is in pain."

Again, the concept of health appears in terms of the relationship between "feeling" and the state of the physical body. For Amalia, the absence of pain is what determines not only being healthy but *feeling* healthy. Consequently, feeling healthy is also what helps her to be at ease and manage her everyday life.

Whilst these two informants view health as the absence of disease and pain, which in turn serves as the vehicle to *feel* healthy, Norma's account goes a step beyond and reflects the absence of disease/pain as a desired goal that requires active management. More specifically, to Norma, being "healthy" is being regularly monitored by her medical doctor; the fact that she stresses how important it is for her to get vaccinations and regular check-ups in order to "keep illness away" conveys a narrative of prevention. Furthermore, her account carries an implicit sense of wellbeing derived from the reassurance of being taken care of, as she referred to how fortunate she was "for having a private doctor that takes care of my health and is always checking in." Accordingly, to be healthy, to maintain health, and to avoid illness, takes on the symbolic value of an interpersonal relationship built on trust.

Health as Attitude

Thus far, these notions of health differ greatly from one another; however, they all are conceptualized upon the daily experience of embodiment in which the relationship between the body and emotions is crucial. Interestingly enough, so far none of the women's definitions of what "healthy" means made any reference to age, let alone to old age and aging. However, there is still a significant narrative of health to discuss: health as attitude. This category is important for two reasons: (1) a considerable number of informants (eleven) shared this view, and (2) it provides an opportunity to examine the mind-body relationship and issues of agency and emotion.

In sociology, traditionally, to discuss the mind-body dualism is certainly problematic. The reason for this, Crossley ("Embodiment" 81) would argue, is that sociologists have primarily focused on people's behavior, actions, interactions and practices by which, almost inadvertently, they have managed to transcend the distinction between mind and body. The foundations for such a distinction are attributed to Descartes' reflections on the existence of God and human nature in which he provided modern Western culture with an epistemological notion of the body as an *object*, a *mechanical* entity separated from the *soul* or *mind* that was clearly elevated as an *inner substance* rooted in thought and knowledge and distinct from the *corporeal* body (see Crawford, "Boundaries"; Crossley, "Social body"; Tulle). Even though sometimes there is a tendency in contemporary theoretical approaches to demean "Cartesian dualism" (Csordas 7), this shift has been a valuable aid for analyses with practical consequences for human agency as it marked the rise of –Western – individualism (Tulle 19). Moreover, this radical separation of mind and body gave way to a new kind of knowledge aimed at mastery and control of the newly objectified body. Thus, "when the body became an abstracted entity, identical to all other bodies, detached from living situations, health became a concept for describing its normal state." (Crawford, "Boundaries" 1350).

Accordingly, the account of health as attitude appears to be a "mind over matter" narrative; the body is objectified and the self is the conscious mind that "has" an objective body (Jackson 207). For these women, attitude is a key signifier of health. More specifically, a healthy body seems to depend on a healthy mind first, contrary to the famous dictum of *mens sana in corpore sano*. However, this construct of health as attitude is rather complex and needs to be unpacked in detail. Florencia's (age 72 D) description summarizes this notion of health: "The thoughts, the mind, the attitude is what determines to feel good or bad; good thinking and bad thinking are reflected in yourself. We are creations of our own thoughts."

This account shows clearly how it is through the mind – good or bad, positive or negative thinking and attitudes –that the person is affected and becomes either a healthy or an unhealthy body. In this sense, such a notion of health is in line with an act of management; Florencia sees being healthy as the result of an active "integration" of mind and body into her lived processes. This is of course where this mind-body dynamic becomes quite complex, as Florencia in fact is not merely talking about the body as an object, but instead she appears to be talking about the whole person, the *self* as being affected by both positive and negative attitudes. This notion of being "creations of our own thoughts" is expressed by many of my informants, for instance Evelia highlighted how important it is to have a "peaceful mind" in order to be physically healthy. Furthermore, Evelia as well as Florencia, Luisa, Raquel, Adela, Isabel, Elena, and Matilde all share the idea that leading a stressful life, having a negative attitude or being bad-tempered cause illness or disease. Bertha, for example stated that worrying too much is one of the reasons some people develop cancer. And thus she, as well as the informants mentioned above, claimed that in order to avoid ill-health one should "take it easy" or be *"conchuda"* [laid-back], as Evelia notes, and not be thinking about illnesses at all.

Apparently, for these women being healthy is a matter of personal responsibility, the ownership of a positive mental attitude has a positive impact on the physical body. One could argue that the emphasis on the mind over the body appears as a result of these women being aware of their aging bodies. Their bodies are increasingly vulnerable to disease, distress and dysfunction, prone to fail and "dys-appear", as Leder (89) would argue. In fact, Leder's "dys-appearing body" seems to constitute the experiential core of Cartesian dualism by explaining why there are times when people experience the self as separated from the body. When the body functions properly and without pain or discomfort, when it is absent from experience in the sense that no pain is felt, body and the self (mind) are fully integrated in a harmonious performance. When the opposite is the case, the dys-appearance of the body brings the notion that self and body exist separately, invoking aspects of subjectivity (the "I") and objectivity (the "me") (Hepworth 38; Csordas 8). As these women lose control over their bodies, they turn to their minds as the ultimate site of personal agency in an attempt to claim an identity of an aging but competent self. Nevertheless, the notion of health as attitude can be considered a strategy to manage one's own identity as agent in control of one's health despite physical decline in old age.

Whether the key aspect defining health was the ability to function independently, God's will, or genetics, freedom from pain and disease, or the consequence of a positive attitude, the women formulated their accounts based on their everyday experiences of embodiment. Clearly, the meanings of "healthy" discussed so far reveal the ways in which these women retain or redefine their self-identity in old age, and claim agency for having health. Yet, we can also find the notion of "renegotiation of a healthy self." Amongst some women, we can find awareness that not being *completely* healthy was rather *normal*. This is evident in Felícitas' (age 75 W) account: "Well, totally healthy no one can be; that I've learnt in all these years, right? But healthy is not only in the physical aspect, it's emotional, spiritual, mental, right? And people are never at 100%, we always have something, some fault, spiritual, mental, or emotional or physical, always, always there is something in which one fails."

Although there was no allusion to aging and old age, all these accounts were informed by the women's current lived experiences. The age factor became evident once I asked them to describe their own health status. Interestingly, at the *individual* level most of the women do make references to the physical aspects of their aging bodies and elaborate on the absence or presence of certain disease, illness or (physical or emotional) pain, which were missing for the most part in their definitions of what being "healthy" means.

(Un)Healthy Bodies

When specifically asked about their own health status, most of my informants reported having "good health," or "very good health." I opted for using a literal translation of "*tener salud*" [having health], as it provides the cultural context in which particularly health ideas and behavior (Kleinman 146-7) can be identified and discussed. Moreover, the phrase "*tener salud*" [I have health] is not the result of Spanish linguistic rules, as one can also say "estoy sano" [I'm healthy]. Rather, it appears that most of these women talk about health as something one *has* (attains and maintains) and that could be separated from what one is or becomes, from *being*.

Most women gave positive answers regardless of whether or not they had a chronic or degenerative disease, or were in fact undertaking medical treatment for such conditions. Very few acknowledged their health status as "normal." Another informant defined her health as "very poor" and one defined herself as an "ill" person. The subjectivity of the informants' answers about their health status denotes how individual meanings are embedded in particular social interactions and cultural settings. Most informants took into consideration the interaction of the self (mind) and the physical body, the role of emotions and embodied experiences, and therefore were able to normalize illness and disease and give an overall "positive" account of their health status.

More specifically, some participants considered themselves healthy as a result of being able to engage in social and caring activities; others viewed themselves as healthy persons despite the "presence" of disease, pain or impairment, whilst some participants thought of themselves to be in "ill-health" due to their suffering from a disease, pain or distress. Finally, others considered their age and claimed to have "normal" health for an old person. Within each of these health narratives there was a salient aspect: most of the participants' accounts were embedded in the material aspects of aging and old age and engaged in personal agency, showing the potential to adapt to the changes that accompany old age, and also challenging the socio-cultural discourses that see aging and old age in negative terms. Whilst an in-depth discussion of each of these narratives is beyond the scope of this chapter, in what follows I concentrate on the fourth narrative in order to show the interplay of age and health perceptions amongst my informants.

"Normal Health" for an Old Person

Many scholars have critically discussed how the cultural "narrative of decline" (see Gullette; Twigg), which associates loss, physical decline, frailty and poor health with old people, has become the *dominant* narrative for interpreting aging and old age. However, at the empirical level, it is necessary to uncover how old people themselves make the connection between their age and their health status. Amongst the informants, only Cecilia (age 80 NM) stated this relationship, and in a subtle way. She does not mention her age per se but attributes her health status to what seems to be the "normal" or common consequence of old age: "I still feel strong and I feel good, I don't have any other disease, I don't have anything! Well, sometimes I get rheumatics and my knee hurts, but it's only because of the weather and the old bones, there is no remedy but to soldier on!"

Beyond the clear references to physical capabilities, emotional state, and absence of disease/illness used to define her own health, what is relevant in this account is how she explains her at times *dys-appearing* condition, arthritis, not merely as a disease but as something that is a direct consequence of the changes in weather and the "old bones." Although she might not be referring directly to her own age, the use of the term "old bones" evokes her experience of an aging body. Moreover, it is in the last part of her statement where a salient discourse is revealed: "there is no remedy but to soldier on." There is an acceptance of the new circumstances of the body, the rheumatism and the pain. Cecilia sees these as normal. So, arguably, hers is a normative discourse of the body and its correlation with health and old age.

Other informants, although initially evaluating their health as "not so good," considered themselves to be in "normal" health for their age. Interestingly, they all used the expression *"los achaques normales de la edad,"* which could be translated into English as: "the normal travails of old age." Beyond the obvious references to bodily experiences of aging, the most significant part of that expression was the term "normal." Elena's (age 79 W) account is a good example: "Well, definitely I have bad health, I am telling you, having pain here or there and there that is not very good health. Although it's not, how can I say? It's not like I can't move at all! I think my health is very normal at my age, like I say, at my age and with all the things I've been through and everything, I think it's normal!" Elena is giving a coherent description of her health status as it is based on her health problems: she is on medication for hypertension, has a prosthesis in her right leg, suffers from a stomach ulcer and also from thrombophlebitis in both of her legs. Interestingly, she constructs the notion of her health by integrating two elements: "my age" and "all the things I've been through." She recognizes that her age is not the exclusive cause of her current health but merely another factor along with other issues and previous experiences in her life course. As Sidell (33-4) would argue, disease and decline are not "naturally" attributable to old age but rather the result of close interactions between the physical, social and emotional environments. Elena is somewhat aware of this dynamic and its impact on her health. Furthermore, she seems to overcome her health problems (e.g. pain) by attributing them to her age, and in doing so, she takes a "healthy" outlook.

In their accounts, these women were explicitly acknowledging their old age and clearly assessing their own health in a different way to what I presented in previous sections. Apparently, for them the various physical changes and more specifically "health problems" often – but not exclusively – take place in old age. Having problems was something "expected" as a consequence of the passage of time and their various life experiences. Hence, they interpreted their biological/physical difficulties as part of the normal process of aging and old age, as long as they continue to function. Raquel's (age 81 W) comments are pertinent here as she contested that old age is not the cause of her feeling unwell or unhealthy: "I have this pain in my [right] hand, it comes and goes, and the doctors keep telling me [it] is because of my age; so is that it? Only because one is old then there is no cure or treatment? There must be a valid reason for my pain, not just my age!"

Certainly, these accounts are more focused on the physical/biological aspects of health and do not fully integrate the emotional or social context of the women's experiences when compared to those in previous sections. Nonetheless, their perception of their own current health is in relation to being an old person and their life course experiences as a whole. For these women seeing *"los achaques de la edad"* as "normal" is definitely not a narrative of conformity to the physical and biological changes that commonly accompany old age but rather a personal coherent account grounded in the reality they experience every day through their own bodies.

CONCLUSION

In this chapter, health is a dynamic concept old women explain by making references to the daily experience of both the physical body and the social-emotional body. Given the interpretations of what being healthy means to these women (e.g. function; attitude) it seems that the concept of health takes on physical, moral, emotional and spiritual dimensions and is thus also constructed as an *ideal*. However, their individual perceptions of their own health were mainly affected by their sense of reality embedded in their personal experiences of disease, impairment or pain and the social and cultural contexts they live in. Then, it is not surprising that many of the women's ideas and behavior regarding health are also embedded in Mexican religious values.

Conversely, the women's health talk is also quite complex. Most of them appear to make sense of health by emphasizing a mind-body dualism, usually giving a privileged status to the mind. Moreover, it is also helpful to consider the role of language in this process. For these Mexican women health is something one *has*, something apart from the self. In other words, they "have health" and consequently they objectify their bodies. Yet, paradoxically it is by experiencing their own corporeality that they "separate" their bodies from their minds. Their bodies are increasingly vulnerable to disease, distress and dysfunction and that is why oftentimes most of them construct their minds as the site of personal agency for their everyday life experience. Evidently, their bodies are central to both the experience and feelings associated with illness and disease and to the processes involved in their management (Kelly and Field 262). Thus, a mind-body dualism is an essential management strategy not only for constructing an identity of a healthy self but also for making sense of aging and old age. In doing so, they feel in control of their aging bodies, their pain, illness or disease.

Being in control is also the reason why most of these women had a positive outlook in relation to their health and highlighted the importance of "feeling good" by focusing on the positive aspects of their lives, by relying on their emotional and physical capital, instead of focusing on the physical symptoms or limitations they may experience. In sum "feeling good" derives from wanting and having the attitude to "feel good." That is why the majority of the informants considered themselves to be in "good health." It is not that they deny their experiences of pain, impairment or disease; on the contrary, they are aware of their vulnerability to illness, disability, decline, and ultimately death. As these narratives reveal, most of these women show a resilient attitude toward the changes and issues they face in old age. In this context, the investment in their social, emotional, religious and physical capital represents for these women the mechanism for managing their lived experiences and maintaining their self-identity, so that they are able to make sense of health, illness and bodily changes.

REFERENCES

Blaxter, Mildred. "Why do the victims blame themselves?" *Sociology of Health and Illness. A Reader.* Ed. M. Bury and J. Gabe. London: Routledge, 2004. 36-46. Print.

Chambers, Pat. *Older Widows and the Life Course: Multiple Narratives of Hidden Lives.* New Perspectives on Ageing and Later Life Series. Hants, England: Ashgate, 2005. Print.

Crawford, Robert "A cultural account of health, control, release and the social body." *Issues in the political economy of health.* Ed. J. McKinlay. London: Tavistock Publications, 1984. 60-103. Print.

———. "The boundaries of the self and the unhealthy other: reflections on health, culture and AIDS." *Social Science & Medicine,* 38 (1994): 1347-65. Print.

Crossley, Nick. "Researching embodiment by way of 'body techniques'." *Embodying Sociology.* Ed. C. Shilling. Spec. issue of *The Sociological Review* 55.S1 (2007): 80-94. Print.

———. *The Social Body: Habit, Identity and Desire*. London: Sage, 2001. Print.

Csordas, Thomas. "Introduction: the body as representation and being-in-the-world." *Embodiment and experience. The existential ground of culture and self*. Ed. T. Csordas. Cambridge: Cambridge UP, 1997. 1-24. Print.

Elizondo, Virgilio. *Guadalupe: Mother of the New Creation*. New York: Orbis, 1997. Print.

Gullette, Margaret Morganroth. *Declining to Decline: Cultural Combat and the Politics of the Midlife*. Age studies series. Charlottesville: U of Virginia P, 1997. Print.

Hepworth, Mike. *Stories of Ageing*. Buckingham: Open UP, 2000. Print.

Jackson, Jean. "Chronic Pain and the Tension Between the Body as Subject and Object." *Embodiment and experience. The existential ground of culture and self*. Ed. T. Csordars. Cambridge: Cambridge UP, 1997. 201-28. Print.

Kelly, Michael and David Field. "Medical Sociology, Chronic Illness and the Body." *The Sociology of Health and Illness. A reader*. Ed. M. Bury and J. Gabe. London: Routledge, 2004. 256-65. Print.

Kleinman, Arthur. *Patients and Healers in the Context of Culture: An Exploration of the Borderland Between Anthropology, Medicine, and Psychiatry*. Berkeley: U of California P, 1980. Print.

Krause, Neal and Elena Bastida. "Religion, suffering, and health among older Mexican Americans." *Journal of Aging Studies* 23.2 (2009): 114-23. Web. 23 Aug. 2010.

Leder, Drew. *The absent body*. London: U of Chicago P, 1990. Print.

Leon, Luis. *La Llorona's children: Religion, life, and death in the US-Mexican Borderlands*. Berkeley, CA: U of California P, 2004. Print.

Lupton, Deborah. *The Imperative of Health: Public Health and the Regulated Body*. London: Sage, 1995. Print.

Lyon, Margot and Jack Barbalet. "Society's body: emotion and the 'somatization' of social theory." *Embodiment and experience. The existential ground of culture and self*. Ed. T. Csordas. Cambridge: Cambridge UP, 1997. 48-66. Print.

Paz, Octavio. *El Laberinto de la Soledad*. México. D.F: Fondo de Cultura Económica. (2004 [1959]). Print.

———. "Reflections: Mexico and the United States." Trans. R. Phillips. *The History Teacher* 13.3 (1980): 401-15. Web. 24 Aug. 2011.

Reeve, Joanne et al. "Revisiting biographical disruption: exploring individual embodied illness experience in people with terminal cancer." *Health* 14.2 (2010): 178-95. Web. 24 Nov. 2011.

Rodríguez, Jeanette. *Our Lady of Guadalupe: Faith and empowerment among Mexican American women*. Austin, TX: U of Texas P, 1994. Print.

Sidell, Moyra. "Older people's health: applying Antonovsky' salutogenic para-digm." *Debates and dilemmas in promoting health. A reader.* Ed. M. Sidell et al. London: The Open University/MacMillan Press, 1997. 33-9. Print.

Spilka, Bernard et al. *The Psychology of religion: an empirical approach.* 3rd ed. New York: The Guilford Press, 2003. Print.

Twigg, Julia. "The body, gender, and age: Feminist insights in social gerontolo-gy." *Journal of Aging Studies,* 18(1): 59-73. Web. 19 Sep. 2010.

Tulle, Emmanuelle. *Ageing, The Body and Social Change.* London: Palgrave MacMillan, 2008. Print.

WHO. WHO definition of Health as appeared in Preamble to the Constitution of the World Health Organization as adopted by the International Health Conference, New York, 19-22 June, 1946; signed on 22 July 1946 and en-tered into force on 7 April 1948 (2003). Web. 14 Jul. 2010.

ANNEX

Table 1. Transcription notations

Notation	Definition
[word]	Material within square brackets represents the transcriber's clarification of an unclear part, or a change made to preserve anonymity.
"*Italics*"	Italics within quotation marks used to denote Spanish words, followed by the English translation within square brackets.
M	Within brackets denotes being married.
NM	Within brackets denotes having never married.
D	Within brackets denotes being divorced.
W	Within brackets denotes being widowed.

Kwik-Fit versus Varying Speeds of Aging

Elena Bendien

INTRODUCTION

In the interdisciplinary field of Aging Studies, aging is often addressed as a temporal phenomenon. The concept of time when applied to old age varies between measurable time, time as a subjective experience and existential time, to name just a few possible approaches (Birren, Dittman-Kohli, Hendricks and Peters). At the same time little research has been done on the relation between the individual experience of time and the speed of aging. In this article not time itself but the dynamics of temporal experiences that a person has at a later age will be the focus of my attention. This shift can be productive because the images of aging that are often marked as the images of weakness and disease, when depicted within a particular speed frame, create openings for a richer and more appreciative interpretation.

The emphasis on speed and intensity comes forth from my understanding of aging as a process (Bendien 253) or, to be more precise, as "the experience of time passing"[1], which has its roots in process philosophy (Middleton and Brown 62). The attention to the speed of aging is triggered by a phenomenon called *acceleration,* which is defined here as an on-going compression of experience into a unit of clock-time within an increasingly shrinking space[2]. Acceleration in its mundane as well as its historical meaning (as acceleration of history) has already been known since the mid-eighteenth century (Koselleck 241, 242), but its influence on the pace of human development still seems to be increasing (Rosa 3). This article will assess the relation between the process of human aging and acceleration. My starting point is that people possess, or more precisely, are possessed by the ability to age, each with a speed of their

---

1 | This is a definition of the concept of duration used by Middleton & Brown in their discussion on the process philosophy of H. Bergson (62).

2 | This definition is generic; it is inspired by other definitions of social acceleration. See e.g. Koselleck (269), Rosa (7), Leccardi (30) and others.

own. The differences in speed with which people can age can be viewed as a homogeneous process that is measurable and predictable and that in politics tends to form synonymic relations with ageism. But aging can also be seen as an experience that differs from one individual to another and constitutes a fascinating heterogeneous domain, the complexity of which a researcher can only approximate.

Human aging is in fact a heterogeneous process, marked by both acceleration and slowing down. For most of us the later stages of life are associated with decreased mobility, whereby especially fragile older people can evoke the images from a slow-motion film. The question I want to address in this article is whether the change in the speed of living influences the intensity of the experiences of the aging person. The goal of this article is to show that the experience of slowing down, when set off against social acceleration, does not refer to a single homogeneous process of lessening within the process of aging. In order to do this I shall provide examples explaining the divergence in the approach to speed within the policies on aging and in the lives of individuals.

The objectives of the article are: to outline the relations between acceleration and the velocities of aging; to show how living and aging complement each other by using the process approach towards the notion of change; to introduce the *kwik-fit* concept as antipode to the diversity of speeds of aging; and to demonstrate how insight in the divergence of those speeds can enrich and diversify the notion what it is to become old. The discussion will be opened with an empirical introduction of the concept kwik-fit. It will be followed by theoretical reflections on acceleration and change in relation to aging. Acceleration will be shown to reflect changes that have an effect on people, whereas change as understood within process philosophy will be given an ontological status in the context of an individual human life. Acceleration will stand for the quantitative density of one's life, whereby change will emphasize the qualitative intensity and diversity of the life rhythms according to which we age. Examples from on-going international debates on retirement policies, longevity and anti-aging culture will be used to illustrate *acceleration in action* and to frame the concept of kwik-fit. I shall demonstrate that kwik-fit solutions are based on one-size-fits-all strategies in regard to aging. As an alternative to kwik-fit I shall underline heterogeneity as a basic premise in our experience of aging. Some examples from ethnographic studies (one was concluded and one is still in progress (Bendien, *The Art of Remembering*)) will be used in order to show how the images of age-related decline can be transformed into a more subtle narrative of frailty by applying the principle of divergent life rhythms and speeds with regard to aging. Finally, the question whether speed-related notions can be used successfully for (self-)care strategies will be discussed, along with a possible follow-up of this study in other cultural contexts.

Empirical Introduction of Kwik-Fit:
Quick but Not Fitting

The debate on aging in all its manifestations, be it the discussion about obligatory retirement, longevity or anti-aging strategies, shows a friction between
the complexity of the issues at stake and the crude ways in which they are often
being addressed. Those fixing efforts can be called kwik-fit techniques. Their
main feature is derived from the infamous principle "one-size-fits-all," which
can be re-formulated as "one-speed-fits-all." The following example will illustrate this point (Bendien 176-77).

I met Rebecca while conducting an ethnographic research project in the
residential complex for older people in Rotterdam, the Netherlands. Rebecca
was 73 years old. The awkwardness of her movements was caused by progressive Parkinson's disease, which influenced her speech as well. She had been
living alone, but because of the disease she had temporarily been placed in the
nursing home, which she did not like very much. We met, talked and became
friends for the period she spent there. I traveled to Rotterdam for my research,
which meant I was mainly there to see and to listen. Bit by bit she shared with
me the facts of her life. Her stories fluctuated with her wavering voice and
the logic of the connection between the various fragments was sometimes as
awkward as the disobedient movements of her body. From a pleasant story of
her granddaughter who came to visit her, she could switch to an account about
her diminishing health and the growing restriction in her movements, which
she now was feeling more often. Her joyful hope for a nice apartment in one of
the central locations (*because the shops were close by there and the children could
visit her by bike*) was clouded by the realization that a large part of her furniture
would be left behind. The stories about her distant and recent past became a
colorful patchwork. Gradually, I learned how to anticipate emotions that would
make her uneasy by offering her another theme to talk about. She would pick
that up gratefully, calming down, her body and expression relaxing, her voice
returning back to normal and her face smiling at me again in its sharp-witted
way.

Our conversations turned into a mixture of reminiscences about her youth
and events that occurred more recently. She took my attention very seriously
and used every opportunity to teach me things (expressions, traditions) that
were unknown to me. The clock-time we spent together did not matter, probably because neither of us ever abused each other's time. Her inner clock was
perfectly tuned. She moved between the different planes of her memory quite
easily, at one moment telling me about her work, and at another switching to a
story about the night before, when she had not been able to sleep and had gone
to the kitchen to fetch a cup of tea. The nurses had been startled and looked unhappy because they had not expected to see her or any of the clients at that hour.

She wondered why: what could be wrong about fetching a cup of tea or warm milk in order to fall asleep again? Calling the staff and asking for a sleeping pill was not a better alternative. Experiences like that made her sound critical from time to time. One of her stories I remember particularly well.

Some of the nurses required the clients to select the clothes they wanted to wear the next day already the evening before. Rebecca, who still regularly received attention from men, cared for her appearance. Choosing the clothes for the next day was a moment she cherished in her own way. While telling her story she looked at me in desperation, explaining that the unpredictability of Dutch weather prevented her from making the right choice in advance. The planning that was demanded from her was maybe in the best interest of the institution, but it made her uneasy. Then she paused, her expression changing as I had seen many times before. In a rather sharp-witted and humorous way she told me that she had found a solution. At about four o'clock every morning she would secretly switch her radio on and listen to the latest weather forecast. Whenever necessary, she would change the clothes she had selected the previous evening and then return to bed again satisfied. She looked at me triumphantly, and we both burst into laughter.

It was this story that set me thinking about the discrepancies between our experience of time and the speed of life that often underlines our attitude towards older people. The nurses of the home think and act within the frame of their time schedule. This schedule defines how much time they can spend per client, especially during the rush hour in the morning. Their suggestion to select one's clothes for the next day in advance seems to be quite an efficient strategy that can save time and speed for the entire department at the start of the day. And yet, Rebecca remains unsatisfied and disturbed by their request. Rebecca refuses to be an average client, she is Rebecca with her own priorities. The major discrepancy here is not about different aims which an individual and the organization pursue, but the difference in time experience and its value for all parties involved. The nurses try to manage time per client, in other words the speed and the efficiency of their handlings. Rebecca, to put it very simply, takes care of herself. She does not want to be rushed, and the decision she takes requires time and slow consideration.

The interactions with older people that are based on homogenization I shall call here kwik-fit techniques. In the following paragraphs, the theoretical and empirical grounds on which the concept kwik-fit is based will be presented in detail. For now I shall define kwik-fit as an attitude directed at achieving quick results by applying standardized actions to a supposedly malfunctioning person, organization or system without consideration for the diversity of processes which underlie or cause the initial questions in the first place.

SLOW FOUNDATIONS

Acceleration

The phenomenon *acceleration* is important for our discussion about the rhythms of life and velocities of aging. To put it concisely, social acceleration generates a quick change, as a result of which historical time-intervals become shorter (Koselleck 241). In the life of an individual, this leads to a structural lack of time, resulting in an accumulation of superficial homogenized experiences. Koselleck strikingly calls it consumption of experience (242), which in the long run is expected to have a disintegrating effect on one's identity. The possible consequences of acceleration for the erosion of one's identity had already been made public at the end of the 19th century, when the American physician George M. Beard introduced the term "American nervousness" in order "to capture emotional flatness and exhaustion from a life increasingly mediated by the mechanized acceleration and time pressure of the industrial age" (Aho 25). More recent publications investigate the phenomenon of acceleration in the context of historical, sociological and anthropological studies. The French historian Pierre Nora defines acceleration of history as a "rapid slippage of the present into a historical past," resulting in "eradication" of tradition, customs and social memory (7), aspects, I shall add, that are of ultimate importance in later life. Using Nora's arguments, the French anthropologist Marc Augé develops the idea further: "the *acceleration* of history corresponds to a multiplication of events" and their consequent "overabundance" (28). In order to keep up with this development, people try to give a meaning to each of them, thereby creating an excess of meaning and at the same time losing the most important one, namely knowing who they are. Paradoxically then, acceleration stimulates our commitment to almost any token of the past, because those tokens tell us "what is different about us now" (26). Individuals and especially the older generation often feel that their own slow history has been plugged into the accelerating history of the world. They have seen and experienced it all: political regimes taking turns, changing social conditions, and the sprint of economic development. On the surface of this ocean the aspects of aging can hardly be distinguished from because everybody, irrespective of their age, is subject to social acceleration. But for certain groups acceleration means that they are not part of the (accelerated) system any longer. They are forced to decelerate and to them that change of speed can present serious challenges. This is especially the case for the generation with an extended lifespan. The switch from the intensity of their work lives to what is felt as the emptiness of retirement can lead to isolation, loneliness, and depression (Victor, Scambler and Bond, Phillipson). The fact that processes of acceleration and deceleration are interconnected has been analyzed in detail by Hartmut Rosa (14-17). And we can see the dynamics of their intersection when the question is raised in which manner the younger generation will be able to care for the growing number of older people.

Living and Aging: Process Approach

Acceleration and deceleration as described above can have a disturbing effect on the later stages of life, when the physical and mental capacity of older people to manage their own lives dwindles. The negative image of an older person does not have just one source. The government, the local authorities, the media – we all are co-creators and receivers of that image, although we don't always realize it. Is the timing of the green light for the pedestrians long enough for an older person to cross the street without getting nervous? And why do the traffic boards that are placed to warn the drivers about a zebra crossing show images of crippled persons when older people are concerned? And even when we are brought to a halt because an older lady is crossing the street we usually reflect on her failing speed and fail to criticize ourselves for stereotyping.

But velocities of aging can be interpreted differently, namely by shifting the emphasis from speed to process. By doing this I shall highlight where the relations between living and aging complement each other, which is usually experienced as an integral process. At the core of this notion lies the concept of change[3] as it was introduced by the French process philosopher Henry Bergson at the beginning of the 20th Century (*CE*[4] 4,7). To put it concisely, change is both constant and accumulative. When we pass from one state to another, for example from feeling energetic to growing tired, or from feeling young while we are talking to our parents to feeling adult when addressing our children, we are continuously changing. There is no tangible marker saying that one state ends and another begins, but in our self-reflection we clearly separate those states, drawing distinctive lines between *then* and *now*, as if each of those states "formed a block and were a separate whole" (*CE* 3). According to Bergson, we usually understand change as a "passage from one state to the next" (3), assuming that the state itself has its own length and therefore can be measured and, to use a modern term, managed. The same kind of thinking, which is based on stereotypes, justifies the division of our lives into stages, whereby old age for example is more often than not characterized by a chronological (65+) frame, an average (and often slow) speed, as well as deteriorating health conditions. Bergson warns that if we agree that aging is just a stage in the course of life, then we are forced to see it as "the constant accumulation of loss of a certain

---

3 | One of the central concepts of Bergson's philosophy is duration. The interpretation of change that is used here forms an intrinsic part of the definition of duration (*Time and Free Will* 101, 105, CE 7).

4 | Creative Evolution

kind of matter" (22). Then "the frame of the explanation has been furnished *a priori*" (22) and aging is nothing else but a gloomy prospect of gradual dying. But this is not Bergson's aim.

The gradual character of change is difficult to catch. We notice that change has taken place post-factum, almost as if it had occurred all at once: we suddenly notice a couple of grey strands in our hair; we are suddenly not able to stay awake anymore on New Year's Eve, and suddenly three flights of stairs leave us out of breath. *Suddenly* is in fact a continuous change in disguise. Living and aging have no breaks, because the process of change is continuous, accumulative, qualitative, and heterogeneous by nature. Bergson's reasoning about puberty or menopause, which he calls "crises" (22) of our organism and at the same time "part and parcel of the process of our aging" (23), are exemplary for the process-bound understanding of aging and are worthwhile quoting at length:

Although they occur at a definite age and within a time that may be quite short, no one would maintain that they appear then ex abrupt, from without, simply because a certain age is reached, just as a legal right is granted to us on our one-and-twentieth birthday. It is evident that a change like that of puberty is in course of preparation at every instant from birth, and even before birth, and that aging up to that crisis consists, in part at least, of this gradual preparation. In short, what is properly vital in growing old is the insensible, infinitely graduated, continuance of the change of form. Now, this change is undoubtedly accompanied by phenomena of organic destruction: to these, and to these alone, will a mechanistic explanation of aging be confined. It will note the facts of sclerosis, the gradual accumulation of residual substances, the growing hypertrophy of the protoplasm of the cell. But under these visible effects an inner cause lies hidden. The evolution of the living being, like that of the embryo, implies a continual recording of duration, a persistence of the past in the present, and so an appearance, at least, of organic memory. (23)

Thus, even biologically predictable changes in a human organism cannot be inferred from the chronology of one's life. It would be preferable to use a pattern of our biological changes in order to define the abstract phases of human life, and not the other way round. Another of Bergson's important ideas is that any qualitative change is an intrinsic part of the entire process of living. In other words, change always contains the accumulated "information" of all changes that have taken place in the past and this "memory" is unique for any course of life. That means that aging is not just one single change; it is infinitely many. And it is not in antagonism with living that we come to age, but aging (= change) embodies the ontology of living.

This process approach towards living and aging allows for a critical look at modern policies regarding aging. In the Netherlands, for example, the attitude of the government towards life expectancy and care for older people deals with age-phases that are artificially separated from their continuous stream of life, without consideration for the unique path of each individual life, or for the changes that a person undergoes before, during and after being labelled as "retired," "old," "impaired" or "dependent." In the following section, I shall discuss a few examples, where the process aspect of becoming older is disregarded, whereas acceleration, i.e. a measurable and speedy approach towards an aged person, is selected for efficiency reasons.

Severing Aging from Living

Egalitarian Retirement

The clock-driven approach to work participation and retirement, which over the years has turned into a compulsory method to achieve an overall equilibrium in terms of demand and offer of employment, has been strongly criticized, but the contrast between government policies and individual aspirations regarding employment and retirement is still very strong (Hardy, Hendricks and Peters, Itzin and Phillipson, Townsend). The recent Dutch debate on the postponement of retirement age was a clear example of a paradox-in-progress (Groothoff, van der Klink, and Sorgdrager 296). While politicians, supported by several leading economists, were strongly in favor of new legislation that would compulsory prolong work life in the Netherlands by two years, the labor unions, supported by other economists, put up quite a fight against those plans. This polarization was not surprising, especially since heterogeneous working conditions (for example, blue-collar versus white-collar work) were not sufficiently being taken into account. The picture becomes more complex when we look at the questions on websites for 65+ers, as they are called in Holland, that were flooded with questions like "Can I keep working after my 65th birthday? What are my options? What are the working conditions, social security, fiscal terms?"[5]

The limitations of compulsory retirement are not an exclusive feature within the Dutch pension debate and the need to adopt a more sophisticated tailor-made approach towards pension regulations is becoming urgent world-wide (Bonoli and Shinkawa; Borghans 7). The UK report "Coming of age" (Bazalgette et al. 40) shows that in cases where possibilities are provided for flexible working arrangements, the number of people who want to work past the age

---

5 | http://www.socialezekerheid.nl/smartsite.dws?id=106409; http://www.plusonline. nl/geldenrecht/artikelen/artikel/1489/na-uw-65ste-toch-doorwerken. Web. 28 Mar. 2013.

of 65 has increased significantly (see also an example of the flexible retirement system in Finland in Gould 519).

The shortcomings of the retirement systems are to a large extent rooted in homogeneous thinking, i.e. the premise that aging has one single speed, coinciding with the measured ticking of a clock. Yesterday, the clock was set at 65 and today it points at 67, which illustrates exactly Bergson's point of critique: the process character of life manifests itself in gradual change, and where change remains a blind spot, something abrupt takes place that I call a kwik-fit technique. To avoid over-simplification, I should add that the debate on retirement addresses a complicated mixture of political, demographic, and cultural issues, whereby the intergenerational relations, the redistribution of work in the labor market and the allocation of the available public resources all play an important role. What I am pointing at here is not the necessity to adjust the retirement system, but the lack of vision in terms of its implementation. Kwik-fit solutions aiming at egalitarian retirement rest on the artificial separation of *aging* from *living*. They embrace average figures and render an older person anonymous. Thus, the differences in health and living conditions between a 65-year-old scholar, a 65-year-old nurse who has been working in the care sector her entire life and a 65-year-old insurance agent are smoothed away in order to meet the organizational challenges of macro-economy and the legislative system.

Uncelebrated Longevity

Another example is about discrepancies in speed in relation to rapidly growing longevity, notwithstanding the lagging improvement of health conditions in later life. The paradox that appears here lies in the societal interpretation of the findings produced by biological science. In 2006, Thomas Kirkwood wrote that "human life expectancy in developed countries has not bumped into a ceiling, but continues to increase by around two years per decade - or five hours per day" (1015). Kirkwood's accounts echo Bergson's ideas when he presents his dynamic approach towards the pivotal issue of the varying rates of aging. Kirkwood explains that in contradiction with the notion of the pre-programmed aging process, there is no evolutionary pre-installed or genetically driven "inner clock" that determines the limits of our lives. Even the heritability factor is not strong enough to sustain any reliable forecast about longevity. Kirkwood indicates that the rate of aging is influenced by a variety of factors "ranging from intrinsic and extrinsic stressors, nutrient levels, temperature, the hazards of reproduction, and so on, but at its heart, aging is about damage and repair" (*Asymmetry* 533-34). Taking into account that the processes of damage and repair are subject to different speeds, Kirkwood's conclusions advocate a heterogeneous approach towards aging. There is no universal rate of aging, and the issue of improving one's health condition in later life is a matter of varying speed since, "if we can slow the onslaught of damage, or boost repair capacity, we can aspire to live longer, healthier lives without altering our genetic make-up" (*Too fast by mistake* 1015).

These findings could have led to a discussion on the broadening diversity of the speeds of aging in the world population, but until now they have only proved to be relevant for reports that provide us with a dim view on longevity in regard to the quality of people's health (Coote 55). According to this extended morbidity theory, while the length of our life-span extends, also the number of years that older people suffer from one or more disabilities increases (review in Derkx 178).

Thus another speed discrepancy manifests itself. We have been told that our lifespan increases faster than the quality of later life, and that soon the older generation will claim a major part of our public resources, leaving a shrinking number of younger people more or less empty-handed. Beside the fact of being another badly presented argument (for more detailed criticism see Neuberger 105, 115; Appleyard 128), this kind of reasoning suffers from the same lack of heterogeneity in its attitude towards aging as we have seen above. It is based on the prejudicial assumption that all older people are in need of care and that they are the most expensive users of public resources such as social security and health care. This homogenization therefore ignores the diversity of the aging population, their voluntary input in various public activities and the perspectives of a longer and healthier life that biological science is aiming at. The kwik-fit answer to the prolongation of our life span is as follows: longevity is supposed to be a success story, which means that living longer and staying healthy should become synonyms, otherwise there is no need for such longevity at all. But as empirical material will show, the rapidly increasing lifespan is rather in need of slow (= taking time), tailor-made care strategies that are adjustable to individual velocities.

Anti-Aging Culture

This example is about techniques that commercial structures use in order to attract older customers. It is obvious that the slogan *"towards decelerating care"* is unlikely to win a new client, but the promise of eternal youth, however improbable, does reap its fruits. The inconsistency of such a fancy story is not difficult to unravel. Instead of embracing aging in all its complexity, the commercial approach advocates to fight it, delay it, defer it, in other words to slow it down at all costs. And there is no doubt that the costs are very high indeed. As Gilleard and Higgs formulated it, "for now, at least, resisting age rather than ageism greases more palms, oils more deals and turns more dollars" (71). The discrepancy between the message and reality unfolds itself at various levels. The combination of product development and marketing strategies has led to the invention of so-called anti-aging solutions, where the negatively connot-ed image of old age plays a central role. The unattractiveness of older age is being emphasized and simultaneously it is offset by the advantages that the advertised products at hand can offer (Ring 597; Williams, Virpi, and Wadleigh 2-3). By now these advertisements have acquired a more subtle approach, not about the ways in which people and/or their bodies age, but by propagating an expensive way to keep one's good looks (Zhang et al. 6). The people who create this kind of clichés are not naïve. They select their examples carefully, give them younger faces and fitter bodies and then sell the photo-shopped images as a choice that *everybody* can make (Mol 16). Setting aside the ethical side of such presentations for a different kind of discussion, we can call them kwik-fit techniques. They concentrate on quick sales, a high turnover, and a steadily increasing stream of new anti-aging products.

There is no need to simplify the matter. Technological progress, molecu-lar genetics, and cosmetic surgery speak of *break-through achievements*. But it would be more realistic to use the terminology proposed by Kirkwood and talk about varying rates of damage and repair instead of some miracle-working pan-acea (see also critique in Olshansky and Carnes 134, 147; Weiner). Moreover, submitting oneself to the *anti-aging fever* does not lead to a slowing down of the aging process, but it certainly does nibble at one's self-confidence, which in turn stimulates the pursuit of eternal youth. Taking fitness exercises as an example, Gilleard and Higgs show that "age-resisting fitness regimes promote a positive self-image of non-agedness that further reinforces the undesirability and fear of old age. Rather than transgressing the current social construction of old age, such practices subtly reinforce it" (81). The discrepancy between the goals and the results is obvious. The stronger our efforts to slow down our aging process become, the sooner our hopes for an easy victory over time wear out. But disappointment is the least of our problems. The underlying and more fundamental issue is that the older generation is presented as a bunch of youth addicts, whose values and happiness are linked to the earlier periods of life, whereby appearances must be kept up at all cost.

KWIK-FIT

Homogenization of experience is closely linked to acceleration and kwik-fit. Already in 1938, Martin Heidegger pleaded against the phenomena of "calcula-tion, acceleration" and the "claim of massiveness" (84-85), which according to him concealed the de-humanization of our society. "Calculation" is rooted in mathematically grounded planning and control, where no space is left for un-predictability. As a result "massiveness" breaks out; it grows, "because numbers and the calculable already count as what is equally accessible to everyone" (85).

This inference is traceable in the examples that were given above: kwik-fit techniques are based on a calculation of averages and mass-bound thinking. Heidegger's elaboration on acceleration goes even deeper in mapping its destructive power for the human character. He describes it as "not-being-able-to-bear the stillness of hidden growth and awaiting; the mania for what is surprising, for what immediately sweeps [us] away and impresses [us . . .]" (84). Heidegger's explicit appeal is to distinguish between "the genuine restlessness of the struggle" and "the restlessness of the always inventive operation, which is driven by the anxiety of boredom" (85). The restlessness of the struggle correlates with what can be called deceleration, or taking time. Aging for example can be experienced as a slow or slower, or a fast or faster process. Deceleration emphasizes here that aging as a quality time *takes time*. The example about the pursuit of eternal youth represents the second kind of restlessness and the anxiety that is connected to it. It conceals the existential dimension of growing older that can be revealed in an unhurried effort of self-reflection and (self-)care.

To summarize, kwik-fit is a set of superficial fixing measures based on a homogeneous view of the world that lacks diversity, process approach, and a flexible perspective to the future. The kwik-fit techniques related to aging do not restrict themselves to the given examples. They can be found in the uniform living conditions in residential-care facilities (the same food and the same schedule for all residents), in the public image of older people as presented by the media ("All older people need care and will claim most of our public resources"), and even in our everyday conversations ("They do not need much," "They always complain"). In each of these examples kwik-fit doesn't allow us to take the time to look into the essence of the problem. It tends to provide easy solutions that nevertheless shape our long-term thinking. Kwik-fit is about products and not about processes (Mol 22). It is about homogeneity instead of the heterogeneity of the speeds of life. Whenever the kwik-fit approach is used in regard to aging, it tends to trivialize aging in general, skips the aging process and develops one homogeneous "solution" for everyone, i.e. one age/speed for all of us. The kwik-fit remedy against aging symptoms is denial, followed by some anti-aging formula that is implicitly directed against the experiences of being old and therefore is discriminative by nature.

TACTICS OF DECELERATION

Remembering

While kwik-fit appears in various domains of public life, people are aging at their own pace, using their own tactics to protect themselves from homogenization. One of the tactics that people – and not the authorities – often turn to is remembering the past, individually or collectively. Remembering is a very important source for continuation of our identity at any age, but it becomes particularly significant in old age (Bendien 285). It is a natural means against homogenization, since there will never be two identical memories about the same event, whereas each account can present unique features of the remembering person's identity. Remembering also provides leverage that we can use against acceleration, by reminiscing in times when the on-going events tend to drown our personalities. Understanding remembering as quality time brings us closer to Bergson's interpretation of gradual accumulative change. Just like aging is the ultimate proof of living, remembering is a precondition for the continuation of one's identity. Both processes integrate continuity with change and both are characterized by an unhurried gradual growth from within.

This interpretation of remembering resonates with Foucault's contemplations on self-care and the preparation for old age that aims "to turn time around, or at any rate to tear ourselves free from time thanks to an activity of memorization that [. . .] is the remembering of past moments. All this in fact places us at the very heart of this activity, of this practice of the care of the self" (88). Foucault presents freeing ourselves from time and remembering as mutually dependent activities that are especially valuable in relation to the practices that we see as specific tactics to maintain our identities in later life. Kwik-fit aims at solutions, but fails to provide a secure environment, whereas continuation and change within one's character can enhance each other. Personal care takes time that cannot be downgraded to a calculation of intensity or speed, variables on which the bureaucracy of many organizational care organizations is based nowadays. The following account will underline this point. It is taken from a large ethnographic study that has been conducted in one of the residential complexes for older people in Rotterdam (Bendien, Brown, and Reavey 149). It describes a group visit to a place called the *Reminiscence Museum*. The Museum is located within the premises of a care-providing organization and reconstructs the atmosphere of middle-class domestic life in the Netherlands in the first part of the 20th century. By the time the dialogue takes place, the visitors have already spent an hour at the museum. Most of them have gone on to have a cup of tea, but two women, L1 and L2, both in wheel-chairs, and one nurse N, stay behind in the museum. An old photograph of a woman peeling potatoes attracts the attention of L1. She studies it intensively and calls to her friend: "Look at this. Oh, how nice!" L2 reacts melancholically: "Yes, that is how we were sitting there then, right?" L1 adds: "And there were three gas stoves [. . .] three gas stoves [. . .]" The ladies talk slowly in an almost meditating way. Suddenly, N invites herself to the conversation:

N.: We shall definitely return here with a very small group.
L1: And then the pan on the floor, right?
L2: Yes, look.
L1: And then you peel ten, ten kilos of potatoes a day.
L2: Exactly.
N: And we shall take one room at a time. That is more than enough. Because these were very many impressions all at the same time. Right?
L1: So.
L2: Gosh, 10 kilos of potatoes a day.
L1: A day.
L2: Large families [. . .]

What takes place in this dialogue can be called the coexistence of two entirely different temporal streams which do not intersect. The two visiting ladies are absorbed by their memories of the days when domestic work was a harsh and heavy responsibility. They interact by using very concise remarks, but the emotional tension of their memories increases considerably because they are building it up together, each of them repeating, complementing or adding a detail in order to reconstruct the entire picture as precisely as possible. They are not in a hurry, so there are frequent pauses in their dialogue. Those intervals are used by the nurse who is accompanying them. Her time pattern is quite different. She feels the need to be in charge of the time issues and wants to make it clear that the visit is over now. According to the agenda, they have other things to do. Following her schedule, which is based on the usual hour division of activities, she tries to kwik-fit the potential delay. Moreover, she looks back at the visit which has just taken place and is kwik-fitting that as well by indicating that coming with a "large group" was not such a good idea, while "very many impressions all at the same time" could somehow be harmful as well. The two ladies do not hear her, or maybe they do not want to hear what she is saying. In their own slow mode of remembering they are enjoying the stream of unmeasured time that belongs to them and they don't allow themselves to be disturbed by an unwelcome intrusion. The example is instructive because it shows an everyday setting that often passes by unnoticed. But precisely during such "slow" moments the frail pace of aging can be spotted and understood.

Personal Ties

Remembering the past often is a welcome asset that can help us to preserve the unique pace of our lives later on and to resist the acceleration that organizational systems and policies tend to impose. But sometimes, when one's memory is under attack, this natural protective means of old age becomes useless and other tactics must be found. The following account is taken from an ethnographic research-in-progress about informal care and self-care of older people with dementia. Mary was 87 when the following situation took place. We were neighbors. We had known each other for more than 10 years and she had been fully in charge of her own life, living with dignity and in accordance with her own habits and wishes. After her 87th birthday her mental health had changed radically. She was still living independently, but by then her autonomous life had been carefully and continuously reanimated by her relatives, friends, and neighbors. One of the consequences of her reduced mental health was that Mary could not remember anymore what day or which date it was. She started coming to me on a daily basis, sometimes even several times a day, carrying a notebook to write everything down. Since I was living according to my own time pattern I experienced this as a problem, or her problem to be precise, and I almost unconsciously started looking for a solution. And there it was. The next time she complained about the fact that she could not remember the dates, I asked her (not without some self-satisfaction) whether she would like to have a large wall calendar. Then she could cross off the past days so she would know what day she was enduring at that moment. She looked at me a bit surprised but without much enthusiasm. So I enquired: *"Don't you like the idea?"* and she replied: *"Not really, I would rather keep asking."*

What has taken place during our dialogue cannot simply be discarded as a result of the generation gap or a difference in lifestyle. The crucial issue here is our individual experience of time and the power of the clock which we are constantly exposed to. The paradox is obvious. Because of the dementia process that prevented Mary from remembering the exact date, she had as it were come free from the overwhelming power of clock-bound time. By the same token she was experiencing this freedom as a problematic development, since freeing herself from the power of the hour-glass has not set her free from her socially embedded habits. But the most remarkable part was her refusal to surrender to the rule of the calendar. One could call it an ingenious decelerating strategy which allowed her to maintain regular contact with me, instead of submitting herself to the silent routine of crossing off the days of her life.

This interpretation leads to another important issue. The failure of my *helpful* idea rests on a fundamental problem, namely my disregard of the difference between living a good life with dementia and living a healthy later life. In Mary's case, while thinking in terms of my own organizational efficiency and a speedy result, I came up with a kwik-fit solution by trying to treat the untreatable. But in spite of its obvious (to me) advantages, it didn't work. If Mary had accepted my proposal, our daily communication would have decreased and her incalculable lonely hours would have become even longer.

Aging as a process of change and the issues of care in later life in particular do not go well with kwik-fit solutions. In my story about Mary, my kwik-fit proposal had transparent goals and a logical solution, but they failed. While a number of people had become closely involved with Mary's life, she was still living alone in her apartment, taking care of herself as she had done for more than 60 years already. The way Mary had arranged her life had its own rhythm which fitted within what, following Bergson, we can call her own duration. It was neither slow nor fast. There was no hurry to it, and as a result of Mary's mental health problem there was no such thing as calculable speed to it either. Her way of living at that point in time could be seen as a good illustration of what Foucault, with reference to Seneca, called "a focal point of life, a positive focal point towards which we should strive," where old age is understood as "a safe shelter" (110). This may sound like a contradiction because looking at it from the outside, we may wish Mary to lead another kind of life. But this is exactly where the problem with kwik-fit solutions starts. We presume to know best what an older person wants and how (s)he should live. Yet, the manner in which Mary was coping with her life had been harmoniously synchronized with what can be called her personal unique pattern of living. She had lost the ability to measure the days, but she had not forgotten how to *live* them. Her *living* had become purely qualitative. When she woke up, it had to be morning. When she found that her thermos flask with tea was empty, she realized that it was probably the end of the day. Whenever she found a second tray of ready-made food in her refrigerator, she could conclude that she had forgotten to eat on the previous day. And whenever she was referring to recent events, she compressed them all into a simple "yesterday." It was a fascinating heterogeneous relational world without measuring in which Mary was living quite happily for some time. Perhaps she would not have chosen it rationally, but that was the way she was reassembling her identity on a daily basis, in order to come to terms with a new balance between living and aging.

We can look at these two examples as a quite innocent manifestation of kwik-fit techniques, but we should also realize that they reflect the inconsistencies and rigidness of many regulations that pretend to be supportive to the older generation. One of the reasons why various systems fail is because they do not *distinguish* clearly whom they are supposed to support in the first place. The older generation cannot be represented by one average man or woman with a certain speed of living and aging. The diversity of the ways in which older generations want to live their lives already contains some hints as to how the system can approach and support them: by allowing them to cherish their memories and by letting them make their own decisions about the pace of their lives. A good later life requires time that cannot be measured in terms of hours. It is impregnated with emotional reverberation and incalculable values that can be reflected in a smile, a hug or a small word of gratitude.

CONCLUSIONS

In spite of the universality of aging processes, there is a broad variety in the speed and manner in which people grow older. Given the latest world trends which include the rapid increase in longevity on the Asian and African continents, we shall without any doubt be facing more cultural diversity in aging processes than ever. The response from the West-European countries to their populations that are growing older and the societal issues that this entails can be called pioneer work. This has not been easy, but we learn as we are aging. In this article, I have looked at one aspect of later life, namely the experience of time passing, and I have tried to see how official policies and organizational structures are responding to that. Their tactics based on the "one-speed-fits-all" principle have been labeled as kwik-fits. They are more often than not developed at a macro-level and they are based on average variables which usually fail to provide a proper response to the needs of an individual.

The strategies with which I propose to counterbalance the kwik-fit techniques are based on the diversity of aging experiences that literally mean taking time. Aging is not a discovery of the past hundred years and changes in the experience of time as one of its features has been reported throughout the centuries. It seems as if the tactics of an older person to take more time are in the first place a form of self-preservation or even retaliation against kwik-fit solutions that (s)he is confronted with. By winning our time back (from the clock and the calendar), and by indulging ourselves with memories and self-reflection, we can suppress the rush of acceleration that is forced upon us, in order to enhance the individual rhythm of our lives. This rhythm is unique for everyone, which is why there will never be a system that is perfect enough to match the aging rhythm of each individual. But we can become aware of this in order to achieve more tolerance and flexibility towards older people.

Another important inference is the necessity to pay more attention to the ways in which older people are already dealing with time and speed, in order to adapt the existing policies accordingly. A *conditio sine qua non* is to understand living and aging in terms of process and change. It would allow for flexibility and heterogeneity in the depictions of old age, as opposed to the rule of *average-ness*. The refreshing influence of this approach can be recognized when "freeing from time" or remembering practices of the older generation are observed. During those moments the unique experience of timelessness becomes almost tangible. They can be used to fight back the nerve-wrecking acceleration. We can define them in terms of deceleration or taking time. And because the older generation often "forgets" time and "indulges" in remembering, we should be able to connect the processes of *time experience, living,* and *aging* in order to disconnect the terms *speed* and *care.* I am reminded of this every day when I am talking to older people who don't want any kwik-fitting, but simple and unhurried personal consideration and interest.

REFERENCES

Aho, Kevin A. "Acceleration and Time Pathologies: The critique of psychology in Heidegger's Beiträge." *Time & Society*, 16.1 (2007): 25-42. Web. 30 Jan. 2010.

Appleyard, Bryan. "A life worth living? Quality of life in older age." *Unequal aging: The untold story of exclusion in old age*. Ed. Paul Cann and Malcolm Dean. Bristol: Policy Press, 2009. 141-58. Print.

Augé, Marc. *Non-places: Introduction to an Anthropology of Supermodernity*. London: Verso London, 1995. Print.

Bazalgette, Louise, John Holden, Philip Tew, Nick Hubble, and Jago Morrison. *Coming of Age*. London: Demos, 2011. Print.

Bendien, Elena. *From the Art of Remembering to the Craft of Ageing: A Study of the Reminiscence Museum at Humanitas, Rotterdam*. Rotterdam: Humanitas Foundation, 2010. Print.

————, Steven D. Brown, and Paula Reavey. "Social remembering as an art of living: Analysis of a 'Reminiscence Museum'." *New Technologies and Emerging Spaces of Care*. Ed. Michael Schillmeier and Miquel Domenech. Hants: Ashgate Publishing Ltd., 2010. 149-67. Print.

Bergson, Henry. *Time and Free Will: An Essay on the Immediate Data of Consciousness*. 1913. USA: Kessinger Publishing, 2008. Print.

————. *Creative Evolution*. 1911. New York: Cosimo Classics, 2005. Print.

Birren, James E. "Theories of aging: A personal perspective." *Handbook of Theories of Aging*. Ed. Vern L. Bengtson and K. Warner Schaie. New York: Springer Publishing, 1999. 459-71. Print.

Bonoli, Giuliano, and Toshimitsu Shinkawa. *Aging and Pension Reform Around the World: Evidence from Eleven Countries*. Cheltenham: Edward Elgar Publishing Limited, 2005. Print.

Borghans, Lex. "Tijd voor maatwerk in arbeidsmarktbeleid." *Economisch Statistische Berichten*, 93.4533S. (2008): 4-9. Web. 28 Mar. 2013.

Coote, Anne. "The uneven dividend: health and well-being in later life." *Unequal Aging: The Untold Story of Exclusion in Old Age*. Ed. Paul Cann and Malcolm Dean. Bristol: Policy Press, 2009. 53-75. Print.

Derkx, Peter. "Engineering substantially prolonged human lifespans: biotechnological enhancement and ethics." *Valuing Older People: A Humanist Approach to Ageing*. Ed. Ricca Edmondson and Hans-Joachim von Kondratowitz. Bristol: Police Press, 2009. 177-98. Print.

Dittman-Kohli, Freya. "Temporal References in the Construction of Self-Identity: A Life-Span Approach." *Aging and Time: Multidisciplinary Perspectives.* Ed. Jan Baars and Henk Visser. New York: Baywood Publishing, 2007. 83-120. Print.

Foucault, Michel. *The Hermeneutics of the Subject: Lectures at the Collège de France 1981-82.* New York: Picador, 2005. Print.

Gilleard, Christopher, and Paul Higgs. *Cultures of Aging: Self, Citizen and the Body.* Harlow: Person Education Limited, 2000. Print.

Gould, Raija. "Choice or Chance – Late Retirement in Finland." *Social Policy and Society,* 5.4 (2006): 519-31. Web. 28 Mar. 2013.

Groothoff, Johan W., Jac J. L. van der Klink, and Bas Sorgdrager. "Beroepsbevolking vertoont krimp noch vergrijzing." *Tijdschrift voor Bedrijfs- en Verzekeringsgeneeskunde,* 17.7 (2009): 294-97. Web. 27 Mar. 2013.

Hardy, Melissa. "Older workers." *Handbook of Aging and the Social Sciences.* Ed. Robert H. Binstock and Linda K. George. Boston: Academic Press, 2006. 201-18. Print.

Heidegger, Martin. *Contributions to Philosophy (From Enowning).* 1938. Bloomington, Indiana: Indiana UP, 1999. Print.

Hendricks, Jon, and Calvin B. Peters. "The times of our lives." *American Behavioral Scientist* 29.6 (1986): 662-78. Web. 28 Mar. 2013.

Itzin, Catherine, and Chris Phillipson. *Age Barriers at Work.* London: METRA, 1993. Print.

Kirkwood, Tom. "Aging: Too fast by mistake." *Nature* 444 (2006): 1015-16. Web. 28 Mar. 2013.

––––. "Asymmetry and the origins of aging." *Mechanisms of Aging and Development* 126.5 (2005): 533-34. Web. 28 Mar. 2013.

Kosselleck, Reinhart. *Futures Past: On the Semantics of Historical Time.* New York: Columbia UP, 2004. Print.

Leccardi, Carmen. "New Temporal Perspectives in the 'High-Speed Society'." *24/7: Time and Temporality in the Network Society.* Ed. Robert Hassan and Ronald E. Purser. Stanford, California: UP, 2007. 25-36. Print.

Middleton, David, and Steven D. Brown. *The Social Psychology of Experience: Studies in Remembering and Forgetting.* London: Sage Publications, 2005. Print.

Mol, Annemarie. *The Logic of Care: Health and Problem of Patient Choice.* London: Routledge, 2008. Print.

Neuberger, Julia, Baroness. "What does it mean to be old?" *Unequal Aging: The Untold Story of Exclusion in Old Age.* Ed. Paul Cann and Malcolm Dean. Bristol: Policy Press, 2009. 101-21. Print.

Nora, Pierre. "Between Memory and History: Les Lieux de Mémoire." *Representations* 26 (1989): 7-24. Web. 28 Mar. 2013.

Olshansky, S. Jay, and Bruce A. Carnes. *The Quest for Immortality: Science at the Frontiers of Aging*. London: W.W. Norton, 2002. Print.

Phillipson, Chris. *Transitions from work to retirement: Developing a new social contract*. Bristol: Policy Press, 2002. Print.

Ring, Anne L. "Using 'anti-aging' to market cosmetic surgery: just good business, or another wrinkle on the face of medical practice?" *Medical Journal of Australia* 176 (2002): 597-99. Web. 28 Mar. 2013.

Rosa, Hartmut. "Social Acceleration: Ethical and Political Consequences of a Desynchronized High–Speed Society." *Constellations* 10.1 (2003): 1-33. Web. 28 Mar. 2013.

Townsend, Peter. "The Structured Dependency of the Elderly: A Creation of Social Policy in the Twentieth Century." *Aging & Society* 1.1 (1981): 5-28. Web. 28 Mar. 2013.

Victor, Christina, Sasha Scambler, and John Bond. *The Social World of Older People: Understanding Loneliness and Social Isolation in Later Life*. Maidenhead: Open UP, McGraw-Hill, 2009. Print.

Westendorp, Rudi, G.J., and Thomas B.L. Kirkwood. "The Biology of Aging." *Aging in Society: European Perspectives on Gerontology*. Ed. John Bond, Sheila Peace, Freya Dittman-Kohli, and Gerben J. Westerhof. London: Sage, 2007. 15-37. Print.

Weiner, Jonathan. *Long for This World: The Strange Science of Immortality*. New York: HarperCollins, 2010. Print.

Williams, Angie, Virpi Ylänne, and Paul Mark Wadleigh. "Selling the 'Elixir of Life': Images of the elderly in an Olivio advertising campaign." *Journal of Aging Studies* 21.1 (2007): 1-21. Web. 28 Mar. 2013.

Zhang, Yan Bing, Jake Harwood, Angie Williams, Virpi Ylänne-McEwen, Paul Mark Wadleigh, and Caja Thimm. "The Portrayal of Older Adults in Advertising: A Cross-National Review." *Journal of Language and Social Psychology* 25.3 (2006): 264-82. Web. 28 Mar. 2013.

Preemptive Biographies

Life and the Life Course in the Age of Security Administration

Rüdiger Kunow

1. Lively Capital

In this paper, I will follow up the proposition that the mapping of the human genome together with breakthroughs in the biotechnical sector have fundamentally changed our understanding of human life and the life course, especially their later and more precarious stages. However plausible this proposition may be, it is also incomplete without acknowledging the wider societal context in which this refashioning is going on. This is important because the "biotech gold rush in medicine" (Elliott 110) is co-evolving with another equally transformative development: neoliberal governance. The latter's unrelenting drive to downsize "big government" has likewise changed the public understanding of human life: by targeting health care and social security programs for the ill and the elderly, neoliberalism has eroded "one of society's most basic covenants – to care for the helpless [. . .]" (Giroux 173). Instead of succor, neoliberal governance is offering "security"; recent years have seen, especially in the United States but other states of the Global North as well the administrative build-up of a surveillance apparatus against perceived outside threats (especially by terrorists) so that "the politics of the public domain does not just have to do with property but also [with] security" (Rajan 443).

The nexus of security and property manifests itself very forcefully also in the field of the biological. These developments are well-documented and need not be described here once again. What seems reasonably clear at this point is that both have had far-reaching resonances even beyond politics and the market. It is certainly no exaggeration to say that both have generated altogether new epistemologies of human life, emphatically including elder life,[1] with a profound impact on the ways in which people are dealing with their bodies in

---

1 | In recent years the presence of elderly populations, and especially their growing numbers, have come to be viewed first and foremost as a problem, and a "pressure

areas such as reproduction, illness, old age and death. And the effects of these new epistemologies do not exhaust themselves in subjecting human physicality to the calculus of the market (which would be bad enough): they are turning life itself, whole or aggregate parts (cells, blood, tissue or body organs), the prophylaxis as well as the treatment of bodily malfunctions, into capital, *lively capital*.[2]

In other words, human life has become the scene, and a very lively one at that, of capitalist activities. Growing amounts of capital worldwide are invested into biotechnological R&D. In a recent statement the United States Internal Revenue Service found:

The Biotech Industry within the last 5 years has seen a significant influx of capital into their firms due to their cutting edge technologies, the mapping of the human genome and a wave of new biologic drug product approvals by the FDA. This influx of capital, which has come from venture capitalists, private investors, off balance sheet financial arrangements, convertible debt instruments, alliance revenue and product sales, has changed the Biotech business model. (Biotech Industry Overview – Trends)

The IRS also quotes a Standard and Poor's estimate that aggregate earnings of the biotech industry will grow at rates of approximately 25 per cent annually. After the bursting of the IT bubble and with other insecurities unsettling the market, human life, especially in its precarious forms, seems to be one of the few remaining sound investment opportunities. It is no surprise, therefore, that the Organization for Economic Co-Operation and Development (OECD) has launched a "Proposal for a Major Project on the Bioeconomy in 2030" which is geared to capture "the latent value in biological processes and renewable bioresources to produce improved health and sustainable growth and development" (Proposal).[3]

There is, I want to argue, a common logic at work in this multi-factor and multi-sector re-calibration of the biology of human life into lively capital. The physical, the economic and the political domains are here being brought together and mutually imbricated in new and intense ways that the mechanistic Foucauldian notion of biopolitics does not capture. What is at stake in the cur-

---

on a country's resources and government budgets [which] hinder[s] economic growth" (World Bank 2, xiii).

2 | Although the term has many uses, its presence in this argument here references a recent collection of essays edited by Kaushik Sunder Rajan, Lively Capital: Biotechnologies, Ethics, and Governance in Global Markets (2012).

3 | Cf. Nicolas Rose's observation that "the capacities of certain things – such as organs and tissues – to produce surplus value" has produced a global market in "biocommodities" (9).

rent political bio-economy of life is no longer "the entry of phenomena peculiar to the life of the human species into the order of knowledge and power" (141), but the conscription of this life into a new logic. This new logic is no longer content with knowledge and control of life as *is*, but seeks to know and control life in its future, "demanding action in the vital present in the name of vital futures to come [. . .]" (Clarke et al. 7). In the argument that follows I seek to capture this new logic of radicalized anticipation of human life-in-the-future by organizing my argument around the term *preemption* as master trope.

2. Managing the Future in the Now: Preemption

Preemption is a concept which originated in the context of contractual law but is now circulating widely in many areas of public debate, more so, in fact, in the United States than in other capitalist countries. Its currency in political theory and the political culture is of rather recent, post 9/11 date, when preemption has figured most prominently in the context of the Bush Doctrine's advocacy of preemptive war and the establishment of the Homeland Security Administration as linchpin of the "national security state" (Stuart). In a 2002 speech at West Point, President Bush established a link between preemption and national security administration which has continued to dominate the debate: "We cannot defend America and our friends by hoping for the best [. . .] . If we wait for threats to fully materialize, we will have waited too long – Our security will require [. . .] all Americans to be forward-looking and resolute, to be ready for preemptive action when necessary to defend our liberty and to defend our lives" (Graduation Speech at West Point).[4]

Bush's choice of the term "preemption" is most certainly not accidental; preemption can indeed be usefully understood as a particular mode of security administration (Sofoer). Security (private or public) is intimately bound up with the not-yet, and preemption promises an administration of this not-yet. Its *modus operandi* consists in anticipatory measures that are geared toward the elimination of a given risk before it has a chance to fully manifest itself, "catching it 'before it actually emerges' (as the Bush doctrine of preemption instructs)" (Massumi 30). What is important about this anticipatory action from the American Studies point of view is the fact that it is based on a different understanding of individual and collective temporality: time, seen through the

---

4 | Preemption was given the status of official government policy later that year in a National Security Council paper where it says: "It is an enduring American principle that [. . .] to forestall or prevent such hostile acts by our adversaries, the United States will, if necessary, act preemptively in exercising our inherent right of self-defense" (United States National Security Council).

lens of preemption, is no longer a gradual flow moving from past via present toward the future. In the perspective of preemption, the future is always already there, requiring action in the here and now. Preemption's "intricate speculative operation [. . .] no longer leaves the future unoccupied and open" but seeks to control it in the present (Parisi and Goodman 166).

In my own argument, I will contend that preemption is an extremely useful concept also for coming to terms with the new epistemologies of life emerging in the wake of the biotech and neoliberal revolutions. It is certainly no accident that even in its more narrowly political usages, preemption has often been given a decidedly biological inflection.[5] Perceived threats to human lives have since time immemorial been the cause for individual or collective preemption. In our own time, the specter of terrorism, represented in the public sphere in terms taken from medical epidemics with terrorists likened to sleeper cells is probably the example coming most readily to mind (Mitchell xv). Preemption produces the very opposite of Nietzsche's antiquarian sentiment; its teleology is the future-present which must be brought under control even before it actually arrives.[6] This view is essentially that of a security utopia, made possible and sustained by technologies whose "key feature is their forward vision: these technologies of life seek to reshape the vital future by action in the vital present" (Rose 18). Preemption, strictly speaking, amounts to an attempt at colonizing the future. Such a project has both become feasible in the wake of the biotech revolution and is even called for in the context of neoliberal governance.

What I find useful, even attractive about the term for a discussion of changes in the understanding of the human life course, is, first of all, the rigorous future-directedness of the practices which the term designates. Viewing the biological basis of human life in terms of preemption takes us, broadly speaking, from the field of political prudence to biographical prudence,[7] from the contingencies of the political world at large to those of the life-course. What remains invariant in such a re-contextualization is the emphasis in preemption on risk management or security administration, to be achieved through a pro-active intervention in the status quo. In both cases, the future is no longer a distant

---

5 | Melinda Cooper. "Pre-empting Emergence: The Biological Turn in the War on Terror." *Theory, Culture, Society* 23 (2006): 113-35. Print. For an example of the traveling of the term to other disciplines cf. Anderson 2010.

6 | Eric Cazdyn has presented such an argument at more length than is possible here: "there is a shared logic in the way preemption was employed by the Bush administration to justify its attacks on Iraq and the way preemption is now employed in economics, psychiatry, ecology, culture, and the medical sciences" (130).

7 | Nicolas Rose even speaks of "an age of biological prudence" (29).

horizon of possibilities but a "nested future"[8] which has moved closer to the present or is already present.

Thus understood, the logic of preemption can be observed at work in public and private documents, in the media as well as in expert papers. Preemption surfaces in debates about the promises and premises of genetic intervention, pre-implantation diagnostics, assisted reproduction, life-extension medicine, psychopharmacology, and a host of related issues.[9] Age is not a totally new identity marker but relates in interesting ways with the other identity markers currently in use – most famously race, class, and gender. What preemption adds to this is a perspective asking not who a person *is* vis-à-vis others (difference) but who s/he *will be*, sometime (not too much) later on. Preemption thus looks at the individual self in terms of the latter's future perfect, both time-wise (the perspective of the future) and status-wise (a more perfect self as status to be achieved). With such a concern about the individual self and its potential, preemption might even be read as a latter-day variant of the self-help ideology that has been a cornerstone of the US-American culture of the self. These Weberian echoes get particularly important if we focus – as I will in this paper – on human life in its *longue durée*. Here, preemption will take us right away to the inescapable future awaiting all forms of life, aging and old age. These are "risks" awaiting all human beings at some point in the future to be administered in the present. A preemptive attitude toward a person's life-in-time thus is, I will argue, a specific form of giving or forming a person's identity through strategies of anticipatory action on the human body. In this context, it is perhaps worth noticing that preemption is, after all, an argument of the slippery slope type. It operates with the ominous signifier: "if we wait" – which was also used in George W. Bush's speech.

3. IN ORDER TO FORM A MORE PERFECT BODY: HUMAN LIFE IN THE AGE OF ITS BIOTECHNICAL PRODUCTION

From very early on in their history human beings have tried to modify their biological endowment – through magic, cosmetics or other means, invasive or incantational. What is different today is that modification has become a bio-

---

8 | Cf. also nested futures, "A Standardized Representation of Asynchronous Operations." open-std.org. Web. 6 Nov. 2012.

9 | Preemption also plays a great role in the growing healthcare market where corporations purchase "sole supplier status" in search engines, here preemption means to control, the flow of information to consumers before they have the chance to make an – informed? – choice (Clarke et al. 73).

technical feasibility. "Life is not imagined as an unalterable fixed endowment. Biology is no longer destiny" (Rose 39-40). The ongoing bio tech revolution is rapidly expanding the discretionary autonomy of human beings over life, their own and that of others. Modifications on the body are being or soon will be possible which human beings have long hoped for and new ones will soon become available that are surpassing our wildest dreams.

The process of producing recombinant DNA, a.k.a. molecular cloning which had begun with plant and animal species has since the 1980s reached the human body. This is making available new technologies of or rather on the body that go far beyond the areas of organ transplants and body replacement parts – hips, hearts, kidneys, IVF – towards producing new "technological forms of life" (Clarke et al. 6). Interventions into the human genome can proceed along various routes, through gene cutting and splicing, genetic screening, genetic therapy, etc. Reproductive cloning – made iconic by Dolly the Sheep – has had the highest profile so far, but other, potentially more important new technologies including bio-banking (the storage of biological samples for later genetic modification) and bio-pharming (molecular-based targeted drugs) are entering the field. Most recently, the discovery of how human-induced pluripotent stem cells can be turned into nerve cells was awarded the Nobel Prize for Medicine. This list is by no means exhaustive.

What can be said about a great many of the new biotechnological processes is that their purpose is no longer exclusively curative in the traditional sense; they go beyond what is necessary to repair bodily malfunctions or to sustain heath; instead they ameliorate or optimize the body's physical function and status with the perspective of creating a body that is "better than well."[10] Whereas previously medicine was by and large an on-demand business seeking to control and contain certain bodily malfunctions, its new biotechnical version has become, at least tendentially so, a proleptic project to re-engineer human life altogether. This has a dimension that spans not a single human being but many, not one generation but the following ones as well: Chapman and Frankel are calling this "designing our descendants" (qtd. in Clarke et al. 19). Gene transfer at the embryonic stage would be a step toward producing children with desired features, such as phenotypical characteristics or body build. Such an "enhanced" child could be expected to have certain advantages over other whose genetic make-up does not include the desired optimizations.[11]

---

10 | This argument is more fully unfolded in Elliott's book by that title.

11 | "The questions raised above also create significant new challenges to our regulatory capabilities. On September 11, 1997, the National Institutes of Health (NIH) convened a conference on genetic enhancement. The meeting was prompted by a request to NIH to approve a protocol for conducting a gene therapy experiment on healthy volunteers, rather than on patients. Although the experiment was part of an effort to

The ways in which people actually engage in the new and exciting biotechnical potentialities in their daily lives are of course manifold and often contentious.[12] "[T]he intense investment of bodily markers with social [and I would add personal] anxieties [. . .]" (Sielke and Schäfer 27) is not at all abating, rather, it is intensifying under the domain of preemptive intervention. It is a little observed fact that the public debate about biotechnical interventions in the human genome has been going on along lines similar to discussions about the practicality and desirability of environmental engineering. So, if improving on Mother Nature by creating genetically modified plants and foods is regarded as ok, then improving people's lives by modifying their bodies (through body design) is also ok – or, inversely, both are seen as equally reprehensible. Genetic and biotech changes in general are often represented in the public sphere as questions of mere technological feasibility. This public presence is not mere expert talk; it is performing important social and cultural work investing human life, especially in its less than optimum, precarious, and later stages, with new urgencies and ambiguities, urgencies and ambiguities which I would like to capture by the term preemption.

What seems especially noteworthy about all this from an American Studies or Cultural Studies point of view is the degree to which the brave new biotech world is captivating the imagination also of lay people. Biomedicine and biotechnology, especially genetic sequencing and body design, are fast becoming "one of the key sites for the fabrication of the contemporary self" (Novas and Rose 239). Accordingly, a wide range of narratives has emerged which registers both the excitement and the anxieties, also the ethical conundrums that accompany the new achievements of biotechnologies. A whole new *biological imaginary*, more specifically perhaps, a "genetic imaginary" (Franklin in Clarke 19) has been forming, in which the logic of preemption is wedded to important concerns about what makes up a good human life, worth having and living.

There is no space here to deal with this preemptive imaginary in all its details and filiations. It has left its mark on key areas of cultural production, life-writing and science-writing, literature, film and the social media. The following brief overview can do little more than offer a glimpse of the various ways in which the lure and the dread of preemption are capturing people's minds.

---

develop treatments for cystic fibrosis, the proposed use of healthy subjects raised, for the first time, the questions of whether and in what circumstances it was appropriate to use gene insertion technology in healthy volunteers. Exactly how to regulate this potential use of genetic technology remains unclear" (National Human Genome Research Institute).

12 | Clarke et al. have noted growing resistance against biotech measures and a "(re) emergent public discourse that 'more (bio)medicine is not necessarily better' [. . .]" (Clarke et al. 14).

Life Writing

Alice Wexler, in *Mapping Fate: A Memoir of Family, Risk, and Genetic Research* (1996)[13], a half-autobiographical, half-documentary tale, probes how the new biotechnological knowledge, in this particular case, allowing people to test for Huntington's Disease (or Chorea Huntington), impacts on the lives of the Wexler family – her own family. The high probability of children "inheriting" HD genetically from an afflicted parent, Alice Wexler's mother Leonore, introduces new concerns for that parent's own future and that of her children. In her Introduction, Wexler speaks of seeing "chorea memories written on [their] mother's [Leonore's] face" (xvii). It is worth noting here that this phrase addresses a condition yet to come in her mother's life, a nested future which I identified above as characteristic of preemptive thinking. And preemption is also guiding the Wexlers' response: "[Dad] is going to save Mom, save us, save everyone else who is at risk for Huntington's. The genetic revolution has begun [. . .] and everything is possible" (44). In this spirit, the Wexler family decides to put their money and influence to use in combating the disease. Even though there is as yet no cure for the disease, by founding and funding the Hereditary Disease Foundation, the Wexlers help achieve a major breakthrough in research which will make a genetic cure more likely in the future. All this comes too late for Leonore but perhaps not too late for her children. As the text progresses, one can notice a change of perspective, from the "silver bullet" solution sought initially (and registered in the quote above) to the more sober, incremental procedures of scientific research. In this way, *Mapping Fate* offers a nuanced narrative which avoids the over-hyping so characteristic of much genetics-related life writing and presents instead a perspectival, stereoscopic vision, which is constantly oscillating between personal experience and "objective" medical facts, between the private and the public, between hope and frustration.

Science Fiction

The natural "habitat" of a preemptive biotech imaginary is of course the field of science fiction, films and novels alike. *Rollback,* a 2007 novel by Canadian writer Robert J. Sawyer, uses the alien encounter plotline to discuss the ethical challenges of biotechnical interventions into the human life course. Sarah Halifax, age 87, is a high-caliber astronomer who years ago decoded a message from an extraterrestrial source. As the novel opens in the year 2048, a second message from the same source, an answer to Sarah's earlier reply, is just being received, and only Sarah can decode it – provided she lives long enough to do the complicated deciphering work. She is the only person living who can con-

---

13 | My thanks to Ariane Schröder for alerting me to this text.

tinue communication with this alien star system. This is where the "rollback" which gives the novel its title comes in; state of the art genetic modification plus biotechnical surgery take Sarah and her husband back to their twenties, but not for long. In Sarah's case the procedure fails and she dies soon thereafter, while her husband is left living the unhappy life of a 20 year old with the experiences of an old man. In this text, Sawyer is splicing together two plotlines, each organized around the idea of preemption, the familiar save-the-world-at-the-last-instance katechontic story and the ancient human desire to escape the aging process, and both are given a sardonic twist.

A good example of a technically ambitious novel crafted around the idea of preemption is Kazuo Ishiguro's *Never Let Me Go* (2005). The novel which was also made into a film (2010; Mark Romanek dir.) is so well-known by now that I can restrict myself to a few general observations. While the novel clearly is a coming-of-age tale, it is also an avoid-age story concerned in important ways with the ethics of organ donation and reproductive cloning. The initial setting of the novel is Hailsham House, a boarding school of sorts where there is a forcible intergenerational bond between the young and the old which is forged and which is getting revealed as the story progresses. The Hailsham children are, in a very direct sense, "there" for the sake of others (the novel calls them "possibles"). They are brought up to be "donors," even multiple "donors," and when their organ supply is exhausted, they have reached "completion" and die. The young people exist as resources, according to the logic of what is now called "biopharming," a process whereby "[b]ody parts are *extracted* like a mineral, *harvested* like a crop, or *mined* like a resource" (Andrews and Nelkin 39; emphasis original) with the exclusive purpose of playing a trick on Mother Nature. *Never Let Me Go* takes to the limit, in a carefully restrained narration and without paying much attention to scientific detail, the nexus of bioeconomy and security administration discussed at the beginning of this paper. Hailsham is an experiment which fails and is later abandoned, but it is in an important sense also the site of a biotechnical utopia organized around the idea(l) of preemption, where a select few are spared the physiological deteriorations associated with "natural" aging.

Social Media

Questions surrounding the scientific ability to fundamentally alter human life and the lifespan are unsurprisingly flooding the social media. They offer lots of material, most of it in narrative form, as in "Our Genes, Our Choices," a PBS series with a website where the reader can access a "Read Real Stories" section of often heart-rending tales about "families who have grappled with the complex implications of genetic information" (Lieber). Genetic information and genetic counseling, as already Alice Wexler's *Mapping Fate* has shown, are all "about" preemption, catching or averting a serious disease before it manifests itself. And in many of the narratives to be found on the "Our Genes, Our Choices" site, testing is the moment when preemptive thinking enters individual lives. This is so, for example, in the case of a 35-year-old mother whose father had been diagnosed with Huntington's and who is herself also tested positive. Subsequently, she wants her children to be tested as well. "As a parent, she felt she had a right to this information [. . .] and wanted to be able to allocate her limited financial resources accordingly." However, this request is denied by the genetic counseling institution. Where she goes from here and which way the story goes, we don't get to know.

There is much hype surrounding the power of the genes, and so it may be too early to assess how much social and cultural work the emergent capacities of the biotechnological sciences are already doing and will do in the future, by enforcing a logic of preemption.[14] But already now it is clear, as Stephen Collier and Andrew Lakoff argue, a new "bioethics of technoscience" is emerging [. . .]" (Collier and Lakoff 19) whose contours are as yet blurry but which will soon turn the simple act of living into an ethical problem.

It is certainly no coincidence that these bioethical quandaries are affecting the human life course unequally, with special emphasis on its two liminal conditions, reproduction and aging. Much has been written about IVF and pre-natal genetic diagnostics which are turning women into "moral pioneers" (Rapp 3). But ethically charged situations and decisions occur also at the other end of the life course.

4. ALIVE AND KICKING FOREVER? AGING AND OLD AGE

Aging and old age are in important ways the ultimate frontier of genetic enhancement and biotech intervention. It is here that their Promethean potential to transform human life could unfold itself most forcefully. After all, the idea of life's inevitable progression from womb to tomb is still regarded as part of a natural order of things. "Over the course of time, all living organisms undergo progressive physiological deterioration that results in increased vulnerability to stress and an increased probability of death. This phenomenon is commonly referred to as aging [. . .]" (Cristofalo, Tresini, Francis and Volker 98). To preempt that very process would mean that the ancient dream of humanity of eternal youth, if not eternal life, would at long last come to be realized. Some

---

14 | Nicolas Rose has repeatedly insisted on the debit effect of these processes: "the reorganization of many illnesses and pathologies along a genetic axis does not generate fatalism. On the contrary, it creates an obligation to act in the present in relation to the potential futures that now come into view" (107).

geneticists are actually convinced that this will indeed be possible in some not-too-distant future, for example, by unlocking the secrets of the "aging gene" (Sinclair and Guarente).

The last 15 years have already seen astounding innovations in the genetics of aging so that there is now available a growing number of medical and genetic interventions in the aging body whose principal aim is no longer restorative (ameliorating the physical impairments coming with age) but transformative (rejuvenating the body) by preempting the onset of deteriorative organic processes. This is not a matter anymore of cosmetic surgery or cochlear implants. Beating the biological clock is the promise offered by the new life enhancement and life extension practices – among them gene therapy, stem cell grafts, pharmacogenomics or anthropo-technical devices (e.g., computerized limbs). All this is becoming increasingly available to older Americans, even those with more moderate, middle-class incomes. One of the modifications that is likely to enter the scene soon is an anti-aging procedure based on a gene called MGF (Mechano-growth factor). This gene regulates a naturally occurring hormone produced after exercise that stimulates muscle production. Levels of MGF fall as people age. MGF-treatment to build up muscles would allow older people to remain able-bodied and independent much longer. IGF-1, another muscle-building hormone, has produced increased muscle mass in laboratory mice. Theoretically, gene insertion of IGF-1 could produce an equally impressive effect in humans.

In other words, new intersections of senescence and technology are opening up which bring new challenges to the cultural critique of aging and old age. Kelly Joyce and Laura Momo call this "graying the cyborg" (Joyce and Momo 121-22). Even though studies as theirs are most welcome, they remain incomplete if they do not attend to the material basis of these options which are part and parcel of a commodification of life choices: only those who are willing and able to "invest" into their bodies are given a chance to delay the restraints of human embodiment and especially those restraints deriving from their growing old.[15] In the perspective offered by these anti-aging procedures, aging and age are on their way of being no longer a universal condition ("we all age") but a form of life that replicates, even reinforces, the unequal distribution of life chances in capitalist societies.

It is true that most of the new anti-aging biotechnologies still are in their experimental stage, technically possible but not (yet) widely put in operation. Nonetheless, the contours of a techno-scientific utopia in which humans may

---

15 | There is an important shift in emphasis involved in all this, "a move away from concerns with humans in society and social salvation and towards ideals of individual perfectibility and enhancement [. . .]" (Clarke et al. 11).

one day be able even to preempt the aging process are looming large. What seems reasonably certain even at this moment is this:

Technoscientific innovations are pushing when old age is believed to begin further into a receding future. Late life is transformed into a mutable and reversible state [. . .] At the same time, through a discourse of health and risk, old age per se is biomedicalized [. . .] aging patients themselves take up a new kind of 'clinical life,' using biomedical interventions to rejuvenate bodies from the inside out [. . .]. (Clarke et al. 25-26)

Preempting aging through biotechnical means is already changing the public image of senescence in important ways. A case in point here is Viagra, often billed as the "wonder drug" that enables old men to retain or regain their sexual potency. Possible side effects such as heart attacks have recently brought Viagra under attack. What is important about the drug from a cultural point of view is that it has delinked impotence and aging and supported a new vision of positive aging based on continued sexuality (Fishman 290-92). In doing this, Viagra has dovetailed nicely with popular discourses about "new aging," "positive aging," or "best agers" based on continued consumption of anti-aging products and procedures, thus putting pressure on older people to intensify their participation in the market. These pressures are not always imposed on old people "from above" but have also become part of the agenda of old age advocacy groups such as the American Association of Retired Persons (AARP).[16]

At the same time, the availability of biotech anti-aging technologies does not overcome, rather it reinforces the cultural ambiguities attending senescence. When human life-in-time has entered the domain of intervention and choice, this will increase the pressure on people to actually put to use the available procedures in order to preempt bodily shortcomings, and certainly those associated with aging. Observers have noted that this is already indeed the case and point to a growing willingness among the elderly to allow preemptive interventions. They even found a growing sense of being somehow ethically obligated to do so, in order to avoid being a burden on others or society at large. Seniors under the perspective of biotechnical perfectibility do age or are being aged "in a political and ethical field in which individuals are increasingly obligated to form life strategies, to seek to maximize their life chances, to take actions or refrain from actions in order to increase the quality of their lives [. . .]" (Rose 107; Kaufman et al. 738; Clarke et al. 48). The upshot of this process might well be called *coercive fitness*.

Coercive pressures of this kind can be expected to mount as more preemptive measures become available in the future. The flip side of this biotech coin is then a new form of bio-based techno-governance over the individual body as a result of which the

---

16 | For details cf. Gullette, 124-25, 141, 154, 217.

primary responsibility for successful ageing [is getting assigned] to the individual who can be blamed for failing to comply [with recommended enhancement procedures or products]. Those who retain their fitness and active engagement in life are praised, whereas those who lose their vitality or disengage from society are marginalized, pitied and ridiculed. (Hodgetts et al. 419)

In this way, the ideal of preemption applied to the aging process is also well on its way of producing new forms of biocultural otherness.

5. CONCLUSION: FIXING AGE?

The genome revolution and the biotechnologies emerging in its wake have transformed the biomedical architecture of life and of the life course. They have also profoundly affected individual and collective understandings of what it means to be human in the direction of some free-market, free-enterprise version of human life. The essence of this version, I propose, can be captured by the term "preemptive biography" which for this reason is also the title of this paper. A preemptive biography turns the quondam injunction of the Delphi Oracle, γνῶθι σεαυτόν, know yourself, into a biotechnical imperative: know your body. The quest for such knowledge brings with it constant self-surveillance and an anticipatory watchfulness toward the future and its potentialities. And the need for such watchfulness is growing in proportion with the accumulation of possible health risks over the human life course, especially during senescence. This amounts to a form of personalized security administration.

Aging and old age have for the longest part of human history been understood as *fate*; genetics and biotech are in important ways turning that into *choice* – if they have not already done so. A whole new "regime of living" (Collier and Lakoff 22, 39) is emerging for the elderly organized around prudent decision-making and even more prudent planning ahead. And both planning and choices are already at every step of the way penetrated by market relations. This situation raises important ethical issues.

Preemption, looked at from an ethical point of view is not unrelated to the Nietzschean will to power, the power of *fixing* things, in the context of the present paper, *fixing bodies* in and over time which is the same as *fixing age*. Biotechnical and cultural innuendos suggesting security from the ravages of aging or old age by means of a customized version of optimum self-performance are far too important for what Habermas calls "the future of human nature" to be left to coteries of experts or the biomedical industrial complex, which is, after all, an industry, an industry that is bent on generating profit. Against this background, the question what in the future will constitute a "secure old age" calls for the special competence of the Humanities in reading public representations of human life and its options – representations here understood in both the semantic and the political senses. The ascendency of bio-tech and of neoliberal governance with a poignant preemptive logic all their own is making it extremely urgent to reflect again and anew on "the relationship between representation and humanization [. . .]" (Butler 140). Public representations of human life in its less-than-perfect forms and stages are indeed showcase examples of how the nexus between representation and humanization (or, rather, de-humanization) can do important social, cultural, and also political work. The idea that we in American Studies or Cultural Studies may have something to say about these matters is not the conceptual over-reaching of disgruntled academics. In fact, when the President's Council on Bioethics was established in the US in 2001, it began its work with a discussion of Nathaniel Hawthorne's story "The Birthmark" – which may suggest that the biotechnological imaginary does not hold an exclusive monopoly over how human life is defined, in an age of politically and bio-technically administered security.

REFERENCES

Anderson, Ben. "Preemption, precaution, preparedness: Anticipatory action and future geographies." *Progress in Human Geography* 34.6 (2010): 777-98. Print.

Andrews, Lori, and Dorothy Nelkin. *Body Bazaar: The Market for Human Tissue in the Biotechnology Age*. New York: Crown, 2001. Print.

Bush, George W. "Graduation Speech at West Point, 1 June 2002." *Voices of Democracy*. Web. 20 Oct. 2012.

Butler, Judith. *Precarious Life: The Powers of Mourning and Violence*. New York: Verso, 2004. Print.

Cazdyn, Eric. *The Already Dead: The New Time of Politics, Culture, and Illness*. Durham: Duke UP, 2012. Print.

Clarke, Adele E., Janet K. Shim, Laura Mamo, Jennifer Ruth Fosket, and Jennifer R. Fishman. "Biomedicalization: A Theoretical and Substantive Introduction." *Biomedicalization: Technoscience, Health, and Illness in the U.S..* Ed. Laura Mamo, Jennifer Ruth Fosket, Jennifer R. Fishman, Janet K. Shim. Durham: Duke UP, 2010. 1-44. Print.

Collier, Stephen J., and Andrew Lakoff. "On Regimes of Living." *Global Assemblages: Technology, Politics, and Ethics as Anthropological Problems*. Ed. Aihwa Ong and Stephen J. Collier. Malden: Blackwell, 2005. 22-39. Print.

Cooper, Melinda. "Pre-empting Emergence: The Biological Turn in the War on Terror." *Theory, Culture, Society* 23 (2006): 113-35. Print.

Cristofalo, Vincent J., Maria Tresini, Mary Kay Francis, and Craig Volker. "Biological Theories of Senescence." *Handbook of Theories of Aging.* Ed. Vern L. Bengtson and K. Warner Schaie. New York: Springer, 1999. 98-112. Print.

Elliott, Carl. *Better Than Well: American Medicine Meets the American Dream.* New York: Norton, 2003. Print.

Fishman, Jennifer R. "The Making of Viagra: The Biomedicalization of Sexual Dysfunction." *Biomedicalization: Technoscience, Health, and Illness in the U.S.* Ed. Laura Mamo, Jennifer Ruth Fosket, Jennifer R. Fishman, Janet K. Shim. Durham: Duke UP, 2010. 289-306. Print.

Giroux, Henry A. "Reading Hurricane Katrina: Race, Class, and the Biopolitics of Disposability." *College Literature* 33.3 (2006): 171-96. Print.

Gullette, Margaret Morganroth. *Agewise: Fighting the New Ageism in America.* Chicago: The U of Chicago P, 2011. Print.

Habermas, Juergen. *The Future of Human Nature.* Trans. Hella Beister and William Rehg. New York: John Wiley & Sons, 2003. Print.

Hodgetts, Darrin, Kerry Chamberlain, and Graeme Bassett. "Between television and the audience: negotiating representations of ageing." *health: An Interdisciplinary Journal for the Social Study of Health, Illness and Medicine* 7.4 (2003): 417-38. Print.

Joyce, Kelly, and Laura Mamo. "Graying the Cyborg: New Directions in Feminist Analyses of Aging, Science, and Technology." *Age Matters: Realigning Feminist Thinking.* Ed. Toni Casalanti and Kathleen F. Slevin. New York: Routledge, 2006. 99-122. Print.

Kaufman, Sharon R., Janet K. Shim, and Ann J. Russ. "Revisiting the Biomedicalization of Aging: Clinical Trends and Ethical Challenges." *The Gerontologist* 44.6 (2004): 731-38.

Lieber, Caroline. "Who Gets to Know? Genetics and Privacy." *pbs.org.* pbs. Web. 11 Jan. 2012.

Massumi, Brian. "National Enterprise Emergency: Steps Toward an Ecology of Powers." *Beyond Biopolitics: Essays on the Governance of Life and Death.* Ed. Patricia T. Clough and Craig Willse. Durham: Duke UP, 2011. 19-45. Print.

Mitchell, William J.T. *Cloning Terror: The War of Images, 9/11 to the Present.* Chicago: U of Chicago P, 2011. Print.

National Human Genome Research Institute. "Ethical Boundaries Workshop. Genetic Enhancement." Web. 10 Oct. 2012.

Novas, Carlos, and Nikolas Rose. "Biological Citizenship." *Global Assemblages: Technology, Politics, and Ethics as Anthropological Problems.* Ed. Aihwa Ong and Stephen Collier. Oxford: Blackwell, 2004. 439-63. Print.

Organization for Economic Co-Operation and Development. "Proposal for a Major Project of the Bioeconomy in 2030." *Oecd.org.* OECD. Web. 21 October 2012.

Parisi, Luciana, and Steve Goodman. "Mnemonic Control." *Beyond Biopolitics: Essays on the Governance of Life and Death.* Ed. Patricia T. Clough and Craig Willse. Durham: Duke UP, 2011. 163-77. Print.

Rajan, Kaushik Sunder. "Epilogue: Threads and Articulations." *Lively Capital: Biotechnologies, Ethics, and Governance in Global Markets.* Ed. Kaushik Sunder Rajan. Durham: Duke UP, 2012. 437-51. Print.

Rapp, Rayna. *Testing Women, Testing the Fetus: The Social Impact of Amniocentesis in America.* New York: Routledge, 1999. Print.

Rose, Nikolas. *The Politics of Life Itself: Biomedicine, Power, and Subjectivity in the Twenty-First Century.* Princeton: Princeton UP, 2007. Print.

Sielke, Sabine, and Elisabeth Schäfer-Wünsche. "The Body as Interface: Dialogues between the Disciplines. Introduction." *The Body as Interface: Dialogues between the Disciplines.* Ed. Sabine Sielke and Elisabeth Schäfer-Wünsche. Heidelberg: Winter, 2007. 11-30. Print.

Sinclair, David, and Lenny Guarente. "Unlocking the Secrets of Longevity Genes." *Scientific American,* 20 Feb. 2006. Web. 20 Nov. 2012.

Sofoer, Abraham D. "On the Necessity of Pre-emption." *European Journal of International Law* 14.2 (2003): 209-226. Print.

Stuart, Douglas T. *Creating the National Security State: A History of the Law that Transformed America.* Princeton: Princeton UP, 2012. Print.

United States Internal Revenue Service. *Biotech Industry Overview – Trends.* LMSB-04-0207-019. *irs.gov.* IRS. Web. 21 Oct. 2012.

United States National Security Council. "Summary of National Security Strategy 2002." *georgewbush-whitehouse.archives.gov.* Web. 21 Aug. 2012.

Wexler, Alice. *Mapping Fate: A Memoir of Family, Risk, and Genetic Research.* Berkeley: U of California P, 1996. Print.

World Bank. *Averting the Old Age Crisis.* Oxford: Oxford UP, 1994. Print.

Internalization or Social Comparison?

An Empirical Investigation of the Influence of Media (Re)Presentations of Age on the Subjective Health Perception and Age Experience of Older People

Julian Wangler

HEALTH COMMUNICATION AND THE MEDIA

Both psychological and communication research consider media communication to play an important role in influencing perception, attitude, and practice with regard to health and disease. Media provide their users not only with information and knowledge but also unleash so-called processes of "mediatization." This means that the diffusion of media communication in society sooner or later alters collective discourses, attitudes, norms, and behavior patterns (Krotz). In particular, the explicit or implicit discourse on health and illness in terms of specific, recurring presentation patterns may – intended or unintended – cause "collective priming conditions" (Filipp and Mayer 212). Hereby, the recipients' attribution of attention and relevance concerning their present and future well-being as well as their health behavior can be changed. Thus, media are in the center of health and health change communication.

Basically, one can distinguish between two types of media health communication: health-related and health-relevant media content. In most definitions and empirical studies the focus is on health-related content. Such media (re)presentations seek to draw the recipients' attention to certain aspects of health, for example in the context of public health campaigns providing education, preventive and therapeutic knowledge. Health-relevant content is not directly related to health issues. Nevertheless, it has an impact on health attitudes, opinions, and behavior as well as on the health status of recipients.

Especially this second type of media health communication has not been adequately explored, although it is obvious that media – due to their potential of collective influence – play a crucial role in health communication. By selecting and emphasizing certain objects and pieces of information (Matthes 28) that show a subliminal reference to health and disease, media create general staging patterns and interpretation frames that can easily be internalized by media recipients in the wake of accumulative and consonant presentation (Gerbner et al.). From the cultivation hypothesis' point of view, media convey a homogeneous mainstream world view and lifestyle, which sometimes differ greatly from real life. However, these media (re)presentations can retroact on the perception of social reality. Against this background, it can be assumed that media-mediated images of age can change ideas and feelings towards health and disease.

MEDIA IMAGES OF OLD AGE

Generally speaking, images of old age refer to opinions and beliefs about presumable characteristics and attributes of aging as well as attitudes towards age, aging, and older people (Schmitt 135). In that sense, such images can be seen as "expectation codes" or role models concerning the elderly that are capable of influencing social relationships in a positive or negative way (Göckenjan, *Das Alter würdigen* 24). Accordingly, they do much more than just reflecting cultural imaginations and stereotypes of old age. Old age pictures are, in fact, communication concepts that have an impact on sociocultural processes and conditions since they affect the social reality they pretend to mirror (BMFSFJ; Femers).

Media (re)presentations of old age, most notably, are said to have a high power of suggestion. On the one hand, this is due to the formation and mass distribution of similar (re)presentation patterns in terms of seniority. On the other hand, it is because both expressive images and striking language are being used in the media. Media-mediated old age pictures are presented as human and physical concepts on all possible communication channels always referring to very general aspects: characteristics of the elderly, perceptions of health and illness, autonomy and dependence, fears, hopes, and thoughts about the finiteness of life (Schmidt-Hertha and Mühlbauer 111)[1]. In this way, media create and offer constructs that allow to scan old age for the most intimate details, to stage it as lived reality (Schroeter 164) and, by doing so, to access our feelings and values towards the process of getting old (Gehlen 71).

---

1 | Also see Göckenjan (*Die soziale Ordnung* 104) who distinguishes between four public discourse types of age and aging: age consolation, age lamentation, age praise, and age scolding. It is likely that these basic discourse types are employed by modern mass media.

POTENTIAL EFFECTS OF MEDIA IMAGES OF OLD AGE

In light of these remarks, Filipp and Mayer (119-20) draw attention to the importance of old age images circulating in the public sphere. Considering the significantly increased public interest regarding demographic change, a strong presence and polarization of the topic can be noted in German media. In the case of negative portrayals of older people, this leads – almost a self-fulfilling prophecy (Ryan and Kwong See) – to an increase of disease probability since the German discussion about nursing is primarily associated with negative and threatening aspects of becoming and being old. According to the *internalization hypothesis,* first and foremost older people tend to identify with negative portrayals of age[2]. Through this identification their self-perception, motivation, and future estimates may be affected (Arnold and Lang; Oswald).

However, it can be assumed that even exaggeratedly positive portrayals of old age can cause problematic effects on the health of seniors, because they create unrealistic expectations and generate guilt on part of those not living up to the ideals and conditions of "successful aging" (Mayer 120). In order to stabilize the welfare state and social security system, it has become a political aim to "activate" older people, for example in terms of volunteering, in order to mainstream their skills according to social demands. Collective effects of media-mediated old age images can jeopardize a society that is trying to adapt to demographic change.

Apart from the widely-used internalization hypothesis one can also think of other and more differentiated modes of influence caused by media (re)presentations of old age. The *resilience theory* assumes a certain barrier regarding the transmission of old age images to older people's selves because seniors tend to shield themselves against an impairment of their self-concept, especially regarding questions of age (Mayer et al. 77; Rothermund and Brandtstädter 549-50). Such a coping strategy is carried out by selecting only positive aspects of age (re)presentations. In regards to media usage of seniors, one can also refer to the uses-and-gratifications approach presuming that selective motivations determine the potentials of influence that media can have on the recipient (Blumler and Katz). The *comparison hypothesis,* in turn, is based on the theory of social comparison processes (Festinger). It considers old age images as reference points for social comparisons: Instead of integrating negative information into their self-concepts, older people conduct a self-esteem promoting downward

---

2 | As old age images are more often seen as referring to personal experiences of aging than as detached external perspectives, older people seem to be more aware of these images (Niederfranke et al. 31). It is assumed that self- and other-images of age inform each other, so that auto-stereotypes adopted in youth become self-stereotypes in old age (Rothermund).

comparison so that counterproductive effects can be limited. Under certain circumstances it is even conceivable that negative images of age can improve self-contentment and life satisfaction of older people (Kessler 152)[3].

EMPIRICAL STUDY:
RESEARCH INTEREST AND METHODOLOGICAL APPROACH

Apart from theoretical assumptions dealing with possible effects that media (re)presentations may have on the well-being of older people, there is currently a lack of empirical studies. Therefore, a questionnaire experiment has been conducted examining in what way and to what extent (re)presentations of old age in news coverage can influence the assessment of seniors' health status and their expectations towards their personal aging processes. The investigation included three experimental groups. The subjects in the first group were given (re)presentations of old age as tragedy and stigma, while the second group received (re)presentations of a successful, juvenile life in old age. The third experimental group was given a placebo, an article about the European debt crisis. The stimulus material of the first and second group comes from a separate textual and visual content analysis of German news magazines in the time period between 1999 and 2010, which identified basic presentation and interpretation patterns (frames) concerning old age and older people. As stimulus material for this study, a staging pattern demonstrating health and social drama in the context of age care ('old age as human demise'), and another focusing on activity, vitality and life opportunities in old age ('old age as new departure') were used (see attachment).

With the aid of an online questionnaire posted in an internet forum for older people, a total of 135 subjects were surveyed in the period between June 14th and July 2nd, 2012. The youngest participant was 60 years of age, the oldest 83 years old. Everybody who was a member of the forum and read the post had the chance to participate in the survey. Each experimental group was limited to 45 participants. It was ensured that the number of women and men were almost even. Age and gender were the only criteria that counted.

The questionnaire consisted of two components. First, health assessments of the subjects were questioned on various dimensions. The scale was adopted from Wydra thus including physical, psychological, and social aspects based on a definition of health not as a static state but a dynamic equilibrium between so-called risk and protective factors (Fromm et al. 17; Bengel et al. 16). The second scale con-

---

3 | A study by Mares and Cantor demonstrates that older viewers feel better after being confronted with a negative media stimulus of old age. This effect was observed only in the case of isolated older viewers. Viewers who were not lonely felt better after being confronted with positive (re)presentations.

sisted of I-related items that were mostly taken from the standard scale *Expectations Regarding Aging* (ERA-38; Sarkisian et al.). Both components were nested in order to disguise the repetition of six items (three for each component, before and after the stimulus). The stimulus was placed in the middle of the questionnaire.

RESULTS

The subjects were asked to assess their personal health. They could gradate their responses on a four-step Likert scale.

Figure 1: Assessment of one's own health, without repetition items (arithmetic average, grey (blue in original) = group 1: negative frame, light grey with stripes (red in original) = group 2: positive frame, black with dots (yellow in original) = group 3: control group)

	1	2	3	4
B: I am physically fit.				
B: I am not comfortable in my own skin.				
B: I feel physically balanced.				
B: My circulation is stable.				
B: When I move I can feel my illness.				
P: In the evening I'm pleasantly tired.				
P: I am in a cheerful mood.				
P: I feel stressed and nervous.				
P: I have little success.				
P: I am able to survey my surroundings.				
S: I cannot rely on my friends.				
S: I feel most comfortable in a crowd.				
S: I am busy enough with myself.				
S: I have no one to talk to.				
S: I would like to help other people.[1]				
		Stimulus		
B: I am self-sustaining.[1]				
B: I am happy with my body condition.[1]				
B: I feel exhausted and tired.[1]				
B: I feel sluggish.[1]				
B: I am in constant pain.[1]				
P: I am not a confident person.				
P: I have everything under control.				
P: I am taking pleasure in a fresh start.				
P: My mood is depressed.[1]				
P: Nothing can wind me up.				
S: Helping other people is a matter of course to me.				
S: It is a pity that almost no one comes to visit me.				
S: I am disappointed by my fellow men.				
S: I feel left behind.				
S: I can easily make the first move on others.				

Superscript numbers indicate the respective experimental group and mark, on a significance level of p <.05, significant mean differences in comparison with the two other experimental groups.

The polarity profile provides an overview of the mean values within and between the experimental groups (see Figure 1). Items checked before and after the stimulus are listed separately (see Table 1). Items relating to physical health are marked with 'B', while statements with regard to psychological and social well-being are indicated with 'P' and 'S'. As one can see, before the stimulus the estimates of the subjects in all groups are mostly similar. After a reading of their respective texts, however, very different health assessments were made. In particular, statements strongly associated with physical performance (*I am self-sustaining, I am happy with my body condition, I feel exhausted and tired, I feel sluggish* and *I am in constant pain*) led to significantly different results of the first group compared to the other two. It is striking that the subjects receiving the negative frame made significantly better estimates than those with the positive frame or in the control group. Interestingly, the most negative outlook could be found in the group with the positive frame.

Table 1: Experimental groups in before-after comparison, perceived health status

		Group 1: Negative Frame	Group 2: Positive Frame	Group 3: Control Group
I feel physically healthy.	before	2.3*	2.2*	2.1
	after	1.8*	2.6*	2.2
I am not happy.	before	3.0*	3.1*	3.1
	after	3.5*	2.8*	3.0
There are people who need me.	before	2.2	2.4	2.3
	after	2.2	2.3	2.4

*Low values indicate high agreement. Only for values marked with an asterisk the estimates between before and after differ on a significance level of p <.05.

Looking at the repetition items separately, it is interesting to note that in the first and second experimental group the statements *I feel physically healthy* and *I am not happy* changed significantly in assessment after the stimulus. Surprisingly, the subjects that were given the negative frame evaluated their health status much better, whereas in the group with the positive frame the items got worse. By comparison, the values in the control group remained fairly constant.

Figure 2: Expectations regarding aging, without repetition items (arithmetic average, grey (blue in original) = group 1: negative frame, light grey with stripes (red in original) = group 2: positive frame, black with dots (yellow in original) = group 3: control group)

When I get older I expect...	1	2	3	4
I will be able to take care of myself.				
I will not be able to work as well as I do now.				
I will become more forgetful.				
I will become more dependent on others.				
I will spend less time with friends and family.				
I will spend more time alone.				
			Stimulus	
my quality of life will decrease.[1]				
I will get depressed.				
I will get tired more quickly.[1]				
I will become lonelier.				
I will not be able to do everything I want to.[1]				
I will become less attractive.				

Superscript numbers indicate the respective experimental group and mark, on a significance level of p <.05, significant mean differences in comparison with the two other experimental groups.

Figure 2 illustrates the mean values in terms of the expectations of the subjects' own aging. As in the first polarity profile, the values before the stimulus differ only insignificantly. In contrast, the values in the first experimental group drift off after the reception of the stimulus. Significant mean differences can be discovered for the items *My quality of life will decrease, I will get tired more quickly,* and *I will not be able to do everything I want to.* Once more it is remarkable that the most significant differences appear with items related to physical performance.

In the assessment of a future state of health, there were significantly fewer people in the first experimental group who believed that their age would be marked by discomfort and pain, or that they would have to cope with difficulties in everyday life after reading the texts. To the same degree, they rather tended to assume that they would be able to enjoy their lives. As the previous results already showed, the opposite can be observed in the second experimental group: Here, after the stimulus application, the approval of the first and third item increased. A deterioration of the ratings regarding the expectations towards subjective aging can be noted even in the case of positive age (re)presentation.

Table 2: Experimental groups in before-after comparison,
expectations regarding aging

When I get older I expect...		Group 1: *Negative Frame*	Group 2: *Positive Frame*	Group 3: *Control Group*
I will have more aches and pains.	before	2.4*	2.5*	2.5
	after	3.0*	2.1*	2.6
I will enjoy my life.	before	2.8*	2.8	2.7
	after	2.3*	2.9	2.7
it will become more difficult to do my daily activities.	before	2.2*	2.5*	2.5
	after	2.7*	2.1*	2.4

*Low values indicate high agreement. Only for values marked with an asterisk the estimates between before and after differ on a significance level of p <.05.

INTERPRETATION AND CONCLUSION

How can we interpret the results of the questionnaire survey in the context of existing theoretical assumptions? There are some indications that the theory of social comparison processes may provide a plausible explanation. According to this theory, media recipients are given benchmarks and ratios that can be used for downward or upward comparisons, always depending on life circumstances, personal characteristics and the reception situation.

In the case of the first experimental group (negative frame), it can be presumed that the subjects perform a downward social comparison. Facing the drama of being old, the subjects become aware of how lucky they actually are – especially with regard to their physical well-being – when comparing themselves with the elderly presented in the article. However, in the second experimental group (positive frame), it can be assumed that the subjects are forced to conduct an upward social comparison that does not turn out in their favor. Presentations of "best agers" with a high level of activity and vitality make traditional age notions seem absurd. In comparison to ordinary women and men facing age-related challenges and restrictions, such portrayals of age fall short and lead to feelings of frustration.

The empirical study on journalism-mediated age (re)presentations led to two important conclusions. First, the findings show that images of old age – because they illustrate human and body concepts – can affect an individual's subjective health experience as well as his or her personal view of getting old. Therefore, it can be concluded that old age images are an important part of health-relevant communication and should be dealt with accordingly. Yet, the way old age images influence older recipients is more than unexpected. Age-euphorically tuned (re)presentations showing modern and youthful best agers do not necessarily cause positive effects on people's self-perception but actually have negative effects. Conversely, negative images of old age do not automatically trigger frustration and self-doubt but can remind recipients that – in comparison to the persons depicted – they should be content with their health status. Furthermore, these results clearly indicate that it is not enough to simply rely on content analysis results and theoretical assumptions concerning the effects of media portrayals of old age. Actually, extensive empirical studies are required that attempt to clarify under which circumstances media (re)presentations of the elderly can unfold negative or positive effects on older people. It would also be very interesting to find out how younger people's attitudes towards age are being changed by media images of the elderly, since the current state of research does not yet provide an answer.

REFERENCES

Arnold, Klaus, and Erich Lang. *Wie sieht man die Älteren, wie sehen sie sich selbst?* Erlangen: Hamburg-Mannheimer-Stiftung für Informationsmedizin, 1989. Print.

Bengel, Jürgen, Regine Strittmatter, and Hildegard Willmann. *Was erhält Menschen gesund? Antonovskys Modell der Salutogenese – Diskussionsstand und Stellenwert.* Köln: Bundeszentrale für gesundheitliche Aufklärung, 2001. Print.

Blumler, Jay G., and Elihu Katz. "Foreword." *The Uses of Mass Communications. Current Perspectives on Gratifications Research.* Ed. Jay G. Blumler and Elihu Katz. Beverly Hills/London: Sage, 1974. 13-16. Print.

BMFSFJ [Bundesministerium für Familie, Senioren, Frauen und Jugend], ed. *Sechster Bericht zur Lage der älteren Generation in der Bundesrepublik Deutschland. Altersbilder in der Gesellschaft.* Berlin: BT-Drs., 2010. Print.

Femers, Susanne. *Die ergrauende Werbung. Altersbilder und werbesprachliche Inszenierungen.* Wiesbaden: Verlag für Sozialwissenschaften, 2007. Print.

Festinger, Leon. "A Theory of Social Comparison Processes." *Human Relations* 7, 1954. 117-40. Print.

Filipp, Sigrun-Heide, and Anne-Kathrin Mayer. *Bilder des Alters. Altersstereotype und die Beziehungen zwischen den Generationen.* Stuttgart: Kohlhammer, 1999. Print.

Fromm, Bettina, Eva Baumann, and Claudia Lampert. *Gesundheitskommunika-tion und Medien. Ein Lehrbuch.* Stuttgart: Kohlhammer, 2011. Print.

Gehlen, Arnold. *Anthropologische und sozialpsychologische Untersuchungen.* Reinbek: Rowohlt, 1986. Print.

Gerbner, George, Larry Gross, Nancy Signorielli, and Michael Morgan. "Aging with Television. Images on Television Drama and Conception of Social Reality." *Journal of Communication* 30, 1980. 37-49. Print.

Göckenjan, Gerd. *Das Alter würdigen. Altersbilder und Bedeutungswandel des Alters.* Frankfurt a.M.: Suhrkamp, 2000. Print.

—–—. "Die soziale Ordnung der Generationenfolge." *Bilder des Alterns im Wandel. Historische, interkulturelle, theoretische und aktuelle Perspektiven (= Akademiengruppe Altern in Deutschland, Bd. 1).* Ed. Josef Ehmer and Otfried Höffe. Stuttgart: Wissenschaftliche Verlagsgesellschaft Stuttgart, 2009. 103-14. Print.

Kessler, Eva-Marie. "Altersbilder in den Medien: Wirklichkeit oder Illusion?" *Medien und höheres Lebensalter. Theorie – Forschung – Praxis.* Ed. Bernd Schorb, Anja Hartung, and Wolfgang Reißmann. Wiesbaden: Verlag für Sozialwissenschaften, 2009. 146-56. Print.

Krotz, Friedrich. *Mediatisierung kommunikativen Handelns. Der Wandel von Alltag und sozialen Beziehungen, Kultur und Gesellschaft durch die Medien.* Wiesbaden: Verlag für Sozialwissenschaften, 2001. Print.

Mares, Marie-Louise, and Joanne Cantor. "Elderly Viewers' Response to Televised Portrayals of Old Age: Empathy and Mood Management Versus Social Comparison." *Communication Research* 4, 1992. 459-78. Print.

Matthes, Jörg. *Framing-Effekte. Zum Einfluss der Politikberichterstattung auf die Einstellungen der Rezipienten.* München: Reinhard Fischer, 2007. Print.

Mayer, Anne-Kathrin. "Vermittelte Altersbilder und individuelle Altersstereotype." *Medien und höheres Lebensalter. Theorie – Forschung – Praxis.* Ed. Bernd Schorb, Anja Hartung, and Wolfgang Reißmann. Wiesbaden: Verlag für Sozialwissenschaften, 2009. 114-29. Print.

—–—, Christina Lukas, and Klaus Rothermund. "Vermittelte und individuelle Vorstellungen vom Alter – Altersstereotype." *SPIEL* 1, 2005, 67-99. Print.

Niederfranke, Annette, Reinhard Schmitz-Scherzer, and Sigrun-Heide Filipp. "Die Farben des Herbstes. Die vielen Gesichter des Alters heute." *Funkkolleg Altern. Vol. 1: Die vielen Gesichter des Alterns.* Ed. Annette Niederfranke, Gerhard Naegele, and Eckart Frahm. Opladen/Wiesbaden, 1999. 11-50. Print.

Oswald, Frank. "Das persönliche Altersbild älterer Menschen." *Zeitschrift für Gerontologie* 5, 1991. 276-84. Print.

Rothermund, Klaus. "Effects of Age Stereotypes on Self-Views and Adaptation." *The Adaptive Self: Personal Continuity and Intentional Self-Development.* Ed.

Werner Greve, Klaus Rothermund, and Dirk Wentura. Göttingen: Hogrefe, 2005. 223-42. Print.

——, and Jochen Brandtstädter. "Age Stereotypes and Self-Views in Later Life. Evaluating Rival Assumptions." *International Journal of Behavioral Development* 6, 2003, 549-54. Print.

Ryan, Ellen B., and Sheree T. Kwong See. "Sprache, Kommunikation und Altern." *Sprache und Kommunikation im Alter*. Ed. Caja Thimm and Reinhard Fiehler. Radolfzell: Verlag für Gesprächsforschung, 2003. 57-71. Print.

Sarkisian, Catherine A., Ron D. Hays, Sandra Berry, and Carol M. Mangione. "Development, Reliability, and Validity of the Expectations Regarding Aging (ERA-38) Survey." *The Gerontologist* 4, 2002. 534-42. Print.

Scheufele, Bertram. *Frames – Framing – Framing-Effekte. Theoretische und methodische Grundlegung des Framing-Ansatzes sowie empirische Befunde zur Nachrichtenproduktion*. Wiesbaden: Westdeutscher Verlag, 2003. Print.

Schmidt-Hertha, Bernhard, and Catharina Mühlbauer. "Lebensbedingungen, Lebensstile und Altersbilder älterer Erwachsener." *Individuelle und kulturelle Altersbilder (= Expertisen zum Sechsten Altenbericht der Bundesregierung, Vol. 1)*. Ed. Frank Berner, Judith Rossow, and Klaus-Peter Schwitzer. Wiesbaden: Verlag für Sozialwissenschaften, 2012. 109-49. Print.

Schmitt, Eric. "Altersbild – Begriff, Befunde und politische Implikationen." *Enzyklopädie der Gerontologie*. Ed. Andreas Kruse and Mike Martin. Bern: Huber, 2004. 135-47. Print.

Schroeter, Klaus R. "Altersbilder als Körperbilder: Doing Age by Bodyfication." *Individuelle und kulturelle Altersbilder (= Expertisen zum Sechsten Altenbericht der Bundesregierung, Bd. 1)*. Ed. Frank Berner, Judith Rossow, and Klaus-Peter Schwitzer. Wiesbaden: Verlag für Sozialwissenschaften, 2012. 153-229. Print.

Wydra, Georg. *Der Fragebogen zum allgemeinen habituellen Wohlbefinden (FAHW). Entwicklung und Evaluation eines mehrdimensionalen Fragebogens*. Saarbrücken: Sportwissenschaftliches Institut der Universität des Saarlandes, 2005. Print.

ANNEX: STIMULUS ARTICLES

1. *Old Age as Human Demise*

Where Even Dignity Comes to Death

The last way is long and shabby. Hundreds of thousands of elderly doze in German homes and hospitals with their lives very slowly coming to an end that holds no dignity. They are well managed but physically and emotionally neglected. Resigned caregivers and experts complain: Even animals are better protected.

The older one gets, the greater the probability of dying in a nursing home. However, the process of dying does not take hours any more as it used to. The result: Many months, sometimes years, of vegetating. The body cannot go the way your mind has already taken when forgetfulness becomes dementia. Then the last possibility is the nursing home.

Malnutrition, dehydration, damage of health by sedatives, large-volume incontinence pads which are used against the patients' will and not being changed for a long time, violations of personal integrity and dignity to the deprivation of liberty. All that is the norm. Care expert Claus Fussek escapes to black humor when he says: "What is the difference between old oil and old people? Disposing old oil means to follow certain standards."

Fussek once asked the head of a charity organization whether he could guarantee the following minimum standards in his old age homes: eating and drinking in a chew and swallow pace, washing, dressing, inserting dentures, going to the toilet as often as needed, keeping fresh air once a day, holding the hand of a dying person. Unfortunately no, the honest man answered.

Many care home residents are confined to bed. Their everyday lives are monotonous. Nurses only stop by to take a blood sample and to change diapers. Relatives do not visit these old people because the seniors are confused and no longer recognize familiar faces. In addition, hospitals dismiss care cases rigorously, often in a deplorable state. They are deported to nursing homes. There, a clientele accumulates that is increasingly older and sicker.

Horrible, but not uncommon is the example of Michael Nunhofer from Munich. He had to take his 87-year-old mother Mary from hospital although her back was still marked by a huge gaping wound the size of a hand. It was so deep that the spinal column was shimmering through: a purulent decubitus ulcer that the old lady had suffered from by a fatal care failure. A month later she was dead.

The younger the ill, the more likely they will find their ends in hospital. More than fifty percent of people between 60 and 80 years are going to die in a hospital. Regarding 85 year-olds, the proportion drops to one quarter. Experienced home managers try to avoid that their suffering and dying nurslings are transported to hospital because they would only be attached to pipes there.

Given the 150,000 people who already are in need of care a nightmare scenario is looming: One day there will be wards with food lines as in a cowshed. Pipes go to every care bed, and in the basement there is a computer controlling everything.

2. *Old Age as New Departure*

Golden Oldies: Generation Happy End

'Old age' no longer exists. Today, middle age lasts until at least 70. This is the report of a social revolution.

Where are the perms? We do not find them anymore. The 'new old' are going to mark society in the years to come: They have more money available than younger people. They could benefit from decades of a favorable economic development without wars and extreme inflation.

They are as fit as no old generation before them since they profit from the blessings of modern medicine, are sensitive to health matters and appreciate fashion. In particular, old men still do intensive physical activity, some of them are even running marathons. Moreover, in recent decades the jobs that incorporated hard physical labor heavily decreased. Experts estimate that age-related decline tends to begin about ten years later than in previous generations.

They are mentally active and mobile as old people have never been before. Almost 25,000 seniors are guest students at German universities. They surf the internet and join social networks. Most of the older Germans still drive their cars. They travel and consume as long as there is money on their credit cards.

Age: Only 30 years ago was a period of modest claims and low zest for action: small apartment, crossword puzzles, watering the plants, hearing Heino on the radio, taking the dog for a walk, making a short trip from time to time. The current generation of retirees is fundamentally different and often looks like this: Mechthild Gerdes, director of a residential project, has many interests and is so socially engaged that sometimes her schedule collapses. Patent attorney Utz Kador, 65, wants to work until 85 and loves all kinds of sports. 70-year-old Helga Hermann is learning four languages. In addition, she has begun to write her first novel.

"Other people label you 'old'," Helga Hermann, a highly attractive woman, complains. "People say: 'Can you still do this and that at your age?' 'At your age' – just to hear that! There is the accusation that our society has an obsession with youth but in my opinion that is wrong. It is a fear of aging which we suffer from, the idea that older people should not do this and should not do that."

Experts are pretty sure: The new seniors create an entirely new vision of life in old age which is no longer limited to disability, pain, sadness and loneliness. Today-old age means to be active, vital and hopeful for the future.

Combating Age Discrimination in the Workplace

A Study of the United States' Rights-Based Response

Elisabeth Boulot

In 1967, Congress passed the *Age Discrimination in Employment Act* (ADEA). The twin goals of this new piece of legislation were to address the problem of the long-term joblessness of older workers perceived to result from employers' misconceptions about the value of their contribution to the workforce and to "uphold the dignity" (Rep. John Dent, House Report 6) of these workers by preventing stereotypical thinking about age and aging. The purpose of this paper is to examine whether this rights-based legislation has proved to be an adequate tool to persuade employers to hire unemployed older workers as well as fight age bias in the workplace and to explore the reasons accounting for the difficulties still experienced by older workers, 45 years after the passage of the Act. The first part will provide an overview of the history of the ADEA and an outline of the changes in its coverage. In the second part, I will discuss its impact on employers and workers. Through a comparison of the US experience with that of other nations which have enacted age discrimination legislation, the question of the efficiency of a rights-based response will be raised in the last part of this article.

1. History and Purpose of the ADEA

The first attempt to have Congress pass an Age Discrimination in Employment bill dates back to 1951, when Jacob Javits submitted one to the House of Representatives. In 1962, an Equal Employment Opportunity bill which would have prohibited employment discrimination on the basis of age, race, color, national origin, or ancestry was drafted by the House Education and Labor Committee but never emerged from the Rules Committee which sets the House's agenda (Macnicol 234). Another attempt to legislate on this issue was made when Congress debated the text of Title VII of the *Civil Rights Act* in 1964. Though

Senator Smathers of Florida proposed to add age as a form of discrimination prohibited in section 703(1), it was mainly to derail the passage of the bill which he opposed[1]. Consequently, supporters did not include it. It was also felt that specific legislation should address this issue, since unlike racial or sex discrimination at work, age bias could affect anyone. As a result, section 715 of the *Civil Rights Act* enjoined the Secretary of Labor, Willard Wirtz, to "make a full and complete study of the factors which might tend to result in discrimination in employment because of age and of the consequences of such discrimination on the economy and individuals affected." The report to Congress had to be completed by June 30, 1965 and needed to contain "recommendations for legislation to prevent arbitrary discrimination in employment because of age as [the secretary] determine[d] advisable." Available evidence showed that older workers, when they were laid off, had much greater difficulties to find another job and were thus unemployed for longer periods[2]. Yet, by 1965, 20 states had passed age discrimination legislation. The bill submitted to Congress was voted without controversy on December 15, 1967 and attracted little attention from the media. No one seemed to anticipate the number of claims which grew in the first ten years from 1031 in 1969 to 5374 in 1979 (O'Meara 30).

The Act prohibits age discrimination in advertising jobs, hiring, termination of employment and layoffs as well as promotion and wages. Section 623(d) protects any employee from retaliation for "participat[ing] in any manner in an investigation, proceeding, or litigation" in order to defend his rights[3]. It applies

---

1 | It was outvoted in the Senate by 28 votes.

2 | By the 1960s, the issue of unemployed older workers was well documented. It appeared as a serious concern in congressional debates about the Social Security Act in 1935. A National Conference on Aging was convened in 1950 by Oscar Ewing, the head of the Federal Security Agency. Michael Harrington dedicated a whole chapter of the Other America: Poverty in the United States (1962) to jobless older people living in poverty without health insurance. In the 1940s and 50s gerontologists analyzed the problems of older workers. The bibliography compiled in 1958 by Joseph. T. Drake highlights this interest.

3 | Harassment on the basis of age is prohibited under Title VII of the Civil Rights Act and by Section 623a (2) of the ADEA: "It shall be unlawful for an employer [. . .] to limit, segregate, or classify his employees in any way which would deprive or tend to deprive any individual of employment opportunities or otherwise adversely affect his status as an employee, because of such individual's age." EEOC regulations specify: "Harassment can include, for example, offensive remarks about a person's age. Although the law doesn't prohibit simple teasing, offhand comments, or isolated incidents that aren't very serious, harassment is illegal when it is so frequent or severe that it creates a hostile or offensive work environment or when it results in an adverse employment decision (such as the victim being fired or demoted). The harasser can be the victim's supervisor,

to workers employed in US companies of at least 20 employees[4] affecting interstate commerce, labor unions and employment agencies. This means that small businesses are not covered by the ADEA. Initially, it applied to workers from 40 to 65 years of age, and only to private companies.

The Act has been amended several times since its passage. Coverage was enlarged in 1974 to employees of federal, state, and local government, and to US citizens working for US corporations overseas in 1984. Because of a rise in life expectancy, the upper age limit for retirement was raised to seventy in 1978. Since 1986, the Act covers workers 40 years of age and older; mandatory retirement is limited to a small number of professions, usually on grounds of public safety (i.e. bus drivers, fire-fighters, law enforcement officers and air pilots[5]). In 1990, further protection was provided for older workers against employers' staff-cutting and discrimination in benefits which had become a very common practice in large companies aiming at reducing their payroll costs[6]. That same year Congress passed the *Americans with Disability Act* (ADA). Employers were required to make reasonable adjustments to enable such workers to enter or stay in the workforce regardless of their age. Enforcement was transferred in 1978 from the Wage and Hour Division of the Department of Labor to the Equal Employment Opportunity Commission (EEOC) which also investigates complaints under Title VII of the Civil Rights Act. Trial by jury and class actions are available for these cases.

Under the ADEA (§ 623f), employers have five possible defenses against a claim of age discrimination. These are the three main ones:

1. Prove that the action taken against an employee "was reasonably necessary to the particular business" i.e. a bona fide occupational requirement (BFOR).
2. That the employer's decision was based on "reasonable factors other than age" (RFOTA).
3. To discharge or otherwise discipline an individual for good cause.[7]

---

a supervisor in another area, a co-worker, or someone who is not an employee of the employer, such as a client or customer."

4 | In 1967, the Act applied to private companies employing at least 25 workers. It was amended in 1973.

5 | Though challenged in court, the Federal Aviation Authority (FAA) has refused to amend its 1960 regulation requiring air pilots to retire at sixty. It argued that the age sixty rule is a bona fide occupational qualification (BOFQ).

6 | The *Older Worker Benefit Protection Act* (29 U.S.C. § 623, 626 and 630). It also regulated the legal waivers that employers are increasingly asking employees to sign in connection with so-called early retirement programs.

7 | See Feder 5. The text of the ADEA provides these specific defenses whereas defenses under Title VII were created by courts (Johnson 1422-27).

Lyndon Johnson pointed out, when he signed the Act into law on December 19, 1967, that it was part of his administration's overall struggle for equal opportunity in employment and meant to address a pervasive form of discrimination "which had long been ignored, and about which little was known." He stressed its economic cost – 1 out of 4 workers between 45 and 65 was unemployed and billions of dollars paid each year for unemployment insurance – as well as its human price: "men and women who need to work – who want to work – and who [are] able to work, [are] not being given a fair chance to work." The president believed that, as a result of this "practical and humane" piece of legislation, this portion of the American workforce would have "a better chance to go on working productively and gainfully [and] the country [would] gain, as well, from making better use of their skills and experience." He also hoped that it would change the public's views about older workers.

2. The Impact of the ADEA on Age Discrimination in the Workplace

Labor Department statistics as well as those of the Employment Equality Opportunity Commission (EEOC) provide valuable information to assess whether the ADEA protects older workers and is effective in combating age bias at work today. In March 2013, according to the Bureau of Labor Statistics, the unemployment rate dipped to 7.6 percent and the jobless rate for workers aged 55+ slid to 5.5. It is lower than the rate of workers under 50 (6.3 percent) and teenagers (24.2 percent). The average duration of unemployment is however longer for the 55-65 year-olds (49.2 weeks) than for those under 50 (35.7 weeks). Moreover, one has to bear in mind that some of these workers are unable to find full-time jobs and usually experience a significant drop in wages. What has changed is their participation in the labor force (Eglit, "Age Bias" 105-6; Neumark, "Challenge of Population Aging" 43). While it steadily declined until 1993, it has been growing since then to peak at 40.4 percent in May 2009. During the continuing recession it has only slightly decreased to 40.1 percent in 2011 (Sok; GAO Report 9-10) but demographic projections show that the trend should increase in the next decade (Heidkamp, Mabe and DeGraff 3-4). According to Emy Sok, "the move by employers to replace defined-benefit retirement plans with defined-contribution retirement plans, allowing employers to shift more responsibility for retirement income to the employee" is one of the underlying reasons for "the increased labor force participation of older workers." As opposed to the 1960s, older workers today are faced with losses in their retirement accounts and with the necessity to ensure adequate postretirement income. Moreover, the number of women in the workforce explains this change in demographics since there is a higher rate of women in managerial positions and they often have to work in their later years in order to make up for the years during which they stopped working because of family responsibilities (Eglit, "Age Bias" 110-11). There is also another factor: a study conducted by the Pew Research Center stresses that among the 54 percent who work after 62, which is the median age for retirement, "attitudes about work also play an important role – in particular, the growing desire of an aging but healthy population to stay active well into the later years of life."[8]

Labor Department statistics, however, show that employers' hiring practices do not seem to have improved; though the Act has been enforced for over four decades now, it has failed to fulfill its main goal: preventing age discrimination against *older applicants* who are still experiencing long periods of unemployment when laid off. EEOC data about age discrimination complaints highlights a steady increase of claims brought on this ground[9], though it is difficult to prove (Posner 426; Neumark, "Challenge of Population Aging" 46). Moreover, many interviews of workforce professionals and testimonies of jobless older workers corroborate employers' reluctance to hire older workers (GAO Report 29-30); numerous studies stress this as well (T. Butler 5-7). While they point out that, as a result of federal and state legislation, manifestations of age bias are less "blatant" (Macnicol 26; Neumark, "Challenge of Population Aging" 50), they underscore that employers prefer to hire young workers for entry level jobs rather than the age group protected by federal legislation and workers in their 40s for managerial positions, men being less affected than women (Lahey, "Age, Women, and Hiring"). Invoking economic motives is often a subterfuge:

There is overwhelming evidence that older people are now living more active and longer lives, mainly due to advances in medicine, healthcare, and lifestyle choices. Although employers should be aware of these trends, there are those who continue to carry out acts of ageism, "discriminatory beliefs, attitudes, and practices regarding older adults as part of their way of doing business." (T. Butler 6; Rothenberg and Gardner 11)

Nonetheless, a group of workers has benefited from the ADEA. It has partly acted as a deterrent against firing older workers; in particular white males aged 55-59 in managerial or salesmanship positions for fear of the cost of being sued (Neumark and Stock). After that age, though mandatory retirement has been abolished, employers still tend to offer attractive retirement packages. And in

---

8 | In 2007, Michael Smyer and Marcie Pitt-Catsouphes examined the key elements which affect the meaning of work for older workers and raised the issue of the impact of this data on employers in the twenty-first century.

9 | See Overman: "The Equal Employment Opportunity Commission (EEOC) reports that the number of age discrimination charges has increased over the past few years, rising from 16,548 charges (21.8% of all claims) in 2006 to 22,778 (24.4% of all claims) in 2009."

spite of the passage of *The Older Worker Benefit Protection Act* in 1990, it is risky to refuse such an offer, as threats of demotion or termination are quite likely.

One cannot ignore that the financial cost of hiring or keeping an older worker is high and often presents one of the prime motives for severance or refusal to hire: this includes healthcare costs[10], (Lahey, "Age, Women, and Hiring" 20-21; Neumark, "Challenge of Population Aging" 59), rules under the Americans with Disabilities Act (Neumark, "Challenge of Population Aging" 60-61), pensions (though defined-contribution plans are now rare, at least in the private sector) and salaries. The state of the economy is also a factor to take into account; the downsizing of corporations in the 1980s was a case in point. However, there is ample evidence that ageism is rampant and condoned, as opposed to racial and sexual discrimination and harassment[11]. Although life expectancy, fitness and health have significantly increased since the 1970s, older people on the job as well as older applicants are still mainly perceived as likely to be absent for health reasons and accident-prone. Employers argue that older workers often lack motivation and are more difficult to train. They also view them as less productive, enthusiastic or creative. Such negative generalizations are largely disproved by collected data but they are still pervasive and take their toll on older workers' career prospects and perception in the workplace as well as on their own perception of their ability in an environment where everyone is rated according to his or her performance (Eglit, "Age Bias" 128-33; Levy; Roscigno et al.; Shore and Goldberg). Moreover, employers have learnt to use the defenses available to them and can easily argue that termination is due to rational factors other than age. This partly explains why the winning rate of these actions is low[12].

It must also be underscored that the Supreme Court's and federal courts' jurisprudence has been less than favorable to claims made by workers on the basis of age rather than race or sex. Justifications for specific legislation, made by the Secretary of Labor distinguishing age from race, are often quoted in their decisions:

1. "The gist of the matter is that "'discrimination'" means something very different, so far as employment practices involving age are concerned, from

---

10 | Until workers can access Medicare insurance at 65; see Retired Persons v. Equal Employment Opportunity Comm'n, 489 F.3d 558 (3rd Cir., 2007), certiorari was denied by the Supreme Court in 2008 (Neumark, "Age Discrimination Legislation" 48-49).

11 | Stephenie Overman stressed that EEOC statistics showed a constant decrease in sexual harassment claims whereas age discrimination claims are on the rise (14% compared to 24.4%. in 2009). See as well *Ageism in America* 78-79.

12 | 2.8% of age discrimination claims brought for refusal to hire and 11% of those brought for termination (Posner 426).

what it means in connection with discrimination involving – for example race."

2. "Employment discrimination because of race is identified, in the general understanding of it, with non-employment resulting from feelings about people entirely unrelated to their ability to do the job. There is no significant discrimination of this kind as far as older workers are concerned."

3. "The most closely related kind of discrimination in the non-employment of older workers involves their rejection because of assumptions about the effect of age on their ability to do the job when there is in fact no basis for these assumptions." (U.S. Department of Labor 1965, *The Older American Worker* 1-2)

4. "Age, as opposed to race, is not an 'immutable' characteristic since aging is experienced by everyone. It is not 'animus' which causes discrimination against older workers but rather assumptions about the effect of age on their ability to do the job." (U.S. Department of Labor 1965, *The Older American Worker* 20)

The report acknowledged that older workers could be victims of stereotypes and prejudice but it stated that there was no history of past discrimination like in the case of race. One cannot fault Willard Wirtz for making such arguments. His analysis reflects the prevailing view of the times: age bias in the workplace was seen as less pernicious than other forms of discrimination (listed in Title VII). It was also grounded on the *Fair Labor Standards Act*, a heritage from the New Deal, and meant to foster fairer employers' practices towards older workers. That is why the Secretary of Labor's report ended on the necessity of legislating promptly:

First: *Action* to eliminate arbitrary discrimination in employment.
Second: *Action* to adjust institutional arrangements which work to the disadvantage of older workers.
Third: *Action* to increase the availability of work for older workers.
Fourth: *Action* to enlarge educational concepts and institutions to meet the needs and opportunities of older age.
(US Department of Labor 1965, *The Older American Worker* 21)

Unfortunately, Wirzt's assertions have proved detrimental, in particular since the 1990s. Conservative judges appointed by Republican presidents relied on them to undermine the scope of some ADEA provisions and not to afford the same protections to older workers under the equal protection clause of the

Fourteenth Amendment[13] or as Title VII claimants. The legal consequences are as follows:

1. The constitutional test applied by the Supreme Court to examine age discrimination is the most lenient one[14] – older workers are not a "suspect class" like workers victims of race or sex discrimination.
2. Employers' Bona Fide Occupational Qualification defense is taken great account of.
3. Awards of damages under the ADEA are based on the system which exists under the *Fair Labor Standard Act*. They are limited to compensatory damages putting the plaintiff "back to whole" – to his situation before the prejudice occurred. Punitive damages as such[15] are not awarded against employers, which means that they are not under the same pressure to comply as in the case of race or sex discrimination.

---

13 | See *Massachusetts Board of Retirement v. Murgia*, 427 U.S. 307 (1976) and Eglit, "Age Bias", 145-46.

14 | *Massachusetts Board of Retirement v. Murgia*, "Equal protection analysis requires strict scrutiny of a legislative classification only when the classification impermissibly interferes with the exercise of a fundamental right or operates to the peculiar disadvantage of a suspect class. Mandatory retirement at age 50 under the Massachusetts statute involves neither situation" (427 U.S. 307, 313). Justice Marshall dissented, arguing: "Not only are the elderly denied important benefits when they are terminated on the basis of age, but the classification of older workers is itself one that merits judicial attention. Whether older workers constitute a 'suspect' class or not, it cannot be disputed that they constitute a class subject to repeated and arbitrary discrimination in employment" (427 U.S. 307, 324). The ADEA was amended to provide for the early retirement of fire-fighters and law enforcement officers in 1983.

15 | Justin A. Walters' study of remedies under the ADEA shows that juries have granted "unpaid minimum wages and unpaid overtime" (Section 626b) known as "back pay." The Act provides, like the Fair Labor Standards Act, for an award of "liquidated damages" when the employer acted "willfully" but as the author points out: (1) "Unlike the FLSA, [. . .] the ADEA requires a heightened level of culpability before statutory liquidated damages may be awarded" and since the amount of liquidated damages cannot exceed damages awarded for back pay (Section 216b), this limits awards. (2) "In addition to the remedies explicitly authorized, the statute leaves judges with a great deal of freedom to fashion alternative relief on a case-by-case basis." This is known as "equitable relief." The Act does not provide, like Title VII, for compensatory and for punitive damages (257-59). Punitive damages in such cases can be very high and only require a finding by the jury that the employer's conduct was "onerous."

The Court upheld safety as a reasonable cause for mandatory retirement[16], decided that the use of factors closely related with age by employers was not discriminatory *per se* (*Hazen Paper Co. v. Biggins*, 507 U.S. 604 1993[17]) and ruled that state employees cannot sue states for monetary damages under the ADEA (*Kimmel v. Florida*, 525 U.S. 62 2000). What is also telling is that it has taken years for the Supreme Court to acknowledge that age discrimination in the workplace could result in indirect discrimination (*Smith v. City of Jackson*, 544 U.S. 228 2005[18]). Moreover, a majority of justices has shown little sensitivity to claimants' arguments and made these cases more difficult to prove (*Gross v. FBL Financial Services Inc.*, 557 U.S. 1 2009[19]). In other words, the jurisprudence as well as the language used by the Supreme Court of the land have often served to perpetuate prejudice rather than suppress it, as this passage from *Gregory v. Ashcroft* (501 U.S. 452 1991) on mandatory retirement of state judges highlights: The statute draws a line at a certain age which attempts to uphold

---

16 | The Burger court reversed the Court of Appeal's decision in *Massachusetts Board of Retirement v. Murgia*, and under "the rational basis test" decided that mandatory retirement at 50 for state policemen was not violating the Equal Protection Clause of the Fourteenth Amendment. The vocabulary used is quite revealing in regards to the view held by the Court about policemen at fifty. Though conceding that Massachusetts may not have used "the best means to achieve its purpose," it argues: "since physical ability generally declines with age, mandatory retirement at 50 serves to remove from police service those whose fitness for uniformed police work has presumptively diminished with age and is, therefore, rationally related to the State's announced legitimate objective of protecting the public by assuring the physical preparedness of its uniformed police" (427 U.S. 307, 316 1976).

17 | Until then, decisions based on pension status, retirement legibility and seniority were equated by courts as unlawful age discrimination prohibited by the ADEA. Howard Eglit and Judith J. Johnson stress that the Court embraces a view defended in dissent by then-Justice Rehnquist in 1981.

18 | This legal rule was established under Title VII for race discrimination in *Griggs v. Duke Power Co.* (401 U.S. 424 1971) and extended to sex discrimination. Its scope was so narrowed in Wards Cove Packing Co. v. Atonio (490 U.S. 642 1989) that Congress voted the *Civil Rights Act* (1991) to amend Title VII and counter the Court decision but it failed to directly amend the ADEA. Consequently, in ADEA cases, it is the Wards Cove ruling which applies. It is another instance of the negative impact of a conservative court on age discrimination jurisprudence (Webb 1386, 1398).

19 | The year before, in *Meacham v. Knolls Atomic Power Laboratory* the Court had ruled in favor of the plaintiff relying on the EOOC guidelines. The only dissenter was Justice Thomas, once chairman of the EEOC under Regan's presidency. He penned the 2009 decision.

the high competency for judicial posts and which fulfills a societal demand for the highest caliber of judges in the system;

"the statute [. . .] draws a legitimate line to avoid the tedious and often perplexing decisions to determine which judges after a certain age are physically and mentally qualified and those who are not"; "mandatory retirement increases the opportunity for qualified persons [. . .] to share in the judiciary and permits an orderly attrition through retirement"; [. . .] any one of these explanations is sufficient to rebut the claim that "the varying treatment of different groups or persons is so unrelated to the achievement of any combination of legitimate purposes that we can only conclude that the [people's] actions were irrational." (501 U.S. 452, 472)[20]

This can be interpreted as a rather cynical reasoning from the part of life-tenured justices, especially as Congress amended the ADEA in 1986, in order to prevent this practice. Nonetheless, if the Court can express itself in this way, it reflects the general tolerance for such negative views and the belief that older Americans enjoy privileges that younger Americans do not have[21], as conservative jurists such as Richard Posner, Samuel Issacharoff and Richard T. Ford have argued. They fault the powerful American Association of Retired Persons (AARP)[22] for the so-called rule of a "gray lobby." Finally, in 2010, the California Supreme Court held in *Reid v. Google Inc.* (235 P.3d 988, 50 Cal. 4th 512, Cal. 2010) that "an age-based remark [. . .] uttered by a non-decision-maker may be relevant circumstantial evidence of discrimination [. . .] because discriminatory remarks by a non-decision-making employee can influence a decision maker".[23] It was interpreted as a warning to companies in that state since the ruling

---

20 | Justice O' Connor, who penned the majority opinion in this case, quotes a decision of the Missouri Supreme Court (O'Neil v. Baine, 568 S.W.2d 761 (Mo. 1978) and the U.S. Supreme Court's holding, in the wake of *Massachusetts Board of Retirement v. Murgia*, that Section 632 of the *Foreign Service Act* of 1946, which requires persons covered by the Foreign Service retirement system to retire at age 60, though no mandatory retirement age is established for Civil Service employees, including those who serve abroad, did not violate the equal protection component of the Due Process Clause of the Fifth Amendment, (*Vance v. Bradley*, 440 U.S. 93, 97 1979).

21 | The way the ADEA is built does not allow someone to sue for reverse discrimination.

22 | It was founded by Ethel Andrus and Leonard Davis in 1958 to cover the risk of accidents, illness and disability in old age; it began putting pressure on governments to improve the situation of older Americans.

23 | This issue divides federal circuits (Cohen). The 3rd circuit ruled the contrary (*Hyland v. American International Group Inc.*, 2010WL 95059, 3rd Cir. 2010) disregarding the "stray remark doctrine" as defined in the Supreme Court ruling in *Price Waterhouse v. Hopkins* 490 U.S. 228 1989. The EOOC expressed concern about this trend when

suggests employers should train their employees to avoid multi-generational tensions in the workplace.

3. AGE DISCRIMINATION
AND THE RIGHTS-BASED RESPONSE

The US was a pioneer in resorting to a rights-based response and pass sweeping legislation[24] to remedy the ills of discriminatory practices against older workers perceived as a disadvantaged group (Macnicol 225; Friedman 177). The ADEA is a child of the "rights" revolution of the 1960s. Congress enacted it in the wake of the Civil Rights Act when, as Paul Burstein points out, "discrimination at work" and "equal employment opportunity" were "salient issue[s]" (xx.). It has been the target of conservatives and progressives alike. During the Reagan years it was attacked by employers and free-market economists[25]. In the midst of a recession which led to widespread downsizing of firms, corporate mergers, and massive lay-offs, it was criticized by conservatives as an ill-conceived piece of legislation enacted under the pressure of the Civil Rights

arguing before the federal appeals court in New York the *Fried v. LVI Services* case (11-4791, 2nd Cir. 2010) in October 2012. The Court nonetheless ruled against the appellant upholding the trial court's decision. Such rulings play a significant part in perpetuating stereotypes against older workers and justifying ageist comments as mere "jokes" even when evidence shows that they played a part in the decision to terminate the older worker and replace him by a younger one.

24 | Even the 1958 Discrimination (Employment and Occupation) Recommendation issued by the International Labor Organization (ILO) – a UN specialized agency – did not include age in its definition (Meenan, "The Future of Ageing" 9).

25 | In 1978, the age for mandatory retirement was raised to 70. Edward Lazear defended businesses' support for mandatory retirement in 1979, arguing that older workers, because of their age and seniority, were paid more than their marginal value and productivity. He laid the blame on "lobbying groups which represent the elderly" (1277), correlated the difficulty of older workers to be hired to this change in the law and predicted that "[i]f the ability to enter mandatory-retirement contracts is eliminated through legislation [. . .] current older workers will enjoy a small once-for-all gain at the expense of a much larger and continuing efficiency loss that affects all workers and firms adversely" (1284). Such arguments have since then been supported by Issacharoff and Posner. Neumark and Song's review of his arguments drew more positive conclusions. In 2009, Neumark re-examined Lazear's "life-cycle model" of employment, in the context of an aging population and of a shift from defined-benefit to defined-contribution pension plans ("Challenge of Population Aging" 58-9).

Movement[26] by liberals who had a simplistic view of economics and believed the federal government could solve all social problems. Richard T. Ford, in his recently published book *Rights Gone Wrong: How Law Corrupts the Struggle for Equality*, reiterates these arguments: "although older workers fare well, jobless older people still face high odds in finding employment. Most of these problems require nuanced and comprehensive institutional changes – not individual entitlements" (245). Countering Conservatives' views, their opponents claim that the rise of neo-liberal economics has favored the employment of low-paid and flexible workers since the 1980s. They denounce the continuing prevalence of the employment-at-will doctrine, the difficulty to prove age discrimination, the EEOC's lack of means to pursue claims and adverse judicial doctrine as key factors in the ADEA's failure to protect older workers from age discrimination in the workplace. They also underscore employers' reluctance to develop better intergenerational cooperation (Eglit, "Age Bias" 704-05; Rothenberg 25-26; T. Butler 9). Raymond Gregory believes that baby boomers should be better informed about age bias in the workplace and encouraged to pursue claims to fight pervasive age stereotypes. For David Neumark, policies must be crafted to improve hiring while being "mindful of underlying economic barriers [. . .] and try to focus on rooting out only discriminatory behavior" ("Challenge of Population Aging", 63, "Reassessing Age Discrimination" 31). These studies highlight that a rights-based response to age discrimination at work could be more efficient if enforcement mechanisms imposed more stringent control on employers' conduct and the likelihood of prevailing in court was reasonable so that attorneys would be less reluctant to bring claims. They also provided and still provide insights to countries which have implemented rights-based legislation and are now faced with the problem of older workers' self-sufficiency, livelihood and dignity.

If the US was a trailblazer, Canada prohibited unequal treatment based on age in section 15(1) of the text of its Charter of Rights and Freedoms in 1982. Yet, it is currently considering the issues of early and mandatory retirement as

---

26 | One example of this type of criticism is Posner's depiction of the ADEA in 1999: "The Act was 'sold' by means of emotional rhetoric concerning the plight of the elderly, in 1967 still viewed as a disadvantaged segment of American society" (425). He underscores its limited scope: "The first thing to note is the misfit between the scope of the law and the concerns of the elderly. The law kicks in when a worker turns 40 years of age, and only 10% of the plaintiffs in a recent sample of cases, [. . .] including those plaintiffs who challenged mandatory retirement, are 65 or older – a smaller percentage than the percentage of elderly people in the US population as a whole" and argues: "The main reason is plain enough: most people who are 65 or older are voluntarily retired, and so are not protected by the *Age Discrimination in Employment Act*" (425). He is also the author of *Age and Aging*. Age Discrimination is dealt with in chapter 13.

baby boomers push back against such rules. In 1993, New Zealand enacted a Human Rights Act and created a Human Rights Commission whose powers of enforcement have recently been extended. When the European Union's Council issued The Equal Treatment in Employment Directive (2000-78 EC), which had to be implemented in member states by 2006 at the latest, the American experience served as a reference. The United Nations Second World Assembly on Ageing[27], held in Madrid in 2002, adopted an International Plan of Action on Ageing, with the specific aim of ensuring that persons everywhere are able to age with security and dignity and can go on working as long as they feel able to (Meenan, "Age Equality" 11, "The Future of Ageing" 16-18). Two years later, Australia included age as a ground for discrimination in its 2004 Human Rights Act (Field). So the idea that older workers should be protected from age discrimination in the workplace has gradually become accepted by international and European decision-making bodies. These legislations apply to younger and older workers and prohibit all kinds of discriminations.

European countries are used to imposing rules on companies in exchange of incentives (such as tax breaks)[28] to prevent layoffs before retirement and increase the hiring of older workers. Their policies also reflect concerns about saving and transmitting industrial skills to younger workers. The Directive provided that member states had to lay down rules on court actions, sanctions and compensation. Some have penalized discrimination against workers on the ground of age[29] in order to promote equal treatment. Others created a single Rights Commission to investigate complaints on the model of the Equality Authority set up under the *Employment Equality Act* in Ireland in 1998 (Meenan, "Age Equality" 4, "The Future of Aging" 20). Most states also chose to raise retirement age. It remains to be seen if the combination of these policies will fare better in preventing stereotypes, keeping workers employed and help jobless workers over fifty to find employment[30]. Changing laws is one step but changing customs and views is more complex (Lahey, "International Compari-

---

27 | The first World Assembly on Ageing took place in Vienna in 1982. It adopted the International Plan of Action on Ageing, providing guidance to international and global levels. Neither these recommendations nor the ones in the Madrid Plan are legally binding as Helen Meenan underlines ("The Future of Ageing" 5-6).

28 | When the House debated the Age Discrimination bill, tax-credit for employers was proposed but this measure was rejected "as too radical" (Macnicol 233).

29 | French Penal Code 2002. Age discrimination can entail a three-year prison sentence or a 45000E fine (Art. 225-1C). It is also prohibited by the Labor Code, Art. L 1131-1 (Drouler and Pie Guiselin 109). Age discrimination in employment is also an offence in Finland.

30 | Decisions of the Court of Justice of the European Community since 2005 show its will to fight age discrimination (Brisse 289).

son" 683). Yet, a European study of employment trends of older workers shows that a significant share of these workers remains in the workforce longer now than ten years ago. The rules about eligibility for full benefits were altered; consequently older low-income workers, once retired, often take a job and find a part-time less paid one to complement their pension, like in the United Kingdom. More surprisingly, though the state of the economy varies significantly in member states, middle-aged and elderly workers have been relatively spared from unemployment in 2010, in spite of the economic crisis. However, according to the 2011 OECD statistics[31], the percentage of Americans aged 55-64 in the workforce is higher. What probably explains the gap is that, at least in some European countries, there is still a safety net, and generous retirement packages are offered.

Longer life expectancy, increased fitness, and better health are common features of the US population as well as European societies. European countries face the challenge to devise ways of keeping an aging population in the workforce and to fight against Ageism[32], in the context of "differences in cultures ideologies and political systems" (Hudson 20). US lawmakers at the end of the Sixties argued that the ADEA was a way to "re-educate" the nation in a period when the predominant youth culture claimed that no one over thirty could be trusted (Macnicol 229, Eglit, "Age Bias" 102)[33]. Today, as life spans lengthen, Catherine Mayer points out that "the ages of man have started to elide" (38). Yet

---

31 | The OECD average is 53.6 % and the US rate is 60.6%.

32 | It was coined in 1968 by Dr Robert Neil Butler, a pioneer in gerontology and the author of *Why Survive? Being Old in America*, chapter 4 deals with the right to work.

33 | Macnicol quotes the following statement made by William R. Hutton, Executive Director, National Council of Senior Citizens, before the General Subcommittee on Labor of the Committee on Education of the House of Representatives, in August 1967: "We have permitted our entire society to become so youth-oriented that those over 45, without jobs, have been swept away in the backwash." Eglit points out that there are numerous negative "epithets" to depict older men and women but none about young people; he also stresses that negative images are associated with the elderly in the media and consumer advertising (103-4). A study of ageism conducted in Europe in 2012 shows vast differences from one country to another: Portugal has the most positive image of older people and the Czech Republic the most negative one. This report also points out, in a comparative study of US and UK legislation, that anti-ageism is "a double-edged sword" because it entailed, according to John Macnicol, "a significant reduction in welfare rights" because state pension age has been risen in line with gains in life expectancy. He is also suspicious of predictions of an impending economic catastrophe stressing that in Japan, Sweden and Germany about 22% of the population is already over 65 (Hudson 24).

when "amortality"[34] becomes a denial of aging rather than the acceptance of it, it becomes a pernicious illusion. For Margaret Morganroth Gullette, the American age narrative is one of "decline" and in *Agewise. Fighting the New Ageism in America* she warns that it should be a greater source of concern, showing the devastating effects and far reaching consequences of the prevailing alarmist stance about a graying America in the workplace and beyond[35].

The entire decline system – innocent absorption of cultural signals, youthful age anxiety, middle-ageism, ageism – infiltrating our society from top to bottom, is increasingly a threat to psychological well-being, to healthy brain functioning, public health, midlife job growth, full employment and a growing economy, intergenerational harmony, the pursuit of happiness, the ability to write a progressive narrative, and the fullest possible experience of life itself. (Gullette, *Agewise* 15)

John F. Kennedy observed in a 1963 address to Congress: "it is not enough for a great nation merely to have added new years to life. Our objective must be to add new life to those years" (Mayer 42). The passage of the ADEA was one of the measures taken by the Johnson administration to achieve this goal for older workers. It has partly succeeded, though in an unforeseen way. As we saw, one of the outcomes of the Act and subsequent amendments prevented the termination of many older workers. One possible explanation of the recurrent difficulty of those over 50 to be hired, once they have lost their jobs, is the lack of legal means to impose sanctions on employers. In this respect, one can say that, if age as a ground for discrimination had been included in Title VII of the *Civil Rights Act*, enforcement would have been more effective. However, fighting this form of discrimination, though it is difficult, can be done by other means. For instance, many older workers change careers; as Barack Obama pointed out in his 2012 State of the Union Message, those over 55 can be an asset if retraining programs are developed and improved to facilitate their re-entry on the job market. David Neumark suggests that in order to keep more workers over 65 employed, changing rules about Medicare for these employees would reduce healthcare costs and that the combined protections of the ADEA and ADA should be put to better use for encouraging employers, in particular

---

34 | Term coined by the author to define "the burgeoning trend of living agelessly" (38).

35 | According to the Pew Research Center, on January 1, 2011 baby boomers born in 1946 reached retirement age. The 46-65 age groups represent 79 million Americans (26% of the US population). By 2030, when the last ones retire, they will represent 18% of the population as opposed to 13% today. This survey stresses their pessimistic view of the future: "Perched on the front stoop of old age, Baby Boomers are more downbeat than other age groups about the trajectory of their own lives and about the direction of the nation as a whole."

in the manufacturing sector, to alter working conditions, which would enhance the productivity of this age-group and, in return foster a desire to stay on the job ("The Challenge of Population Aging" 60)[36]. Businesses in the US can certainly find creative and innovative ways to demonstrate that – as the President asserted – an aging workforce is a competitive advantage instead of bemoaning the rising cost of its aging population.

REFERENCES

Ageism in America. International Longevity Center-USA (ILC). Anti-Ageism Taskforce (2006). Web. 8 July 2011.

Brisse, Mathieu. "La jurisprudence européenne sur les discriminations fondées sur l'âge." *Retraite et Société* 51 (2007): 286-91. Print.

Burstein, Paul. *Discrimination, Jobs and Politics: The Struggle for Equal Employment Opportunity in the United States Since the New Deal*. 1985. Chicago, IL: U of Chicago P, 1998. Print.

Butler, Thomas H., and Beth A. Berret. "A Generation Lost: The Reality of Age Discrimination in Today's Hiring Practices." *Journal of Management and Marketing Research* 9 (2012): 1-11. Web. 5 Oct. 2012.

Butler, Robert N. *Why Survive? Being Old in America*. (1975). Baltimore, MD: Johns Hopkins UP, 2002. Print.

Cohen, Richard B. "EEOC 'Stray Remarks' Troubles Continues With New Ruling." Employment Discrimination Report, 16 Oct. 2012. Web. 5 Nov. 2012.

Drake, Joseph T. *The Aged in American Society*. New York: Ronald Press Co., 1958. Print.

Drouler, Olivier, and Emmanuel Pie Guiselin. *Regards croisés sur l'influence de l'âge en sciences humaines et sociales*. Paris: L'Harmattan, 2010. Print.

Eglit, Howard C. "The Age Discrimination Act at Thirty: Where It's Been, Where It Is Today, Where It's Going." *The University of Richmond Law Review* 31 (1997): 579-756. Print.

———. "Age Bias in the Workplace." *The Journal of International Aging Law and Policy* 3 (2009): 99-167. Print.

"Employment and Labour Markets: Key Tables from the OECD 2010, Employment Rate of Older Workers; % of Population Aged 55-64." *OECDiLibrary*, 3 Jan. 2011. Web. 5 Mar. 2012.

"Employment Trends and Policies for Older Workers in Recession." *European Foundation for the Improvement of Living Conditions*, 1-12, 18 Jan. 2012. Web. 10 Oct. 2012.

---

36 | Faced with the challenge of an aging population, businesses in Germany, France and Finland have already explored such solutions and shown that they work.

Feder, Jodie. "The Age Discrimination in Employment Act (ADEA): A Legal Overview." *Congressional Research Service*, 7-5700, 23 June 2010. Web. 5 Mar. 2012.

Field, Sue. "Issues Facing Older Australians: Legal, Financial and Societal." *The Journal of International Ageing Law and Policy* 1 (2005): 95-113. Print.

Fried v. LVI Services Inc., Case n°11-4791 (2nd Cir. 2012). Web. 5 April 2013.

Friedman, Lawrence M. "Age Discrimination Law: Some Remarks on American Experience." *Age as an Equality Issue: Legal and Policy Perspectives.* Ed. Sandra Fredman and Sarah Spencer. Oxford, UK: Hart Publishing, 2003. Print.

Ford, Richard T. *Rights Gone Wrong: How the Law Corrupts the Struggle for Equality.* New York: Farrar Straus and Giroux, 2011. Print.

Gregory, Raymond F. *Age Discrimination in the American Workplace: Old at a Young Age.* New Brunswick, NJ: Rutgers UP, 2001. Print.

Gullette, Margaret Morganroth. *Aged by Culture.* Chicago, IL: U of Chicago P, 2004. Print.

———. *Agewise: Fighting the New Ageism in America.* Chicago, IL: U of Chicago P, 2012. Print.

Heidkamp, Maria, William Mabe, and Barbara DeGraff. "The Public Workforce System: Serving Older Job Seekers and the Disability Implications of an Aging Workforce." NTAR Leadership Center (May 2012): 1-52. Web. 27 Nov. 2012.

Hyland v. American International Group Inc., 2010 WL 95059 (3rd Cir. 2010). Web. 5 April 2013.

House Report No. 805, 90th Cong. 1st Sess., 23 Oct. 1967. *Age Discrimination in Employment Act* of 1967. Report from the Committee on Education and Labor, in US Equal Employment Opportunity Commission, Legislative History of Age Discrimination in Employment Act. Washington D.C.: 1981. Print.

Hudson, Robert B., ed. "Cross-National Perspectives on Age Discrimination." *Public Policy and Aging Report* 22.3 (2012): 1-25. Web. 6 Oct. 2012.

Issacharoff, Samuel, and Erica Worth Harris. "Is Age Discrimination, Really Age Discrimination? The ADEA's Unnatural Solution." *New York University Law Review* 72(1997): 780-838. Print.

Johnson, Judith J. "Rehabilitate the Age Discrimination in Employment Act: Resuscitate the 'Reasonable Factors Other Than Age' Defense and the Disparate Impact Theory." *Hastings Law Journal* 55 (2003-2004): 1339-448. Print.

Johnson, Lyndon B. "Statement by the President After Signing the Age Discrimination in Employment Act of 1967." December 16, 1967. Online by Gerhard Peters and John T. Woolley, *The American Presidency Project.* Web. 5 Mar. 2012.

Lahey, Joanna N. *"How Do Age Discrimination Laws Affect Older Workers?"* Center for Retirement Research at Boston College, Series 5 (Oct. 2006): 1-8. Web. 26 July 2011.

––––. "Age, Women and Hiring: An Experimental Study." *The Journal of Human Resources* 43.1 (2008): 30-56. Print.

––––. "International Comparison of Age Discrimination Law." *Research on Aging* 32.6 (2010): 679-87. Print.

Lazear, Edward P. "Why Is There Mandatory Retirement?" *Journal of Political Economy* 87.6 (1979): 1261-84. Print.

Levy, Becca R. "Eradication of Ageism Requires Addressing Enemy Within." *The Gerontologist* 41.5 (2001): 578-79. Print.

Macnicol, John. *Age Discrimination: An Historical and Contemporary Analysis.* Cambridge, UK: Cambridge U P, 2006. Print.

Massachusetts Board of Retirement v. Murgia, 427 U.S. 307 (1976). Print.

Meacham v. Knolls Atomic Power Laboratory, 128 S. Ct. 2395 (2008). Print.

Mayer, Catherine. "Amortality: Why Acting Your Age Is a Thing of the Past." *Time* April 25 2011: 37-42. Print.

Meenan, Helen. "Age Equality after the Employment Directive." *Maastricht Journal of European and Comparative Law* 10.1 (2003): 9-38. Print.

––––. "The Future of Ageing and the Role of Age Discrimination in the Global Debate." *The Journal of International Aging Law and Policy* 1 (2005): 1-41. Print.

Neumark, David. "Age Discrimination Legislation in the United States." *Contemporary Economic Policy* 21.3 (2003): 297-317. Print.

––––. "The Age Discrimination in Employment Act and the Challenge of Population Aging." *Research on Aging* 31.1 (2009): 41-68. Print.

––––, and Joanna Song. "Barriers to Later Retirement: Increase in the Full Retirement Age, Age Discrimination and the Physical Challenges of Work." *14th Annual Joint Conference of the Retirement Research Consortium*, Washington, D.C. August 2-3, 2012. Web. 5 Nov. 2012.

––––, and Wendy A. Stock. "Age Discrimination Laws and Labor Market Efficiency." *Journal of Political Economy* 107.5 (1999): 1081-125. Print.

O'Meara, Daniel P. *Protecting the Growing Number of Older Workers: the Discrimination in Employment Act.* Labor Relations and Public Policy Series 33. Philadelphia, PA: Pennsylvania UP, 1989. Print.

Obama, Barack. "State of the Union 2012: Obama speech transcript." 24 Jan. 2012. *The Washington Post* 24 Jan. 2012. Web. 25 Jan. 2012.

Overman, Stephenie. "Age Discrimination at Work Complaints Have Increased in the Past Few Years and It's Only Getting Harder to Prove You Have Been Wronged." *Fortune,* 21 June 2011. Web. 27 Nov. 2011.

Posner, David. "Employment Discrimination: Age Discrimination and Sexual Harassment." *International Review of Law and Economics* 19 (1999): 421-46. Print.

———. *Age and Ageing in America.* Chicago, IL: U of Chicago P, 1995. Print.

"Recession Turns a Graying Office Grayer: America's Changing Work Force." *Pew Research Center,* 3 Sept. 2009. n. pag. Web. 8 Feb. 2012.

Price Waterhouse v. Hopkins, 490 U.S. 228 (1989). Print.

Roscigno, Vincent J., Sherry Mong, Reginald Byron, and Griff Tester. "Age Discrimination, Social Closure and Employment." *Social Forces* 86.1 (2007): 313-34. Print.

Rothenberg, Jessica Z., and Daniel S. Gardner. "Protecting Older Workers: The Failure of the Age Discrimination Act 1967." *Journal of Sociology and Social Welfare* 38 (2011): 9-30. Print.

Shore, Lynn M., and Goldberg Caren B. "Age Discrimination in the Workplace." *Discrimination at Work: The Psychological and Organizational Bases.* Ed. Robert L. Dipboye and Adrienne Colleta. NJ: Lawrence Erlbaum Associates, 2005. 203-26. Print.

Smyer, Michael A., and Pitt-Catsouphes Marcie. "The Meanings of Work for Older Workers." *Generations* 31.1 (2007): 23-30. Print.

Sok, Emy. "Record Unemployment among Older Workers Does Not Keep Them Out of the Job Market." *United States Bureau of Labor Statistics* (2010). n. pag. Web. 16 Feb. 2012.

Unemployed Older Workers: Many Experience Challenges Regaining Employment and Face Reduced Retirement Security. United States Government Accountability Office (GAO), Report to the Chairman, Special Committee in Aging, U.S. Senate April 2012: 1-90. Web. 5 Aug. 2012.

United States Department of Labor. *The Older American Worker: Age Discrimination in Employment.* Report to Congress under Section 715 of the Civil Rights Act 1964, Washington DC: Government Printing Office, 1965. Print.

Walters, Justin A. "Drawing a Line: the Need to Rethink Remedies under the Age Discrimination in Employment Act." *University of Illinois Law Review* 1 (2012): 257-85. Print.

Webb, Kelli A. "Learning to Stand On its Own: Will the Supreme Court's Attempt to Distinguish the ADEA from Title VII Save Employers from Increased Legislation?" *Ohio Law State Law Journal* 66 (2005): 1375-414. Print.

Cultural Representations

"There's a reason we're here"

Performative Autobiographics and Age Identity in Performer-Created Intergenerational Theatre

Sally Chivers, David Barnet, Jacquie Eales, and Janet Fast

> We're here because we're NOT invisible.
> ("Am I Invisible?")

INTRODUCTION

This paper emerges from a large collaborative research project, "Health and Creative Aging: Theatre as a Pathway to Healthy Aging," that works with an intergenerational theatre company in Edmonton, Alberta to study the potential for participation in seniors theatre to contribute positively to health outcomes. The theatre company, GeriActors & Friends (GF), unites seniors from the Seniors Association of Greater Edmonton (SAGE) with university students (working with award-winning Professor David Barnet) in exploring issues and stories common across generations in performer-created plays. GF work in a tradition of community-based theatre: plays are devised by a dramaturge based on the actors' own experiences and, as such, tend to convey their values, interests, and concerns. The resulting oeuvre reflects an engaging combination of humour, reminiscence, and serious commentary in plays that depict the experience of aging through self-images that challenge pervasive stereotypes of late life as necessarily a time of physical decrepitude and social isolation.

After joining GF, a university student recorded in her journal (kept as part of an assignment for her community-based theatre course), "Seniors are a library of experience" (Drama 459 student). This statement demonstrates that the student values the knowledge she might gain from her engagement with the senior participants whom we call GeriActors in this paper, even as she perhaps idealizes it. Yet, the GF's archival materials indicate that the GeriActors do not typically feel valued for their contributions in a broader social context. Instead, GF repertoire repeatedly turned to themes related to invisibility in their early years, resulting from seniors' expressions during the devising process, and to the importance of finding a voice, particularly for the seniors.

While the act of performing on stage is one means of finding a voice, the GF repertoire also makes the process of devising theatre from performers' experiences an explicit theme. GF's signature piece in the first decade of performances is entitled "Invisible," in which twinned overlapping narrative vignettes depict seniors as ignored in favour of their younger family members. This central theme aligns with the ways in which social gerontologists have commented upon the ways in which various ageist stereotypes and social views render older women invisible across realms such as the fashion industry (Freixas, Luque, and Reina 48; Lewis, Medvedev, and Seponski 102; Falcus 4; Biggs 49; Twigg 62). What is more, critical gerontologists show that older adults, especially women, are usually noticed only in the context of their existence as a physical burden requiring care and costing the system time and money (Freixas, Luque, and Reina 53; Woodward). The GF turn these perceptions on their head by reinforcing their visibility and by situating themselves as caregivers as well as potentially requiring care.

Our textual analysis of archival materials shows how GF, in making the seniors' "library of experience" public, attenuate the challenge of becoming visible in a culture determined to see older adults as physically problematic, if they are noticed at all. That is, the archival materials show how the GeriActors struggle and to some extent manage to be seen without being seen to be grotesque, expensive, pathetic, or just objects of humour. For GF, especially but not solely the GeriActors, the very act of being on stage announces an increasingly commanding cultural and social presence regardless of their physical state. Artistic director David Barnet explains that seniors' participation in creating theatre that is meaningful to them is in itself a challenge to stereotypes. As he tells the *Vegreville Observer*:

Audiences are clearly delighted to see aspects of their own lives portrayed on stage, partly because it's so rare to see it in mainstream culture [. . .] when on TV or in movies, for example, do you see senior citizens and their issues – issues of Alzheimer's and death and dying and romance and so on – being played truthfully, by true seniors? You might see it, but you'll see it from the point of view of a scriptwriter or of a young actor in their 40s or 50s portraying someone in their 70s or 80s. ("Geriactors Perform" A7)

Former GeriActor, Joan (now deceased), puts it more bluntly: "There's a reason we're here" (GeriActors Typing 4.2). A chronological analysis of the play scripts and ancillary materials amplifies the significance of that seemingly simple statement as it relates to purpose, stage presence, and social presence.

GERIACTORS & FRIENDS AND ITS ARCHIVE

Research for this paper primarily comes from textual analysis of archival materials gathered since the inception of GF, including play scripts, student journals, rehearsal and performance videos, other participant notes, and typed transcriptions of pre-production conversations among the GF from which Barnet crafts the plays. In addition, we draw on material obtained through a community-based participatory qualitative research project that included interviews with current and former members of the GF, including performers and staff. The multilayered archive gives voice to members of GF who were no longer alive when we conducted interviews, and whose voices may otherwise be missed. In this way, we are able to bring in the voices of participants from a variety of sources, analyzing the ways in which certain voices and themes become public.

GF not only offers older adults an opportunity to participate in drama with an expert theatre artist and drama "teacher," it also has developed an intriguing means by which to involve its members in the play creation process, usually based on their own past and current personal experiences. The GF archive offers a way to capture in part the process of play development because it houses different script versions as they have collaboratively evolved over a number of rehearsals, writing sessions (by Barnet), and performances. In this paper, we analyze the group's signature piece "Invisible" as a key stage of that evolution, and supplement our analysis by looking at significant companion pieces. Our research into the first decade of GF performances, as documented in their archives, reveals a progression from reflecting common experiences to a more deliberate practice of collective and collaborative autobiography, focused on actors' life stories, including a reflexive element about their inclusion in the play development process. We argue that this progression offers insight into the role of age identity in contemporary theatre practice and the potential for overtly intergenerational collaboration to result in the telling of new stories of growing old in a greying world that challenge images of aging as tied only to physical decrepitude and disease, without ignoring that health is a key part of aging.

Acting in stories that come from the actors' own lives is tied to a growing sense of purpose. Indeed, for the GF, the notion of being "here" has transformed into a manifesto and even an anthem for seniors in the Greater Edmonton Area where creative aging thrives. The GF archive provides further evidence that a clear sense of self and purpose emerges for seniors who participate in collaborative intergenerational theatre based on their own lives. The emergence occurs because of creative engagement, cultural expression, and enhanced visibility for a segment of the population too often assumed to have run out of ideas, to be not worth hearing from, and to be invisible.

Fig. 1: "GeriActors"

AUTOBIOGRAPHICS

In an early newspaper interview, Barnet says of GF, "They're good because they're real" (qtd. in Rankin C2). He in part captures the character of GF and the ways in which they are genuine to each other during rehearsals. But he is also referring to the collaborative practice of creating theatre directly from the experiences of the actors. Such structured collaboration has been part of the GF's creative process from its inception, but it has changed over time. In the early years, general conversations were transcribed and Barnet subsequently transformed them into scripts or wrote scripts based on them. After conducting research trips to observe other similar theatre groups, especially Age Exchange in the UK who uses techniques from reminiscence theatre, Barnet has increasingly adopted methods tied to storytelling, particularly stories based on memories of past experiences. As a result, the plays performed by GF increasingly tend to tell stories from and of the actors' lives. Thus, what began as Barnet's gentle nudge to GF to consider repertoire beyond slightly revised Shakespeare scenes has transformed into an intriguing collaborative autobiographical practice.

In this paper, we think through the transformative effects of seniors' participation in theatre production and presence on stage and contemplate the ways in which GF increasingly draws directly not just on conversations about seniors' experiences but on stories from their lives. To do so, we turn to a theoretical frame from auto/biography theory. Speaking specifically of contemporary Canadian theatre, Sherrill Grace says,

> The play, like all auto/biographical activity, is reproducible but always different, always open to reinterpretation, at least until the final curtain ends the life. To speak this way of performance, of course, is to speak in metaphors. But when such metaphors are grounded in auto/biographical plays, then they underscore the theatre's representation of what I call performative autobiographics: the creation of identities that exist in performance, that challenge fixed notions of the self and of subjectivity, and that are new each time the story is performed. (18)

The autobiographics lens offers a way to read the GF archive as reflecting a process that gives the actors a sense of significance not only from "being real" but also from engaging with discourses of truths about aging and identity (to play with the words of auto/biography theorist Leigh Gilmore). As such, the GF performances, like the autobiographical writing about chronic pain that is Gilmore's focus, "[shift] the focus from [. . .] exemplary selves to an engagement with selves in conditions of alteration and relations of interdependence" (84). The GF staying "real," as Barnet puts it, depends upon the ways in which enacting stories from their past conjures up new understandings of the self, and the self in relation to others.

THE EARLY YEARS

What is now the GF began in 2001 when members of what was then called the Society for Retired and Semi-Retired in Edmonton, Alberta (now SAGE) expressed a desire to begin a theatre/drama group for older adults. Barnet was introduced to them as a "volunteer" who might be willing to work with them. Now artistic director, Barnet embarked on the project due to an interest in community-based theatre piqued by his past involvement in social and political theatre. The invitation offered him an opportunity to consider a new creative research direction at a pivotal career moment. The project offered a means for continuing his development of meaningful theatre with new and marginalized communities. The group began as a small (<10) group of seniors meeting with Barnet with the initial goal of doing drama in the spirit of enjoyment, while playfully engaging with stereotypes associated with aging.

Billed as "The Society Players," the group's first performance took place at the SAGE Christmas show in December 2001. Five actors appeared in a program that included a performance of the balcony scene in *Romeo and Juliet*, an excerpt from *Macbeth*, and "The Seven Ages of Man" from *As You Like It*, a piece which in its original (turn of the seventeenth-century) context is spoken by "very much a senior citizen" and is about the stages of life, offering alternate voices (12). The excerpts included in the inaugural performance contain subtle script gestures to the age of the actors in that the couple meets at a seniors' dance, rather than at the Capulets' masquerade feast. The GF Romeo and Juliet are attracted to each other despite being lodged in rival seniors residences, rather than being members of feuding families. The *Macbeth* scene was included in the show because actor Carmela had learned the play in high school and always wanted to perform it, an early indication of the ways in which the GF has come to fulfill a longstanding goal of many of the seniors to participate in the theatre in some way. The 2001 program also included two original plays, one being a somewhat gritty "episode" of a seniors' soap opera in which central character Marie rebuffs George's marriage proposal and informs the audience (in an aside): "Well, would you get married again? He told me last week I was nicer than his dog. I'd rather have a new stove than a new husband" (11). The other play was an intriguing piece about an older woman sneaking a cow embryo through airport security by concealing it within her bra, based on the actual experiences of Lucille from her days working as a security scanner at the airport. As Barnet later explained in a University of Alberta ExpressNews story, "Initially, they asked whether they could do Shakespeare, but I encouraged them to draw on some of their own life experiences and write their own scripts" (qtd. in Vivequin). The Shakespearean scenes draw on a long theatre history, and the Soap Opera and security scanner plays have the sense of being part of a series such that the archival traces of this early performance reveal a very inviting sense of continuation.

In their second season, the group of seniors partnered with four students to put on a December show, performed both at SAGE and at the University of Alberta. The central theme of seniors' invisibility – and its important counterpoint of commanding presence – clearly emerges in that show. The scripts are part of the presentation for University of Alberta students from a fourth year theatre course who joined with the GF for their class project. The students' goal was to create a one-hour performance, in collage form, including intergenerational material. In student journals, they express their long-term goal, "to try and hear other stories from other seniors of different backgrounds and demographic groups, and then create a comparative piece" (Drama 459 student). As a result, the show is framed by explicit commentary about aging and the age differences between the students and the seniors. The scripts that comprise the show indicate that the students did well in turning to seniors as what the student cited above refers to as a "library of experience" and that they fulfill their goal of "paying attention to individuals who deserve to be heard," while ironically reinforcing the underlying implication that seniors are not always heard.

The students conclude that their own work with the GF is important because they "are appreciating people who do not have a voice, and that is crucial.

They want a voice, and want to be heard." The archival record demonstrates that embarking on intergenerational theatre shifted their material and the audience. The student journal comments, "we're dealing with seniors' taboos, so in many ways, this [SAGE] audience could understand the issues so much more than the audience yesterday [U of A]." Influenced by the practices of Roots and Branches, Barnet later made the union of University of Alberta drama students and GeriActors a yearly practice, and the company became intergenerational in 2006. While the inclusion of students in the GF season has become a permanent fixture, the audience outside of the University of Alberta performances has tended to be seniors, or those interested in seniors issues, rather than intergenerational.

Fig. 2: "StoryTelling"

"A QUICK TRANSACTION," "1984," AND "THE BUREAU OF VITAL STATISTICS"

Two plays of particular note emerged during the collaboration with the early group of students from a fourth year University of Alberta Drama course entitled "Collective Creation." In each, the GF depict situations that try to make seniors legible in an economic system that refuses to value them any more. The short play "A Quick Transaction" fits into a pattern of GF repertoire that illustrates the exaggerated effect the increasing bureaucratization and automation of service industry has on seniors. "A Quick Transaction" is a humorous piece about the automation of the service industry and the disrespect for seniors' time (and everyone's by extension) shown by the humans working within that system. That disrespect is almost enough to motivate one to use the bank machines after all, since the human touch is so uninspiring. For example, the main character is sent to the "You Are Not a Big Corporation And We Could Care Less" department, a unit designated to work with "common folk." The character is eventually told explicitly, "All of us here are very busy and believe your time is worthless." Just by creating and performing a play that parodies the increasing depersonalization of the business world, the GF demonstrate that their own time and existence is in fact worthwhile. The play is a small act of defiance against the perceived invisibility of seniors, and it shows the importance of that theme to the theatre company from an early date.

Another play that first appeared in 2003, "1984," comes from a discussion amongst the seniors and students about the change in policy whereby pre-1984 birth certificates had to be renewed. As Joan had explained to the students, "If you take away the certificates, you take away old people." The play features a woman trying to renew her birth certificate. Mrs. Green has to produce to the authorities her mother, Mrs. Buggs, in order to verify that Mrs. Green does indeed exist in a way that the state can recognise. But Mrs. Buggs's dementia complicates that process and so the civil servant suspects Mrs. Green of attempting to make a fraudulent claim about her own existence. In the course of the play, the receptionist makes the humorous yet chilling demand of character Mrs. Spencer: "You will need to validate your existence." This leads Mrs. Green to ask, "Could it be that my existence is merely a figment of my imagination?"

A 2004 version of the play offers a new title of "The Bureau of Vital Statistics." The order is greatly changed to allow for more commentary on the existential aspect of the piece. The perspective of the civil servant is more sharply insulting: "If you don't have a valid birth certificate and you are not in our computer and you can't find anyone to say who you are, you don't really exist. Are you sure you were ever born? Have a nice day." One typed copy of the script in the archive includes an undated handwritten addendum following this passage:

This is all very confusing – what happened to my original Birth Certificate? It was good enough when I was born. How come it isn't good now. Frankly I haven't heard that I have died lately – so why do I need a new one. I think it's a shame you were born – where's my mother [. . .]

The addition indicates that at least one GeriActor wanted to insert the older adult character's voice back into the script to speak back to the offensive bureaucratic perspective.

These plays demonstrate the GF's early interest in the effacement of seniors within bureaucratic frameworks – wherein their time is not valued within a busy and efficient modern work world. However, these three plays were written drawing from general conversations amongst GF about contemporary issues and are not autobiographical. They very much incorporate seniors' perspectives, but they are not telling the GeriActors' stories in the way that subsequent repertoire does. They are about the effacement of identity more than about the flexible exploration of subjectivity. As Kathleen Woodward explains in a different context, "Their words [. . .] necessarily lack the sense of a vital connection to a unique life, to a voice that articulates the tone and tenor of a particular experience" (65).

"AM I INVISIBLE?"

A "vital connection" to unique lives and particular voices becomes more apparent in "Am I Invisible?" – a key play performed beginning in the 2006/07 season. "Invisible" continues the theme of seeming effacement but is written from conversations about specific GeriActors' experiences. The play that grew into a very well-structured eight-minute piece of theatre was developed differently from those previous, in that its creation was based on storytelling and improvisation. The archive contains records of the conversations that led to the play. The documented conversations include comments about what participation in the theatre company means to the members. Joan explains, "There's a reason we're here [. . .] it is the fact that people want to be seen. They want to get out there – recognition. To get up there and be in front of people, to be seen to be doing something."

Another GeriActor reflects on a moment when she felt invisible while telling a story about a time when her mother took her to the doctor:

Sometimes all they see are wrinkles, white hair and liver spots sitting in the chair before them. Wrinkles, white hair and liver spots don't have treatable illnesses. "It's old age!" They throw their hands up and say, "It's old age. It's old age."
Well I don't accept that from my doctor! Not from any doctor! I am more than wrinkles and white hair and symptoms. I won't let you make me invisible.

While the setting of the doctor's office receives only brief mention in the resulting play, the theme of invisibility becomes the play's central preoccupation. The play employs an opening chorus featuring intergenerational banter about various instances when both seniors and students encounter invisibility. Then it switches to two distinct autobiographical narratives: one is set at a gas station where a female senior is ignored because the station attendant fancies her daughter; the other takes place during a shopping trip wherein both daughters invite the attention of the store clerk to the exclusion of another female senior who is in fact the one who has money to make a purchase. After these two scenes, the company comes together to sing "Watching all the girls go by." The play closes with a chorus, countering the opening by citing instances of either *not* being invisible or embracing invisibility. Two poignant lines from that chorus are "I'm not invisible when I'm on stage" and "I'm not invisible when I'm crazy." At the end of "Invisible," the actors join triumphantly in a final song, Barnet's adaptation of Behan's "We're here because we're queer": "We're here because we're here because we're here because we're here" because "we're NOT invisible." That song has become an anthem of sorts for seniors in Edmonton and has exceeded the bounds of the play perhaps because it offers a bold yet joyous enunciation of Joan's comments: "There's a reason we're here [. . .] recognition."

Fig. 3: "Am I Invisible?"

The central vignettes of "Am I Invisible?" reflect dominant views on the diminished value of women as they age due to the social value of youthful beauty. That dominant view is refracted through seniors and students singing "Standing on the Corner," a song that celebrates the male gaze. As a whole, drawn from conversations among seniors and students about the moments across the life course when people become invisible and visible, the play calls attention to and questions the set of taken-for-granted assumptions that also propel it. In the opening chorus, the pain of seniors being ignored by grandchildren is foregrounded by students being ignored by their parents, so that the story is not simply one of neglect of older adults. The pain of seniors becoming invisible in a crowd is balanced by the new reality of the huge classes faced by students in the current university system. Based on the experiences of the individual actors who initially performed it, "Invisible" takes unique lives and shows the connections among them to offer a view of aging that insists on a cultural presence beyond that dictated by the holders of the gaze.

A Play about Alzheimer's

Following the success of "Invisible," the GF ambitiously took on a topic often associated with aging and with which many members had some personal experience: dementia and related caregiving practices. While they unearthed some surprising intergenerational connections, the conversations that were part of the development of the multi-scene play contain a considerable amount of disagreement, some of it so strong that Barnet felt it should be incorporated into the self-reflexive structure of the play, which includes elements of the rehearsal and creative process in its performed versions. Developed over a period beginning in 2006, the play reflects especially the group's awareness, noted by Barnet, that there was a deep need to speak to caregivers. The play's development captures GeriActor Janette's key point that Barnet explains as pivotal also to his 98-year-old mother: the play needed to be about "having value, being a contributor, not being a throw-away person." Perhaps paradoxically, working together on a play about an illness that is typically associated with doom led Barnet to explain the GF's purpose as tied to hope: "It's very important that I believe we can open a window of light onto lives and not present the darkness of life, if there is a darkness, however true it is, I believe we have to offer the possibilities of joyfulness."

We focus here on part 1 of the play, entitled "Que Sera," which over time developed such that it combines the tensions among family members who need to decide how much and what care a mother figure needs with tensions among the actors, playing themselves, about the purpose of performing such a play, about its viability, and about how to be respectful within it to the members of the GF whose stories it tells. "Que Sera" pushes this further to openly contemplate the effect the GF might have on the people who come to watch them perform, as conveyed in the line, "What I'm wondering is, can we do a play like this [. . .] Is there some audience we can do something powerful for?" The power of "Que Sera" comes partly from a decidedly sympathetic portrayal of the mother figure with Alzheimer's, who explains to her daughter, "See, I may be ill but I'm not as crazy as you think I am." While momentary lucidity is often a fantasy perpetuated by Hollywood portrayals of dementia patients (*The Notebook* and *Away from Her* are two prominent examples), "Que Sera" makes clear its origins in lived experience, offering the line: "In real life not every story has a happy ending." As such, the play demands a reckoning with a range of perspectives that are never quite resolved but that each arise from individual experiences with people who have dementia.

This challenging structure comes from a need Barnet perceived after "Que Sera" was performed by the two students who initially wrote it at a GF rehearsal at SAGE on November 13th, 2008. As the students explained, the script came from their performer created theatre class, and "some of the ideas for [the mother] character came from [. . .] things that [the GF] have talked about." The two students then took on the role of a daughter conversing with her mother who has dementia and is standing on the roof of her house. The scene as performed prompted Barnet to express his view that "we can't do a scene like this because it would leave our audiences with unresolved sadness [. . .] if we take this anywhere, it would be left without, without kind of, a resolution [. . .] I think whatever audience we would do a scene like this for, it would need to end up with opening a window of possibility," which he is later pushed to qualify as "an ending with possibilities of bouts of joy and love, positive forces, and certainly the happiness must not be trite, because that would be a total disservice and a lie to everybody." The transcripts indicate that at least one GeriActor voiced agreement, saying, "Put some love into it. Put some love into it, go and get your mother, and bring her down," referring to a possible plot development that has the daughter help her mother down from the roof upon which she is perched. Drawing from these ideas, Janette (now deceased) expands the concept of the need for an ending that offers some possibility for resolution, saying, "I think we need to experience some kind of joy, some sense of quality of life, this is what is lacking as you get older, and especially because you have a mental illness of any sort." Speaking from her own related experiences, she is able to draw together the conversation about Alzheimer's with the need for joy in late life.

At the subsequent rehearsal on November 20th, 2008, the GF discussed their mixed reactions to having watched the students perform "Que Sera." They tried to parse the significance of how they had responded, and they discussed how they might reshape the play based on their own experiences with people with dementia. A combination of annoyance with and sympathy for the daughter figure provoked a need for a form of theatre that could capture, even more readily than usual, contradictory perspectives on a deeply provocative topic. One GeriActor who has been a caregiver of a son with a serious mental illness points out a grave lack in social supports: "We have to have more understanding for the caregivers, where they're coming from. We have to give them support. We talk big about volunteering and having the family be caregivers, but do we support them? Do we really give them the emotional support that they need?" Another GeriActor reinforces this view, explaining, "The caregiver is totally alone." Both of them are referring to scenarios in which a family member is called upon to play the role of caregiver so that a family member does not slip through the cracks into an unwieldy care receiving situation, quite possibly institutional care. The discussion leads David to conclude, "I think we know where our path is. And our path is in the protection of the caregiver. And we're not just talking about people with dementia, although that's one aspect of it. But we're talking about all caregivers."

By 2010, the GF had incorporated subsequent scenes that capture their disagreement about the representation of the daughter's approach to her mother and their debate about whether or not they could or should produce a viable play about Alzheimer's. They transform "Que Sera" into one where the daughter joins the mother in an attic, rather than on top of a roof, and sees the world as her mother might, and an alternate version where her son-in-law makes an appearance and saves her, to his wife's chagrin at him stealing the glory, thus offering a version of what Augusto Boal calls metaxis, "the state of belonging completely and simultaneously to two different, autonomous worlds" (43). The alternate scenes, performed sequentially, are followed by a discussion about whether or not the play needs the happy ending because "it's life" and "in real life, not every story has a happy ending." The process that is evident in the archive is represented in the play, so that the audience has a clear view into the ways in which this particular performance has the "vital connection to a unique life, to a voice that articulates the tone and tenor of a particular experience" that Woodward refers to (cited above).

With "Que Sera" the process of play creation becomes part of the play itself showcasing the ways in which the GeriActors and the student members struggle to convey a sense of authenticity as well as respect for the people for whom they have cared. It is important that this self-reflexive mode appears in relation to the play that is most overtly about health and, even more so, about a health concern associated with late life: Alzheimer's disease. When it came to that trigger issue, the GeriActors most defiantly needed to convey the differences among them rather than come to a simpler unified message for their audience, members of whom are sure to also have had varied experiences with caregiving as well as with different forms of dementia. Thus, "Que Sera" takes what some GeriActors initially perceived to be an unduly negative portrayal of a woman with Alzheimer's and inserts a constructive ambiguity as well as a sense of hope to portray their own ongoing group collaborations about topics relevant to the life course.

CONCLUSION

The archive shows that the early GF repertoire repeatedly turned to themes of invisibility and the importance of finding a voice, particularly for the seniors. The triumph of the "I'm here" anthem is playful and exuberant, but it is more than just play. As David Barnet states in a recent interview, "It's fine to have high culture or established culture [. . .] that which is represented by the symphony, the opera, the Citadel, and other theatres. But cultural expression, meaningful expressions of art can be found in the community and can speak to the people who perform it and the people who receive it." Or, as Leigh Gilmore explains, "Autobiographical accounts are efforts to say 'who I am' that are always addressed to another. Thus, autobiographical accounts travel a social circuit: they circulate senses of the social world, they seek connection, they translate" (94). The selective trajectory we outline in this paper shows a progression from socially relevant narrative commentary on the position of seniors in an increasingly bureaucratic world through exuberant expressions of presence to a self-reflexive commentary on the challenges posed to caregivers in a greying world. While all the plays we discuss are drawn from material gleaned through conversations with the actors, the plays become progressively more based on personal narratives over time. As Grace argues,

At their best, auto-biographical plays [. . .] challenge the social construction of identity by staging processes of identity formation that invite audiences to see themselves and others as able to recreate identity and to reassert personal agency. At their best, these plays use the facts of a personal story to make us rethink the concept of *self* and the relationship of *self* to other. (15)

The GF archive demonstrates an increasing move towards this type of reflexive performance offering GeriActors the opportunity to reassert the personal agency they gain through finding creative forms through which to express their experiences as older adults, in the case of "Que Sera" encouraging a reconception of the *self-other* relationship by inviting experiences with dementia.

As the student member noted, the GeriActors provide a "library of experience," but that experience is not always valued or expressed in a broader social context. The modes of play development employed by GF in their first decade have provided ways to convey senses of purpose and self in late life that challenge pervasive stereotypes about aging and that counter the more dominant form of representations of aging, as Barnet describes it, "the point of view of a scriptwriter or of a young actor in their 40s or 50s portraying someone in their 70s or 80s." Instead, the GF have found ways to perform aging that allow them to inhabit and explode common viewpoints in order to offer new authentic perspectives not only of growing older but of being older actors finding ways to express their new place in the world. Thus by "being here," as actors telling their own stories, the GF offer a legible form of visibility for Edmonton seniors that is culturally and socially significant: "a whole way of life."

Fig. 4: "GeriActors"

REFERENCES

"1984." Part of December 2, 2002 script. GeriActors and Friends print archive. Binder 1. Print.

"A Quick Transaction." Part of December 2, 2002 script. GeriActors and Friends print archive. Binder 1. Print.

"Am I Invisible?" undated 2006 & 2007 scripts. GeriActors and Friends print archive. Binder 2. Print.

Barnet, David. Research Team Interview. February 7, 2012.

Biggs, Simon. "Age, Gender, Narratives, and Masquerades." *Journal of Aging Studies* 18.1 (2004): 45-58. Web. 13 Aug. 2013.

Boal, Augusto. *The Rainbow of Desire.* New York: Routledge, 1995. Print.

"The Bureau of Vital Statistics." February 2004. Script. GeriActors and Friends print archive. Binder 1. Print.

Drama 459 Students. Student logbook. October-December 2001. Print. GeriActors and Friends print archive. Binder 1. Print.

Falcus, Sarah. "Unsettling Ageing in Three Novels by Pat Barker." *Ageing and Society* (2011): 1-17. Print.

Freixas, Anna, Bárbara Luque, and Amalia Reina. "Critical Feminist Gerontology: in the Back Room of Research." *Journal of Women & Aging* 24.1 (2012): 44-58. Web. 13 Aug. 2013.

"Geriactors Perform at St. Michael's Care Centre." *Vegreville Observer*. May 5, 2004: A7. Print.

"GeriActors Typing 4." October 2004. 1-2. GeriActor and Friends print archive. Binder 2. Print.

Gilmore, Leigh. "Agency Without Mastery." *Biography* 35.1 (2012): 83–98. Print.

Grace, Sherrill. "Theatre and the Auto/biographical Pact: An Introduction" *Theatre and Autobiography : Writing and Performing Lives in Theory and Practice*. Ed. Sherrill Grace and Jerry Wasserman. Vancouver : TalonBooks, 2006. Print. 13-29. Print.

Lewis, Denise C., Katalin Medvedev, and Desiree M. Seponski. "Awakening to the Desires of Older Women: Deconstructing Ageism Within Fashion Magazines." *Journal of Aging Studies* 25.2 (2011): 101-09. Web. 13 Aug. 2013.

"Que Sera." November 2008 through April 2009. Scripts and conversations transcribed. GeriActors and Friends print archive. Binder 3. Print.

Rankin, Bill. "Older Actors find their calling: Seniors enjoy putting their stories on stage." *Edmonton Journal* March 29, 2005: C2. Print.

"Society Players: December 2001." December 2001. 1-17. Script. GeriActors and Friends print archive. Binder 1. Print.

Twigg, Julia. "The Body, Gender, and Age: Feminist Insights in Social Gerontology." *Journal of Aging Studies* 18.1 (2004): 59-73. Web. 13 Aug. 2013.

Vivequin, Wanda. "Geriactors Bring Experience to the Stage." *ExpressNews*. University of Alberta. Fall 2003. Web.

Woodward, Kathleen, ed. *Figuring Age*. Bloomington: Indiana UP, 1999. Print.

Images of Living and Ageing

Counter-Cultural Constructions of Health and Wisdom

Ricca Edmondson and Eileen Fairhurst

Practitioners of life-course studies are repeatedly reminded to avoid treating older people as "other" – but without very clear accounts of what this might entail. To the extent that either academic or everyday discourse envisages older age positively, use may be made of references to "wisdom" – but, again, without consensus about what the term implies. This article examines two contrasting attempts to *intervene* in the ways in which older people are perceived – and, by extension, treated. These attempts are specifically not academic, but take the form of calendars, particularly interesting artefacts because they are intended for everyday use. Here we examine two calendars intended for daily use that feature older people, their activities, and how they should be seen. These calendars – one from the UK, one from Ireland – are specifically intended to impact on public perceptions of older people. In different ways, they offer creative subversions of everyday expectations about the life course and what it has to offer. We shall argue here that, using dynamic interplays of words and images, they in effect urge counter-cultural ways of imagining the activity, the health and also the wisdom of older people – at the same time accentuating productive, mutual social and intergenerational relationships, which take different forms in their different cultural contexts.

Calendars are made to take part in the lives of those who purchase or are given them, used for recording appointments or birthdays. They are treated in everyday life as *aides mémoire*, but it is their potential for impacting on the views or perceptions of those who use them that gives these two calendars their initial interest. One was produced as part of an ongoing "Valuing Older People" initiative in Manchester, and the other by the Dean Maxwell Community Nursing Unit in Roscrea, Ireland. Each is committed, in different ways, to deconstructing stereotypes of older people as vulnerable and uninteresting, and to implicitly or explicitly critiquing the prevailing culture as far as ageing is concerned. The Manchester calendar in particular subverts taken-for-granted assumptions about living and ageing, focusing explicitly on interplays between continuity and change to endorse constructive images of health and wisdom in later life. Both these calendars tell us more about what ageing and wisdom might – in the context of different states of health and in different cultural settings – be expected to entail.

The positions conveyed in each of these calendars are complex, exploring diverse positions on how older people ought to be seen. Each raises questions about what older people can be expected to convey to each other and to other generations. Since they are primarily visual forms of communication, we shall draw out what the images seem to us to convey and how they interact with written texts provided. Our mode of interpretation aims to reconstruct meaning on the basis of verbal and pictorial implications that are largely public, extrapolating from what the calendar pages can arguably *be taken* by viewers to communicate. Tracing public meanings in this way does not centre on imputing subjective intentions to the teams of authors concerned; the concern is, rather, what members of the public might reasonably infer.

Strikingly and at the same time engagingly, the Manchester calendar exhibits combinations of images and words connected with ageing in which active acceptance of reality is combined with a theme stressing constructive reciprocity in relationships, and the co-creation of different forms of insight. In the Irish calendar, older people in more infirm states of health are still represented as creative and communicative, though perhaps in less practically counter-cultural ways. Both calendars take up public discourses related to insight and ageing, and in so doing extend and alter them. The Irish calendar entails an implicit criticism of contemporary materialism, especially given the fact that the quotations it uses, though presented anonymously, are in fact taken from the work of the spiritual writer, the late John O'Donohue. While many Irish people might recognize O'Donohue's authorship, the anonymity of the attribution in a sense accentuates its authority, bestowing on it almost Biblical status. The idea of wisdom is thematised here, sometimes implicitly and sometimes explicitly, but it is presented as a significant spiritual aim for older people's own life development rather than centrally as a capacity they offer others – which, we shall argue, is a more vibrant presence in the Manchester calendar.

"Wisdom" has in the past been associated with types of insight into the conduct of life that may be expected to increase, all other things being equal, with age. Both these calendars contribute to a wisdom discourse that continues to be present in everyday interactions, perhaps more prominently than in academic commentary, where revival of attention to the concept is relatively recent. It has not as a rule been claimed that people *necessarily* grow wiser as they age (Pasupathi, Staudinger, and Baltes 251), though some non-Western or non-modern cultures may incorporate a presumption in favour of assuming so as a basic guide to social interaction with older people (Chandler). The term "wisdom" is used with implications that remain comparatively general. They may include comprehending the meaning and conduct of life (Baltes and Smith, 1990), an orientation to "the fundamental pragmatics of life" as manifested in the practical and empathetic understanding of other people, combined with an ability to discern the best course of action in ethical terms (Baltes and Staudinger 122), a capacity to balance different aspects of a situation so as to perceive what should be done for the common good (Sternberg), or the activation of particular traits in similar connections (Ardelt). All these approaches assume some blend of thought, ethical reflection, interactive ability and feeling (Edmondson; Ardelt). Here, we shall explore what we can learn about wise and other capacities these calendars attribute to older people or to processes of ageing, and in particular how this can amount to a strikingly counter-cultural account of constructive ageing.

The Calendars

The Manchester calendar derives from an ongoing multi-agency "Valuing Older People" initiative dating from 2003, which aims to place older people at the centre of plans for reshaping the city and the opportunities it offers citizens.[1] A "positive images of ageing" campaign was launched in 2004 as part of an overall programme promoting "a positive and healthy attitude towards ageing", challenging "negative stereotypes" and persuading the public "to re-evaluate their attitudes towards older people". It stresses that positive attitudes towards ageing can add up to seven and a half years to life; attitudes, in other words, are deeply serious in their effects.[2] This calendar was sponsored, as one of its concluding pages makes clear, by four organisations relevant to older people, and it offers phone numbers so that readers can get in touch with them, as well as personal messages of support to the project. The calendar series is described using terms such as "challenging" (employed here in a double sense), "bolder", or "all ages", probably not typically connected with being "older": this implies an effort to *shift* readers' expectations about the separateness of later life stages. The images included, we can infer, have been chosen carefully, with the overall intention of inducing change.

The 2005 calendar ("Challenging Older People in Manchester") accompanies each image with a quotation from a prominent older person, such as Nelson Mandela. The 2006 calendar ("Growing Older with Attitude in Manchester") dispenses with quotations in favour of unpacking the "attitude" part of

---

1 | <www.manchester.gov.uk/site/scripts/documents_info.php?documentID=3428>, 23 Aug. 2013.

2 | <www.manchester.gov.uk/site/scripts/documents_info.php?categoryID=500 099>, 23 Aug. 2013.

the theme. Thus, for February, an older woman (ethnically Asian) is portrayed holding chopsticks and beaming; the caption is, "Like life, food is best shared with friends." For June, a Caucasian woman directing a garden hose at a man is depicted with the caption "The joy of never growing up." The 2007 calendar ("Older and Bolder in Manchester") quotes from the individuals it depicts – with commentaries often stressing novel activities adopted after retirement (Fairhurst; and Fairhurst and Baines also examine these calendars).

The 2008 calendar, "Manchester – a City for All Ages", is composed of photographs that have been commissioned; they are "documentary" (see Johnson and Bytheway), depicting everyday life or activities in some way, rather than being obviously staged or posed. Each case offers different combinations of quotations, as contextualisations of the scene or image depicted, and names of the individuals portrayed. We stress the 2008 calendar here for its deliberate thematisation of how continuity and change interact in ways that not only subvert negative expectations of ageing but explore specific benefits of later life – not only for those concerned but also, crucially, for others. Like the others, its images and texts interact; participants in the pictures are identified, but it also uses quotations from well-known people for each month, together with verbal accounts on each calendar page, guiding what the image can be taken to convey. Such verbal supplements to the images modify them directly, hints to the "reader" on how to see them (Zalot).

The Irish calendar we analyse was produced by and on behalf of a nursing home, the Dean Maxwell Community Nursing Unit in Roscrea, for the year 2010. We should resist comparing the two as productions, since the Manchester calendar is a highly professional product, avowedly attempting to impact on social attitudes and featuring highly independent individuals, while the Irish calendar deals with people in more fragile stages of health, who need much more support. It is local and low-profile in nature, and part of its aim seems to be to reflect something of the ambience of the Dean Maxwell community that produced it. Nonetheless it also intervenes into the ways in which older people are regarded, supporting specific values and relationships. Its approach might be termed gentle: the illustrations for each month are paintings by nursing home residents, with the painters' photographs inset. The paintings are unsophisticated and unpretentious; inside the front cover there are further paintings, interspersed with photographs of the painting classes involved. On each calendar page, there is a small photographic view of the nursing home, the same in each case, with a spiritual quotation (in fact from Donohue's *To Bless the Space Between Us*): "May there be kindness in your gaze when you look within" (June) or "May you know wisdom of deep listening, the healing of wholesome words" (October). The delicate balance attempted here is reflected in the make-up of the calendar, which tells us nothing about the artists involved. It is silent, for example, about their level of (in)dependence. This makes it impossible to judge their achievements; but it is part of the ethos of this document that judging achievements is not intended to be at the forefront of our minds.

LEARNING FROM THE CALENDARS

In the interpretations that follow, we ask reiterated questions of the pages of the Manchester calendar, and follow this with a briefer set of reflections on the Irish calendar. For the Manchester calendar, we start from what the image depicts in the simplest sense: who is in it, who is old and who young, what their family or community relationships seem to be, and what they are doing. We then infer what sort of generational transaction is at the centre of the piece – where the piece will include the text that accompanies the image. It will be important to attend to non-verbal aspects of the transaction, and whether shared activities are involved. We shall find that the transactions in question often include knowledge or experience, but at least two recurrent features are significant. First, the initial impact of the piece may be a relatively conventional portrayal of "knowledge" as transmitted from older to younger generations; but this is modified, after reflection, by the fact that both the knowledge and the relationship in question are a good deal more complex and considerably more mutual than this impression might have suggested. Here, questions about what wisdom might be and how it is conveyed are revealed as much more closely related to social and interpersonal processes than we might have expected. The older people are not defined by their health status or ages; rather, the intergenerational relationships involved are central: mutually enriching and highly active. Secondly, the "knowledge" involved in these pieces is not separated off from questions relating to feeling and relationships. Thirdly, there is the question of the *cumulative* effect of each calendar. The individual pieces for each month are not the sole sources of impact; we shall need to consider what impacts each calendar has overall.

The piece for January, 2008 shows four young people in various poses in a garden, one older woman (Emily) and a black cat – which one of the younger children is in the process of stroking. This is clearly a town garden on a fairly sunny day, with the brick of the house and its neighbour in the background. The woman and the child stroking the cat are squatting down or sitting, the other three standing. All the young people are male, and all of Asian ethnic origin; two stand together, one in front of the other, the back figure with his arms round the younger one. It is clear, therefore, who is old and who young, and that at least two ethnic groups are involved. While the woman is smiling, only the child stroking the cat has a pleased expression on his face. There is a quotation in the picture, attributed to Angela Schwindt: "While we try to teach our children about life, our children teach us what life is all about." On the calendar page for January, we read that "Emily has shared her home with language students from China for the past four years", with "laughter" and "tears" a constant feature. "She still receives phone calls from China four years on."

Fig. 1: January 2008

As in most of the pieces here, the written texts are crucial to interpreting this scene: there is a reciprocal relation between language and image. Throughout this calendar the words and images collaborate; the words draw out implications of the image, first by offering information which cannot be conveyed in the picture (such as the length of a relationship, for instance); secondly, by pointing to elements in the image rather than merely instructing the reader what to see; and, thirdly, by adding to the complexity of the piece, offering the reader more to reflect upon. In addition, verbal corrections are offered in case readers misunderstand the visual pieces (important in the case of April, where the activity portrayed needs linguistic identification). Fourthly, all this extends the real time-frame of the reader's response to the piece, creating space for more complex reflection and interpretation. Thus, in this case, it becomes plain that the gain in this set of relationships is not one-way, that Emily learns from what is going on as much as her visitors do, that this learning is a matter of insight as well as more conventional knowledge and that it is not separate from emotional relationships. How does this reciprocal learning take place? The implication, strengthened by the quotation, is that children (can) put adults in a position where they are forced to understand, both intellectually and emotionally, that their own orientations to life are not the only possible or acceptable ones. They provide, or impose, access to a view of the world from the position of "the other" – which the adult, as learner, otherwise might not have acquired. At the same time, Emily is clearly an unusual woman, not only in taking on the work of welcoming young strangers into her house but also, importantly, in the extent to which she has made herself *open* to this form of learning.

Against the background of this point of view, it is possible to discern more in the image. We can see that this is an informal garden. Effort has been made to plant bright flowers, but they are in moveable containers; the garden is child-friendly, then, one in which football can be played. Even the fact that not all the children have felt obliged to smile may show a certain acceptance of the reality of relationships. While the young people in the image are showing their relations with each other, and with the pet cat, it is clear that no false impression of cosiness has been imposed and the young people were permitted to appear as they chose. This seems to indicate something important: it is not only *learning as such* that is reciprocal here, but the entire set of relationships involved. The children must respond to what the adult does, and vice versa, or the whole enterprise will not take effect. That it does take effect is stressed on the calendar page, which underlines that continuous physical contiguity is not essential for the continuance of the relationship. This piece certainly touches on the gradual and mutually supported achievement of complex forms of wisdom or insight, therefore; it is presented as a complex intergenerational transaction arising from ordinary, everyday actions.

The February piece is perhaps more complex still. It shows two men, one clearly younger than the other, sitting together on a sofa; their body-language suggests a reciprocal relationship in which the participants feel at ease, for their poses reflect each other: each rests one arm on the back of the seat and has the other hand on his knee, their bodies almost touching and turned towards the centre of the image. They are clearly in smart working clothes, tactful rather than ostentatious though each wears cufflinks and a tie, but they are relaxing, having taken off their jackets. The older man wears a waistcoat. The setting is relatively unusual: it is clearly an old-fashioned tailor's workshop, comfortable (with standing lamp) and traditional: even the buildings visible through the window are of an old-fashioned and elegant design. The quotation reads "What cannot be achieved in one lifetime will happen when one lifetime is joined to another" (Harold Kushner). On the calendar page we learn that this is a father and son. The father, James, established the firm, and for nine years now he also "has been sharing his extensive knowledge and imparting the skills of a traditional trade to his son". But it is not only the son who is benefiting from this relationship; the quotation on the image makes clear that the father needs his son for the completion of his own life's project. This is reinforced on the calendar page: their cooperation will "ensure the continuation of the business down the generations".

Fig. 2: February 2008

This emphasis opens the way to further considerations about the reciprocity of learning (and family) relationships like this one. Wisdom, conventionally, may possibly be envisaged as involving "sitting at someone's feet", as in a traditional apprenticeship. But the image itself conveys the idea that the transaction is more complicated than this might suggest. It appears to be a much more balanced relationship than merely passing knowledge down the generations would suggest. The older man, indeed, is portrayed as retreating somewhat into the background of the image, with his son, both more brightly dressed and more visible, towards the centre of the scene. Lastly, there is a third element to the relationship, in the form not only of the knowledge that is involved but also of the fact that it is set into a tradition of feeling and behaviour. This can only be hinted at: by the workmanlike orderliness of the bales of cloth set into shelves, the careful mastery of symbolism in the men's self-presentation, and not least the fact that on the sofa is an embroidered cushion, on which the word "LORD" is visible. These details again remind us that "knowledge" may not most productively be thought of merely in cognitive terms; the tradition in which each of these generations engages is richly multi-dimensional.

While "March" presents age "as a new stage of opportunity and strength" (Betty Friedan), illustrating a dance and exercise class for people with diabetes, "April" presents an image of two older Caucasian men on the ground in a project entailing moving earth.

Fig. 3: April 2008

In the middle background is a small girl of Asian ethnic origin and in the foreground is an even smaller white child, sitting on the earth. The caption runs "There are no seven wonders of the world in the eyes of a child. There are seven million" (Walt Streightiff). The two figures in the foreground, the man (in a baseball cap which shades his face) and the child, are both moving earth with trowels. One might at first glance take this project to be connected with gardening, but the next page makes clear, perhaps to the reader's surprise, that it is run by the South Manchester Archaeological Research Team. The bearded man in the background, Andy, who is looking up and smiling, was a founder member. In fact, at least three of the four figures in the scene are wearing identical tee-shirts (they function as overalls in the children's cases), presumably associated with the dig. The youthful interests of the children are not denied – a glove puppet is lying on the ground – but each child is clearly absorbed in the dig itself. The people here, despite their different ages, genders, and backgrounds, are sharing in common membership of a group. Their differences in effect become less important than their shared interest – and perhaps too their shared humanity, as curious inheritors of a common past.

In one sense, this piece is more literally about knowledge transfer down the generations than most others in this collection. At the same time, it complicates the question of what this involves, taking up the theme in the January piece: that children show us "what life is all about". While clearly the adults know more about archaeology than the children do, the showing can still be reciprocal in that the children are compellingly conscious of the *wonder* of what is shown (the image suggests that one of the children may be showing Andy what she has found). Moreover, Andy's interest in archaeology is described on the calendar page as "passionate": it belongs to a set of practices, in other words, involving emotional as well as cognitive vectors. This is a serious intellectual endeavour, but its profundity extends to its connectedness to the humanity which the children represent.

These are themes which continue throughout this collection. "May" shows an older and a younger boxer, with the quotation "The greatest good you can do to another is not just to share your riches, but to reveal to him his own". (This is ascribed to Disraeli; it is sometimes also attributed to Jean Vanier, the founder of the L'Arche movement.) The surprise for the reader here is that it is the younger man who is the coach; here, knowledge goes *upward* through the generations. "June" shows different generations engaged in "Hawaiian dancing". Both the image and the quotation echo the theme in "March": "Life is available to anyone no matter what age. All you have to do is grab it." "July" presents what first appears a conventional pose, two older adults in a garden surrounded by young people and children. The surprise here is that these are not grandparents; they are a retired printer and his wife, who have deliberately decided to take up child-minding. Ron "left full-time employment" to do this. "He considers it a fantastic alternative to retirement and loves the house full of children." This piece is not about family but about intergenerational community relationships, then. The caption to the image runs, "For a community to be whole and healthy, it must be based on people's love and concern for each other." Underlying this is an implied contrast between Ron's very competent, masculine profession and the (stereotypically) "softer" avocation he has chosen. The effect of this piece is, importantly, to broaden "love and concern" for others outside the confines of family, to place them in a setting of wider concern for other human beings. One of the children in the picture is holding another; this is not solely an intergenerational issue, but includes relationships across generations.

Succeeding months' images reinforce the themes not simply of fun between the generations but of the genuine depth of what each can learn from their joint activities. "December" reinforces the exploration of education, though emphasizing that "knowledge" is a multifaceted phenomenon.

Fig. 4: December 2008

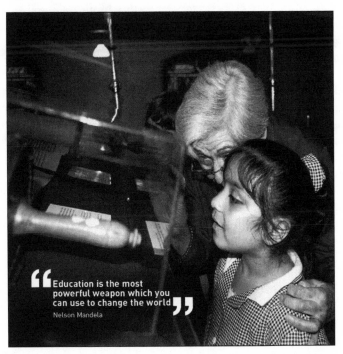

It is very clear here who is old and who young: an older woman seems to be showing a little girl something in a museum. The two seem friendly; the woman has her hand on the child's shoulder, expressing a physical connectedness which joins the two. The child seems interested in what is being said to her, straining to see and understand the object in front of them that is under discussion. The caption quotation, by Nelson Mandela, says, "Education is the most powerful weapon which you can use to change the world." As we may by now have come to expect, the calendar page pinpoints the dialectic between image and text. The setting in question is the Manchester Jewish Museum, "telling the story of the Jewish population in Manchester over the past 200 years"; many older people work there as guides. We may presume that the older woman in the image is Jewish; but the little girl appears to be Middle Eastern or Asian in ethnic origin. The last page of the calendar names participants, and if we turn to this, it appears that she has a Muslim name. The interaction here is not only intergenerational, then, but intercultural in a challenging way. That image and text elaborate each other in the way suggested allows the "reader" to see this not just in terms of intergenerational but also of intercultural relations in all their complexity. The fact that little fuss is made about these challenges possesses its own eloquence.

It is evocative too that this is the last picture in the collection and that it focuses so explicitly on education and the future – reinforcing the fact that time, and the relations between past, present, and future, have been themes permeating this collection. The links involved most certainly do not depend on simple forms of continuity, sameness and control, but entail creativity, freedom, development and change. The quotation on this last image is taken from Mandela, who is associated with political struggle for freedom and also with the idea of reconciliation. The intergenerationality expressed in this collection is above all complex; its success depends on a warm and supportive co-operation which may make use of the experience of the past, but in which each generation is open-minded towards what happens next. Whether or not wisdom is mentioned explicitly, all these are processes and capacities often mentioned in connection with wisdom. It is, though, the mutuality stressed here which is of special importance, and we shall recur to this below (Edmondson; Fairhurst and Mairs Slee).

THE IRISH CALENDAR

As in the UK, Ireland contains organisations whose purpose is to promote "positive images of ageing", as, for example, Age Action Ireland does with its "positive ageing week" or Age and Opportunity, with its Bealtine (May) festival of creativity and the arts. The Dean Maxwell Community calendar, however, is connected only with the "community" that has produced it. Yet, it conveys the message that being older or in ill health, a wheelchair-user like some of the artists, need not restrict creative endeavour. The calendar begins with photographs of the painters in action, sitting in natural surroundings and hunched over their work. They do not appear posed; the aim seems to be to show them in action. The paintings themselves are naïve in style and most are of flowers; one depicts a bluebell wood (May), one a scene suggesting Tuscany (July), one is abstract (August), one shows a weeping willow by a pond (October), and one a lighthouse (November). The last image, for December, is expressly Christmassy and involves a robin, hawthorn, and holly berries, and snowed-upon Christmas trees. Only the first six of the paintings are signed. Clearly, they refer heavily to natural objects and views, rather than overt forms of communication. Ancient philosophers such as Socrates advised the contemplation of nature for a wise person, and connections between wise older age and nature recur in the history of Western thought, as in the work of Cicero or Montaigne. Such associations are part of the heritage of a culture in which the appreciation of nature is often associated with serenity; but they function at most as background atmosphere in the present instance.

The texts in this calendar do not appear to relate specifically to the images; in fact, they appear on the calendar pages, as if to imply that they are connected less with the paintings themselves than with the way the reader might spend his or her month. They take "spiritual" form, explicitly evoking "you" and "your" reactions, and are "blessings" from the work of John O'Donohue. Hence they echo the liturgical pattern of statement and refrain or response, often us-ing three threefold repetitive patterns common in sermons and public speak-ing – as in "May you allow the wild beauty of the invisible world to gather you, mind you, and embrace you in belonging" or "May you know wisdom, deep listening, the healing of wholesome words." Note this overall impression is not as anodyne as non-Irish readers might suppose. John Donohue was a theolo-gian and ex-priest, engaged to be married at the time of his premature death from illness in 2008. He was extremely popular, in Ireland and worldwide, for his re-presentation of an eclectic combination of spiritual and psychological insights in a "Celtic" form that made them attractive and accessible to readers. He was also someone who expressed a deep consciousness of the difficulty and pain ordinary individuals endure in their attempts to negotiate contemporary life. His views were, to this extent, strongly counter-cultural: not only did he himself leave the formal structures of the Catholic Church, he excoriated the materialism and stressfulness of modern Irish life. On the whole he linked this to a "spiritual search" (Dillon) rather than to political action, even though he was, for example, part of a group which took the Irish Government to the Supreme Court in a successful bid to prevent the building of an "interpretive centre" in the Burren, in his native County Clare.

Hence the Irish calendar needs to be interpreted more holistically than does the Manchester one. For each month the picture, the fact that an older person has painted it, and the text may work together to convey an attitude the recipient can choose to connect with the life course as such. From this point of view, the calendar may be taken to convey an attitude of hope, creativity, or se-renity, which can be attached to older age by the recipient, and perhaps applied to his or her own life as well as to those of the painters. Such effects may be to a certain degree culture-specific: readers from other countries, or with other ages or backgrounds, might find such a meaning-complex intrusive in respect of their own self-understanding, or may simply feel it does not apply to them. Yet, the texts in this calendar convey a more general message: the suggestion that the life-course can be experienced as a spiritual journey, in which conventional expectations can be set aside and in which ageing – even vulnerable ageing in terms of health – has a positive and even crucial part to play.

Conclusions

These calendars show contrasting approaches to creativity and wisdom as means of dealing with ageing at different stages of life and health, and in different cultures. The texts and images of the Manchester calendar stress vibrantly constructive activities across and between different generations and the consequent interaction points to co-creation of meaning between participants; the Irish calendar is more "spiritual" and reflective, though also convivial. Each relates to its particular social setting and the relative states of health of participants, helping to understand different ways in which "wise" interventions can be constructed. In each case, continuity and change are drawn upon in different ways; time and experience are interpreted as positive resources for ageing individuals and also – crucially – for those around them.

The depiction of lively and original forms of transferring knowledge and skills between generations is a pervasive theme of the Manchester calendar's images. Individual details supply often-surprising insights into how wise actions and relationships work. They are more interactive than we might have expected, enhancing the status of partners from both generations, and take place *in the setting of relationships*: the "knowledge" involved in wisdom, it becomes clear, is not just cognitive. Text, which is linked to each monthly image, elaborates our understanding of wise actions: knowledge or "learning" is not the sole preserve of "the old" but rather an intergenerational process. This relationality is underlined by the fact that recognising or "seeing" wisdom in action requires the "reader's" involvement. Pictures are constructions of the world initiated by those involved in making them (Radley), but they are co-constructed in addition by readers or seers. These calendars enable us to explore details of how people bestow meaning on their and others' lives as they grow older; this includes developing wisdom among individuals and in certain social processes.

Our approach here, using calendars to "unpack" or access views on wisdom in contemporary life, contrasts with social-scientific methods focusing on academic analyses of texts, or testing what individuals say under controlled conditions. Since "wisdom" arguably became occluded by more rational and instrumental approaches during the 20th century (Edmondson; Marcel), we need to excavate for what are in effect uses of different interpretations of "wisdom" in everyday life – even though these often remain fragmented and implicit. These calendars are arresting sources, produced by (different groups of) individuals committed to older people: highlighting what is good about their worlds. At the same time they are aimed at wider audiences and intended to communicate directly, even though some of their implications are more explicit than others.

In these ways both calendars cast light on what it entails to "put human activities at the centre of theorising" – reasoning about vital social and political values as bound up with good communication (Woerner and Edmondson). This has been central to the humanistic emphasis on exploring and supporting what binds people together in terms of the common good, even while seeking to identify significant structural barriers to bringing this about. Thus, the calendars suggest clearly that older people should not be expected simply to make positive contributions all by themselves, independent of their circumstances. The ways society and social processes treat older citizens can support them as full contributors to society, acknowledging their wisdom and making possible their involvement, or it can do the opposite. The reciprocity involved in constructive rather than repressive interactions can lead to explicitly making active use of what has been learnt from different generations (Fairhurst *et al.*).

This article raises a variety of questions for further work. The Manchester calendar was created as part of a long-term series of interventions designed to impact on public perceptions of older people. In Ireland, there are also groups charged with policy interventions of a similar kind. But the calendar we have accessed does not draw on this context, nor does it make use of resources we have analysed elsewhere in terms of rural Irish understandings of wisdom (Edmondson). Its context seems to relate strongly to a church-related discourse of spiritual searching (Dillon), but it is important to remember that such discourses may be more relevant and helpful to some populations of older people than even the Churches themselves may recognize (Coleman). In each case, therefore, the calendars are created within an impactful social discourse, but it remains to be explored how each discourse relates on the one hand to the older people immediately associated with producing the calendar, and on the other to the wider populations of older and other people to whom the calendars may relate.

The Manchester Calendar production, including choice of photographs, is steered by the Positive Image task group of the *Valuing Older People Programme*, to which a number of older people belong. The older people pictured in these calendars, some of whom are actively involved in the wider *Valuing Older People Programme*, have volunteered themselves rather than being hired from a modelling agency. These particular older people, through their membership of the Positive Images task group, have participated in the production process of calendars and, consequently, have had some control over images found in them. It is not known, though, the extent to which they have chosen quotations accompanying the images, nor who took the photographs.

The participation of the Irish residents is equally strong in that it is clearly in some sense "their" calendar: the calendar is composed of pictures they have painted, a photograph, presumably of the painter, appears on each page in connection with the calendar, and the back page of the calendar shows a series of photographs of people, many of them artists. But there are more pictures of people than there are months in the year; this underlines the activities of others also living in the community. There is nothing to suggest, in either case, that the people connected with the calendar would repudiate its language or implications – even if it may be language they have been offered, rather than what they would (for whatever contextual reasons) have chosen. The agency of the older people involved in each case here, nonetheless, remains more to the forefront of these calendars than in most conventional social-scientific or literary accounts. This reinforces the compelling accounts of ageing, and ageing well, that they offer.

REFERENCES

Ardelt, Monika. "Wisdom as expert knowledge system: A critical review of a contemporary operationalization of an ancient concept." *Human Development* 47.5 (2004): 257-85. Print.

––––. "Experience and the beginning of wisdom." *The Sage Handbook of Social Gerontology*. Ed. Chris Phillipson and Dale Dannefer. London: Sage, 2010. 306-16. Print.

Baltes, Paul, and Jacqui Smith. "The Psychology of Wisdom and its Ontogenesis." *Wisdom: Its Nature, Origins and Development*. Ed. Robert Sternberg. New York: Cambridge UP, 1990. 87-120. Print.

Baltes, Paul, and Ursula Staudinger. "Wisdom: A Metaheuristic (Pragmatic) to Orchestrate Mind and Virtue Toward Excellence." *American Psychologist* 55 (2000): 122-36. Print.

Chandler, Albert R. "The Traditional Chinese Attitude Towards Old Age." *Journal of Gerontology* 4.3 (1949): 239-44. Print.

Coleman, Peter. "Religious Belonging and Spiritual Questioning: A Western European Perspective on Ageing and Religion." *Valuing Older People: A Humanist Approach to Ageing*. Ed. Ricca Edmondson and Hans-Joachim von Kondratowitz. Bristol: Policy Press: 2009. 23-50. Print.

Dillon, Michele. "Incorporating the Sacred in Creative Ageing." *Valuing Older People: A Humanist Approach to Ageing*. Ed. Ricca Edmondson and Hans-Joachim von Kondratowitz. Bristol: Policy Press, 2009. 51-72. Print.

Donohue, John. *To Bless the Space Between Us: A Book of Blessings*. London: Doubleday: 2008. Print.

Edmondson, Ricca. "Practical Reasoning in Place: Tracing 'Wise' Inferences in Everyday Life." *Practical Reasoning and Human Engagement.* Ed. Ricca Edmondson and Karlheinz Hülser. Lexington: Rowman and Littlefield, 2012. 111-30. Print.

———. "Wisdom: A Humanist Approach to Valuing Older People." *Valuing Older People: A Humanist Approach to Ageing.* Ed. Ricca Edmondson and Hans-Joachim von Kondratowitz. Bristol: Policy Press, 2009. 201-16. Print.

———. "Wisdom in Later Life: Ethnographic Approaches." *Ageing in Society* 25.3 (2005): 339-56. Print.

Fairhurst, Eileen. "'Positive Images' and Calendars: Explorations in 'Agelessness' or 'Ambiguous' Identities?" *Representing Aging: Images and Identities.* Ed. Virpi Ylänne. London: Palgrave-Macmillan, 2012. 189-206. Print.

———, and Sarie Mairs Slee. "The Hive in the Cliff: A Case Study in Intergenerational Relations and Culturally Led Regeneration." *Active Ageing and Intergenerational Solidarity Between Generations in Europe: Celebrating the European Year 2012. Special Issue of the Journal of Intergenerational Relations* 10.3 (2012): 246-60. Print.

———, and Sue Baines. "Positive Images of Ageing and the Production of Calendars." *Valuing Older People: A Humanist Approach to Ageing.* Ed. Ricca Edmondson and Hans-Joachim von Kondratowitz. Bristol: Policy Press, 2009. 277-82. Print.

———, Sue Baines, Marilyn Fitzpatrick, Julia Ryan, Tracy Williamson, Jan Reed and Glenda Cook. "Older People, Participation and Collaborative Governance in Post-Industrial Cities in England." *First International Sociological Association Association World Forum, Barcelona, Spain, 5-8 September 2008.* Unpublished paper.

Marcel, Gabriel. *The Decline of Wisdom.* London: Harvill, 1954. Print.

Johnson, Julia, and Bill Bytheway. "Illustrating Care: Images of Care Relationships With Older People." *Critical Approaches to Ageing and Later Life.* Ed. Anne Jamieson, Sarah Harper, and Christina Victor. Buckingham: Open UP, 1997. 132-42. Print.

Moody, Harry R. "Overview: What is Critical Gerontology and Why is it Important?" *Voices and Visions of Aging: Toward a Critical Gerontology.* Ed. Thomas. R. Cole, W. Andrew Achenbaum, Patricia. L. Jakobi, and Robert Kastenbaum. New York: Springer, 1993. xv-xli. Print.

Pasupathi, Monisha, Ursula Staudinger, and Paul Baltes. "Seeds of Wisdom: Adolescents' Knowledge and Judgement About Difficult Life Problems." *Developmental Psychology* 37.3 (2001): 351-61. Print.

Phillipson, Chris. *Reconstructing Old Age: New Agendas in Social Theory and Practice.* London: Sage, 1998. Print.

Radley, Alan. "What People Do With Pictures." *Visual Studies* 25.3 (2010): 268-79. Print.

Sternberg, Robert. "A Balance Theory of Wisdom." *Review of General Psychology* 2 (1998): 347-65. Print.

Woerner, Markus H., and Ricca Edmondson. "Towards a Taxonomy of Types of Wisdom." *Yearbook of the Irish Philosophical Society* (2009): 148-63. Print.

Zalot, Michael. "Wall Calendars: Structured Time, Mundane Memories and Disposable Images." *Journal of Mundane Behavior* 2.3 (2001). n.p. Web. 14 Aug. 2013.

She's Been Away

Ageing, Madness and Memory

Sherryl Wilson

Television is a popular medium that, despite its cultural centrality and significance, is rarely taken seriously. The reasons for this are many but include elitist
attitudes to "mainstream tastes" and because, despite the ubiquity of screens
outside of the home, it is still regarded as a domestic (and therefore feminine)
medium. The general disparagement of television ignores the (many) instances
of political interventions that are made across a range of genres. In this paper,
I focus on a single TV drama that challenges dominant paradigms of both
ageing and madness which has, therefore, the potential to intervene in social
consciousness and the formation of social memory. *She's Been Away* (BBC 1,
1989) was written by Stephen Poliakoff, directed by Peter Hall and broadcast as
a part of the BBC's *Screen One* (1989-1997) series. The play of memory in *She's
Been Away* reverberates with the cultural fear of ageing coupled with that other
unthinkable, mental illness.

   In the years since *She's Been Away* was first broadcast we have witnessed
a proliferation of images of older people (especially women) across a range of
media and genres, but rather than presenting us with new ways of thinking
about age and ageing, representations cohere to a series of somewhat retrogres-
sive images. (There is a debate to be had about the ways in which men as well
as women are represented as equally narrow/reductive constructions, but for
the sake of consistency with my case study, I want to focus on women here.)
The contemporary figures are familiar to us: the woman who has aged "successfully", she who is young-looking, full of youthful vigour and conventionally
attractive; all traces of life experience are erased. This construct is a repudiation
of the horrors of ageing. The other enduring trope is older woman as ancient
crone, enfeebled and vulnerable; again, experience and history are eradicated.
Both constructs are two sides of the same coin that carries a lot of currency: the
strenuous disavowal of ageing processes. Commonly in developed economies
age and ageing elicits disgust and fear, a problem to be solved, the older person
a presence to be repelled; we must not be reminded of our mortality. But this

may also be linked to what is seen as a "problem" of an ageing society where we are living longer and threaten to drain on precious resources.[1]

It is against this background that I consider *She's Been Away*. Rather than acting as a cipher for a denial of mortality through the effacement of history and experience, the older woman is constructed with the positive hue of the Bakhtinian grotesque body. A feminist critique of contemporary patriarchal structures is mounted through the mobilisation of an elderly woman's memories that, once excavated, liberate her and act as a force for empowerment for a younger woman. Here we are presented with a model of female friendship formed *because* of the old age of one of the protagonists, not *despite* it. As such, this drama is unusual in that it offers possibilities related to ageing – the space to be unruly, to produce something new – that are often absent from mainstream representations that are mostly narratives of decline and loss.

THE PLAY

Some broadcast context: As with any television production, there is a long history that gives shape and form to it. The political economy of the television industry and broadcasting policy, shifts in aesthetics and the development of technologies all impact on a production as much as cultural tastes and contemporary social concerns. This is no less true of *She's Been Away*, and although there is not the space to fully discuss the historical dimension here, it is important that we understand something of the context in which it was broadcast. As stated earlier, *She's Been Away* was broadcast as a part of the BBC's anthology series *Screen One* meaning that it was devised for a mainstream audience in the UK. With the introduction of *Screen One* in 1989 the BBC had an already established reputation for producing challenging dramas (albeit of uneven quality) through its anthology series of plays such as those that comprised *The Wednesday Play* (1964-1970), *Play for Today* (1970-1984) and *Play of the Month* (1965-1983), the authors of which embraced television as a platform for social engagement and a

---

1 | On International Women's Day this year (2013), BBC Radio 4's news programme World at One promised a discussion on "whether the ageing female workforce is blocking new female talent". It is hard to know where to start with this but it is astonishing that the recognition of a day celebrating women's achievements demonises the very age group that helped call this kind of celebration into being. The older woman here is positioned as a problem, as an impediment to younger women's aspirations. She is, in fact, being excluded from the meaning of Women's Day. In fact, the discussion was actually between two generations of female journalists who reflected on the changing nature of their profession. But the hook for the item is an example of the powerful discourse that constructs older women as a problem.

means to address the popular imagination. According to Lez Cooke, one of the reasons for the demise of the single play on British television in the 1980s was the political climate that made it difficult to get "radical or progressive drama commissioned [. . .] and virtually impossible after *Play for Today* ended in 1984" (141). However, against the backdrop of increasing conservatism Channel 4 was launched in 1982. As a public service broadcaster, the new channel had (still has) a remit to cater to diverse tastes and audiences and to represent minority voices; Channel 4 had to broadcast material that offered a different diet to that which was available through the BBC and ITV. The advent of Channel 4 not only increased competition to the already established broadcasters through its diet of edgy and innovative programming, it also had a commitment to film production allowing for its commissions to have a theatrical release as well as being shown in its *Film on Four* series.[2] *Screen One* was the BBC's response to this changing ecology of the television landscape by providing a showcase for feature-length, made for TV films.[3] This is the context in which *She's Been Away* was produced.

Critical reviews of the play were mixed. It was described by Andrew Lycett as "a notable coup" for the BBC Drama department because *She's Been Away* was chosen as "the official British" entry for the Venice Film Festival in September, a month before it was broadcast on television; it won Best Actress prize for both Dame Peggy Ashcroft and Geraldine James. A rather more negative position was adopted by Hugh Herbert who said, "Whatever its effect in the foetid atmosphere of Venice, in the corner of the living room this oversold mush of realistic social comment, fantasy, and Laingian psychology only works at all for me because of Ashcroft. To whom many thanks." (*The Guardian* October 9, 1989). On the other hand Richard Jeffery commented that

[i]t's typical English BBC drama stuff. Tightly scripted by Stephen Poliakoff, invisibly directed by Peter Hall, impeccably acted by a top-class cast of stage and small-screen professionals too rarely seen on the big screen. "She's Been Away" is a funny anecdotal, thought-provoking drama of a woman liberated-and, almost incidentally, a scathing critique of Britain today, and particularly the ruling class. (*The Daily Yomiuri* October 27, 1990)

---

2 | Although being launched just as the conservative policies of Thatcherism were beginning to take a hold, Channel 4 with its sometimes edgy and controversial programming was the result of a long process that began in the 1970s when a Labour government was in power.

3 | For the sake of consistency, I will refer to *She's Been Away* as a drama or play rather than introduce the term "film", but I should note that the production is indeed feature-length and did have a limited theatrical release.

I have been unable to access audience responses to the drama, but *She's Been Away* is now available through YouTube where comments are posted by viewers. One response is as follows: "Thanks for posting this. I watched it probably 20 years ago on PBS, and it's haunted me ever since" (Youtube). The notion that the play has remained in the subconscious of at least one viewer is perhaps an indication the power of a television text to produce (haunted) memory. It is not my intention to rehearse the strengths or weaknesses of the play; I merely offer these as examples of the ways in which it was received at the time. My intention is to focus on the figure of the older woman and the interesting ways in which she mobilises questions concerning patriarchal structures, our approach to the "mad", and our understanding of how memory works to construct a sense of ourselves.

The narrative: *She's Been Away*'s narrative centres on Lillian (Peggy Ashcroft) and begins with her ejection from the psychiatric hospital where she had spent more than 60 years of her life. With no other family, and despite being all but strangers, Lillian is sent to live with her highly successful City financier nephew Hugh (James Fox), his wife Harriet (Geraldine James), and their young son Dominic (Jackson Kyle). The family's nervousness of this mad old woman, irritation by the moral obligation to house her, and fear of the disruption she signals are counterbalanced by their well-meaning attempts to reintegrate her into everyday life. Nonetheless, despite their efforts, Lillian remains frustratingly mute and a mystery to her hosts. However, her back story, the reason for her confinement as a young girl, is revealed through a series of flashbacks triggered at key moments following her discharge from hospital and signal the gradual unlocking of her own memories while at the same time equipping the audience with insight into and knowledge of the conditions that produced the aberrant behaviour that resulted in years of hospitalisation. The series of flashbacks to Lillian's past reveal the young Lillian's (Rebecca Pidgeon) unruly refusal to conform to traditional constructions of femininity, her argumentative, sexually desiring, and defiant self displayed through her distain for, and resistance to, normative structures. This gives shape and meaning to the now mostly mute older woman who still displays defiance and resistance through her silence and an apparently naïve series of misbehaviours. Lillian's past and her present combine to provide a narrative of female subjugation that mirrors that of Harriet who, despite (because of?) her privilege and wealth, is stifled by her kind but patronising husband and infantilised by her very young son, both of whom embody the patriarchal order and symbolise the ways in which it is reproduced across generations. Over time, a bond between Lillian and Harriet is formed that works to liberate both women. The combined forces of Lillian's age along with her refusal to conform to discourses of traditional femininity are those which eventually work to liberate the unfortunate Harriet. As such, this is both a celebration of the unruly older woman and a meditation on the power of memory to produce counter-discourse. And it is the mobilisation of memory that is the catalyst for development and movement.

Prosthetic Memory

Returning to the play's narrative, Lillian's disruptive presence and 'out of place behaviour' is made intelligible through the movement between Lillian's old and young self which operates as the vehicle through which a powerful argument emerges. As a narrative device this works because of prosthetic memory defined by Alison Landsberg as that memory which

emerges at the interface between a person and a historical narrative [. . .] In this moment of contact, an experience occurs through which the person sutures himself or herself into a larger history [. . .] [T]he person [. . .] does not simply apprehend a historical narrative but takes on a personal, deeply felt memory of a past event through which he or she did not live. The resulting prosthetic memory has the ability to shape that person's subjectivity and politics. (2)

Enabled by cultural technologies such as film (and in this case, television), Landsberg argues that the "circulation of images and narratives about the past" (2) offer the possibility of an "interface between a person and a historical narrative about the past, at an experiential site" (2). This formulation of prosthetic memory offers a vital key to the understanding of the processes at work in *She's Been Away*. The play is an experiential site in which an older woman is positioned as powerful, as transgressive, and whose memories are shared with the audience (but not the other protagonists in the play), meaning that we become sutured into the disruption. The sociopolitical importance of this is evident because as Annette Kuhn says, memory has social as well as personal resonance (298). And according to Anna Reading, "the concept of social memory signals that what is being addressed is beyond but not distinct from the individual [. . .] Social memory is taken to include aspects of culture as well as social practices and structures" (5). So, in this play the figure of the mad old woman reverberates with familiar but unspoken fears of ageing and decline, but our ideas of what she represents undergo transformation as the narrative unfolds creating a new set of prosthetic and social memories that reposition the older woman in an entirely different light: as Lillian reconstitutes herself through her memories she is reconfiguring our expectations as an audience.

The opening sequence of any TV programme is designed to position the audience, to set up expectations and to lead us into the narrative/s. That memory is important to *She's Been Away* is signalled right at the start as the credits accompany a slow pan across a collection of old broken stuff discarded on a table in a gloomily lit room, a jumble of belongings – bric-a-brac, pictures, hats, a doll - all dust and decay – accompanied by the elegiac music which returns at points throughout at moments when memory is evoked. The series of inanimate objects provides what Kuhn calls a "performance of memory" described as a series of snapshots, flashes, vignettes "which are not sequential and have more in common with poetry than classical narrative" (299). It is the poetry of the discarded belongings and the memories they symbolise that produces the affect that frames the ways in which we see and experience much of the play.

The long forgotten items displayed at the beginning are present again when Hugh and Harriet arrive to collect Aunt Lillian. The objects stand in for the past residents of the hospital and their stories; glancing over them the nurse says, "isn't it odd what some people want to keep" as they move on to meet Lillian: Lillian who "doesn't understand anything," "Doesn't remember anything." There is an equivalent here made between the apparently valueless but once treasured belongings and the empty vessel that is the old woman as she is removed from the hospital in which she has lived for 60 years. The refrain "she doesn't remember anything" is repeated throughout the drama as Lillian's silence is interpreted as emptiness, symbolic of old age, especially female old age, which has nothing to say, no wisdom to impart. As such, the lack of memory signals, to the other characters in the play, an evacuation of self. More, Lillian triggers the dynamic of disgust and fascination that mark her as abject, an issue I will return to later.

Returning with Hugh and Harriet to their home, the same home that Lillian had grown up in, memories are activated not through a guided tour through the family tree or the old family photographs that Hugh shows her in his attempt to engage (Hugh to Lillian as she stares mutely at the images, "You really don't remember anything, do you?"), but through the shape and structure of the house itself – the doors peered through, the encounters with individuals who peopled her past, and the repetition of events: the spaces in which the young and old Lillian disgraces herself. These memories become prosthetic through a layering in which the past and present-day are co-present suturing the audience experience into Lillian's own. The first time this occurs is when Lillian catches sight of the now old Edward with whom she was in love when they were both young. This memory is particularly potent because it is triggered by being at a party held in the same rooms as the one held 60 years before during which the young and excitable Lillian declared her love and sexual desire for Edward, and in a near-delirious state disrupts the polite calm of the gathered adults. Now, peering through the doorway, Lillian pauses as she sees elderly Edward and his brother. Unnoticed by anyone apart from the audience, Lillian closes the wooden framed doors so that we see her in mid-close up framed by the glass and wooden bars as the memory music fades in. What follows is a sequence that takes us through the narrative of Lillian's young self and the events leading to her incarceration. Viewed as an object of curiosity by guests at the long-ago party and the source of embarrassment and shame for her father, Edward publicly spurns her – "Edward, why are you doing this?" – his rejection, his complicity with normative structures, provoke Lillian's virulent anger and distress.

IMAGES OF MADNESS

What is striking is the ways in which Poliakoff draws on familiar tropes of madness and old age and then subverts them by the process of prosthetic memory through which viewers confront their own expectations and cultural knowledge. The date of this production is not coincidental: in the UK during the 1980s and into the 1990s, many of the Victorian psychiatric hospitals were closed down with patients being tipped out to be cared for in the community. On the one hand, by the late 1980s, the ideas of controversial psychiatrist R. D. Laing are more widely known. Even if the audience is unaware of the specifics of Laing's work, the debate that took place during the 1960s and 1970s continues to have resonances well beyond the moment at which Laing was held in high esteem. His claims that mental illness is a product of toxic cultural and social forces continues to have a purchase both on the psychiatric profession and in the popular consciousness (hence the rather sniffy reference to Laingian psychology in Herbert's 1989 review cited above).

On the other hand, this move to close hospitals increased the anxieties that linked mental illness with violence (Philo *et al.*) as well as giving rise to more subtle worries: how can we tell who are the mad Other now that there are no boundaries separating Them from Us? As Simon Cross argues, the popular imaginings of madness have deep and complex historical roots that, despite shifts in definitions (from mad to mentally ill), diagnoses and treatments, remain tied to traditional notions of the mad as criminal, violent, as objects of fear. These discourses of madness work to position the mentally ill person as Other, the ones outside offering a reassuring difference that suggesting that the "devastation of mental illness is not likely to happen to ourselves or the people around us" (Cross 199).[4] So, in the social context of late 1980s Britain, the repeated scenes in *She's Been Away* of the hospital building in a state of collapse

---

4 | There is a large body of research exploring media representations of the mentally ill that focuses on (a) the accuracy (or otherwise) of clinically determined pathological symptoms and (b) the erroneous and highly disproportionate of linkage of mental illness with violence (Philo, Henderson, and McLaughlin; Diefenbach; Rose; Paterson and Stark). The overall conclusion is that there are a range of stereotypes (most frequently

and decay provoke memories of these places as the stuff of gothic fiction, of horror and darkness, as spaces that contain the otherwise uncontainable. This popular imagining is then is coupled with the figure of the mad old crone, the despised (a "gentle vegetable") or simply ignored older woman rendered invisible because of her age. The stuff of horror indeed!

The confluence of old age and madness threatens to produce an abject figure occupying an "'uninhabitable' subject position, eliciting shame and disgust that must be cast outside the sense of self and identity" (Ringrose and Walkerdine 234). And the abject performs a powerful regulatory purpose.

The boundary of the body as well as the distinction between internal and external is established through the ejection [. . .] of something originally part of identity into a defiling otherness [. . .] What constitutes through division the "inner and "outer" worlds of the subject is a border and boundary tenuously maintained for the purposes of social regulation and control. (Butler cited in Ringrose and Walkerdine 234)

In the context of *She's Been Away*, the young and old Lillian are, initially, clearly abject, but the process of abjection is disturbed because of the use of memory and the ways in which it becomes prosthetic; Lillian's memories are a part of the narrative known only to the audience making us complicit in both her silence and her knowledge. And because of this complicity Lillian can no longer be outside the symbolic order, the space she occupies may be liminal in terms of how she is positioned by the other protagonists, but we share that space with her. Her refusal to be charming or grateful or communicative gradually repositions Lillian from object of abject horror to a coherent subject.

INTERGENERATIONAL CONTINUITIES

This is all well and good but these processes might have remained at the level of the unintelligible if it were not for the dynamic between Harriet and Lillian through which narrative progression occurs. Difficult to characterise, their relationship is not quite that of mother and daughter as a familial tie is evidently absent, neither is it a friendship between peers. What links them is the continuity of a feminine self repressed by patriarchy. Where Lillian's excitability and artistic potential were obstructed by the construction of her as insane and resultant confinement in a psychiatric hospital, Harriet's acting career was thwarted through entombment in a marriage with a well-meaning but ultimately controlling husband; it is as if the feminist movement of the 1970s

violent) deployed across the media along with representations of mental ill-health sufferers as having a poor quality of life (Signorielli; Diefenbach).

had not taken place. Now Harriet's new pregnancy will perpetuate the order of things reproducing the generational line and reinforcing the containment within which she finds herself. We already know that Harriet's precocious son Dominic is an echo of his father – concern that the family home is properly insured; warnings to the (male) obstetrician of possible law suits should the gender of the unborn child be mistaken [. . .] So what if this next baby is male also? Delighted by the pregnancy, Hugh and Dominic accompany Harriet to the first scan. The hospital room in which the procedure is being performed is so dark that the faces of the doctor, husband, and son are barely visible. The rest of the room is in complete darkness producing a claustrophobia that we imagine is a reflection of Harriet's state of mind as she lies motionless on the hospital bed. "She's doing everything alright, is she?" whispers Hugh to the physician as they gather in a conspiratorial huddle away from the bed. Off camera, Hugh discusses his wife's progress while the screen is filled with a close up of Harriet as she overhears: "My wife can be, how shall I put it [. . .] my wife can be, um, a tiny bit scatty". Harriet, however, remains silent.

This scene is evocative of the atmosphere of suffocation and hopelessness articulated in Charlotte Perkins Gilman's novel *The Yellow Wallpaper* (1892) in which a woman is driven insane by her well-meaning but paternalistic husband described by the first person narrator as "very careful and loving" (5) and who refers to his wife as "a blessed little goose" (6). Both texts present men speaking while the women do not. However, in *The Yellow Wallpaper* the unnamed woman is alone with her silence having only her diary to record her thoughts, while the narrative of *She's Been Away* offers the outlet of sharing repressed rage with an older woman; Lillian's refusal to communicate mirrors Harriet's inability to speak. And this is the point of connection that ultimately liberates both.

Particularly useful in thinking about this intergenerational relationship is Kathleen Woodward's concept of sociality. Recalling a day, a moment that best expressed her relationship with her grandmother, Woodward says that what she (Woodward) experienced was "certainly nothing less than a palpable *sociality*, a convivial ease" (81). She describes this inter-generational sociality as a "plumb line – one that has specific gravity and weight to it" (84). Drawing on Jessica Benjamin's term "emotional attunement" and Lawrence Grossberg's "theorization of the affective economy of mood (in its 'positive' manifestation)", Woodward describes the mood of her memory as one of "fluent companionship" (82). If not exactly fluent, Woodward's formulation helps us understand the kind of companionship based on an emotional attunement that characterises the friendship emerging between Harriet and Lillian despite and because of the years that separate them in age. The convivial ease between them is gradually emerging, producing a plumb-line that joins them and which is eventually characterised by grit and steel. This is made apparent during the scene in the family home immediately following the hospital scan when Harriet and Lillian sit together in silence while the extra-diegetic memory music plays linking the two women in the present day. The silence is broken when a panicked Harriet rehearses the mantra: "I mustn't panic, I mustn't panic, I mustn't panic, I mustn't panic, I mustn't panic." That this is uttered in the presence of the older woman at least suggests a sense of safety, a sense of sociality premised on shared emotional experience. Without knowing each other's story, the two women understand each other. Earlier in the play, a knowing Harriet speaks to the forever silent Lillian: "You don't fool me, Lillian. You haven't fooled me from the start. Because you know far more than you pretend, don't you. You understand everything, don't you, but you are refusing to show it. You prefer to seem an idiot. [. . .] I don't mind. No one else need ever know."

Continuing to express no gratitude for the efforts to reinstall her into society, Lillian remains largely silent and uncommunicative, her silence is defiance, resistance, the performance of madness irritating the smooth social body. However, the audience becomes sutured into Lillian's history simultaneous to Harriet's own developing understanding of the older woman, so that the two women's narratives of repression merge while the silence provides the plumbline, a continuity blending past and present, the one informing the other.

THE ROAD TRIP

The scan proves to be the tipping point, the moment in which repressive practices of patriarchy propel Harriet into a sort of "mad" response to her situation. To describe her reaction to her pregnancy as undelighted is an understatement: the baby will either perpetuate the male lineage and all that comes with that or, if a girl, will inhabit the same social and cultural paradigm as Harriet. What is interesting about this moment is that it is the first time we hear Lillian speak spontaneously to the younger women. Having watched Harriet's frantic search for suitcases and now on the point of leaving the house, she calls out:

Lillian: Harriet!
Harriet: I'm just popping out, just for a minute.
Lillian: I think I could pop out, too. It would be nice to pop out.
Harriet: I'm only going round the block. To the shops.
Lillian: I'll pop out to the shops, too.
Harriet: I'm not going far; you'll see.

The next shot is of Hugh's very expensive, very shiny car being driven recklessly out of the drive, denting and scraping the whole of the driver's side along the wall. So, a now seven months pregnant and frustrated Harriet takes herself and Lillian on a mad car journey to nowhere in particular (a kind of deranged Thelma and Louise).

Frantic with worry over the disappearance of his wife, Hugh is mystified. "Maybe Lillian did something to her," he says. And of course, Lillian has done something to his wife, but not in the way that he had imagined. After crashing and abandoning Hugh's (much beloved) car, the dishevelled women hitch a lift and check into an upmarket hotel. Posing as mother and daughter, Harriet tells the surprised looking male receptionist: "We're here for pleasure!" The liminal space of the hotel offers Harriet the liberty to express her hatred of her unborn child, to reflect on her own compliance within a system she despises. Harriet: "It's very unattractive, I know, being full of hate. Is there anything worse, worse feeling in the world than hating the child you are about to have, without knowing why?" Without fully knowing the details of Lillian's adolescent misdemeanours or present thought processes, Harriet nonetheless intuits: "You can't forgive; why should you ? [. . .] I'm not as brave as you are [. . .] You did what you had to do. It didn't exactly get you very far, but that is something else." The hotel operates as a liminal space in which rebellion is fostered, strengthening the plumb-line, the bond of a sociality premised on shared experience. It is here that the unsayable can be said: Harriet loathes her husband, and Lillian can, for the first time, speak her story, tell how she gradually made herself get smaller, become more "locked away" over the many "little" years in the hospital.

Still at the hotel and after much alcohol and wild dancing, Harriet collapses resulting in a rush to hospital and a diagnosis of eclampsia. The ensuing emergency caesarean delivery of her baby saves Harriet's life, but it is Lillian who saves Harriet. The scenes of Harriet being rushed into theatre for the caesarean delivery are juxtaposed with scenes of an emotionally fraught Hugh and calm, reasoning Dominic discussing wife/mother. As Hugh gains awareness that his wife ran away rather than being kidnapped, his shame (shame because everyone would know, it has been reported on the television) frames his fury: "God, she's got some explaining to do. These last weeks until the baby is born she will never be out of my sight!" A crushing claustrophobia is conveyed, once again, by the darkness of the room in which Hugh has this exchange with his son mirroring the moment of the hospital scan where Harriet had no say, was rendered voiceless. What punctures this relentless regulation and control is the moment when Lillian's' memory is stirred, once again acting as the catalyst that ultimately offers the possibility of rescue for both women. This is key to the play.

As Harriet is rushed into the hospital theatre, a (male) doctor asks Lillian if she is the patient's mother – "I'm not, not quite her mother" – because she (Harriet) has a life-threatening condition and they must "get the baby out now".

Lillian: "I must see her."
(Male) Doctor: "I'm afraid that is impossible [. . .]"
Lillian: "I must see her. I have something to give her."
Doctor: "You don't understand [. . .] that woman could easily die [. . .] Now stop wasting our time."

As these final words are spoken, Lillian is manhandled away from the theatre entrance and towards a seating area. The grip of the doctor's hand on her hand, restraining her, the owner of the hand refusing to listen to her words of protest. Memory music fades in as we watch Lillian being led away, a tight close up of the male grip on her wrist. As they walk, the performance of memory is activated as images of her young self merge with the music so that we, as well as Lillian, are transported back to the day when, as a young girl, she was taken away, incarcerated. This is powerful because we not only witness what did actually happen to Lillian at the moment of her removal from society, but also how she responded, how she felt, what she said. The brutal physicality of her incarceration is evoked, then the remembering of her "interview" with the two psychiatrists. Lillian: "You don't know what you are talking about. That's the trouble. And I know you don't; that's what you don't like." What follows is a tight close up of the young Lillian undergoing tests, again in a dark room, while the unseen examiner poses diagnostic questions:

Psychiatrist: "Who is the Prime Minister of this country?"
Young Lillian: "A kind of monkey."
Psychiatrist: "What do we call a man who looks after our teeth?"
Young Lillian: "A blood-thirsty man."

As the camera pulls back, we see the male doctor on one side of a large wooden desk as the resistant Lillian is seated opposite.

Psychiatrist: "What is the name of this country where we live; what do we call it?"
Young Lillian: "I don't know. Black Islands. Some name like that. A place that you fall through [. . .] and come out the other side."
Psychiatrist: "Why do you think you are here?"
Young Lillian: "Because I am cleverer than you. Because I am meaner than you. Because I see through you. It would be much easier if I wasn't around, wouldn't it? But most importantly because you do not feel [. . .] Just like my father."

At this point, memory music fades in as old Lillian recalls her sexual encounter with the much-wanted Edward. Young Lillian [excitedly]: "They will come soon, find out where we are." Lillian's refusal to hide, to not worry that they will be found is both a sign of her individuality and the cause of her subsequent powerlessness. More memories: renouncing her father, she says, "I can no longer believe you exist. I have lost my faith. I can't believe such a boring, small minded, lumpy man can be my father. So I have decided you aren't my father." These memories are recalled as taking place in darkened spaces indicating Lillian's internal processes intensifying her declarations as she refutes the Law of the Father both at home and in hospital. We, too, are drawn into Lillian's narrative through the process of prosthetic memory, enabling us to understand both the root of her "madness," able to see it as socially constructed, and to position us with Lillian rather than with the technologies of regulation (Foucault) that work to position her as abject.

The memory sequence triggered by the restrictive hand on Lillian's arm is the longest and most expository in the drama and leads to the denouement. We still have flashes and poetic images, but the performance of memory here tells us the most complete story suturing us into Lillian's back-story: images of young Lillian being restrained are fused with images of old Lillian being restrained as we cut between the present day – Lillian in the hospital prevented from being with Harriet – and the past and young Lillian screaming through the bars of a cell-like hospital room. Old Lillian is silent, while her not-yet-shattered young self is imprisoned but defiant: "Bastards! Bastards!" Ultimately, the two Lillians merge as, in the present, she soliloquises, "What happened to all that time? It was just [. . .] taken [. . .] away"; her anger and distress are palpable. (Ellipses in original). What is significant here is that the old Lillian could not have the force that she ultimately does, if it were not for the recollections of the injustices meted out to her young self. While her young self is disempowered, her old self claims an agency and defiance *because* of her age. The closing six minutes of the play are enacted in the postoperative room in which Harriet is recovering and the newly self-empowered Lillian takes charge. Shoving a nurse out of the way – Nurse: "You can't go in there"; Lillian [pushing the nurse aside]: "Oh rubbish" – we understand that a profound shift has occurred.

Harriet: "So what the hell are we going to do now, Lillian? Haha. Listen to me, I'm asking you that."
Lillian: "Yes. [pause] I don't know why you're laughing."

Barricading the door so that "they" cannot get in, Lillian stands guard, watching as echoes of the memory music play over images of a contented-looking Harriet and a vigilant Lillian. Hints of the music are heard as the camera pulls back to reveal Lillian and Harriet behind a wall of glass, sharing the space separating them from us. As we look, we hear footsteps approaching the room. This is the sound of the as yet unseen Hugh approaching. Now, as the footsteps get louder and more pronounced, a succession of shot/ reverse shots switch our points of view between that of Lillian looking down the corridor and that of the approaching threat. These shots merge with a series of memories of young Lillian looking through the bars of her cell/room, jumping in ecstasy on her bed, having sex with Edward, an unruly presence at her parents' party [. . .] all these are shown overlaid with the sound of the footsteps and mingled with faint snatches of memory music blurring the boundary between past and present. Finally, when Hugh comes into view, he is seen marching down the corridor with a fleet of medical and nursing staff in his wake (Hugh is a very influential man after all), his feet making the same noise pattern as that of the old clock in young Lillian's memory tick-tocking the years away. Finally, as the play comes to an end, we are left with Hugh and Lillian staring at one another through the glass.

I hope that I have shown how it is possible for a mainstream television drama to offer a discourse of ageing and mental illness that stands counter to those most prevalent in contemporary culture. The narrative is made profound through the processes of prosthetic memory enabling Lillian's subject position to become sutured into the audience experience. Rather than made abject, the confluence of madness, old age, and memory disrupts expectations and punctures the consciousness. As Landsberg states, prosthetic memories enable a sensuous engagement with past lives and past experiences that, she argues, can serve as "the basis for mediated collective identification" offering the ethical, social, and political potential for "unexpected alliances across chasms of difference" (3). Television drama of this kind offers the possibility of (re)creating a social memory that reconfigures madness and old age as wisdom and powerful unruliness – a source of celebration.

References

Cooke, Lez. *British Television Drama: A History*. London: BFI Publishing, 2003. Print.

Cross, Simon. "Visualising Madness: Mental Illness and Public Representation." *Television and New Media* 5 (August 2004): 197-216. Web. 11 Aug. 2013.

Diefenbach, Donald. "The Portrayal of Mental Illness and Prime-Time Television." *Journal of Community Psychology* 25.3 (1997): 289-302. Print.

Foucault, Michel. *Discipline and Punish: The Birth of the Prison*. London: Allen Lane, 1977. Print.

Herbert, Hugh. "The Meek Shall Inhabit the World." *The Guardian* (London) 9 October 1989. Web. 29 May 2013.

Jeffery, Richard. "She's Been Away." *The Daily Yomiuri* 27 October 1990. Web. 29 May 2013.

Kuhn, Annette. "Memory Texts and Memory Work: Performances of Memory in and with Visual Media." *Memory Studies* 2010 (3.4): 298-313. Print.

Landsberg, Alison. *Prosthetic Memory: The Transformation of American Remembrance in the Age of Mass Culture.* New York: Columbia UP, 2004. Print.

Lane, Ann (ed.). *The Charlotte Perkins Gilman Reader: The Yellow Paper and Other Fiction.* London: The Women's Press, 1980. Print.

Ley, Shaun. *The World at One.* BBC Radio 4. 8 Mar. 2013. Radio.

Lycett, Taiwo Ajai. "Drama at the BBC." *The Times* (London) 2 August 1989. Web. 29 May 2013.

Philo, Greg, Leslie Henderson, and Greg McLaughlin. *Mass Media Representations of Mental Health/Illness: A Study of Media Content.* Glasgow: Glasgow University Media Group, 1993. Print.

Reading, Anna. "Editorial." *Media, Culture and Society* 25 (2003): 5-6. Print.

Paterson, Brodie, and Cameron Stark. "Social Policy and Mental Illness in England in the 1990s: Violence, Moral Panic and Critical Discourse." *Journal of Psychiatric and Mental Health Nursing* 8.3 (2001): 257-67. Print.

Ringrose, Jessica, and Valerie Walkerdine. "Regulating the Abject. The TV Make-Over as Site of Neoliberal Reinvention Toward Bourgeois Femininity. Feminist Media Studies." *Feminist Media Studies* 8.3 (2008): 227-46. Print.

Rose, Diana. "Television, Madness and Community Care." *Journal of Community and Applied Social Psychology* 8.3 (1998): 213-28. Print.

Ross, Karen, and Tim Healey. "Growing Older Visibly: Older Viewers Talk about Television." *Media Culture and Society* 24.1 (2002): 105-20. Print.

She's Been Away, BBC1 (1989), and YouTube.com. Web. 28 Mar. 2013.

Signorielli, Nancy. "The Stigma of Mental Illness on Television." *Journal of Broadcasting and Electronic Media* 33.3 (1989): 325-31. Print.

"Slowdiving." YouTube.com. Web. 21 Aug. 2013.

Vernon, JoEtta A, J. Allen Williams, Terri Phillips, and Janet Wilson. "Media Stereotyping: A Comparison of the Way Elderly Women and Men are Portrayed on Prime-Time Television." *Journal of Women and Ageing* 2.4 (1991): 55-68. Print.

Woodward, Kathleen. "Tribute to the Older Woman." Ed. Mike Featherstone and Andrew Warnick. *Images of Ageing: Cultural Representations of Older Life.* London: Routledge, 1995. 79-96. Print.

Illness and Love in Old Age

Jonathan Franzen's *The Corrections*
and Elizabeth Strout's *Olive Kitteridge*

Meike Dackweiler

There are remarkably few positively connoted examples of love in old age in literary history: Besides the mythological couple Philemon and Baucis (Ovid), old lovers often appear in the form of stock characters. For centuries, the luckless *senex amans* has been the dominant literary motif combining love and old age. It is usually typified by the amorous old woman or the dirty old man (Fiedler). These characters typically desire characters many years their juniors and are often ridiculed by their false belief in the remains of their own (erotic) attractiveness (Meyer 210). Prominent stereotypes are the procuress or the rich old man who foolishly married a young woman and is being conspicuously cuckolded for the amusement of the audience (Featherstone and Hepworth 739).

Fictional literature tends to present erotic love and old age as mutually exclusive. This finding is astonishing, bearing in mind that human beings usually strive to live as long as possible and erotic love as one of the most important subjects of Western literature since the 11th century (Lewis 3) is thought to enhance life's quality greatly (Traupmann and Hatfield 268). According to Murray S. Davis, the reason for the disproportional ratio of negative types of old lovers is the belief that the sexual attractiveness of a human body declines within the process of aging: "Aging switches off the physical features that generate erotic reality one by one, though it may increase the power of personality and social generators almost enough to compensate for their loss. If personality and social characteristics may age like wine, bodies must always age like milk" (38). Davis' explanation of the tabooing of erotic love in old age hints at evolutionary psychology. In this field the instinctive and thus subconscious urge to reproduce is seen as one of the roots of sexual desire. Thus, a potential mate's attractiveness depends on the perceptible indications of his or her ability to produce healthy offspring. A certain age, waist-hip-ratio, thick hair, smooth skin, or full lips are characteristics that suggest fertility and health (Henss 289-90).

Healthiness of one's mate increases the likelihood of this mate's ability to provide high-quality parental care and one's offspring to inherit genetic protection
from diseases (Singh and Young 485, 503).

Hence, wrinkles, grey, thinning hair, and an incomplete set of teeth reduce
the physical attractiveness of an individual as they signal diminished fertility
and declining health (Singh and Young 503). Although obviously healthy sev-
enty-year-olds exist and people in their thirties suffer from (fatal) diseases,[1] old
age and illness are often seen as synonymous in the Western World. According to Bryan S. Greene, the idea of old age as "one long progressive disease"
(Haber 67) emerged with the conclusions observers drew from medical statistics on populations: Due to the advances in public health and hygiene, the pro-
fessionalization of medicine and the discovery of cures in the nineteenth century, the mortality rates in children and middle-aged adults significantly dropped
(Fischer 108). Thus, "fatal illness became more and more a phenomenon of
old age" (Greene 44). When at the beginning of the twentieth century the field
of gerontology took form in the United States, senescence was viewed from a
pathological perspective which was based on a rather "depressing tautology"
(Greene 44): "aging had become defined as a progressive disease that caused a
multitude of physiological and anatomical changes. Growing old was itself the
source of the inevitable organic alterations known as old age" (Haber 76).

The notion of healthy old age seemed to be the positive exception to the
rule (Greene 43). Although in the second decade of the new millennium the
stereotype of old age as a "progressive disease" is prevailing, science and literature scrutinize it. Media and marketing professionals even describe healthy
old age in glowing terms to aim at "seniors," i.e. retirees over 65 (Hopkins,
Roster, and Wood). In this paper, I would like to discuss the possibility to find
and keep a loving relationship for "frail" individuals beyond 65. A study on old
age, love and its effect on health in older Americans suggests that not only the
existence of an intimate relationship is "critically important in securing mental
and physical health" but also the quality of the relationship (Traupmann and
Hatfield 268).

According to the logics of evolutionary biology outlined above, age and diseases have a negative influence on physical attraction. Thus, the chances of an
old individual afflicted by illness to find mutual love are believed to be minimal
(Vincent 156). However, in the first decade of the new millennium a number of
novels by established authors with characters falling or being in love in their
late sixties or beyond have been published. Additionally, their protagonists are
characterized by at least one more or less age-related disease. In which ways

---

1 | This is the case in Philip Roth's novel *The Dying Animal* where the seventy-year old
college professor David Keppesh begins to care about his 30-year old former lover
Consuela who is suffering from a very serious form of breast cancer (Roth 126-56.)

does illness as deviance from the standard of health affect romantic relationships in old age and how is this presented in contemporary American novels?

I will discuss two novels on the basis of socio-psychological conceptions of the nexus of love, old age and illness: The first one is Jonathan Franzen's *The Corrections* (2001), the main characters being Enid and Alfred Lambert, a longstanding married couple. The plot duration stretches from the 1990s to the year 2002, which is roughly two years after the beginning of the economic crisis following the burst of the so-called dotcom-bubble in March 2000 (595-96). The couple lives in their own house in the fictional Midwestern city of St. Jude, modeled on St. Louis, where the author was born and raised (Grewe-Volpp 207, 209). Their marriage can be described as a traditional and patriarchal relationship with Alfred as the dominant breadwinner and Enid as the submissive homemaker and mother of three. The characters are created as antipodes: While Alfred's pessimistic worldview was shaped by his misogynist father and Schopenhauer's pessimism (282), his wife is an enthusiastic optimist with an affinity for luxury articles (124). Enid suffers from chronic pain in her hip (547). After his retirement Enid gradually becomes the sole caretaker of Alfred who displays symptoms of dementia and Parkinson's disease (129, 599).

The situation is a little different for Olive Kitteridge, the main character of the eponymous novel *Olive Kitteridge* (2008) by Elizabeth Strout: The heroine, a former math teacher, ran a double income household and raised one son with her devoted husband Henry, a pharmacist (13). The couple built their own house in Crosby, Maine, where ten generations of their ancestors (145) had already lived their lives. The spouses' characters are also very different, not on a philosophical level as in the case of Alfred and Enid – but on a psychological level: While Olive "is stubborn, impatient, fierce, sometimes even cruel, but also fiercely loving"; her husband is "almost too sweet," always forgiving and forever accepting any hardship imposed on him (Teicher 32). Similar to Enid's situation, in her late sixties Olive becomes a part-time caretaker of Henry's who had suffered a stroke soon after he closed his pharmacy.

Jonathan Franzen's The Corrections

According to psychologist John Alan Lee, six basic styles of love exist: eros (passionate love), ludus (game-playing love), storge (friendship love), pragma (logical, "shopping list" love), mania (possessive, dependent love) and agape (all-giving, selfless love). The love style which describes the foundation of Alfred and Enid's marriage best seems to be pragma. When Enid got engaged with Alfred, she had a distinct wish-list for her future and the man to shape it. Enid wanted to avoid her mother's fate of a marriage with a poor man who died young, and "intended to be comfortable in life as well as happy" (281). Although Alfred's frequent Schopenhauer quotations suggest a rather pessimistic personality, his luxurious wool suits, his good looks and his job as a steel engineer seem to be indicative of him being a good provider (282). While Alfred's criteria for mate selection are never explicitly mentioned within the novel, with Enid he seems to have chosen a pretty, obedient future housewife and mother. Unfortunately, both spouses experience a keen disappointment in the first years of their marriage: While Alfred is unloving and unwilling to invest his money in equities as Enid constantly demands, she is not the plain, dutiful wife he expected her to be (290-91).

In the present of the novel Alfred has retired from his middle management post with the railroad company "Midland Pacific." Most of his adult life, Alfred showed himself a "man" in the public sphere, and believed the right and duty to rule over his household with unquestioned authority to be his natural reward. For many years the prevailing order of the Lamberts' home was discipline and spotless cleanliness (Grewe-Volpp 209). However, after his retirement Alfred gradually loses the capacity to fulfill the role of "the governing force" (6) in the household. Causes for this are his suffering from Parkinson's disease and symptoms of dementia, which his wife Enid hopes to be only the negative side effects of his medication. Because Enid fears the finality of a diagnosis like Alzheimer's, Alfred is evasively deemed by herself and their children (68-69) "to be 'depressed', a supposition which, rather than recognizing an inevitable side-effect of his disease, implicitly pathologizes his old-fashioned patriarchal values" (Toal 311).

Alfred's mode of life consisted of self-denial, strictness, and exertion (Toal 315) before his retirement. His identity as a male, white upper middle class member (302) was for most of his life founded on the grounds of his "manly" ability to work long hours without pauses and he "fought off extracurricular napping like any other unwholesome delight" (296). However, after his early retirement he spends his days watching local news and sleeping in his blue chair (8-9). Alfred's illness does not only affect his performance of gender-adequate behavior (Toal 306), but also the power balance in the hierarchical relationship between husband and wife: Although Enid tries to conceal it for domestic bliss, the couple undergoes a power shift from the sick *pater familias* to his caring wife. Enid, who most of her life had to pay nothing but shopping-bills with the household and pocket money she was given by Alfred (294), now secretly struggles with the cleaning woman's social security contributions, health insurance bills and the money Alfred has been offered for a patented discovery he made in his younger years.

Concerning *The Corrections*, Franzen dubbed the term "social novel," a genre which "connects the private with the public and individual psychologies with material realities" (Annesley 111). Alfred's private struggle with Parkinson's disease and dementia leads to "observations on the ever-greater refinements of consumer society and an exploration into the potential of new and more powerful pharmaceuticals" (111). While Enid cares in every way for Alfred, she pins her hopes on a pharmaceutical cure of his symptoms which their doctor is unable to provide, because no actual cure exists for dementia-related symptoms. When Enid fulfills her long-cherished dream of a so-called Luxury Cruise, Alfred's nightly hallucinations and agitation leave her sleepless and tired throughout the day:

> She found Alfred naked with his back to the door on a layer of bedsheets spread on sections of morning paper from St. Jude [. . .]. Her immediate aim was to quiet him and get some pajamas on him, but this took time for he was terribly agitated and not finishing his sentences, not even making his verbs and nouns agree in number and person [. . .]. Even now she couldn't help loving him. Maybe especially now. Maybe she'd known all along, for fifty years, that there was this little boy in him. Maybe all the love she'd given Chipper and Gary [. . .] had merely been practice for this most demanding of her children. (329-30)

The equation of a demented partner's behavior with a child's is a topos used widely within the discourse on Alzheimer's. When a demented individual's behavior becomes inconsistent with the normative expectations of age-appropriate behavior, the alleged childlikeness can serve as a coping strategy for the caregiver: The comparison reminds the caregiver that high stressfulness and equal amiability are coexisting features of an individual. Like parents caring for "unruly" children, a caregiver married to the patient is supposed to be forbearing and forgiving even under extreme circumstances.

For Enid, who was bored all her life by household and caring chores so much that she needed Alfred's love doubly (262), this metaphor bears a special comfort: As much as Enid longed for tenderness and Alfred's appreciation of her, she suffered from his coldness and his lack of empathy to the point of rape throughout her marriage (295-96). In old age her unsatisfied romantic love for Alfred and her indestructible optimism enable her to satisfy her lifelong "desperate yearning for love and belonging" (Grewe-Volpp 209) with the enforced physical closeness that comes with caring for a chronically ill spouse: "The intimacy of care-giver and patient mimics the relation between mother and child, or rather presents such a relationship in a distorted, reconfigured, or transposed form" (Wiltshire 413). However, in the long run this intimacy is no more than a poor substitute for the loving kindness and sexual pleasure Alfred is forever withholding from Enid (293) on the grounds of his Schopenhauerian reprobation of kindness and affection in general and sexual lust in particular:

> It frightened and shamed Enid, the loving kindness of other couples. She was a bright girl with good business skills who had gone directly from to ironing sheets and table-

cloths at her mother's boardinghouse to ironing sheets and shirts chez Lambert. In every neighborhood woman's eyes she saw the tacit question: Did Al at least make her feel super-special in that special way? (255)

Alfred does not only withhold pleasure from Enid, his nightly deliria – a symptom of early Alzheimer's – also sabotage consumer pleasures like the luxury cruise. Due to her permanent worries about Alfred, sleeplessness, and increasing exhaustion, Enid finds herself unable to enjoy spare time activities such as "education, travel and voluntary service," which resemble "the holy trinity" of the so-called "Third Age" (Kubik 138). Her mood improves when Enid learns from her adult children about "Corecktall," a drug which is in the clinical testing phase that is supposed to reduce the symptoms of Parkinson's and Alzheimer's disease (208). The producer of this 'magic cure' is the Axon Corporation that bought Alfred's patent exactly for the purpose of developing this medication. Unfortunately, Alfred's ability to follow simple instructions rapidly deteriorates in the course of the story (222) and he is finally identified as "an unsuitable candidate for the free clinical trial of Corecktall" (Annesley 114).

Despite her frustration over Alfred's physical and mental incapacities, Enid regards her husband of nearly fifty years as very attractive. According to their oldest son, Alfred is "still an imposing figure. His hair was white and thick and sleek, like a polar bear's, and the powerful long muscles of his shoulders [. . .] still filled the gray tweed shoulders of his sport coat" (16-17). Even in his worst moments Enid registers the "almost youthful beauty" and the "peculiar serenity" (356) of Alfred's face. However, in relation to Enid Alfred's lasting physical attractiveness is an empty signifier due to his lack of empathy, tenderness and sexual interest in his wife. Alfred despises romantic feelings in general and he can see Enid's personal value only in her function as a "pretty" (589) homemaker and mother. While Enid at age 75 experiences desire for intimacy and sexual intercourse (321), Alfred has long chosen sleep as his "invisible mistress" over Enid, whose occasional caressing bewilders and frightens him (296-97).

It is not before Alfred's final institutionalization that Enid's desire for his physical approachability is satisfied. After the "drug holiday," which the three adult children of the Lamberts' encouraged Alfred to take, he is "finally discharged with a diagnosis of parkinsonism, dementia, depression, and neuropathy of the legs and urinary tract" (599).

According to Ott, Sanders, and Kelber, (caring) spouses of patients with dementia tend to suffer from the "losses in the quality of the relationship, roles, control, well-being, intimacy, health status, social interaction, communication, and opportunities to resolve issues from the past" (799). However, in The Corrections the narrator depicts the exact opposite because Enid's situation has actually improved in regard to every single item on the list: Due to the loss of Alfred's ability to communicate his orders, Enid can act on the issue of her suffering from the life-long wrongness Alfred imposed on her. Not only is she relieved from the grueling task of caring for a commanding spouse, she is also able to seek medical help herself and has her hip pain surgically treated (600).

Although Enid is constantly unhappy about Alfred's constitution, she visits him daily "to keep him well dressed, and to bring him home-made treats" (599). While she observes the decencies of the caring wife with her nonverbal actions, her verbal behavior unveils that her image of Alfred has been transformed from 'governor' into 'life-size human doll':

She was glad, if nothing else, to have his body back. She'd always loved his size, his shape, his smell, and he was much more available now that he was restrained in a geri chair and unable to formulate coherent objections to being touched. He let himself be kissed and didn't cringe if her lips lingered a little; he didn't flinch if she stroked his hair. His body was what she'd always wanted. It was the rest of him that was the problem. (599)

Now that Alfred has lost the capacity to control the marital discourse (Kubik 145), Enid turns into the opposite of the Victorian "ideal of womanhood and its adjoining values of dependence, submission, spirituality, and delicacy – so convenient for male comfort and the maintenance of patriarchal hegemony" which "denied women control over their own physical, emotional, or intellectual needs" (Domínguez 24).

Enid uses her newly gained communicative power to lecture her cognitively impaired spouse about his human failure. Although she is aware that Alfred is mostly unable to follow her complaints, she can't help but tell him every single day how wrong he was about not loving and cherishing her, not having sex with her "at every opportunity," not trusting her financial instincts, and spending so much time at work, "and how right she'd been" (600). The time she spends in the nursing home at the bedside of her demented spouse does not serve as quality time for him, but as a therapeutic session for her. Enid, who dwelled during her marriage "in the cellar of [her] wrongness," waiting for someone to take pity on her (264), is unwilling to take anymore pity on Alfred. Like him before, Enid is completely uncompassionate even in respect of his multiple suicide attempts (600).

From a psychological perspective the spouses' mutual lack of empathy may be ascribed to their style of love. Since pragma is a highly conditional love based on a number of desired qualities, this love fails when the partner no longer possesses these qualities. While Enid did not fulfill the role of the devout housewife to Alfred's satisfaction, Alfred betrayed Enid's hopes of a kind and generous husband.

Despite her ethically questionable behavior towards her helpless husband, Enid's character remarkably develops concerning other areas of life and especially in relation to her children. According to Domínguez, the almost exclusive commitment of the traditional house wife to "the family network makes it more difficult to distinguish her own desires from those of husband and children" (23). However, with her children and husband out of the house, the role of the devoted housewife and mother becomes obsolete for Enid.

Alfred's institutionalization does not lead to a life crisis, but Enid actually "succeeds in reconsidering some of her attitudes and opinions, on homosexuality or Jewishness, for example (her son Chip marries a Jewish physician) – and in 'correcting' them to some extent" (Kubik 145). When Enid adjusts the moral and social standards she valued during her marriage, she finds a new approach to interpersonal relationships and is able to enjoy them without moral constraints. Concerning the relationship to her three children Enid's social life significantly improves when she ceases to force her rigid moral standards upon them. It becomes obvious that it was Alfred who prejudiced Enid against alternative lifestyles when she attends the wedding of her elder son with his seven months pregnant wife of Jewish descent:

And it didn't make her proud of herself, it didn't make her feel good about her nearly fifty years of marriage, to think that if Alfred had been with her at the wedding, she *would* have found fault and she *would* have condemned. If she'd been sitting beside Alfred, the crowd bearing down on her would surely have seen the sour look on her face and turned away, would surely not have lifted her and her chair off the ground and carried her around the room while klezmer music played, and she would surely not have loved it. The sorry fact seemed to be that life without Alfred in the house was better for everyone but Alfred. (598)

As much as Alfred suffers, Enid profits from his institutionalization, the consequence of his multiple diseases. Even Alfred's death after two years in the nursing home is narrated as a positive event inspiring hope in Enid, not grief: "And yet when he was dead, when she'd pressed her lips to his forehead and walked out with Denise and Gary into the warm spring night, she felt that nothing could kill her hope now, nothing. She was seventy-five and she was going to make some changes in her life" (601). Enid's unabated optimism and her working class background contrast sharply with Olive Kitteridge's pessimism and her middle class lifestyle. Nevertheless, both characters belong to the same generation and share the experience of the institutionalization of their impaired husbands.

Elizabeth Strout's Olive Kitteridge

The protagonist of Elizabeth Strout's Pulitzer Price-winning novel is presented as a highly impulsive and unpredictable character. Despite Olive's confrontational behavior (122), she and her husband Henry are married till death does them part. The couple remains healthy into their late sixties. During the first months after Henry closed his pharmacy he tries to resume the intimacy of the early years of their marriage:

One day he brought back with him a bunch of flowers. "For my wife," he'd said, handing them to her. They were the saddest damn things. Daisies dyed blue among the white and ludicrously pink ones, some of them half-dead.
"Put them in that pot," Olive said, pointing to an old blue vase. The flowers sat there on the wooden table in the kitchen. Henry came and put his arms around her; it was early autumn and chilly, and his woolen shirt smelled faintly of wood chips and mustiness. She stood, waiting for the hug to end. Then she went outside and planted her tulip bulbs. (145-46)

Not long after this incident Henry suddenly suffers a stroke which leaves him immobile in a wheelchair. Other than in *The Corrections*, in Strout's novel it is the caring spouse who has been the (verbal) aggressor in the family. While her husband is institutionalized as well, the emotional response of Olive Kitteridge to this situation is altogether different from Enid's reaction to Alfred's nursing home future.

Although their social environment is convinced that Henry does no longer "know where he is, or who is with him" (154), Olive spends most of her day in his nursing home. There she helps to care for his physical needs and tries to keep him company as good as possible. The stroke irreparably destroyed his abilities to communicate in any way (147), but he smiles all day. While Olive holds the hand of her spouse day after day, she reconsiders her relationship to this man once handsome and now "half-dead" (158). It is then that Olive realizes and shamefully regrets her coldness towards him (160): "What she minded now was how Henry had bought her those flowers. How she'd just stood there. She'd kept the flowers, dried them out, all the blue daisies brown now, bent over" (152). Olive's daily visits and her caring for him satisfy her need to compensate for her lifelong coldness towards Henry.

The incurable disease of her spouse is the starting point of a new line of action in the novel: The main character undergoes a process of self-reflection concerning her behavior in intimate relationships. From a psychological point of view the Kitteridge's style of love can be described in terms of 'storge.' According to the psychologists Hendrick and Hendrick, this term refers to a kind of "love as friendship. It is quiet and companionate" (153). Although Olive and

Henry are aware of each other's physical attractiveness (11, 158), they are only rarely intimate with each other. Hendrick and Hendrick claim that "[t]he fire of eros is alien to storge. Storge has sometimes been dubbed 'love by evolution' rather than 'love by revolution'" (153). Companionate love can be understood as "the affection we feel for those with whom our lives are deeply entwined" (Hatfield and Walster 9). For a long lasting marriage likes Olive's and Henry's this finding reflects a common phenomenon. When Driscoll et al. conducted a study of dating and newlywed college students, they found that most couples experienced romantic, passionate love only within the early stages of their relationships. If their relationships continued and deepened, the subjects reported that their feelings became less passionate and more companionate. According to social psychologists, passionate love is characterized by its fragility, while long lasting relationships depend on the stability of companionate love. This lets the lasting of the Kitteridge's marriage seem plausible, despite the fact that both spouses suffered from passionate, extramarital love interests in co-workers. Both Olive and Henry always considered leaving the other "unthinkable" (26). Although both spouses realized their partner's lovesickness (21, 29), they never spoke about this subject.

At the age of seventy-two and after four years of caring for her husband (215), Olive reflects on her past extramarital desires and feels

glad she'd never left Henry. She'd never found a friend so loyal, as kind, as her husband. And yet, [. . .] she remembered how in the midst of it all there had been times when she'd felt a loneliness so deep that once, not so many years ago, having a cavity filled, the dentist's gentle turning of her chin with his soft fingers had felt to her like a tender kindness of almost excruciating depth, and she had swallowed with a groan of longing, tears springing to hear eyes. (224)

As a vicarious satisfaction for this longing Olive used food throughout her adult life (62, 95, 107, 110, and 168). At the onset of old age Olive's high consume of pastries and other fat-rich foods leads to a large weight gain (62) which makes her feel like a "fat, dozing seal" (62) and later on like a "whale" (261). After Henry's stroke she adds to the "comfort of food" (62) her tending for him as a substitute for her suppressed romantic and erotic wants.

Since Henry already lives in a nursing home, Olive does not suffer the stress typical in caregiving relatives who are solely responsible for a physically and cognitively disabled partner (Wells and Kendig 667). However, Olive suffers from grief about Henry's condition and her growing social isolation (Ott, Sanders and Kelber 803). While she had trouble all her life to cultivate friendships, Henry was the outgoing and popular part of the couple (73). Gone with him is the high social capital Olive benefitted from throughout her marriage and her loneliness becomes a daily ordeal (215): "Satisfaction of the need to belong is associated with subjective well-being, happiness, and positive affects in general. When individuals experience deprivation in belongingness, they are more prone to experiencing negative affect, depression, loneliness, and anxiety" (Stevens, Martina and Westerhof 496). Although Henry is no longer able to act as a loving spouse, his physical presence and the memories of their intimate relationship can satisfy Olive's need of belonging to some extent. This is highlighted in a morbid competition between Olive and a neighbor, the socially isolated mother of the murderer of a local girl. This neighbor claims that she and her incarcerated son 'live for each other,' while Olive's husband does not even recognize his wife, and their son Christopher fails to show proper interests in his parents (154, 156, 159, 168).

Why does Olive continue to love a spouse who is barely recognizable as his former self (Vincent 156)? The philosopher Simon May identifies the most important stimulus of love as the feeling of "ontological rootedness." This feeling conveys a sense of life as not only being rooted in the present but also as being solid and valid:

My suggestion is that we will love only those (very rare) people or things or ideas or disciplines or landscapes that can inspire in us a promise of ontological rootedness. If they can, we will love them regardless of their other qualities: regardless of how beautiful they are; how (in the case of people we love) generous or altruistic or compassionate; of how interested in our life and projects. And, regardless, even, of whether they value us. For love's overriding concern is to find a home for our life and being. (May 6)

So, despite the fact that Henry is unable to respond to Olive, she draws her sense of belonging from his need for her care and attention. Thus the bond developed in a marriage helps not only to provide care for a partner with irreversible cognitive impairment but can also satisfy the need of belonging within the caring spouse.

On a permanent basis neither her dog nor the long distance phone calls from her son or Henry's physical presence suffice to satisfy Olive's desire for intimacy. In the course of her increasing social isolation she develops a routine of long walks with her dog early in the morning to fight the depressive symptoms resulting from her loneliness. Ott, Sanders, and Kelber state a high prevalence of depression in dementia caregivers (805). When Henry finally dies in the nursing home, her only sorrow is that those walks might contribute to her own longevity, for she longs for nothing but a quick death (253).

The risk of depression due to social isolation in caregiving relatives after bereavement is increased for women for two years after the death of their spouse (Utz, Caserta, and Lund 461). In an attempt to evade the hand-holding, elderly couples on her walks in the "gorgeous" springtime, Olive goes to bed with the sun (259). Additionally she feels neglected by her only married friend Bunny who seems to treat her "as though Olive's widowhood was a contagious disease" (257). The comparison hints towards the negative image of the widow in traditional patriarchic societies: Being likely to suffer from poor financial maintenance and the loss of her social status as being solely based on the reputation of the husband the widow is believed to bring ill luck (Ryle 159). Although in the narrated present, the era of President Bush Jr., a woman's reputation does no longer depend on her husband only and Olive is widely respected for her own career as a math teacher, she nevertheless experiences the loss of her husband not only as a loss of her role as a spouse, but also as a diminishment of her social status. Referring to Ryle, Olive's self-perception reflects the maintenance of the centrality of institutions such as marriage to the status of women, as well as the ways in which social inequalities are intensified for women in old age (159).

Olive's depressing routine is disturbed when one day she comes across Jack Kennison, a man her own age suffering from bereavement of his spouse as well (255). Olive finds him lying on the ground, probably due to a heart attack, and accompanies him to a doctor. A week after this event Olive realizes on her lonely early-morning walk by the river "that the time spent in the waiting room while Jack Kennison saw the doctor had, for one brief moment, put her back into life. And now she was out of life again" (257). Although she had already tried several forms of volunteer work (257-58) and actively pursues gardening as a hobby, none of this could inspire in her the hope of belonging like the spontaneous assistance she provided for Jack Kennison.

The widow and the widower begin to invite each other via telephone to walks, dinners, at each other's house and concerts. After one and a half years of mourning (252) Olive is both curious and afraid to get involved with a new partner again. She fears not only to see the reflection of her diminished physical attractiveness in the eyes of Jack, but also the feelings that come with being in love again (261). What keeps Olive's fear of insufficiency at bay is Jack's psychosomatic weakness resulting from the bereavement (261). Although she is familiar with these expressions of grief, Olive silently criticizes Jack for his weakness. Nevertheless, and other than Henry, Jack inspires a desire for romantic love and erotic interaction in Olive she believed to have overcome in old age:

She didn't tell Bunny how they had supper again the next week, how he kissed her on her cheek when she said good night, how they went to Portland to go to a concert, and that night he lightly kissed her mouth! No, these were not things to be spoken of; it was nobody's business. And certainly nobody's business that she lay awake at the age of seventy-four and thought about his arms around her, pictured what she had not pictured or done in years. (261-62)

Although Olive is tempted by Jack's blue eyes (253) and his affectionateness, he also seems to represent everything that is alien to Olive: Jack is a wealthy, white

Republican with a degree from Harvard and a strong bias against his daughter's homosexuality (266). Those discrepancies lead to a fight and the fragile relationship nearly fails due to Olive's unwillingness to accept attitudes different from her own. At the same time she is jealous and feels "like a schoolgirl whose crush had walked off with a different girl" (268). In this passage the comparison of the feelings of the seventy-four-year old protagonist with a dismissed schoolgirl is especially interesting. While it relates to the high intensity of feelings of somebody inexperienced in matters of love and intimate relationships, the comparison also rejects the stereotype of erotic passion "naturally" soothed by old age. The internal focalization of the narrator provokes the reader's realization that "[d]esire or love know no age" (Bureu Ramos 17).

According to Traupmann and Hatfield, the need for intimacy is part of a larger developmental task, namely that of achieving a sense of self while establishing close, fruitful relations with others (265). Olive accomplishes this task when she misses Jack so much after the fight that she sends him an email at midnight (267). The computer-mediated communication seems to have a couple of benefits for Olive: She is able to overcome her inhibitions and get back in contact with Jack, because the inhibition threshold of email-contact seems to be lower than in face to face communication or telephone calls. The process of writing an email gives her more time to think about the things she actually wants to tell him. Jack accepts Olive's insinuated apology of her past behavior towards him and invites her to his home.

When Olive visits his home, Jack is resting on his bed, feeling emotionally poor. Against the laws of physical attractiveness discussed in part one of this essay, Olive's indulgence in her passion for Jack is stimulated by his loneliness, vulnerability, his fear and her memory that "Jack in the doctor's office, had needed her, had given her a place in the world" (269). In this paragraph the traditional sex-role norms, which mandate that men should initiate sexual activity while women should control or resist these initiatives (Byers and Wang 215), are challenged. In contrast to stereotypes of men as aggressive and women as passive in regard to sexual encounters, Jack (passively) encourages Olive to take the first step. When Olive lies down next to Jack she pursues the active role in their first sexual encounter (269).

According to Traupmann and Hatfield, the sexual satisfaction senior women experience with their partners remains a strong, significant component of the overall satisfaction with their intimate relationships (267). Intimacy is not only the necessary requirement for the satisfaction people experience in their intimate relationships; it also is positively related to their mental and physical health (265). With an increase in happiness and satisfaction in senior citizen's relationships, Traupmann and Hatfield found a decrease in the number of their symptoms of depression, anxiety, and self-consciousness (267).

The sexual act of Olive and Jack is solely narrated from Olive's point of view. The narration focuses not so much on sexual pleasure, but on the meaning of sex as a life-affirming act of human interaction. This experience deepens not only her relationship to Jack Kennison, but brings Olive also back in contact with long suppressed feelings: While she is grateful for the love of her present lover, in retrospect, it saddens Olive that she had not made love to her husband many years before his stroke (269-70). The novel ends with Olive's final realization

that lumpy, aged, and wrinkled bodies were as needy as their own young, firm ones, that love was not to be tossed away carelessly, as if it were a tart on a platter with others that got passed around again. No, if love was available, one chose it, or didn't choose it. And if her platter had been full with the goodness of Henry and she had found it burdensome, had flicked it off crumbs at a time, it was because she had not known what one should know: that day after day was unconsciously squandered. (270)

CONCLUSION

In both novels the distribution of the roles of caregiver and patient is clearly gendered. According to Kubik, this is related to the social custom that women marry older men and the higher life expectancy of women (137). While both novels feature elderly married couples struggling with serious diseases, there are huge differences concerning the foundation of their relationships, the concepts of erotic love and the understanding of gender roles.

While the female protagonists of the novels undergo a character development caused by the diseases of their husbands, their emotional responses to their situations differ greatly: Enid's quality of life increases tremendously due to her freedom from Alfred's authority and the rapprochement to her previously estranged children. Olive's quality of life decreases due to the loss of her loving husband and the emotional detachment of her only son. Nevertheless, both novels are stories which have a happy ending concerning the female protagonists. While Enid's hope is inspired by the death of her patriarchic husband, Olive finds a new love.

As examples of contemporary American literature, both novels convey an image of old age that does not affirm stereotypes about the elderly. In the narrated worlds of *Olive Kitteridge* and *The Corrections*, disease and old age do not preempt the experience of romantic love. In fact, the ability to experience romantic love is reserved for characters with diseases that impair cognitive capacities. Since the male characters Alfred and Henry suffer from permanent cognitive impairment, they are bereaved of the capacity to engage actively in a loving relationship. They serve as mute love objects for their wives. Enid and

Olive's minor physical and mental problems – by comparison with their husbands – are not treated before their husbands' institutionalization or death, respectively. Beforehand they were consumed by caring tasks or taken in completely by depression. It is the absence of their husbands that stirs a new perception of themselves and finally gives them self-confidence. The end of their unhappy marriages inspires new hope and – in Olive's case – is even followed by a new relationship in old age.

Especially in *Olive Kitteridge* the physical disease and frailty of Jack do not prevent, but finally encourage Olive's love interest in him. With the romance between Jack and Olive a positively connoted example of love in old age is narrated in Strout's novel that even goes beyond positive stereotyping of the old. The two books are examples of American literature that show that erotic love, old age and illness are far from being mutually exclusive. In the form of the characters Jack and Olive, the reader meets an old couple who despite their decreased physical attractiveness – in relation to Western social standards – is happily in love.

REFERENCES

Annesley, James. "Market Corrections: Jonathan Franzen and the Novel of Globalization." *Journal of Modern Literature* 29.x2 (2006): 111-28. Print.

Bureu Ramos, Nela: "Introduction: The Aching of Desire." *Flaming Embers. Literary Testimonies on Ageing and Desire*. Ed. Nela Bureu Ramos. Bern: Peter Lang, 2010. 7-22. Print.

Byers, E. Sandra, and Adrienne Wang. "Understanding Sexuality in Close Relationships from Social Exchange Perspective." *The Handbook of Sexuality in Close Relationships*. Ed. John H. Harvey, Amy Wenzel, and Susan Sprecher. New Jersey: Lawrence Erlbaum Associates, 2004. 203-34. Print.

Davis, Murray S. *Smut. Erotic Reality/Obscene Ideology*. Chicago: U of Chicago P, 1983. Print.

Domínguez Rué, Emma. "A Woman's Worth: Perceptions of Desire in Mature Women in Ellen Glasgow's Short Fiction." *Flaming Embers. Literary Testimonies on Ageing and Desire*. Ed. Nela Bureu Ramos. Bern: Peter Lang, 2010. 23-38. Print.

Driscoll, Richard, Keith E. Davis, and Milton E. Lipetz. "Parental Interference and Romantic Love: The Romeo and Juliet Effect." *Journal of Personality and Social Psychology* 24 (1972): 1-10. Print.

Featherstone, Mike, and Mike Hepworth. "Images of Aging." *Encyclopedia of Gerontology*. Vol. 1 (A-K). 2nd ed. Ed. James E. Birren. Amsterdam, San Diego: Academic Press, 2007. 735-42. Print.

Fiedler, Leslie A. "Eros and Thanatos, or, the Mythic Aetiology of the Dirty Old Man." *Salmagundi: A Quarterly of the Humanities and Social Sciences* 3 (1977). 3-19. Print.

Fischer, David H. *Growing Old in America*. Oxford: Oxford UP, 1978. Print.

Franzen, Jonathan. *The Corrections*. New York: Picador USA, 2001. Print.

Greene, Bryan S. *Gerontology and the Construction of Old Age*. With a new Introduction by Roberta R. Greene, Robert G. Blundo. New Jersey: Transaction Publ., 2009 (1993). Print.

Grewe-Volpp, Christa. "Jonathan Franzen, 'The Corrections'." *Novels: Part I. Teaching Contemporary Literature and Culture*. Ed. Susanne Peters, Klaus Stiersdorfer, Laurenz Volkmann. Trier: wvt, 2008. 207-25. Print.

Haber, Carol. "Geriatrics: A Specialty in Search of Specialists." *Old Age in Bureaucratic Society*. Ed. David Dirck van Tassel, Peter N. Stearns. New York: Greenwood, 1986. 66-84. Print.

Hatfield, Elaine, and G. William Walster. *A New Look at Love*. Reading, Mass.: Addison-Wesley, 1978. Print.

Hendrick, Clyde, and Susan S. Hendrick. "Styles of Romantic Love." *The New Psychology of Love*. Ed. Robert J. Sternberg and Karin Weis. New Haven, London: Yale UP, 2006. 149-70. Print.

Henss, Ronald. *"Spieglein, Spieglein an der Wand..." Geschlecht, Alter und physische Attraktivität*. Weinheim: Psychologie Verlag Union, 1992. Print.

Hopkins, Christopher D., Catherine A. Roster, and Charles M. Wood. "Making the Transition to Retirement." *Journal of Consumer Marketing* 23.2 (2006): 87-99. Print.

Kubik, Andreas. "Gender, Aging and Spirituality in 'The Corrections'. Gerontological and Theological Observations." *Geschlecht – Generation – Alter(n)*. Ed. Hella Ehlers, Gabriele Linke, Beate Rudlof, Heike Trappe. Berlin: Lit Verlag, 2011. 133-48. Print.

Lee, John Alan. *The Colors of Love: An Exploration of the Ways of Loving*. Don Mills, Ontario: New P, 1976. Print.

Lewis, Clive S. *The Allegory of Love: A Study in Medieval Tradition*. Repr. London: Oxford UP, 1973 (1936). Print.

May, Simon: *Love. A History*. New Haven, London: Yale UP, 2012. Print.

Meyer, Uwe. "'My libido [. . .] has always been quite normal': Love and Sexuality Among the Elderly in the Works of Alan Isler." *Old Age and Ageing in British and American Culture and Literature*. Ed. Christa Jahnson. Münster: Lit Verlag, 2004. 197-211. Print.

Ott, Carol H., Sara Sanders, and Sheryl T. Kelber: "Grief and Personal Growth Experience of Spouses and Adult-Child Caregivers of Individuals with Alzheimer's Disease and Related Dementias." *The Gerontologist* 47.6 (2007): 789-809. Print.

Ovid. "Philemon and Baucis." *Metamorphoses. A new Translation by A.D. Melville*. Oxford: Oxford UP, 1998 (1986): 190-93. Print.

Roth, Philip. *The Dying Animal*. London: Vintage, 2002. Print.

Ryle, Robin. *Questioning Gender: A Sociological Exploration*. Thousand Oaks, London: Pine Forge Press, 2012. Print.

Singh, Devendra, and Young, Robert K. "Body Weight, Waist-to-Hip Ratio, Breasts and Hips: Role in Judgments of Female Attractiveness and Desirability for Relationships." *Ethology and Sociobiology* 16 (1995): 483-507. Print.

Stevens, Nan L., Camille M. S. Martina, and Gerben J. Westerhof. "Meeting the Need to Belong: Predicting Effects of a Friendships Enrichment Program for Older Women." *The Gerontologist* 46.4 (2006): 495-502. Print.

Strout, Elizabeth. *Olive Kitteridge*. London: Pocket, 2008. Print.

Teicher, Craig Morgan. "Author Profile: Maine Idea." *Publishers Weekly* (February 4, 2008): 32. Print.

Traupmann, Jane and Elaine Hatfield. "Love and Its Effect on Mental and Physical Health." *Aging: Stability and Change in the Family*. Ed. Robert William Fogel, James G. March. San Diego: Academic Press, 1981. 253-74. Print.

Toal, Catherine. "Contemporary American Melancholy." *Journal of European Studies* 33. 3-4 (2003): 305-22. Print.

Utz, Rebecca L., Michal Caserta, and Dale Lund. "Grief, Depressive Symptoms, and Physical Health among Recently Bereaved Spouses." *The Gerontologist* 52.4 (2012): 460-71. Print.

Vincent, John. *Old Age*. London and New York: Routledge, 2003. Print.

Wells, Yvonne D., and Hal L. Kendig."Health and Well-Being of Spouse Caregivers and the Widowed." *The Gerontologist* 37.5 (1997): 666-74. Print.

Wiltshire, John. "Biography, Pathography and the Recovery of Meaning." *The Cambridge Quarterly* 29.4 (2000): 409-22. Print.

Uncanny Witnessing

Dementia, Narrative, and Identity in Fiction
by Munro and Franzen

Amelia DeFalco

In his personal essay documenting his father's struggle with Alzheimer's disease, Jonathan Franzen explains the necessity of his narrative intervention: "This was his disease," he writes. "It was also, you could argue, his story. But you have to let me tell it" (*How to Be Alone* 11). Franzen's remarks invoke the widely held connection between lives and stories, the idea that, "[t]o be a person is to have a story. More than that, it is to *be* a story" (Kenyon and Randall 1). Annette Kuhn reiterates this association in her own family memoir, claiming that "[t]elling stories about the past, our past, is a key moment in the making of our selves" (2). But this theoretical truism, the belief that identity is based on, if not comprised wholly of, narrative, becomes problematic for those who are alienated from narrative and narration by illness and disability. Recent fiction by Alice Munro and Jonathan Franzen depicts the repercussions of dementia for subjectivity and narrative, exploring characters' struggles with conventions of selfhood altered by cognitive disability. These fictional narratives posit an evolution of the role of witnesses, transformed from observers to participants, forced to grapple with new modes of meaning and being. These fictional representations of dementia suggest the precariousness of collaborations between givers and receivers of care, and the risks to self-involved in witnessing the transformation of an intimate into an uncanny stranger. My use of the term draws upon Freud's famous exploration of the uncanny as "that class of the frightening which leads back to what is known of old and long familiar" (340). In Freud's eponymous essay, the uncanny is the resurfacing of buried beliefs, of that which is deeply "known" but repressed. It is not merely the strangeness of an event or experience that generates its uncanniness, but the degree to which it disturbs and dredges up something submerged within the psyche.

The uncanny is at once strange and all-too-familiar.[1] In Munro's and Franzen's fictional interpretations of the condition, dementia's destruction of memory, language and narrative is a destabilization of the apparatus of identity that introduces both the afflicted and their caregivers to uncanny selfhood.

1. Narrative, Identity and the Uncanny

The narrativity of human lives is the effect of human temporality. As Paul Ricoeur explains, narrative and time form a hermeneutic circle in which "time becomes human time to the extent that it is organized after the manner of narrative; narrative, in turn, is meaningful to the extent that it portrays the features of temporal experience" (*Time* 3, 3). As a result of this hermeneutic concomitance, human beings recognize and know their lives, their "selves," in and through narrative. This narrativity of selfhood often becomes more and more prominent as one ages since as one accumulates time, one inevitably accumulates narratives. Indeed, the psychological theory of "life review" is posited on the assumption that aging into old age involves sifting through one's many stories of self, a practice of reassessment and analysis that reaffirms popular associations of old age with summing up.[2]

As both Munro and Franzen demonstrate, in later life, illusions of singular identity, of true "core" selves[3] and reliable, teleological life narratives often begin to unravel as the temporality and resultant mutability of subjectivity be-

---

1 | In Freud's oft-repeated description (itself a reiteration of the work of Friedrich Schelling), the "uncanny is in reality nothing new or alien, but something which is familiar and old-established in the mind and which becomes alienated from it only through the process of repression" (363-64). It is here, I argue, that aging and human temporality intersect with Freud's theory of the uncanny: as one ages into old age, human mutability is precisely that "which ought to have remained hidden but has come to light" (Freud 364).

2 | Robert Butler's seminal article on the practice of life review, which he calls a "naturally occurring, universal mental process" (66), echoes other psychological models, including Erik Erikson's, in its characterization of later life as a time of summation and integration. For a more recent description of life review see Garland and Garland. For an insightful critique of the life review model, see Kathleen Woodward's "Telling Stories."

3 | Descriptions of underlying essential selves abound in aging studies scholarship. Though interpretations of the inner/outer division differ, some notion of a "core" self largely untouched by exterior conditions of aging repeatedly appears as a way of maintaining continuity and integrity in the face of oppressive cultural scripts of decline, and the increasing "inability of the body to adequately represent the inner self" (Featherstone and Wernick 7). See, for example, Biggs, Esposito, Gullette, Hepworth, Kaufman.

come increasingly apparent. In this essay, I explore later-life dementia as a kind of limit test of difference and identity by examining fictional representations of this devastating condition of radical transformation. In these narratives of late-life dementia, aging into old age brings disturbing changes that cannot be contained by facades of permanence. Narrative-based ontologies, such as those described above, imply that selfhood is undermined, if not ruined by dementia: if having a life and making a self relies on storing and shaping stories, many victims of dementia are excluded from living or being themselves. These fictional narratives suggest that dementia may complicate assumptions about "identity" and "selfhood," shifting attention from discrete selves to collaborative relationships. As Munro's stories, "The Bear Came Over the Mountain" and "Spelling," along with Franzen's novel, *The Corrections*, suggest, dementia's transformation of communication and identity tests human structures of meaning and being, revealing both the limits of understanding, and what lies beyond.

2. Dementia and Collaborative Identity

The subjective experience of dementia, particularly in its late stages, remains largely unknown since the condition destroys precisely those tools necessary to produce a coherent life story.[4] What do exist, however, are narratives by the survivors of dementia. Stories in both memoirs and fiction[5] from the point of

---

4 | I have come across a few first-person accounts of Alzheimer's disease: *Losing My Mind: An Intimate Look at Life with Alzheimer's* by Thomas DeBaggio and *My Journey into Alzheimer's Disease* by Robert Davis. The latter includes material written by the author's wife, Betty, continuing the trend of witnesses speaking for the afflicted.

5 | There are a number of nonfictional memoirs written by witnesses. A sampling of titles includes: *Remind Me Who I Am, Again* by Linda Grant, *The House on Beartown Road: A Memoir of Learning and Forgetting* by Elizabeth Cohen, *The Story of My Father* by Sue Miller, *Dancing on Quicksand: A Gift of Friendship in the Age of Alzheimer's* by Marilyn Mitchell, and *Do You Remember Me?: A Father, a Daughter, and a Search for the Self* by Judith Levine. Even novels that attempt to give readers an inside view, as it were, of the disease can only go so far. The final stages of dementia may be beyond the reach of representation or imagination. Novels such as Mordecai Richler's *Barney's Version*, Jonathan Franzen's *The Corrections*, and Jeffrey Moore's *The Memory Artists*, which present compelling self-portraits of dementia in fiction narrated or focalized by victims of the condition, are unable to continue this fictional conceit into the later stages of the disease. The deterioration of language skills is an insurmountable obstacle to narrative communication. In all of these instances the narration is taken over by a caregiving child. Interestingly in all three cases it is a son that provides the primary

view of caregivers speak to the ethical crises provoked by the condition, the difficulty of bearing witness and assisting a person who often cannot acknowledge, or perhaps even tolerate one's help. The impossible yet necessary task of accompanying victims through the alarming disorder of their memory introduces caregivers in painfully real terms to the exhausting demands of ethical responsibility. This is the responsibility of the witness who must, like the psychoanalyst, retain the sufferer's narrative with the hope of returning it to him or her, a gift the sufferer can rarely acknowledge or even accept. Such disability tests the limits of witnessing and testimonial – how does one listen ethically when the sufferer is no longer able to testify?

Later-life dementia often forces the witness into a position of interpreter; merely listening becomes inadequate when the victim can no longer use language to tell stories [6] and at such a point caregivers may provide testimony victims can no longer formulate. As Franzen reminds his readers, it is his father's story, but we must let the son tell it. In other words, Franzen acknowledges how later-life dementia may disrupt the distinct categories of witness and other. The witness can become a medium, but often an originating speaker as well, forced to repair and even create narratives that have been damaged or erased. The

---

(narrative) care, regardless of the sex of the victim. The texts discussed in this essay reveal a continuation of this trend, men caring for afflicted loved ones, both male and female, the only exception being Alice Munro's "Spelling." The preponderance of male caregivers and the possibility that dementia adjusts gender roles is an issue I return to in the essay's conclusion.

6 | The problem posed by subjects unable to tell their stories has been considered by many critics. In particular, trauma theorists, such as Shoshona Felman, Dori Laub, Cathy Caruth and Dominick LaCapra, have theorized the complicated interrelationship of witnessing and testimonial, empathy and identification. Though there are important distinctions between trauma and dementia, there are similarities in the symptoms of trauma and dementia: involuntary repetition, confusion, hallucination, and of course, memory loss. Both conditions inhibit communication and result in the disappearance of memories that may re-emerge unexpectedly, though this is more likely in cases of psychological trauma. Though there can be no "survivors" of Alzheimer's, testimony remains important, the responsibility of witnessing transferred onto caregivers, who are often family members, typically spouses or children of the afflicted. Traditional efforts at witnessing trauma involve "facing loss," those losses too horrific for comprehension that refuse to inhabit the past, persisting instead as ghosts that haunt the victim. For victims of dementia and their caregivers, loss is a continual process and the future can promise only further debilitation and disappearance. Dementia often produces what Felman labels the "involuntary witness: witness to a trauma, to a crime or to an outrage; witness to a horror or an illness whose effects explode any capacity for explanation or rationalization" (emphasis in original, "Introduction" 4).

opportunities for communication and understanding in cases of dementia are seriously diminished. But as Munro and Franzen demonstrate, it is these very difficulties that may increase the potential for, or even enforce ethical insight in the caregiver.

Because of the typically collaborative nature of narratives of dementia – nonfictional and fictional – potential exists for the afflicted to be more than simply a stranger, more than a pathological object bereft of his or her narrativizing autonomy. An ethical, empathetic collaboration can reveal the afflicted as in fact an uncanny subject, an exaggerated embodiment of difference, of radical impermanence that disturbs models of reliable identity. In the fictional texts I explore below, uncanniness is not confined to the sufferers of dementia. "The Bear Came Over the Mountain," "Spelling," and *The Corrections* depict characters confronting the paradoxical knowledge that, as temporal subjects, they are *all* perpetually other than they were, other, even, than they are. In the stories and the novel, compulsory interaction, dependence and responsibility repeatedly undermine individualism, forcing sufferers and their witnesses to reorient themselves within unfamiliar structures of relating and being. Munro's stories suggest that adaptation to the demands of dementia requires a willingness to tolerate, and even accept alterity in both others and the self, while Franzen's novel depicts the failure of adaptation. In *The Corrections*, characters are unable to tolerate difference in others or themselves, a rejection that exacerbates their experiences of alienation and exile. In these fictional accounts, dementia provides dramatic lessons on uncanny identity. Not only is there the obvious uncanniness of the victim whose deteriorated memory produces a frightening strangeness, but there is often self-revelation for the witness who comes to recognize his or her own otherness in the process of collaboration with the afflicted.

3. Care, Collaboration and Ethical Insight

In Munro's 2001 short story "The Bear Came Over the Mountain" (*Hateship*), popularized by Sarah Polley's 2006 film adaptation, *Away From Her*, the onset of dementia disrupts the relationship of an older couple, Fiona and Grant. Institutionalized near the beginning of the story, Fiona's subjectivity remains unavailable to the reader as the narrative oscillates between present and past, between Grant's struggle to comprehend Fiona's altered identity and his ignorance of her experience of their shared past. Through these temporal shifts we learn that Grant is a retired professor of Anglo-Saxon and Nordic Literature, that he had several rather tempestuous affairs with students, that the couple lived in Fiona's parents' house where they led intellectual, reclusive lives. We learn little of Fiona herself in the depictions of the past, which are mostly focalized through Grant. Grant's knowledge of his wife is significantly limited and we find that he has tended to think of Fiona as delightfully foreign, as a dynamic but mysterious being. The scenes from the past expose how Grant has relied on his perception of Fiona's persistent otherness to justify his betrayals, regarding her as a delightfully opaque object, denying her subjectivity in order to indulge his own transgressive desires. Grant discards any possibility of obligation to this other, but Fiona's dementia forces a new engagement with responsibility.[7] In this story, dementia provokes an unexpected call to awareness and responsibility at odds with Grant's history of carelessness and infidelity. Grant's past lacks any evidence of ethical insight or empathetic response. It is only Fiona's dementia, which exaggerates unfamiliarity to a staggering degree, that forces Grant to finally confront alterity, both the otherness of other people and the otherness of the self.

The inclusion of multiple incidents remembered from Grant's past relationship with his wife attests to his ongoing assessment of Fiona as invariably and fetchingly opaque. Grant accepts Fiona's spontaneous proposal because "[h]e wanted never to be away from her. She had the spark of life" (275). Bewitched by her vitality, Grant accepts her subjectivity as entirely mysterious, often quaintly so. In fact this interpretation of Fiona, or more precisely this acceptance of her very *un*interpretability, provokes Grant to perceive her early signs of dementia, what the medical community terms "mild cognitive impairments," as signs of her enduring eccentricity. When Grant notices a proliferation of yellow notes stuck on cupboards and drawers, he sees an extension of her "mystifying and touching" tendency to write all sorts of things down, from book titles and errands to her domestic schedule (276). In fact, as Grant quickly learns, the yellow notes are Fiona's effort to attach signs to their referents; to forestall the disintegration of all connections between words and the everyday world around her, she must literally paste words onto objects. The labelling triggers Grant to recall "a story about the German soldiers on border patrol in Czechoslovakia during the war. Some Czech had told him that each of the patrol dogs wore a sign that said *Hund*. Why? Said the Czechs, and the Germans said, Because that is a *hund*" (276). The story groups Fiona's pathological symptoms with quirky, foreign behaviour, the bizarre traditions of strangers. Fiona has not so much *become* a stranger as been *revealed* as one, the exaggerated idiosyncratic actions distinguishing her as a foreigner.

When Fiona first moves to Meadowlake, an assisted-living facility, there is an imposed thirty-day separation, meant to allow her to adjust to her new environment. On his way to see her for the first time in a month, Grant feels as if

---

7 | According to Naomi Morgenstern, such revelations of responsibility are characteristic of Munro's stories, which "address the question of why it is that the ethical insight - that the other exists beyond the self - needs to be repeated" (72).

he is going to meet a "new woman." Fiona has been transformed into the "other woman," other than his wife, other than herself. The situation provokes Grant to novel gestures: he buys her flowers though "[h]e had never presented flowers to Fiona before. Or to anyone else" (287). Grant himself experiences an unsettling of self, feeling like a character "in a cartoon" (287), engaging in emotions and behaviour other than his own. Upon arrival at Meadowlake, he finds Fiona distinctly familiar yet strange: "He could not throw his arms around her. Something about her voice and smile, familiar as they were, something about the way she seemed to be guarding the players and even the coffee woman from him – as well as him from their displeasure – made that not possible" (289). The reference to Fiona's protective air suggests her position in a community unavailable to Grant, an exclusion that becomes increasingly obvious as the story continues. No longer permitted opportunities to participate in Fiona's life, Grant is consigned to the position of witness, forced to confront Fiona's alterity, a mysteriousness that is no longer quaint and far from comforting. But it is this enforced role of passive observer that arguably introduces Grant to a new ethical awareness, permitting him to acknowledge the incomprehensible subjectivity of the other along with otherness within the self.

In the past, Fiona had provided a useful other, that is, one that reinforced Grant's own selfhood. The disappearance of this stabilizing, benign other whose subjectivity Grant could easily efface disrupts Grant's own selfhood. When Kristy, a staff member at Meadowlake, asks him if he is "glad to see her participating and everything," Grant cannot respond directly, but rather answers with reference to himself: "Does she even know who I am?"(290). In a sense, Grant's question is his only possible response to Kristy's query since he is accustomed to locating himself via Fiona. Much of what follows in the story involves Grant's difficult observations of Fiona as a stranger, existing outside of any relation to himself. Though unable to recognize Grant as her husband, Fiona continues to exist as Fiona, as other, forcing Grant to glimpse his own insignificance.

Fiona's condition initiates an ironic reversal; as reluctant witness Grant comes to occupy the territory he had always reserved for others, in particular for women whom he has typically desired for their intoxicating strangeness. The assisted-living institution's ability to redefine normality thrusts Grant into exile as he can only witness Fiona and her friends from a distance. But normality depends on a majority's ability to exclude others, and an influx of the young and able-bodied on Meadowlake's visiting day reverses the ordinariness of the institutionalized: "And now surrounded by a variety of outsiders these insiders did not look like such regular people after all. Female chins might have had their bristles shaved to the roots and bad eyes might be hidden by patches or dark lenses, inappropriate utterances might be controlled by medication, but some glaze remained, a haunted rigidity – as if people were content to become memories of themselves, final photographs" (296). Newness, strangeness must be contained and hidden, resulting in haunted subjects, people fixed by the oppressive weight of the past. This passage includes the language of traces, of unsettling remainders that infiltrate reassuring facades. The references to haunting, memories, and photographs speak to the permeation of tenses, the failure of attempts to segment and isolate past and present selves. Despite attempts to impose a degree of fixity and conceal the effects of temporal identity, "some glaze remained." The insiders' new identities leave unsettling traces on the performed selves manufactured for the youthful visitors' benefit. In effect, the debilitations of old age transform subjects into imitations of themselves, often highly accurate copies, but copies nonetheless. The not-yet-old, or more specifically, the not-yet-afflicted-by-age, deny the otherness of human temporality by refusing to acknowledge the cohabitation of continuity and change. By opting for one or the other, they deny the more unsettling possibility of uncanny aging, of subjects, of selves, at once familiar and strange, the same and different. In forcing the Meadowlake residents to function as memories and photographs, their visitors deny the otherness of the other.

Grant comes to occupy a kind of liminal space, removed from both sides of the visitor/resident divide. He is privy to various performances in his role as witness. This alternate position facilitates a new ethical awareness in Grant. An ambiguously focalized passage describing the lives of the Meadowlake residents depicts such new insight:

People here – even the ones who did not participate in any activities but sat around watching the doors or looking out the windows – were living a busy life in their heads (not to mention the life of their bodies, the portentous shifts in their bowels, the stabs and twinges everywhere along the line), and that was a life that in most cases could not very well be described or alluded to in front of visitors. All they could do was wheel or somehow propel themselves and hope to come up with something that could be displayed or talked about. (297)

Here we glimpse the disconcerting abjection of old age. If we can detect something of Grant's perspective in this passage, then it is a transformed perspective, showing an emerging willingness to acknowledge the entirely incomprehensible, but nonetheless existent subjectivity of others.

At Meadowlake, Fiona forms a close bond with another resident, Aubrey, an intimacy that excludes her husband. Grant continues to visit his wife, but becomes an outsider, Fiona treating him "as some persistent visitor who took a special interest in her. Or perhaps even as a nuisance who must be prevented, according to her old rules or courtesy, from realizing that he was one. She treated him with a distracted, social sort of kindness" (291-92). So committed is Fiona to her new relationship that when Aubrey is taken home by his own wife she becomes despondent, eating little, barely moving, only "weeping weakly, on a bench by the wall" (306). In an effort to save Fiona from being moved to the second floor where she can get longterm bedcare, a floor reserved for "the people who [. . .] had really lost it" (298), Grant pays a visit to Aubrey and his wife, Marian, asking that Aubrey be allowed to return to Meadowlake, if only as a visitor. After some subtle negotiations and an implied offer of companionship, Aubrey is allowed to return. However, Fiona's allegiances have shifted once more and she rejects Aubrey as a stranger, rejoicing instead at Grant's return:

"I'm happy to see you," she said, and pulled his earlobes.
"You could have just driven away," she said. "Just driven away without a care in the world and forsook me. Forsooken me. Forsaken."
He kept his face against her white hair, her pink scalp, her sweetly shaped skull. He said, Not a chance. (322)

Even this scene of possible reconciliation bears the traces of unsettling strangeness. Though Fiona expresses a familiarity in her ambiguous manipulation of language, Grant is aware of unmistakable alteration, which his focalization associates with decay: "Her skin or her breath gave off a faint new smell, a smell that seemed to him like that of the stems of cut flowers left too long in their water" (321). The unpleasant *new* odour of decomposition coexists with the pleasant familiarity of her "sweetly shaped skull" (322). Though she "retrieve[s], with an effort, some bantering grace," her embrace alerts Grant to the undeniable changes of age. The story leaves us with a glimpse of alterity, the alterity of time manifested in aging, an intimation of radical impermanence.

In "The Bear Came Over the Mountain," later life compels a rereading of life stories that shows us the flexibility of interpretation, and consequently, of identity. Fiona's dementia demands not only rereading, but also a readjustment of expectations and allegiances, a new engagement with ethical responsibility. The process of aging into old age, complicated by Fiona's dementia, introduces Grant to a new awareness of responsibility that moves him to moments of ethical empathy in which he glimpses both his own strangeness, and the familiarity of the other. That is, he becomes fleetingly aware of the possibility of bridging the gap between absolute alterity and the violent containment of the "other's otherness with an economy of the same" (Morgenstern 72). This is what Richard Kearney calls "diacritical hermeneutics": the possibility of "intercommunion between distinct but not incomparable selves" (18). Diacritical hermeneutics depends on a fragile balancing of respect and recognition that introduces subjects to their own uncanniness, an acknowledgement of "strangers in ourselves and ourselves in strangers" (20). Such a precarious position may always be fleeting, but Munro's story shows us how aging and its difficulties, even its pathologies, can cause an often painful transformation of distinct, sturdy identity into murky uncanniness. Fiona's dementia introduces Grant to a new model of relating that provides the potential for ethical witnessing, for empathy and the appreciation of another's needs. Excluded from participation, Grant is forced to assume a role he has refused throughout his life, that of the witness whose job it is merely to listen and observe.

An earlier Munro story, "Spelling," also shows a preoccupation with ethical crises prompted by dementia. One of the final stories appearing in the 1978 collection *Who Do You Think You Are?*, "Spelling" concerns the protagonist, Rose, in middle age, newly responsible for her ailing and aged stepmother, Flo. When Rose returns to her childhood home she realizes the severity of Flo's disability: the house is jumbled and dirty and Flo has difficulty recognizing Rose as her stepdaughter. As well, Flo has developed some bizarre habits: the table is always set; she drinks maple syrup straight from the bottle. Rose's self-serving fantasies of devoted caregiving quickly dissolve as Flo's strangeness triggers the recollection of past narratives of frustration and disappointment, revealing Flo's difficult behaviour in old age as not a departure from, but a disturbing evolution of her character. Flo in the present is often obstinate and demanding to a pathological degree; Flo in the past was wilful, stubborn, and racist. As with Fiona, the afflicted other in "The Bear Came Over the Mountain," Flo's delusional old age modifies a longstanding strangeness, suggesting dementia as a pathological amplification of pre-existing otherness, an exaggeration that forces loved ones to acknowledge such otherness and adapt to its demands.

Rose first confronts the problem of responding to seemingly absolute otherness when she visits the County Home in preparation for Flo's institutionalization. There she meets a woman whom age has transformed into a kind of automated object, an encounter that leads to a revelation similar to that experienced by Grant in "The Bear Came Over the Mountain," a budding awe at the incomprehensible, yet undeniable personhood of those suffering the debilitations of old age and illness: "Taking in oxygen, giving out carbon dioxide, they continued to participate in the life of the world" ("Spelling" 226-27). Rose's visit to the County Home forces her to consider the otherness of persons seriously debilitated by aging, those who are unable to participate in the everyday world of language and movement.

The story's title refers to the only verbal communication still available to a woman Rose meets at the County Home, a communication that becomes an "expression of her humanity" (Redekop 140). "Crouched in her crib, diapered, dark as a nut, with three tufts of hair," the nameless old woman the nurse calls "Aunty," will spell out any word she hears (227). Infantilized and abject, "Aunty" continues to exist, to "participate in the life of the world," though hers is an incomprehensible existence spent "meandering through that emptiness or confusion that nobody on this side can do more than guess at" (228). Rose tries to imagine such an unusual relationship with language, how words might have a kind of foreign vitality to them, making each one seem "alive as a new animal," coming together to form a "parade of private visitors" (228). But this is only one of a list of possible subjectivities Rose imagines. The story's title – "Spelling" – points to the central importance of the scene and its exploration of the difficulties involved in interpreting personhood and subjectivity, and the prevailing tendency to associate identity with vivacious youth. Rose's witnessing of the spelling woman initiates an insight into otherness that makes possible a new kind of respect and communication that will appear in more detail in the story's conclusion.

The majority of "Spelling" shows Rose and Flo at odds, with very little suggestion of understanding or collaboration between the two women. They appear distant, almost strangers, each vaguely ashamed of the other. The story's final pages involve a sequence of scenes depicting failures of communication between Rose and Flo, but culminating in a scene in which the difficulties and demands of aging make possible a new kind of understanding, one able to incorporate miscommunication. The earlier depictions of frustrated communication show how the two women existed at loggerheads, each cocooned in her own resentful superiority. In one episode, the appearance of Rose's bared breast in a televised theatre performance inspires Flo to write a letter of admonishment. The letter does the opposite of communicating, becoming instead a testament to the pair's inability to comprehend one another. The message cannot bridge the gap between them, but rather draws attention to its great expanse, giving Rose a "fresh and overwhelming realization" of that "gulf" (231). Flo's sincere admonishment is so bewildering to Rose that it can only be understood as nonsense: "These reproaches of Flo's made as much sense as a protest about raising umbrellas, a warning against eating raisins" (231). As a result, Flo's letter becomes a kind of party trick for Rose who reads it aloud to her friends "for comic effect," a betrayal that transforms a supposed intimate – Rose's stepmother – into a figure of public mockery (230).

This narrative of Flo's indignation is followed by one in which the shaming is reversed, with Flo committing the humiliating offence. When Rose invites Flo to an award reception where she will be honoured, Flo's racist language exposes her small-town naiveté. "Look at the Nigger!" Flo cries upon glimpsing another award recipient (231): "Her tone was one of simple, gratified astonishment, as if she had been peering down the Grand Canyon or seen oranges growing on a tree" (231-32). The similes construct Flo's outburst as a reaction to something strange and remarkable, and it is this very reaction that ironically exposes Flo herself as exactly that. To the other ceremony attendees, the "bearded and beaded, the unisexual and the unashamedly un-Anglo-Saxon" (232), Flo is something strange, though perhaps more repellent than remarkable.

It is only within the altered circumstances of aging and dementia that the possibility of collaboration and understanding arises as Rose gains new ethical insight, as suggested in her reaction to the old spelling woman. In the story's final scene, a new communicative potential grows out of a shared appreciation of absurdity. When Rose brings one of Flo's old wigs to the County Home where Flo now lives, Flo mistakes the wig for a dead gray squirrel. Rose explains that the hairy thing is, in fact, a wig and the two begin to laugh. Rose looks at the wig and considers that it "did look like a dead cat or squirrel, even though she had washed and brushed it; it was a disturbing-looking object." Flo exclaims, "I thought what is she doing bringing me a dead squirrel! If I put it on somebody'd be sure to take a shot at me." Rose responds by sticking it on her own head to "continue the comedy, and Flo laughed so that she rocked back and forth in her crib" (232). The episode depicts a shared pleasure in slapstick, demonstrating the communicative potential of misunderstanding. Rose not only "humours" Flo's delusions by behaving according to the peculiar expectations of dementia, but also delights her with a comedic display that facilitates a shared pleasure previously unavailable to stepmother and stepdaughter. Rose's increasing openness to the incomprehensibility of the other produces a new experience of collaborative humour far from the comedy that appears earlier in the story when Rose mocks Flo's prudishness to her friends. The unexpected joke suggests that an ethical response may come as the result of an overturning of rational meaning and understanding transpires in moments of non-sense, such as "Aunty's" spelling, or Rose's slapstick. These moments of disrupted communication achieve an alternative form of dialogue, one that allows for a productive space between self and other. The moment of comedy is quickly followed by Flo's delusional references to her gallstones and dead husband:

When she got her breath Flo said, "What am I doing with these damn sides up on my bed? Are you and Brian behaving yourselves? Don't fight, it gets on your father's nerves. Do you know how many gallstones they took out of me? Fifteen! One as big as a pullet's egg. I got them somewhere. I'm going to take them home." She pulled at the sheets, searching. "They were in a bottle."
"I've got them already," said Rose. "I took them home."
"Did you? Did you show your father?"
"Yes."
"Oh, well, that's where they are then," said Flo, and she lay down and closed her eyes. (233)

The story ends here. Her nonsense is not mocked or even interpreted by Rose. The omniscient narrator's remarks are descriptive rather than interpretive: "She pulled at the sheets, searching [. . .] she lay down and closed her eyes." There is no indication that Rose directs the narration. Instead, we are given only her verbalized responses to Flo. By concluding with Flo's language and movements the story privileges incomprehensibility, depicting otherness without a narrator's interpretation or explanation. Not only has Rose taken on the role of witness, willing to listen to uninterpretable testimony, but we too as readers have been pulled toward Flo, fashioned by the narration into witnesses to what Felman calls the "scandal of illness," to the trauma of afflicted old age (Felman 4). Here we see ethical responsibility in action, a respect for otherness that causes Rose to participate in, rather than "correct," nonsense. It is here, in the uninterpreted language of delusion, that we glimpse the positive potential of empathetic witnessing, a dialogic model of relations in which understanding and misunderstanding can coexist.

In Munro's stories dementia diminishes the chasm between self and other by enforcing a subjectivity of exchange. This is counterintuitive since as the many victims of dementia know, and here I refer to both the afflicted and those who care for them, much of the pain of dementia comes from its alienating effect. The opportunities for communication and understanding are seriously diminished. But, as these stories suggest, those afflicted by dementia, in their exaggerated otherness, demand an inexhaustible responsibility and caregivers experience in everyday terms the difficulty, often the impossibility, of responding to the basic obligations that the other represents. Levinas stresses such power imbalances in his theorization of ethics, arguing that ethical relations rely on a "hostaging" of the self to the other: "It is through the condition of being hostage that there can be in the world pity, compassion, pardon and proximity – even the little there is, even the simple 'After you, sir.' The unconditionality of being hostage is not the limit case of solidarity, but the condition for all solidarity" (*Otherwise* 17). Unsettling the "ontological primacy of the meaning of being" (Levinas and Kearney 23), Levinas posits one's obligation to the other as fundamental and all-encompassing. In "The Bear Came Over the Mountain" and "Spelling," later-life dementia has such a rattling effect, enforcing an experience of subordination with ontological implications for both witnesses and sufferers.

Levinas is not alone in emphasizing obligation as primary to humanity, though not all moral philosophers cast responsibility in such severe terms. There is a substantial body of criticism that regards care as a fundamental human need, privileging caring relations as primary, sustaining, and fulfilling. Theorists of the ethics of care, such as Virginia Held, Eva Kittay, Carol Gilligan, and Maurice Hamington, stress that life itself is founded upon caring human relations, insisting that identity is first and foremost relational and dependent. The "hostaging," burdensome obligation that Levinas describes is recast as the source of humanity and meaning. Held describes "persons as embedded and encumbered" (15), drawing on Gilligan's explication of the "paradoxical truths of human experience – that we know ourselves as separate only insofar as we live in connection with others, and that we experience relationships only insofar as we differentiate other from self" (Gilligan 63). As Held, Gilligan and others point out, such "encumbered-ness" is too easily overlooked or dismissed in a culture that privileges independence and individuality. Munro's stories upend illusions of autonomous identity, of persons as discrete, independent, and comprehendible. These stories explore the inevitability of dependence and responsibility, depicting characters forced to confront uncanny identity, "obligated to respond to what is beyond [. . .] comprehension, beyond recognition, because ethics is possible only beyond recognition" (Oliver 106). For ethics of care theorists, obligation to, and dependence on others is neither unusual nor temporary, but is a predictable and necessary aspect of human existence. With "encumbered-ness" comes "embeddedness," that is, with burdensome responsibility come the human relationships essential for life and meaning.

4. ISOLATION AND IDENTITY

An allegiance to independence, autonomy, and separation, those characteristics of individuality so celebrated by western capitalistic culture, can make dependence and obligation appear as failures of identity. In Franzen's novel, *The Corrections*, Alfred, the aging Lambert family patriarch, undergoes a painfully isolated descent into delusions induced by Parkinson's disease. The fleeting insights into otherness that facilitate moments of responsibility and exchange in "The Bear Came Over the Mountain" and "Spelling" give way to terrifying alienation in *The Corrections*. In Franzen's novel, narrative perspective is dispersed among the various family members, allowing the reader to consider events from a variety of angles. However, the varied focalization is countered by a paucity of communication between the family members. To a large degree, these characters are strangers to one another, and there are a number of references to their fear of one another and their trepidation at the prospect of forced interaction. At the head of this detached family is Alfred, whose preference for guarded existence is largely responsible for the family's estrangement. Alfred aligns seclusion with personhood – "Without privacy there was no point in being an individual" (465) – and separation with love – "The odd truth about Alfred was that love, for him, was a matter not of approaching but of keeping away" (526).[8] This ethos of exclusionary identity has serious repercussions as the characters age. For Alfred, the process of aging into old age is complicated by the debilitations of Parkinson's disease; body tremors, hallucinations,

---

8 | Alfred's philosophy of love is in direct opposition to philosopher Kelly Oliver's: "Love is an openness to otherness" (220).

and memory failure undermine his demand for authoritative independence, amounting to a crushing loss of self. In ascribing to a masculine model of rigid, authority-based identity, Alfred inhibits the possibility of collaboration and ethical insight experienced in Munro's stories. Alfred experiences the uncanniness of pathological aging only as a horrifying unravelling of self that leaves him stranded as empowered independence gives way to terrifying alienation. Alfred's later-life illness forces a debilitating confrontation with radical impermanence that is without the consolations of collaborative narrative sometimes found in Munro. He permits no witness to observe and assist his stories, no comedic collaborator. Instead, the abject – his hallucinated excrement – becomes a perverse witness, one that exposes and accuses rather than assists or protects.

Alfred's dementia manifests itself in terrifying, grotesque hallucinations in which the "filth" he has so vigorously rejected throughout his life returns to haunt him: a "turd" appears in the night to terrorize him, screaming obscenities, dirtying the walls and bedding (284-7). These hallucinations reflect the frightening confusion that results from utter separation, crippling privacy, the strictly insular self-reliance of a closed man. Throughout his life he has refused others' attempts to listen and collaborate, resisting the efforts of his wife and children to participate in his life narratives. As his illness worsens the stories he tells himself about his life get out of hand, his suffering aggravated by his devotion to a rigid model of selfhood that relies on impermeable barriers between self and other, in which others are perceived as dangerous opponents, duplicitous strangers.

All that Alfred has rejected, in particular his own difference and desire, returns in his repulsive hallucinations. It is notable that the phantom appears directly after the narration of an episode from the past in which he had reluctantly indulged his sexual desires, which he regards as "a defilement in pursuit of satisfaction" (282). After "defil[ing]" his wife, he imagines his unborn daughter as a "witness to such harm. Witness to a tautly engorged little brain that dipped in and out [. . .] . Alfred lay catching his breath and repenting his defiling of the baby" (281). For Alfred, witnessing is linked to judgement, to castigation and shame and the hallucinated excrement is a manifestation of the judgemental witness he fears, one who will expose his failings. Excrement is clearly abject in Kristeva's terms: at once unavoidably human and utterly other, it exposes the fragility of the border between the "I" and "that which I am not," a boundary necessary for our constitution as subjects (3). The abject reveals the ease with which difference, and therefore meaning can collapse. Alfred's abject turd flouts his longing for order and control by destroying boundaries and abolishing difference. It is "sociopathic," "loose," "opposed to all strictures," promising to sully his clothes with a stinking trace of animality (Franzen 285). In this symbolism, Alfred's aging, his illness – conditions that the novel repeatedly intertwines – produces an utter loss of control that undoes the identity Alfred has worked so hard to preserve.

"Civilization depends upon restraint," Alfred responds to the turd's championing of self-indulgence (285). The hallucination reflects a distinctly Freudian reading of civilization and identity, producing a nightmare vision of emancipation in which the hedonistic Id has entirely overcome the responsible Superego. This symbolic struggle between Alfred's devotion to his "civilized" facade and his own repressed desires participates in the discourse of uncanny age. Alfred's aging and debilitation produce an identity in conflict as the facades of authority and stability give way to chaotic multiplicity. It is significant that "[t]he turd had an attitude, a tone of voice, that Alfred found eerily familiar but couldn't quite place" (286). Alfred hallucinates a confrontation with a narrative of self he would seek to deny, a narrative of licentiousness, eager domination and xenophobic rage. When Alfred exclaims that the hideous intruder belongs in jail, it responds with a page-long tirade that exposes the ugly underbelly of Alfred's exclusionary instincts. Alfred, the turd explains, would see *everything in jail* and it proceeds to list the many offending others: kids "drop food on the carpet," Polynesians "track sand in the house, get fish juice on the furniture," "pubescent chickies" expose their "honkers," "Negroes" drink and sweat and dance and make noise, Caribbeans carry "viruses," the Chinese eat slimy food, women "trail Kleenexes and Tampaxes everywhere they go," and the list goes on (287). This tirade against the perceived excesses of others exposes Alfred's compulsive rejection of otherness as dangerous and vile, a violent refusal that reflects his terror in the face of his own crumbling identity.

Toward the end of the novel, when the family has come together for what promises to be their final reunion, the severity of Alfred's illness is undeniable. As his three children become aware of the painful effects of the disease, they have various opportunities to provide Alfred with care. Gary, Denise and Chip assist their father despite their own unease, even disgust, at the changes of age. They witness their father in abject vulnerability – struggling to bathe, dress, and give himself an enema. Unavoidably, the children adopt, if only briefly, the role of caregiver, a function they find painful and disorienting.

When Gary walks in on Alfred standing naked in the bathtub, hallucinating, he finds his father's uncanniness disturbingly contagious: "Gary himself was infected, there in the middle of the night, by his father's disease. As the two of them collaborated on the problem of the diaper, [. . .] Gary, too, had a sensation of things dissolving around him, of a night that consisted of creepings and shiftings and metamorphoses. He had the sense that there were many more than two people in the house beyond the bedroom door [. . .] phantoms" (501). Such is the dark side of aging's radical instability. Here, collaboration results in a mutual haunting that upsets any sense of stable identity. There is no hope for collaborative levity between afflicted and caregiver as in "Spelling." Rather,

Gary's participation in his father's care precipitates an apprehension of other-ness that disturbs the foundations of his own subjectivity. The world around Gary seems to be in the process of disintegrating, the unified singularity of identity an impossible fiction: there are no longer only "two people in the house beyond the bedroom door" – the world has begun a process of multiplication that destabilizes meaning and identity. The inclusion of the term "metamor-phoses" implies that Gary is taking on, albeit unwillingly, the uncanny vision of radical impermanence, the alterity of human mortality. Gary himself becomes afflicted, in Felman's terms, as "an unwitting, inadvertent [. . .] *involuntary wit-ness*" to "an illness whose effects explode any capacity for explanation or ratio-nalization" (emphasis in original, 4).

When Alfred is finally transferred to Deepmire, a care facility, he regards himself as a prisoner of a brutal authority bent on revenge. His rage at his own helplessness manifests itself in violent racism, this time expressed as a hatred for the black staff. Old age, particularly pathological old age, devastates the power and privilege he has enjoyed all his life as a middle-class, white man. Old age and illness have introduced him to the space of otherness, an otherness he resists by attempting to reinstate the boundaries and hierarchies that have always maintained his identity. Alfred transforms a black, female staff-member at Deepmire into a horrific, vengeful demon: "The big black lady, the mean one, the bastard, was the one he had to keep an eye on. She intended to make his life a hell. She stood at the far end of the prison yard throwing him significant glances to remind him that she hadn't forgotten him, she was still in hot pur-suit of her vendetta" (553). Alfred's delusions suggest a kind of perverted insight into his own culpability, some reluctant awareness of a legacy of domination worthy of revenge. His paranoia seizes upon a figure of marked difference and his racist and sexist, and later homophobic, epithets betray his acute anxiety: "That fat black bastard, that nasty black bitch over there, held his eye and nod-ded across the white heads of the other prisoners: *I'm gonna get you*" (emphasis in original 553). Old age and illness have produced a terrifying inversion. For the Anglo-Saxon patriarch, Alfred, there is danger in confronting radical im-permanence since such fluidity exposes the transience of his power and author-ity. As Alfred enters the space of illness, old age, and difference, he experiences a loss of the prerogatives of strength and youth that he cannot abide.

5. Conclusion: Gendering Collaboration

These three fictional texts present a gendered vision of aging and later-life de-mentia, suggesting that the recognition of radical instability and dependence provokes different crises in men and women. In *The Corrections*, Alfred's rage is largely the result of his suffocating dedication to masculine models of identity based on exclusion and domination, making collaboration an unacceptable adaptation and diminution of power.[9] As a result of his imperial attitudes, becoming a dependent victim devastates his sense of self. Franzen's nonfictional account of his own father's dementia furthers such a patriarchal perspective: the only images of hope in the essay involve Franzen's final accounts of his father's "heroic" persevering power, the triumph of his father's "will" (*How to Be Alone* 34). As Franzen's texts demonstrate, the resilient cultural scripts of masculinity and femininity influence both how "we" (the unafflicted) interpret victims of late-life dementia, and how, through witnessing and care, "we" imagine those victims experience their own disabilities. The moments of pleasure, even grace, afforded the afflicted characters in Munro's stories – Fiona's new love and sudden recognition, Flo and Rose's shared moment of humour – contrast sharply with Alfred's violence and despair.[10] In these narratives, patriarchal models of behaviour inhibit much of the dialogic potential of caregiving: where Rose and Flo may experience a fleeting moment of levity that allows for a kind of communication and understanding that can accommodate difference, the father/son alliance in *The Corrections* involves discrete individuals in distant dialogue.[11]

---

9 | The operations of identity and responsibility in these works by Munro and Franzen lead me to believe that the meaning and function of "care" are fundamental to discussions of subjectivity and alterity, not only as one ages into old age, but throughout the life course. Relationality is central to the condition of identity and the human interaction that occurs in caregiving confirms the fundamental importance of dependence and responsibility in discussions of selfhood. The assertion that human dependence is a fundamental, rather than peripheral aspect of identity is crucial to the growing body of scholarship devoted to the ethics of care. As a number of feminist theorists have recently insisted, human interdependence makes "care" a central concern for moral reasoning. Ethics of care theorists, such as Maurice Hamington, Virginia Held, Eva Feder Kittay, and Kelly Oliver, insist that "[t]he fact of human vulnerability and frailty that dependency underscores must function in our very conception of ourselves as subjects and moral agents" (Kittay and Feder 3).

10 | See also Caroline Adderson's A History of Forgetting for a rather melodramatic vision of dementia as a grotesque exaggeration of patriarchal violence. The afflicted character in that novel is suddenly anti-semitic and homophobic, much like Alfred Lambert in Franzen's novel. Such constructions produce a highly symbolic version of aging and illness as the return of a kind of repressed primitive self, the vicious and destructive Id, unfettered by civilizing forces.

11 | I am not suggesting that women are more capable of constructive collaboration. As Lorraine York points out in her study of women's collaborative writing, too often our interpretations of gendered collaboration have been coloured by romantic visions of maternal kindness. York writes, "for the most part I have found a strong tendency to

In *Writing History, Writing Trauma* Dominick LaCapra proposes a particular definition of "empathy," one that refuses its common association with "identification or fusion with the other" (212). Instead, LaCapra contends that "empathy should rather be understood in terms of an affective relation, rapport, or bond with the other recognized and respected as other. It may be further related to the affirmation of otherness within the self – otherness that is not purely and discretely other" (212-13). It is just this kind of difficult relation, and revelation, that later-life dementia can provoke. The distressingly uncanny vision produced by dementia – the victim is radically other, yet undeniably familiar – is a witnessing of aging and difference that prompts an (often reluctant) awareness of the uncanniness of selfhood in the empathetic observer. In Munro's and Franzen's fictional accounts, dementia poses serious challenges for both its victims and their empathetic witnesses as they struggle to maintain some sense of self or to attain an ethical insight in the face of such an acute demonstration of mutable identity, challenges further complicated by the demands of a patri-

---

celebrate women's collaborations unproblematically and idealistically. This tendency is particularly strong in North America, home of influential feminist theories that see women as more other-directed and caring, and thus more given to relational ethics and collaborative problem-solving" (6). Though I do not subscribe to a model of untroubled fusion, I believe York's observation speaks to cultural expectations for, and even construction of, gendered collaboration. The idealization of women's collaboration suggests that men's collaborative relationships are imagined as the antithesis, that is, as somehow inherently difficult and fraught. Whether intrinsic or not, the belief in the "naturalness" of women's collaboration and the challenge of men's, greatly determines the operation of such partnerships. In novels such as *The Corrections*, collaboration between men carries its own ideological baggage. In his treatment of male literary collaboration, Wayne Koestenbaum establishes the collaborative writer as one "who keenly feels lack or disenfranchisement, and seeks out a partner to attain power and completion" (emphasis added, 2). He continues by proposing that post-1885 (the year of the Labouchère Amendment), collaboration "was a complicated and anxiously homosocial act" (3), claiming that "[c]ertain desires and dreads regularly follow in the double signature's wake: hysterical discontinuity, muteness, castratory violence, homoerotic craving, misogyny, a wish to usurp female generative powers" (4). York and Koestenbaum's divergent critical strategies speak to the divergent cultural scripts that often overdetermine the theory and practice of gendered collaboration, namely, the assumption that women are cooperative and men combative. York often emphasizes conflicts in collaboration and the difficulty of fusion while Koestenbaum is particularly interested in the subversive homoeroticism of men's collaboration, claiming that "men who collaborate engage in metaphorical sexual intercourse" (3). Though the collaborations in these texts are not explicitly engaged with questions of authorship, many of the same anxieties and difficulties plague the participants.

archal culture. In these narratives, later-life dementia confronts sufferers and witnesses alike with the non-fixity of identity, with the uncanniness of others *and* themselves.

REFERENCES

Adderson, Caroline. *A History of Forgetting.* Toronto: Patrick Crean Editions, 1999. Print.

Biggs, Simon. "The 'Blurring' of the Lifecourse: Narrative, Memory and the Question of Authenticity." *Journal of Aging and Identity* 4.4 (1999): 209-21. Print.

———. *The Mature Imagination: Dynamics of Identity in Midlife and Beyond.* Philadelphia: Open UP, 1999. Print.

Butler, Robert. "The Life Review: An Interpretation of Reminiscence in the Aged." *Psychiatry* 26 (1963): 65-76. Print.

Caruth, Cathy. *Unclaimed Experience: Trauma, Narrative, and History.* Baltimore: Johns Hopkins UP, 1996. Print.

Cohen, Elizabeth. *The House on Beartown Road: A Memoir of Learning and Forgetting.* London: Vermilion, 2004. Print.

Davis, Robert. *My Journey into Alzheimer's Disease.* Ed. Betty Davis. Wheaton, IL: Tyndale House, 1989. Print.

DeBaggio, Thomas. *Losing My Mind: An Intimate Look at Life with Alzheimer's.* London: Free P, 2002. Print.

Erikson, Erik H. *The Life Cycle Completed.* Ed. Joan M. Erikson. New York: W.W. Norton, 1997. Print.

Featherstone, Mike, and Andrew Wernick. "Introduction." *Images of Aging: Cultural Representations of Later Life.* Ed. Mike Featherstone and Andrew Wernick. London: Routledge, 1995. 1-15. Print.

Felman, Shoshana. "Introduction." Shoshana Felman and Dori Laub. *Testimony: Crises of Witnessing in Literature, Psychoanalysis, and History.* New York: Routledge, 1992. Print.

Franzen, Jonathan. *The Corrections.* Toronto: HarperCollins, 2001. Print.

———. *How to be Alone.* London: Harper Perennial, 2004. Print.

Freud, Sigmund. "The 'Uncanny'." *Art and Literature.* Trans. James Strachey. Ed. James Strachey and Angela Richards. London: Penguin, 1985. 335-76. Print.

Garland, Jeff, and Christina Garland. *Life Review in Health and Social Care: A Practitioner's Guide.* Philadelphia: Brunner-Routledge, 2001. Print.

Gilligan, Carol. *In a Different Voice: Psychological Theory and Women's Development.* Cambridge, Mass: Harvard UP, 1982. Print.

Grant, Linda. *Remind Me Who I Am Again.* London: Granta, 1998. Print.

Gullette, Margaret Morganroth. *Aged by Culture*. Chicago: U of Chicago P, 2004. Print.

Hamington, Maurice. *Embodied Care: Jane Addams, Maurice Merleau-Ponty, and Feminist Ethics*. Urbana and Chicago: U of Illinois P, 2004. Print.

Held, Virginia. *The Ethics of Care*. Oxford: Oxford UP, 2006. Print.

Hepworth, Mike. *Stories of Ageing*. Philadelphia: Open UP, 2000. Print.

Kaufman, Sharon R. *The Ageless Self: Sources of Meaning in Late Life*. Madison, WI.: U of Wisconsin P, 1986. Print.

Kearney, Richard. *Strangers, Gods, and Monsters: Ideas of Otherness*. New York: Routledge, 2003. Print.

Kenyon, Gary M., and William Lowell Randall. *Restorying our Lives: Personal Growth Through Autobiographical Reflection*. Westport, CT: Praeger, 1997. Print.

Kittay, Eva. *Love's Labor: Essays on Women, Equality, and Dependency*. New York: Routledge, 1999. Print.

——– and Ellen K. Feder. "Introduction." *The Subject of Care: Feminist Perspectives on Dependency*. Ed. Eva Feder Kittay and Ellen K. Feder. New York: Rowman and Littlefield, 2002. 1-12.

Koestenbaum, Wayne. *Double Talk: The Erotics of Male Literary Collaboration*. New York: Routledge, 1989. Print.

Kristeva, Julia. *Powers of Horror: An Essay on Abjection*. Trans. Leon S. Roudiez. New York: Columbia UP, 1982. Print.

Kuhn, Annette. *Family Secrets: Acts of Memory and Imagination*. New York: Verso, 2002. Print.

LaCapra, Dominick. *Writing History, Writing Trauma*. Baltimore, MD: Johns Hopkins UP, 2001. Print.

Levinas, Emmanuel. *Otherwise Than Being: Or, Beyond Essence*. Trans. Alphonso Lingis. Boston: Kluwer, 1991. Print

——–, and Richard Kearney. "Dialogue with Emmanuel Levinas." *Face to Face with Levinas*. Ed. Richard A. Cohen. Albany: State U of New York P, 1986. 3-34. Print.

Levine, Judith. *Do You Remember Me?: A Father, a Daughter, and a Search for the Self*. New York: Free P, 2004. Print.

Miller, Sue. *The Story of My Father: A Memoir*. New York: Knopf, 2003. Print.

Mitchell, Marilyn. *Dancing on Quicksand: A Gift of Friendship in the Age of Alzheimer's*. Boulder: Johnson, 2002. Print.

Moore, Jeffrey S. *The Memory Artists*. Toronto: Viking Canada, 2004. Print.

Morgenstern, Naomi. "The Baby or the Violin? Ethics and Femininity in the Fiction of Alice Munro." *LIT: Literature Interpretation Theory* 14.2 (2003): 69-97. Print.

Munro, Alice. *Hateship, Friendship, Courtship, Loveship, Marriage*. Toronto: McClelland and Stewart, 2001. Print.

———. *Who Do You Think You Are?*. Toronto: Penguin, 1996. Print.

Oliver, Kelly. *Witnessing: Beyond Recognition*. Minneapolis: U of Minnesota P, 2001. Print.

Redekop, Magdalene. *Mothers and Other Clowns: The Stories of Alice Munro*. New York: Routledge, 1992. Print.

Richler, Mordecai. *Barney's Version*. New York: A.A. Knopf, 1997. Print.

Ricoeur, Paul. *Time and Narrative*. Trans. Kathleen McLaughlin and David Pellauer. 3 vols. Chicago: U of Chicago P, 1985. Print.

Woodward, Kathleen. "Telling Stories: Aging, Reminiscence, and the Life Review." *Journal of Aging and Identity* 2.3 (1997): 149-63. Print.

York, Lorraine Mary. *Rethinking Women's Collaborative Writing: Power, Difference, Property*. Toronto: U of Toronto P, 2002. Print.

Shaking off Shackles

LTC Havens in "The Bear Came Over the Mountain"
and *The Other Sister*

Patricia Life

Living environments that to some seem inferior might to others seem superior. An individual's evaluation of a set of conditions depends on the standards already established by that person's life experience. A refugee, for instance, having lost his or her home through natural disaster or war, might consider the meagre accommodations of a prison to be luxurious. Certain desirable features, such as safety, could eclipse supposed insufficiencies. In this article, I explore two Canadian texts in which readers could interpret the protagonists' lives to have improved following admission to late-life-care institutions: Alice Munro's 1999 short story "The Bear Came Over the Mountain," best known for its adaptation as the movie *Away From Her*, and Lola Lemire Tostevin's 2008 novel *The Other Sister*.

For most of the twentieth century, Western society[1] has considered nursing homes to be undesirable, to be places inhabited only by those with no alternative to call home. Margaret Laurence's 1964 novel *The Stone Angel* and texts such as Edna Alford's 1981 short stories *A Sleep Full of Dreams*, Joan Barfoot's 1985 novel *Duet for Three*, and Constance Rooke's 1986 edition *Night Light: Stories of Aging* have reflected and reinforced a negative cultural image of the nursing home. More recently, texts such as Richard B. Wright's 1990 *Sunset Manor*, Carol Shields' 1993 *Stone Diaries*, and Joan Barfoot's 2008 *Exit Lines* have begun to reflect a more positive public perception of late-life housing. However, while the texts suggest that a reasonable maintenance of personal agency is now considered to be possible while living in a care facility, they still assume

---

1 | I use the term "Western culture" as a catch-all term to refer to the norms, values, ideologies, customs, systems, artifacts, and technologies that evolved and are evolving in response to England and its language, origins, and empire; to the larger European context; and to the consequent world-wide influence and counter-influence.

that residents would need to fight against oppressive administrative authorities to avoid the erosion of their independence and the diminishment of their self-hood. In this article, I argue that Munro's and Tostevin's texts both withhold definitive closure and in so doing potentially contest the aging-as-decline narrative; moreover, they take the evolution in the nursing-home-narrative genre one step further by adding an aging-as-opportunity narrative. For these protagonists, admission to a long-term-care facility provides a new and more encouraging environment, a place in which they can find a safe haven and shake off the shackles of their former lives.

Stephen Katz points out that "a nursing home is not simply a building or residence: rather, it is a micro-complex of architectural, administrative, financial, clinical, familial, symbolic, and emotional interactions and power relations" (*Cultural* 204). As a result of becoming a part of this volatile mix, new residents upon admission face the challenge, but also the opportunity, of adjusting their own identities in response. In this paper, I interpret that new home environments allow Munro's and Tostevin's protagonists to focus on certain aspects of their identities while disremembering some others, and that these women both gain by shifting away from earlier modes of being.

In the 2012 article entitled "Embodied Memory: Ageing, Neuroculture, and the Genealogy of Mind," Katz "explores the relationship between the aging mind and cognitive culture, with a focus on the production and distribution of memory as a master metaphor for successful aging" (1). In our ageist Western culture, the loss of a sharp memory is considered to be a sign of a diminished human being, but Katz argues that "our aging and our pasts are molded as much through the work of forgetting as they are through the tracing of memory" ("Embodied" 9). We do not remember every detail of our pasts because we must selectively forget some parts while embracing and remembering other parts in order to shape a narrative history and identity for ourselves. The loss of many memories occurs as a matter of course and is helpful rather than hurtful. Maintaining the full and unfiltered magnitude of our personal history would be overwhelming. Katz points out that "one of the benefits of human brain plasticity is that it allows us to filter, change, interpret, negotiate, and even forget our memories in order to create coherence and stability in our lives, despite social pressures to optimize memory" ("Embodied" 9). For the sake of our own wellbeing, we instinctively shape our own life story, ideally dwelling on the aspects that enrich rather than trouble us. While the extreme and sometimes absolute memory loss associated with a disease such as Alzheimer's undoubtedly constitutes a tragedy, certain types of loss prevent memory overload and other types accommodate the creation of a beneficial self-story. Memory loss in itself is not always a bad thing. In both texts addressed in this article, the selective forgetting, remembering, and refocusing facilitated by living in a new environment allow the protagonist to live to greater advantage. Notably, these texts push aside the home-as-horror nursing home narrative and introduce instead a home-as-haven narrative.

"THE BEAR CAME OVER THE MOUNTAIN"

Alice Munro's 1999 short story/novella "The Bear Came Over the Mountain" has become well known since being adapted as a screenplay for the movie *Away From Her*, directed by Sarah Polley (Jaffe 67). Munro's female protagonist Fiona mirrors Margaret Laurence's Hagar in age and in her growing lack of self-sufficiency. Yet after admission to Munro's version of a care facility, this protagonist creates a new and possibly more fulfilling life for herself. The story suggests that, for some residents, institutionalization could provide more freedom of identity than is available within the more invisible enclosures of their lives outside the care facility. My analysis of this story primarily addresses the story's ambiguous interpretation of the long-term-care facility as a potential site of disruption of patriarchal hegemony, as a place where new personal agency away from an oppressive husband might be enabled.

The story begins with a brief flashback to Fiona's and Grant's courtship prior to their marriage and then abruptly jumps several decades to arrive at the present where they are leaving their long-time home to drive Fiona to Meadowlake for treatment of her recent escalating problems with memory loss and confusion (1-3). In order for Fiona to adjust optimally to her new situation, the facility's administration advises Grant that he should not visit during an initial thirty-day orientation period (8). By this policy, the administration actively discourages residents from dwelling on memories of their previous homes. By the time he sees her again, Fiona has formed a new and intense friendship with Aubrey, a fellow resident and dementia patient, and appears to have forgotten who Grant is – much to his alarm (20). When Aubrey's wife Marion takes him home again at the end of his scheduled respite stay, Fiona, in his absence, falls into a decline. This further frustrates and upsets Grant (41), and so he determines to coax Marion into restoring Aubrey to Fiona (58-63). Ironically, by the time Grant has arranged the reunion, Fiona has forgotten about Aubrey and instead once again demonstrates affection towards her husband (65).

The most obvious interpretation of the story would identify dementia and the demands of institutional living as the negative forces upsetting the couple's life-long love. If readers interpret that Fiona has suffered severe and ongoing memory loss as a result of a disease such as Alzheimer's, then the story should be interpreted as a tragedy with dementia playing the role of villain. The screenplay and other critics of the story have interpreted Munro's work as a poignant love story wherein the husband Grant is as much a victim of his wife Fiona's dementia as is she. In referring to the movie, Ellen S. Jaffe and Ellen Bouchard

Ryan talk of "the grace of love which the couple ultimately salvage" (Jaffe 4). This interpretation is valid and the story can be lauded as an exploration of the losses associated with dementia.

I would argue that because Munro's writing is somewhat impenetrable, this interpretation is debatable. The narration is third-person omniscient with focalization occurring primarily through Grant, but various nuances suggest that the story might differ if readers could hear it through Fiona's voice. As Coral Ann Howells speculates, the story "could be read as the story of a wife's escape through dementia from the prescripted plot of her married life" (75). After her admission, Grant misses Fiona at home, buys flowers to give to her on his first visit to see her at Meadowlake, and apparently attempts to eradicate his wife's unhappiness at Aubrey's absence with no thought to anything except her wellbeing. However, in order to restore Aubrey to her, he is willing (the story suggests) to repeat a life-long pattern of marital infidelity by seducing Marion (61). He relishes the idea of coercing Marion to do his will, saying, "[i]t would be a challenge, a creditable feat. Also a joke that could never be confided to anybody – to think that by his bad behaviour he'd be doing good for Fiona" (61). Many readers will falter here and withhold from Grant the label 'selfless hero.'

The text explains that Grant's reputation as a philanderer had required him to accept a reduced pension and to retire early from his career as a professor of Anglo-Saxon and Nordic literature (35). At this time, Fiona had also given up her job as a "hospital coordinator of volunteer services," and they had moved to the country where there were "no bare female toes creeping up under a man's pants leg at a dinner party" (16-17). The text presents Grant as feeling disgruntled and maligned, justifying his behaviour and musing that he had never treated any of his lovers heartlessly and had "never stopped making love to Fiona in spite of disturbing demands elsewhere" (16). To these thoughts most readers' response would be less than completely sympathetic. The text explains that following his banishment, he "got drunk, and without its being required of him – also, thank God, without making the error of a confession – promised Fiona a new life" (15). What is not explained explicitly is to what extent Fiona has been aware of Grant's repeated infidelity and how she feels about his behaviour and her own exile to the country.

When Fiona first experiences forgetfulness, seems confused, and becomes difficult to interpret, Grant is unsure how concerned to be, thinking that "she's always been a bit like this" (5). He cannot explain to the doctor that he feels

as if she'd stumbled on some adventure that she had not been expecting. Or was playing a game that she hoped he would catch on to. They had always had their games – nonsense dialects, characters they invented. Some of Fiona's made-up voices, chirping or wheedling (he couldn't tell the doctor this), had mimicked uncannily the voices of women of his that she had never met or known about. (5)

Although Grant apparently believes that she had known nothing about these "women of his," the text allows room to interpret that Fiona had known exactly what he was doing all along.

When Grant is given permission to visit Fiona after her initial orientation period at the long-term-care facility, he cannot determine whether his wife's new ambivalence towards him is due to her dementia or whether it is a joke or even an act of cruelty. As Sally Chivers says (albeit in discussing the movie interpretation of the story), "[w]hether she deviously and vengefully plays on her newly acquired unreliability, or whether she genuinely forgets him, does not lessen Grant's suffering" (*Silvering* 90). While Fiona's memory losses precipitated her admission to the home, Munro leaves room for readers to interpret that this dementia patient may not once admitted be quite as overwhelmingly affected by forgetfulness as people think. Chivers thinks that it is possible to speculate that "her attachment to Aubrey becomes a coy yet manipulative way to make Grant reassess, regret, or at least suffer for his own past treachery" (90). Grant himself questions whether Fiona might be playing a game with him: "'I wonder whether she isn't putting on some kind of a charade'" (26).

Munro allows room to interpret that Fiona has embraced a new lifestyle free from Grant's oppressive behaviour. Her relationship with Aubrey may be interpreted as a willful attempt to seek revenge against Grant for his infidelities. Readers could alternatively interpret that she does suffer somewhat from dementia-related severe memory loss and that therefore her behaviour is a less-than-fully conscious, knee-jerk reaction to his previous bad treatment of her.

The text could also be interpreted as saying that, in her relationship with the wheelchair-bound Aubrey, she is enjoying an opportunity to put back into action her former care-giving skills as a coordinator of volunteer services, and that she may simply be enjoying a new and rewarding relationship for its own sake with no particular motivation deriving from her previous relationship with Grant. When Fiona demonstrates affection towards Grant at the end of the story, she may be surfacing from a severe phase in her dementia, or she may have determined – consciously or otherwise – that he had been punished sufficiently.

The ambiguity of the text invites readers to consider whether Grant's and Fiona's marriage has transcended – and will transcend – his tendency to cheat, or whether he is merely demonstrating that he will betray his wife even in her illness. Grant casts himself in the role of hero, but the reader could just as easily interpret him as the villain. Does the relationship transcend monogamy, or is he just proving that he still does not understand what is important in a relationship? Munro's ambivalence invites but does not require readers to see Fiona as a woman who has been previously disempowered in this marriage but who, advantageously, may have "forgotten" her marriage – consciously or otherwise – and who may have redirected the misfortune of being admitted to a care facility towards her own fortunate ends, towards subverting the controlling power of her husband. Her new distanced behaviour and the various visible new markers of her identity associated with living at Meadowlake require Grant to reassess his understanding of Fiona and to reassess his attitudes towards their relationship.

Amelia DeFalco rightly points out that Grant's knowledge of his wife is "significantly limited" and that "he has tended to think of Fiona as delightfully foreign, as a dynamic but mysterious being" (75). At their first meeting when young, he had been "bewitched by her vitality" and had "accept[ed] her subjectivity as entirely mysterious, often quaintly so" (77). DeFalco adds that Grant "relied on Fiona's persistent otherness to justify his betrayals, regarding her as a delightfully opaque object, denying her subjectivity in order to indulge his own transgressive desires," but that "Fiona's dementia forces a new engagement with responsibility" (76). Thus when dementia alters her behaviour, her opaqueness and his inability to see into her are familiar yet also strangely exacerbated and new. When Grant visits for the first time, he finds Fiona's name on the door to her room, but he cannot find the woman he now badly wants to see after being denied her company for the previous month. In a sense, she has become for him the desirable "other woman." The emptiness of her room can be interpreted to represent the erasure of their shared past: "She wasn't there. The closet door was closed, the bed smoothed. Nothing on the bedside table, except a box of Kleenex and a glass of water. Not a single photograph or picture of any kind, not a book or a magazine" (18). He soon finds also that she has donned different clothing, has had her hair cut, and has assumed new behaviours (33). To use Freudian language, his once familiar wife has now been rendered strange and somewhat frightening or "uncanny."

DeFalco interprets that these changes in Fiona and the time he spends following her and her friends around in the care facility eventually cause Grant to see himself as the "other," to catch sight of his own uncanniness or strangeness in relation to the different standard of normal established at Meadowlake. As DeFalco points out, readers can better understand Munro's text by considering Freud's explanation of the significance of disorientation: "the uncanny would always be an area in which a person was unsure of his way around: the better orientated he was in the world around him, the less likely he would be to find the objects and occurrences in it uncanny" (Freud 125). Grant's altered view of his wife and of himself unhinges his self-confidence and sense of place in the world.

Possibly, Grant comes to value his wife and understand himself differently by the final scene of the story when she once again demonstrates affection towards him – or at least seems to demonstrate affection. He suggests to her that he would never abandon her, saying "not a chance," and he keeps his face against her "sweetly shaped skull" (65). Yet he has noted to himself, just before reassuring her, that she smells like "the stems of cut flowers left too long in their water" (77). The text's mention of the yellow of her dress and of her unpleasant scent suggests that Fiona is represented by the previously described yellow skunk lilies in the swamp near their home that may or may not generate true warmth. By this insinuation, the motivation for her behaviour becomes inscrutable, and, as Coral Ann Howells points out, there may be in Grant's final words "an echo of his old duplicitous reassurances" and prevarications in relation to matters sexual (77).

At the time of Fiona's initial admission, sexual intercourse had been an important extra-marital part of Grant's life, but it had been, at least to some extent, a recent part of their marriage as well. Readers are aware that Grant and Fiona have been sexually active recently because, during his period of waiting, he reminisces about the routine he had previously enjoyed with her in the evenings: "[t]his was their time of liveliest intimacy, though there was also, of course, the five or ten minutes of physical sweetness just after they got into bed – something that did not often end up in sex but reassured them that sex was not over yet" (13). When Grant visits following Fiona's orientation period, he becomes worried that Fiona and Aubrey are having an intimate relationship, talking to Kristy "about these affections between residents" and asking "[d]id they ever go too far?" (25). He notes that Fiona and Aubrey spend time together behind closed bedroom doors (32), but he feels reassured when he remembers that Aubrey is in a wheelchair (26). However, readers later see Fiona helping Aubrey to begin walking again, and thus his incapacity is rendered questionable (27). Without explicitly depicting Fiona's sexual experiences, Munro suggests that a long-term care facility could potentially be the site not just for new friendships but also for new intimate relationships that could include sexual intercourse.

The text's depiction of extreme initial limitations on visitation at Meadowlake points out that paired people like Fiona and Grant and like Aubrey and Marion face the likelihood of forced separation when one half of the couple requires admission to a care facility. Thus her text points out a current unaddressed problem in late-life care policy; that is that treatment is individual in nature and does not often consider the needs of coupled individuals. While Munro's 30-day no-visitation rule is stricter than that encountered in real life, by its use she metaphorically references all of the ways admission to a long-term-care facility drives a wedge between partnered individuals. When couples no longer share a home, less obvious losses occur as a result. The non-residential spouse is limited to visiting during prescribed hours, and thus he or she loses the familiarity and intimacy associated with being included in activities of daily living such as bathing, dressing, eating, sleeping, and doctor visits.

On the bright side, Munro's depiction of the tender affection shared by Aubrey and Fiona also suggests that there is a potential for people to begin new and meaningful relationships upon entering care facilities, even though dementia may necessitate an early end-date for that relationship. Munro's depiction of the new relationship between Aubrey and Fiona invites readers to consider the influence of dementia on an individual's morality and ethics. She asks to what extent patients such as these two can be held accountable for their behaviour and at what stage the diagnosis of dementia precludes the application of a charge of adultery. Healthy partners such as Grant and Marion at some point must accept their partners' diminishing mental capacities and associated lost loyalty to former relationships. Munro queries whether healthy partners who have been abandoned as a result of their partners' diseases have the right to begin new relationships without feeling that they are betraying their original partners.

The general public for the most part would prefer to assume that old people are sexually inactive. Thomas Walz, who reports his research findings regarding nursing home sexuality in "Crones, Dirty Old Men, Sexy Seniors: Representations of the Sexuality of Older Persons" (2002), explains that in the late 1970's, while working as a "clinical teaching social worker in a Family Practice Geriatric Clinic," he attended the examination of an eighty-two-year-old woman who had little claim to physical beauty and who had had her left leg amputated. When she responded to an enquiry from her attending physician about the sensation in her leg, Walz inadvertently learned that "Emma" still experienced sexual desire: "'Doctor, the higher you go, the better it feels.'" Walz explains further that "[s]tunned by the sexual connation of her reply, the doctor blushed and remained silent" (105). Walz admits that he too was surprised to consider that she might remain sexually interested. He arranged to interview her formally later and found that she frequently partnered with her late husband's cousin who was living in the same nursing home. Walz's contact with this woman inspired him to join other researchers who were studying late-life sexuality. He reports that

The breakthrough in survey research of sexual behavior in this country is credited to Alfred Kinsey and his reports on male (1948) and female (1953) sexual behavior. In the later report, although only a small segment of his sample were older women, he did find women's interest in sex consistent from the late teens into the 60s, with a modest decline in the frequency of sexual intercourse as women aged. (103)

He also reports that, since that time, *The Hite Report* (1976) confirmed these findings, and that Masters and Johnson (1966) "proved that only rarely does the sexual equipment of the aged fail to allow older persons to remain sexually active" (Walz 103).

As Walz says, the general public prefers to believe that sexual activity is linked to attractiveness, and so, as a result of narratives of positive aging, "there seems to be an increased willingness to credit old people who are aging well (i.e., who look and act young) with being sexually interested and probably active" (101). However, people who look like Emma are assumed by the young to be inactive, despite statistical evidence and qualitative research findings that contradict this supposition.

By her inclusion in a 1999 story of the issue of sexuality in a long-term care setting, Munro should be credited with pushing against then current social awareness boundaries. More recently, attention to late-life sexuality is increasing – both in scholarly texts such as Kate Davidson's and Graham Fennell's *Intimacy in Later Life* (2004) and Stephen Katz's and Barbara L. Marshall's "Forever Functional: Sexual Fitness and the Aging Male Body" in *Cultural Aging* (2005), as well as in popular texts such as Joan Price's *Naked at Our Age: Talking Out Loud About Senior Sex* (2011). In the professional manual *Sexuality & Long-term Care: Understanding and Supporting the Needs of Older Adults* (2012), Gayle Appel Doll stresses that studies show that "libido persists even in frail nursing home residents" and that for care facilities to ignore this fact constitutes neglect (20). She adds that "[u]nfortunately, many expressions of sexuality are seen as inappropriate in nursing homes (6).

The words Munro ascribes to the nurse Kristy allude to a disbelieving or even scornful attitude on the part of the public in regards to late-life sexual expression. Kristy comments:

The trouble we have in here, it's funny, it's often with some of the ones that haven't been friendly with each other at all. They maybe won't even know each other, beyond knowing, like, is it a man or a woman? You'd think it'd be the old guys trying to crawl in bed with the old women, but you know half the time it's the other way round. Old women going after the old men. (27)

Kristy suggests that it is humorous, troublesome, and shocking to think that old people might still seek intimacy. By this quotation, the text invites discussion of the need to change public attitudes and to question the responsibilities of administrations in regard to this topic. It prompts discussion of an administrator's duty to protect residents from each other, to determine a resident's capacity to consent, and to liaise with family members who may have power of attorney and the legal right to limit the sexual activity of their ward.

Gayle Appel Doll points out that the range of sexual expression for older adults can be much broader than for young people, and she thinks that home administrations should accommodate this diversity: "Expressions of sexuality in nursing homes [. . .] might be seen in flirtation and affection, passing compliments, and proximity and physical contact" or in "women dressing up and having their hair and nails done to look attractive." However, she adds that "[k]issing, fondling, masturbation, oral sex, and intercourse are also ways that many persons choose to express their sexual feelings" (5-6). She argues that residents' rights in regard to the sexual expression of their choice should be recognized, although she acknowledges that sensibilities and rights of staff can sometimes make this difficult.

Although the reader is left to interpret whether Fiona's and Aubrey's sexual expression includes intercourse or just flirtation and friendship, Munro's text raises important questions on the topic just because it illustrates residents expressing their sexuality within the walls of the care facility. And if readers interpret that Fiona is not helplessly victimized by severe dementia but instead is making use of her identity as a Meadowlake resident to celebrate her freedom from an oppressive relationship with her husband, then Munro has created an aging-as-opportunity nursing-home narrative.

Lola Lemire Tostevin's *The Other Sister*

Like Munro's protagonist Fiona, Lola Lemire Tostevin's ninety-plus-year-old protagonist of the 2008 novel *The Other Sister* encounters new opportunities following her admission to a care facility – in this case, to Evenholme Retirement Living. Tostevin's protagonist shakes off a mantle of responsibility that she had been shouldering and seizes the opportunity to make new friends, including a fellow resident named Daniel with whom she shares walks, meals, and confidences. Once established at Evenholme, she is surprised to find that it is "not the lonely purgatory she had expected" (3). Thus *The Other Sister*, like "The Bear Came Over the Mountain," can be interpreted to be an aging-as-opportunity nursing-home narrative.

Following her admission, Tostevin's protagonist feels sufficiently free to return to an identity that she had abandoned earlier in life. Although she presents initially as Mrs. Julia Brannon, the text unravels a mystery to reveal ultimately that she is in fact Jane Crane, unmarried identical twin sister to Julia. Once a new resident, Jane rejects the role imposed on her by societal duty and embraces her own individual interests and desires for the first time in fifty years. The reader learns that when Julia had committed suicide at forty and left her four-year-old daughter Rachel motherless, her sister Jane had assumed Julia's identity and had abandoned her own career as a professor of philosophy (201). Jane had thereafter provided a stable home for Rachel, who had grown up knowing Jane as her mother and remaining oblivious to her initial identity as her aunt (169).

In the present time of the frame narrative, the protagonist's granddaughter Thea gives the protagonist a laptop because she thinks that her grandmother is suffering mental confusion, and she asks her to record the events of her life with the hope that her memory will improve (3). By this device, the text inserts flashbacks into Julia's and Jane's past. The reader learns that Rachel's father Wilson Brannon had loved Jane but that she had rejected him, preferring to attend university. At Jane's suggestion, he had married the other more passive twin. Julia's suicide had been precipitated by the death of her two sons and by finding her husband's love letters to Jane, and so Jane's guilt and sense of duty had driven her to snuff out her own life as a career woman and to assume Julia's life as a mother and homemaker (213). In a sense, she had arranged for Jane's life to end instead of Julia's.

Tostevin also incorporates a subplot that places Jane in a meaningful new friendship with fellow resident Lena Kohn, whose dementia causes her to fixate on the torture of herself and her twin in a Nazi concentration camp. By so doing, Tostevin keeps the topic of the Holocaust in front of the reading public, and readers will appreciate that she is compelled by the subject matter and is in large part writing the book as a tribute to those who suffered.

Since this is a 2008 novel, little criticism has as yet been written. The novel's popular strengths are to be found in its unique mystery plot and perhaps in its enquiry into the twin roles (in the home and in the workplace) between which women were torn during the latter half of the twentieth century. In an initial review of the novel, Andrea MacPherson argues that it is the "challenging of gender expectation that sets Julia apart from other characters in the novel," pointing out, however, that Tostevin's "descriptions of her as feisty and forward-thinking no longer feel fresh" (162). She adds that "[t]hese revelations of Julia's life [. . .] sometimes in italicized sections, other times in stiff dialogue, often feel too much like information being fed to readers" (163). Since, as MacPherson points out, the topic of changing roles for women has been addressed by many, I would argue that the greatest significance of the novel may be its contribution of an aging-as-opportunity narrative to the nursing-home narrative genre.

After admission to Evenholme, the protagonist rejects the restrictions of the past, embraces the opportunity to once again become Jane,[2] allows her more assertive nature to resurface, and begins to talk about previous interests such as books and philosophy. Lena's descent into dementia associated with her inability to stop reliving the events of the Holocaust presents a foil against which the

---

2 | It could alternatively be interpreted that she has dementia and, as her granddaughter Thea fears, has become confused about her own identity at this point in her life. Perhaps she has always been Julia the wife and homemaker and has now decided in her nineties to try out the persona of her sister Jane the intellectual.

couple's happiness seems especially fortunate and thus keeps the story from becoming saccharine sweet. However, Daniel's and Jane's lives clearly improve after they meet. Like Jane, Daniel comes to appreciate life at Evenholme: "[t]ake this place, I never thought I'd get used to it, but I'm having a rather nice time. It's awfully good to be able to talk like this, Julia. You're a wise old broad" (104). The two of them enjoy verbal sparring while they share tea in either his or her suite, and, eventually, she reveals herself to him as Jane rather than Julia. At the end of the story, she designates him as the keeper of her laptop – and her true identity – which is not to be shared with her family until after her death (210).

Jane and Daniel illustrate one of Gayle Appel Doll's most important points about sexuality and long-term care, that being that "the longing for a loving relationship does not diminish with age" and that "feelings of homelessness that result from an overwhelming sense of loss of meaning of life" can be alleviated by "promot[ing] intimate relationships for residents" because "[i]ntimacy or emotional closeness can act as a buffer in adaptation to stress and may be a requirement for survival as one grows older" (5). As Margaret Morganroth Gullette puts it, "[c]uddling is the most elemental form of love" (142). Tostevin's text suggests that Jane's growing relationship with Daniel nurtures her willingness to reclaim her own identity. His interest and conversation draw her back into being Jane as she was and help her to develop Jane as she can be in the present.

In the preface to Doll's book, Peggy Brick explains that the "word *sexuality* can be a problem" because many equate it only with sexual intercourse when it in fact also "includes one's feelings about oneself as a male or female person, body image, and the need for intimacy, touch and connection" (viii). Although Tostevin mentions that the residents at Evenholme have a pornographic-film-watching club called The Old Degenerate Club (133), she also describes behaviours not specifically linked to intercourse but that are nonetheless important aspects of what Doll would call "sexual expression:"

There was a fair amount of flirtation at Evenholme, but Julia doubted there was much sex in spite of a few residents who still conducted themselves as if sex should always be on one's mind. Half-a-dozen women behaving like schoolgirls [. . .] The men weren't much better. In fact, they may have been worse, broadcasting their imagined conquests to anyone who cared to notice. Sonny Walsh placed flowers on the dining tables of the women he imagined he was wooing, while Graham Porter left notes under plates and doors. Youth's swagger replaced by the bravado of old age. (87)

As the same passage continues, Tostevin's words begin to sound like Brick's, Gullette's and Doll's opinions about the importance of love: "[m]emories of the flesh carrying their own deceptive rhetoric in order to deal with the palpable dread of being alone. In a setting where people lived together from breakfast to bedtime, there was still the dread of not being loved enough. In this, even the aged were insatiable" (87). In this passage, Tostevin's text presents caring, sexually expressive relationships as an absolute necessity and as a means of eradicating loneliness and creating meaning.

Jane's physical attraction to Daniel as a man is evident when the text says that she "noticed him immediately" and thought that "[h]e owed much of his pleasant appearance to his ramrod posture and his white mane" (88). She also appreciates nonphysical aspects of his identity such as his position as a retired professor of mathematics (88) and his recognition of her as a fellow academic: "I hear you taught at the University of Toronto, he said, then added, As I did" (90). Their thoughtful interactions encourage her to reclaim Jane's intellectual history. As their relationship develops, grapevine talk amongst the other residents links them as a couple, and they enjoy hand holding and sometimes a kiss on the lips goodbye (120). Early on, Jane finds herself "losing interest in life outside Evenholme" (40). When Jane's granddaughter visits and fills her in on family news in the outside world, Jane feels it is "like hearing about strangers" (40). With Daniel's support, Jane throws off the sham widowhood of fifty years, largely unburdens herself of family responsibility, and becomes content living at Evenholme. At least for the present period of her residency prior to transfer, she is able to put to rest and to forget the troubles of her past. Her new life within the walls of Evenholme allows her the opportunity to escape her old sense of responsibility, to find new meaning in life, and to tell her story as she determines it should be told.

CONCLUSION

"The Bear Came Over the Mountain" and *The Other Sister* both withhold closure on multiple fronts and could uphold various readings. That said, readers could interpret that in these two stories admission to care facilities provides the protagonists with opportunities to live more contented lives than they were living prior to residency. Care institutions can be accused of depriving individuals of contact with the outside world, but they also offer shelter from it. Munro's character Fiona provides an example of escape – conscious or otherwise – from the oppression of an abusive husband. The text illustrates that, in certain cases, some forgetting as a result of dementia might provide the benefit of lessened stress. Thus, the text suggests that real-life residents outside of fictional stories might also benefit from forgetting – perhaps, for example, by forgetting about intense grief felt over the loss of something or someone held dear. Both texts illustrate the importance of inter-resident relationships and show how new friendships can create meaning within a care facility environment. Tostevin's text illustrates the sense of freedom from responsibility that some residents might feel upon admission. It also suggests that the unfamiliar environment of a care facility has the potential to nurture new identity development.

Significantly, these two texts add aging-as-opportunity narratives to the nursing-home narrative genre.

References

Alford, Edna. *A Sleep Full of Dreams*. Lantzville: Oolichan Books, 1981. Print.

Appel Doll, Gayle. *Sexuality & Long-term Care: Understanding and Supporting the Needs of Older Adults*. Baltimore: Health Professions Press, 2012. Print.

Barfoot, Joan. *Exit Lines*. Toronto: Alfred A. Knopf Canada, 2008. Print.

Chivers, Sally. *From Old Woman to Older Women: Contemporary Culture and Women's Narratives*. Columbus: Ohio State UP, 2003. Print.

———. *The Silvering Screen*. Toronto: U of Toronto P, 2011. Print.

Davidson, Kate and Graham Fennell. *Intimacy in Later Life*. New Brunswick (U.S.A.): Transaction Pub, 2004. Print.

DeFalco, Amelia. *Uncanny Subjects: Aging in Contemporary Narrative*. Columbus: Ohio State UP, 2010. Print.

Freud, Sigmund. *The Uncanny*. Trans. David McLintock. New York: Penguin, 2003. Print.

Gullette, Margaret Morganroth. "Improving Sexuality across the Life Course." *Agewise*. Chicago: U of Chicago P, 2011: 124-44. Print.

Howells, Coral Ann. *Contemporary Canadian Women's Fiction: Refiguring Identities*. New York: Palgrave Macmillan, 2003.

Jaffe, Ellen S. "The Stone Angel Speaks: Older Women's Voices in Prose and Poetry." *Journal of Aging, Humanities, and the Arts*. 2.1 (Feb 2008): 62-80. Web.

Katz, Stephen. *Cultural Aging*. Peterborough: Broadview, 2005. Print.

———. "Embodied Memory: Ageing, Neuroculture, and the Genealogy of Mind." *Occasion: Interdisciplinary Studies in the Humanities*. V4. 31 May 2012. Web.

Laurence, Margaret. *The Stone Angel*. Toronto: McClelland & Stewart, 1988. Print.

MacPherson, Andrea. "Great[er] Expectations." *Canadian Literature*. 207 (Winter 2010): 161-63. Web.

Munro, Alice. "Away from Her." *Away from Her*. Toronto: Penguin Group, 2007. Print.

Price, Joan. *Naked at Our Age: Talking Out Loud About Senior Sex*. Berkeley: Seal Press, 2011. Print.

Rooke, Constance, ed. *Night Light: Stories of Aging*. Toronto: Oxford UP, 1986. Print.

Shields, Carol. *The Stone Diaries*. Toronto: Random House, 1993. Print.

Tostevin, Lola Lemire. *The Other Sister*. Toronto: Inanna, 2008. Print.

Walz, Thomas. "Crones, Dirty Old Men, Sexy Seniors: Representations of the Sexuality of Older Persons." *Journal of Aging and Identity*. 7:2 (June 2002): 99-112. Web.

Wright, Richard B. *Sunset Manor*. Toronto: McClelland-Bantam, 1990. Print.

"Old women that will not be kept away"

Undermining Ageist Discourse with Invisibility

and Performance

Ellen Matlok-Ziemann

In many literary texts old women are depicted as "ugly old hags," as the embodiment of failing health and death, and numerous literary scholars have criticized such ageist discourse in fiction and other texts.[1] At the same time, many texts have been produced that explore the question of what it means to grow old.[2] As literary critic Anne Wyatt Brown points out, by the 1970s old characters that had earlier only played a minor role "were transformed into central figures" (57). Yet, not only are there now more texts that feature old characters, there are also many texts written by older authors who voice their aging experiences.

However, while these publications have most certainly contributed to a more nuanced picture of aging that sheds light on the diversity of aging experiences,[3] I want to draw attention to two American literary texts from the 1940s that appear to marginalize old women and to depict them as unimportant, even bothersome, or as "old disgusting creatures." As I will show, by skillfully employing elements of ageist discourse, both texts reveal two issues: firstly, they disclose the mechanism of ageist discourse and often the reader's "complicity" with this mechanism and, secondly, they offer means of subverting even conspicuously stereotypical representations of old women and open up ways for a different understanding of usually negative images of age-related weakness and diseases.

---

1 | Apart from literary scholars, many sociologists, historians, and philosophers have discussed Ageism. To name a few, see, for instance, Margaret Morganroth Gullette's *Aged by Culture* and *Agewise*, Margaret Urban Walker's *Mother Time*, Thomas R. Cole's *The Journey of Life*, Mike Featherstone and Andrew Warwick's *Images of Aging*, and Emmanuelle Tulle's *Old Age and Agency*.

2 | See, for instance, May Sarton, Philip Roth, John Updike, and Margaret Drabble.

3 | Of course, these experiences of aging are informed by class, race, and gender. See also Wyatt-Brown 57.

In contrast to texts that are marked by ageist features in character and plot and are, to a resisting literary critic, as such "important for social betterment,"[4] these two texts only *appear* to present ageist features. Instead, they offer valuable insight into how characters, despite and because of their marginalization, are empowered to resist ageist discourse, something that is easily overlooked by readers.[5] Indeed, the short story "The Purple Hat" by Eudora Welty seems to be, at first sight, a blunt indictment of male violence against old women; yet, sexist and ageist discourse, negative images of old age which appear to maintain patriarchal society, become the very tools to subvert the system. The text further intriguingly opens up a possibility of how the "young–old" binary can be undermined. William Faulkner's *Intruder in the Dust* also problematizes stereotypical depictions of old women as "minor characters" and, in fact, uses marginalization, usually one of the many tools of Ageism, to empower an old woman. This novel also illustrates how old age and frailty can be conceived of as a harmonious part of "being-in-the-world."

"MISS HABERSHAM, A KINLESS SPINSTER OF SEVENTY"

Intruder in the Dust, published in 1948, is a murder mystery of sorts. Set in the Deep South, it is a story about old Lucas Beauchamp, a proud and independent black man, who is wrongly accused of having shot Vincent Gowrie, a white man. The publisher's blurb on the back of the 1991 Vintage International edition dramatically states: "Confronted by the threat of lynching, Lucas sets out to prove his innocence, aided by a white lawyer, Gavin Stevens, and his young nephew Chick Mallison." While it is certainly true that Chick and his uncle help free Lucas, they could never have achieved this without Miss Habersham, "a kinless spinster of seventy" (Faulkner 75).[6] She is the one who, in the dark of the night, makes possible the dangerous undertaking of gathering evidence for Lucas's innocence. Interestingly, the publisher's omission of this crucial piece of information renders conspicuous the invisibility of old women. One could also suggest that this omission reveals the extent to which the publisher is embedded in ageist discourse.

---

4 | Barbara Frey Waxman argues that a resisting literary critic "will undermine these sexist and ageist notions in the texts and raise the readers' awareness of how these damaging notions operate both in texts and society" (88).

5 | Whereas literary critic Noel Polk discusses the extreme male violence presented in "The Purple Hat," my reading indicates that the repeated killings undermine and subvert this violence.

6 | Aleck Sander, a black boy, whose assistance is decisive in this undertaking, is equally ignored in the blurb.

Initially it might seem that *Intruder in the Dust* is, like the publisher's blurb, marked by ageist discourse. Despite her crucial role in the novel, Miss Habersham's first appearance occurs only after 73 pages; she is, as Wyatt Brown would put it, only a minor character. The text thus conveys the impression of being yet another example that presents "ageist notions," a text literary critics need to interrogate to "raise general readers' awareness of how these damaging notions operate" (Wyatt Brown 88). In the pages before, we have met Chick, his parents and his uncle; we have also learned about Chick's first encounter with Lucas from four years ago, the murder, Lucas's imprisonment and the imminent threat of his lynching. At length the narrator depicts Chick's ambivalent feelings for Lucas and his uncle's sentiments about Lucas's situation and that of the South in general. When we finally do meet Miss Habersham, on page 74, it is only to lose sight of her again.[7] Chick briefly notices her when he impatiently enters his uncle's office; he sees her "plain dress," her "round faintly dusty-looking" hat, and her watch "suspended by a gold brooch on her flat bosom" (Faulkner 74-75).[8] Yet, the moment he recognizes her, his thoughts immediately digress to old families which once have lived in the county; *men* like Doctor Habersham, Holston, and Grenier. Only after his reflection of these family histories does Chick's attention return to Miss Habersham.

However, the narrative does not simply reflect ageist discourse. On the contrary, Faulkner uses Chick to undermine this discourse by exaggerating his behavior. By having him repeatedly ignore, forget, and not see Miss Habersham, Faulkner discloses one of the tools of Ageism: to render an old person invisible. In fact, on *one* page, page 77, Faulkner has Chick *not* notice her three times. First, eager to tell his uncle about the news from Lucas, Chick ignores the fact

---

7 | Miss Habersham's name inevitably alludes to another character in Charles Dickens's novel *Great Expectations*: Miss Havisham. Yet, while both characters have never been married, are old maids, there are significant differences. Dickens's Miss Havisham lives the life of a revengeful, bitter recluse, "frozen," as Maryhelen C. Harmon puts it, "in the moment of betrayal" (107). Faulkner's Miss Habersham, who does not show any signs of bitterness, shrewdly uses her marginalization to help Chick. Faulkner's depiction of Miss Habersham as one who is in harmony with her aging body contrasts that of Dickens's Miss Havisham who actually stops time, refuses to age, and still wears the dress that she put on for the wedding that never took place twenty-five years ago. Despite their similar names, Dickens's Miss Havisham has more in common with Emily in Faulkner's "A Rose for Emily." For a discussion of Emily and Miss Havisham see Harmon's article "Old Maids and Old Mansons."

8 | The narrator emphasizes the fact that Miss Habersham is indeed a very old woman past menopause by describing her apparel; she is seen in "cotton stockings and a black hat which she had been wearing for at least forty years" and a dress with a "small golden watch pinned to the unmammery front" (76).

that Miss Habersham is actually having a conversation with his uncle; second, his disregard of this "kinless spinster" lets him even forget "her presence" (77); and third, when he opens his uncle's door, Chick instantly dismisses her and "evanishe[s] her not only from the room but the moment too as the magician with one word or gesture disappears a palm tree or the rabbit or the bowl of roses" (77). After Chick's repeated unwillingness to take notice of Miss Habersham, the reader loses sight of her for two further pages until Chick's uncle turns away from him and speaks to Miss Habersham. But Chick does not notice this and still believes that his uncle addresses him because she has "long ceased" to exist (80). "Only later" does he "realize his uncle was speaking" to her (79).

Yet, while Chick constantly dismisses Miss Habersham to the extent that she no longer seems to exist, he is, time and again, forced to take notice of her existence. Her truck, instrumental for the undertaking to save Lucas, is parked in front of his house and although it is "weathered" (73) like her, it cannot be overlooked. Also his uncle's behavior clearly affirms Miss Habersham's existence by simply turning away from Chick and continuing his conversation with her. Even when Chick "evanishe[s]" her like a magician making a rabbit disappear, the narrator insists on the presence of Chick, his uncle, *and* Miss Habersham. The narrator states: "only they remain, the three of them" (77). The text thus creates a peculiar tension: on the one hand, Miss Habersham is constantly ignored and dismissed, yet, on the other, she is never completely invisible. This tension lays bare the fact that Chick's repeated dismissal of Miss Habersham is nothing but ageist behavior. At the same time, this behavior is disrupted, since he is not allowed to succeed in ignoring her.[9]

Chick's (and to a great extent his uncle's) behavior also distinctly illustrates that old women are considered easily frightened, weak, and helpless – too frail. This image of old women is, however, undermined by Miss Habersham. When she approaches him outside and he first fails to recognize her,[10] since he had forgotten her again, he repeatedly misjudges her and is thus surprised by her "not acting her age." He tells her about Lucas's claims and that he will have to see what gun had killed Vincent Gowrie, that he is "just going out there" (87). Yet, he does not finish his sentence, since he fears that this revelation would shock Miss Habersham. Her response, a calm "[o]f course," confounds Chick. As he is convinced that her calmness is not an appropriate reaction for a seventy-year-old woman, he draws the conclusion that she "could not have under-

---

9 | Interestingly, at the end of the novel, Chick's behavior towards Miss Habersham changes dramatically. Although she does not try to draw attention to herself, Chick is acutely aware of her presence.

10 | Chick mistakes Miss Habersham for his mother. See also Doreen Fowler's discussion of Miss Habersham as a mother figure who can be identified as the bearer of death (804).

stood" what he was implying with his unfinished sentence (87). It seems that there are only two possible reactions for an old woman like Miss Habersham: Either she understands the implications and is terrified or she is calm but then her mind cannot have grasped what Chick plans to do.

In fact, Chick seems disappointed by Miss Habersham, a feeling that suggests the extent to which ageist discourse affects sixteen-year-old Chick. When he bluntly reveals that he intends to "go out there and dig him [the corpse] up and bring him to town where somebody that knows bullet holes can look at the bullet hole in him" (88), she again responds with a calm "[y]es. Of course." What is more, she explains to him that, since "it would take a child–or an old woman" like her to find out the truth about the murder, he cannot reveal anything about his plans to his uncle. Chick, however, would have at least expected a shocked gasp.

Instead of being a shocked frail old lady "acting her age," an old woman who cannot be confronted with horrible things such as the uncovering of a corpse in the middle of the night, Miss Habersham is actually the one who rationally tries to foresee the risks in Chick's plan and suggests solutions. Chick, on the other hand, appears slowly to comprehend the difficulty and great danger of his plan, "not the enormity of his intention but the simple inert unwieldy impossible vastness of what he face[s]" (89). He says quietly: "We cant possibly do it" (89). Miss Habersham, however, is not deterred by Chick's doubts and now tells Chick what needs to be done.

Indeed, the text suggests that Miss Habersham's "inappropriate" behavior, her courage and resoluteness, is possible because no one takes notice of her. It is not only Chick who does not see her. His uncle is taken by surprise when he hears Chick's story about their visit to the grave. He realizes the extent of his failure and he also understands that he had completely underestimated Miss Habersham. He says: "Out of the mouths of babes and sucklings" and adds to the saying "*and old ladies*" (emphasis mine, 105). This saying usually conveys that the very young can be unexpectedly wise. As Chick's uncle changes this by adding "and old ladies," he reveals that old women are equally marginalized and not taken seriously, despite their wisdom.[11] Yet, it is precisely this failure to see Miss Habersham that enables her not to act her age. She is, as one of the "Negroes" in the town also remarks, not "cluttered" by norms of Southern society (70). Men, on the other hand, "cant listen. They aint got time. They are too busy with facks [. . .] If you ever needs to get anything done outside the common run, dont waste yo time on the menfolks" (70). Miss Habersham is only too aware of the constraints of norms in a small Southern town. She tells Chick that the reason that Chick's uncle and the sheriff cannot even consider

---

11 | This expression is a shortening and rephrasing of old expressions from the Bible (New and Old Testament), see Psalms 8:2 and Matthew 21:16.

the possibility of Lucas's innocence is that they "have had to be men too long" (88), they have learned to internalize codes and values and act according to these. Old women, however, are less constrained because of their invisibility.[12]

Old age not only renders Miss Habersham invisible but it also seems to "free" her from sexuality.[13] She refuses to be a sexual object, since, as she tells Chick, she is "seventy years old" (97). Her refusal allows her to move her body in ways that, again, are not appropriate. On their way to the grave Chick and Aleck ask her to mount the horse but since there is no side-saddle, she hesitates and suggests that she could walk. They have to save time, however, so Miss Habersham simply mounts the horse "light and fast as either he [Chick] or Aleck Sander could have done" and sits on the horse "astride." Because of the inappropriate position astride the horse her skirts no longer cover her legs, something that Chick notices and who then tries "to avert his face." But Miss Habersham deflects his look and instead has Chick feel hers. She snorts: "Pah [. . . w]e'll worry about my skirt when we are done with this" (97).[14] Since she does not allow her body to be foregrounded, she can use it in ways that permit her to act without inhibition. With her elegant movement Miss Habersham displays a harmonious "being-in-world."[15] Such a harmonious "being-in-the-world," the feeling of the subject as being one with one's body, entails that the body is not noticed.[16] This feeling is disturbed as soon as the focus shifts from the interaction with others to the body, for instance, because of injuries or diseases. As has been widely discussed, to a great extent old age is socially constructed and many of these social constructions in the Western world particu-

---

12 | In contrast to Marie Ticien Sassoubre who discusses the disempowerment of women and children in the South (204), I argue that Miss Habersham is, in fact, empowered.

13 | I do not want to imply that old women in general are burdened by sexuality. Many feminists have discussed this issue and warned of the de-sexualization of women because of their age. In fact, already in 1976 Simone de Beauvoir discussed at length the myth of old men's and women's asexuality in *The Coming of Age*.

14 | According to Leslie A. Fiedler, Faulkner expresses a distinct fear "of the castrating woman and [a] dis-ease with sexuality" in his novels. Fertile women "possess neither morality nor honor" (320). Faulkner's depictions of old women past menopause, however, differ; he treats them with "respect" (320). This respect can clearly be discerned in the depiction of Miss Habersham.

15 | See Maurice Merleau-Ponty's *Phenomology of Perception* and Drew Leder's *The Absent Body*.

16 | A harmonious "being-in-the-world" entails that the body "knows" how to move, to pick up a stick, or how to drive a car. "To get used to a hat, a car or a stick is to be transplanted into them, or conversely, to incorporate them into the bulk of our own body" (Merleau-Ponty 166).

larly foreground the aged female body in a negative manner that obstruct an old woman's interaction with others. However, there are also biological changes in the body that tend to occur in old age such as the fading of strength, eyesight, or hearing. These bodily changes often foreground the body in ways that cause the body-subject to change his or her behavior. Frequently the interaction with others is then inhibited. One could expect that seventy-year-old Miss Habersham also suffers from such complications while interacting with others because of her failing body. Although she shows a high degree of agility when she mounts Chick's horse, there are obvious signs of a weakening of her audiovisual senses. These senses are particularly important as Miss Habersham and the boys undertake their dangerous rescue action in the middle of the night. They have to act secretively while they also have to see and hear if another person approaches or detects them. On their way to the grave, Aleck suddenly stops since he hears a mule coming closer. A little later, when the mule has passed, Chick and Aleck discuss what the mule had been carrying. Miss Habersham, however, failed to hear the mule nor could she see the mule carry anything. This inability, however, does not impede her or the undertaking. Instead she relies on Chick and Aleck; they become her eyes and ears, or, in phenomenological terms, they become her extended body parts that allow her a harmonious "being-in-the-world," to act un-hindered in the dangerous dark.

As we have seen, the decrease of one's physical strength or senses does not necessarily entail marginalization. Chick and Aleck become Miss Habersham's extended body parts in the same way as Miss Habersham becomes their mind by reflecting the dangers and consequences of their undertaking to free Lucas. Neither does invisibility necessarily have to be a means of marginalization of old women. Miss Habersham shrewdly uses her invisibility to not act her age. Interestingly, towards the end of the novel, when Chick's uncle reveals to Chick and Miss Habersham what actually had happened, her presence, although she does not move or speak, is intensely felt both by Chick and his uncle. While earlier Chick had ignored her despite her voice and movements, he is now acutely aware of her presence (Faulkner 222-24). It seems that Chick's attitude towards old women has changed dramatically.

While Chick no longer disregards old Miss Habersham, (in fact, he has learned to trust and to rely on her), the sentiments of the narrator in the second text, Eudora Welty's "The Purple Hat," published in 1941 and little discussed, never change. Ageist discourse is equally discernible and like in *Intruder in the Dust*, it is subverted by exaggeration – despite the narrator's misogynist and ageist demeanor. Yet, what is exaggerated is not the failure to take notice of her but the repeated effort to force her into extreme invisibility, death.

"Drab Old Creatures" that "Would not be Kept Away"

"The Purple Hat" is a "fat man['s]" (Welty 222) narrative told to two other men in a bar in New Orleans. This man tells the story about a mysterious "lady with the purple hat" (Welty 222), a "drab old" creature, a "disgusting" woman who had twice been murdered in the casino, the Palace of Pleasure, but still reappears there with her young lover. The reason for her killing is never stated but what is emphasized is the narrator's dislike for the lady with the purple hat and his strong disapproval of her visiting the Palace of Pleasure. She is "one of the thousands of middle-aged women who come every day to the Palace [. . .] dull enough, drab old creatures" (Welty 223).[17] These women should clearly not visit such a place and the fat man states that "[n]o one has ever been able to find out how all these old creatures can leave their homes like that to gamble" (Welty 223).

In contrast to Miss Habersham in *Intruder in the Dust*, the lady with the purple hat insists on being seen. While Miss Habersham never really tries to draw attention to herself but rather uses her invisibility to act independently, this lady demands her right to (public) space. By visiting the Palace with a young lover, the lady with the purple hat forces everyone to notice her; however, she seems to be in the wrong (public) place. She insists on being there despite the fact that the fat man renders his story as a warning to all women who frequent and seek pleasure in public places.[18] Although the fat man gives the impression that a third killing would be sufficient to rid the Palace of this "drab old" creature, there are several instances in the text that undermine his assuredness and his superiority. The text instead illustrates a powerful performance of death which enables the lady with the purple hat to insist on her place in public.

Unlike Miss Habersham, this woman does not appear to be real. On the contrary, she has been murdered twice by her young lover who accompanies her; the first time the young man shoots her and the second time he stabs her with her hatpin. Violence seems to be necessary to get rid of her, to create a "period of peace" (Welty 225). Yet, she always returns, and although she has done so for thirty years, she does not show any signs of aging. The narrator thinks "she is a ghost" (Welty 223). Her features are also unreal: Her hair is long, thick, and black, the hair of "ghosts that are lovers" (Welty 225). Her head is large, and her face, like cancerous growth on already dead material, "spreads over such a wide area. Like the moon's" (Welty 226). Every time the narrator

---

17 | The fact that she is only middle-aged but a "drab, old creatur[e]" also indicates that it is not chronological age that determines her age but her being in the wrong place with the wrong person. Age is used to derogate and demean her.

18 | Literary critic Noel Polk reads this story as an indictment of male violence against women and thus fails to see the subversiveness in the text.

has observed her in the thirty years, her features seem to have grown, "expanded." They "move further apart from each other" (Welty 226), limitless and beyond control.

One can discern a distinct sense of fear in the story, the fear that the woman with the purple hat cannot quite be controlled despite the narrator's attitude and the tone of his story, and despite the murders. The fat man seems to evince self-confidence and certainty and may be, as Polk frequently emphasizes, "fat [. . .] cosy and prosperous" (Welty 181, 182, 183, 185), but the narrator is not as self-assured as he appears to be. Yes, he does have an "affable look about him" and is, after the first sip of whiskey, "cosy and prosperous" (Welty 222), ready to begin his story. Yet, he merely gives the impression of being in control, of knowing everything that occurs in the casino.[19] He is the armed man standing on a catwalk beneath the dome and watching everyone underneath him in the gambling room. The narrator tells the young, nervous man in the bar that "[he] can see everything *in the world* from [his] catwalk," and, of course, he does not "brag" (Welty 224, emphasis mine). However, his distance from the gamblers underneath is so great that he cannot hear what they say to each other. He implicitly admits that he is not able to follow the woman's and her young lover's conversation by assuring his listeners that he is certain that she "speaks to him, in a sort of purr, the purr that is used for talking in that room" (Welty 226). Yet, as he is just a passive and distant observer who does not interfere, he can only assume this.

There is no doubt that he likes to be in control. The narrator sits at one end of the counter, leans one elbow on it, rests his cheek on his hand, and can "see all the way down the bar" (Welty 223), as if he were on his catwalk. Yet, again there is a detail that undermines his assuredness. As he looks down the bar, his eyes seem "to be dancing there, above one of those hands so short and plump that you are always counting fingers [. . .] really helpless-looking hands for so large a man" (Welty 223). Although he wants his listeners to believe that he could simply "put out [his] finger and make a change in the universe" (Welty 227), as if he were a god, his almost child-like fingers lack the power to do so.

In another incident, his aloofness is clearly troubled. As he tells the young nervous man and the bartender how the lady with the purple hat was murdered the first time, carried away by three strong men, only to reappear within a month, again with a young man, he remarks: "The only good of shooting her was, it made a brief period of peace there" (Welty 225). Yet, the behavior of his

---

19 | Whereas Polk finds that the fat man represents "an agent of social control [. . .] working in the service of the culture to insure that women who take themselves alone to the Palace of Pleasure do not do so without suffering for it" (183) and compares him to the prison guard in Jeremy Bentham's Panopticon prison, I suggest that the fat man only appears to be in control and does not succeed in keeping women away from the casino.

listeners irritates him; since they do not seem to understand the seriousness of his story, he reprimands them: "I wouldn't scoff, if I were you" (Welty 225). He obviously dislikes this "kind of interruption" and appears worried, "fretted"; it is an interruption that questions his authority and brings to light the peculiar tension that can be sensed in the story.

Indeed, this peculiar tension is accentuated by the occasional thunder that interrupts the fat man's narrative. It is not a violent thunderstorm, rather like a "calm roll [. . .] no more than a shifting of the daily rain clouds" (Welty 222). Yet, the thunderstorm does not dissipate; it lingers and the atmosphere is thus tense with electricity and heavy rain. There is only a little sunlight which is "still suspended" in the air and which lights the bar "as a room might have lighted a mousehole" (Welty 222), lengthening shadows and blurring contours in the bar. The thunder not only interrupts the fat man but also seems to affect the young man in the bar. His hands are "shaking" and he looks "fearfully at a spot on the counter before him" (Welty 222). He is "on his guard" (Welty 223) as if expecting a threat. When he finally asks the fat man who he is, he does so calmly. But underneath his calmness lurks "the greatest wildness," like sudden lightning and thunder. Even the bartender, who is probably used to listening to many of his customers' tales, senses the tension and when the narrator is about to leave, he does not dare ask the narrator in a normal voice if this creature is a ghost but does so "in a real whisper" (Welty 227).

This tense atmosphere also strangely evokes the lady's presence in the bar. Although she had been murdered and removed from the casino twice and although she cannot be seen in the bar, the occasional thunder and the electricity distressingly bring her to mind to the three men. The darkness precludes any visual perception. The same presence can also be sensed at the end of Faulkner's novel when Chick and his uncle are acutely aware of Miss Habersham despite her silence and stillness. In contrast to *Intruder in the Dust*, however, the sense of the lady's presence increases the tension among the three men in the bar. She is not only powerfully but also unbearably present.

It is hardly surprising then that, despite their effort to keep their calm, the three men in the bar are uneasy and uncertain as to what will happen when the lady with the purple hat reappears in the Palace. What unsettles them is not just the question of whether or not she is a ghost but whether she will be accompanied by a young lover and whether she will "lea[d] him on" (Welty 226). Although the fat man disapproves of any "drab old creatur[e]" visiting the casino, he regards the lady with the purple hat as particularly disgusting. She would be "like the rest" of these creatures if there was not "the young man she meets there, from year to year" (Welty 223), if there was not the hat which is "ancient, battered, outrageous" (Welty 226), a "monstrosity" (Welty 223).

The purple hat clearly distinguishes this lady from "the rest." This hat is decorated with plush flowers and a glass vial with a plunger, the weight of

which is balanced by a jeweled hatpin. Without the hat she would be inconspic-
uous, merely "one of those thousands" of women whose presence in the casino
is tolerated. Interestingly, while in the past thirty years the lady had not shown
any signs of aging, her hat seems terribly old since it never changes in style and
fashion. This lack of change accentuates its datedness – its old age. It is a hat,
the narrator comments, "the moths must have hungered for" (Welty 223). By
wearing this ancient "monstrosity" on her head she displays old age and clearly
voices her insistence on public space for old women. The lady with the purple
hat not only forces everyone in the casino to take notice of her but also succeeds
in gaining her young lover's appreciation of old age. Every time, usually late at
night, shortly before she leaves the casino, the lady takes off her hat, places it
"on her shabby lap" (Welty 226) and the young man caresses it. He expresses
tenderness and respect for the old hat. It is at this moment, the narrator warns,
that the lady "leads him on." Old battered hats, old age, cannot be caressed; this
must not be tolerated.[20]

This passage also reveals how the binary of young and old can be undermined. As the narrator states in the beginning of the story, the lady with the
purple hat is not really old, merely middle-aged; in fact, she never seems to
age. One could argue that she embodies the dream that many in Western society have: never to become old, to defy death.[21] But her agelessness is juxtaposed with the purple hat, a hat so "ancient and bedraggled" (Welty 223) that
the moths hunger for it. It is precisely this joining of the "monstrosity"– old
age – and middle age in *one* person that upsets the narrator. The lady displays
with her appearance different ages and thus unsettles conceptions of clear age
boundaries. Although she is not old, she is, at the same time, terribly old. The
depiction of her purple hat equally juxtaposes age boundaries but it does not

---

20 | Polk suggests that the purple hat may also represent the woman's genitals, or,
the glass vial her clitoris that the young man fondles underneath the table (182). This
may be possible but the narrator does not convey to his listeners why the young man
then suddenly murders her. It may be that the lady tells the young man to leave her
alone, or to touch her and then leave her alone. The fat man only vaguely states that
"the young lover had learned something, or come to some conclusion" (Welty 226); he
does not know. But, as Polk rightly argues, although she is the one who is murdered
twice, the narrator renders the lady as the victimizer of the young lover (Polk 182). What
incriminates her is, according to the fat man, that "[s]he leads you on," that you "are
never to know whether [. . .]" (Welty 227).

21 | The fear of old age and death is also reflected in Bennett Foddy's article "Enhancing
Human Lifespan." He suggests a re-definition of age-related diseases as congenital
diseases to "make it easier to justify spending money on saving people" (11) who suffer
from dementia or heart diseases. This would extend the number of "years lived in good
health," youthfulness (9).

fuse old age with middle age, but with youth and thus emphasizes further the blurring of the binary of "old" and "young." It is a hat so old that it has "no fashion" (Welty 225). Yet, while the hat's design never changes and thus clearly indicates its age, it is, nonetheless, "in full bloom" (Welty 223), displaying youthfulness. The fact, that the lady can easily take off age, her hat, also underlines a certain fluidity of age, that the boundaries of "young, middle-aged, and old" are blurred. A person is not simply old or young but embodies many different ages.

Although the fat man's narrative can be considered, as Polk does, a warning to women who seek pleasure in public places, that in our culture they will be punished for their outrageous behavior, this story clearly offers another reading. Yet, not only the disturbance of the binary "old–young" and the blurring of age boundaries invite a different reading. As we have seen, "The Purple Hat" has a distinct atmosphere and there is a sense of fear that perhaps, despite the narrator's assuredness, a third killing of the lady will not do the trick and will not prevent this disgusting old woman from insisting on being in public space. As Rosalie Murphy Baum points out in "Work, Contentment, and Identity in Aging Women in Literature:" "[N]either death nor the [thirty] years have stopped her" (98).

The fact that this woman will not let herself be stopped is a trait that Miss Habersham also reveals. However, Miss Habersham shrewdly uses her invisibility to do the unthinkable: to help free a black man by uncovering the corpse of a white man. While no one in town really takes notice of old Miss Habersham, staff and guests in the Palace of Pleasure wish they were able to disregard the lady with the purple hat. This "drab old creature" insists on drawing attention to herself. What is more, the effort to render her invisible is extreme. When she is murdered the first time, the narrator sees her "bleeding from the face," yet he also claims that not only the dead woman but all other signs of her brutal death are removed. Her blood cannot be traced in the "soft red carpet [. . .] There are no signs afterward, no trouble" (Welty 224). No one in the Palace makes a scene, is upset, or calls the police, since her death creates a "moment of peace," restores patriarchal order. However, this "moment of peace" is brief for "within the month she [is] back" (Welty 224). The second time, when her young lover stabs her with her hatpin, it seems as if she had never existed. She simply folds "all softly in on herself, like a circus tent being taken down after the show" (Welty 227). Once more, she is quickly and quietly removed, and patriarchal peace is restored – only, as the fat man senses, to be disturbed again.

Usually death or, seeing the dead body of a human being is something feared and rejected. A corpse becomes, to use Julia Kristeva's theory, the abject, as it sheds light on the breakdown of the distinction between subject and object, the corpse's materiality and one's own eventual death become suddenly very real and threaten one's identity. What causes abjection, according to Kristeva, is the disturbance of identity, system, and order, which "does not respect

borders, positions, rules" (Kristeva 4). Yet, interestingly, in the casino, the lady's death is not something that is feared but wished for. While the death of
the woman who "leads [young men] on" actually maintains patriarchal order,
the presence of this woman alive at the gambling table with her lover becomes
the abject: she threatens men's identity in patriarchal society. As the narrator
warns, her young lovers "can no longer be sure" what her intentions are (Welty
227). With her death, however, these uncertainties are removed and a "moment
of peace is created." This is why the "people at the tables never turn around"
when her corpse is removed from the casino; the lady with the purple hat becomes yet again invisible and the boundaries of everyone else in the casino are
reestablished.

However, the bartender's question: "Is she a real ghost?" reveals the (patriarchal) fear that no matter how many times this woman is murdered, she
will always insist on her place in public. Murder does not have any effect and
"thousands of middle-aged women [. . . will] not be kept away by *anything* on
earth" (Welty 223, emphasis mine). Regardless of how often men kill the lady
with the purple hat, she will "not be kept away." Thus the threat of death or
death itself loses its power. That which maintains patriarchal order, the death
of this woman, actually turns into a performance and as a mere performance
death becomes meaningless and can no longer sustain the system; instead the
performance undermines death.

As we have seen, in both narratives there exists an unwillingness to take
notice of old women, but the narratives discuss this unwillingness quite differently. In *Intruder in the Dust*, the failure to see the spinster Miss Habersham is
emphasized to the extent that ageist behavior becomes painfully visible. At the
same time, the text indicates that it is impossible to ignore her. However, Miss
Habersham shrewdly uses her marginalization to undertake the unthinkable
in the South. Thus Faulkner's text not only sheds light on the disadvantages
and dangers of the marginalization of old women. It also reveals the potential
that such invisibility can offer. The text further illustrates how frailty does not
necessarily entail marginalization. By relying on others who can see and hear
and by incorporating these senses "into the bulk of [one's own] body" so that
they become "extended body parts" (Merleau-Ponty 166) it may still be possible
to interact with others in a harmonious manner even though one might be
physically constrained.

Exaggeration is also employed in "The Purple Hat" and is, in contrast to
Intruder in the Dust, a means of extreme brutality to render a woman invisible.
However, this story is not simply a critique of male violence. The repeated murder of the lady with the purple hat becomes useless and instead empowers her.
The murders turn into a performance that reveals the brutality of patriarchal
society and, most importantly, the powerful and successful insistence of old
women on public space – that old women "will not be kept away." Furthermore,

this story also challenges and undermines concepts of "young, middle-aged, and old," since the lady and her purple hat seem to display all ages at once. The text suggests that age categories such as "old" are fluid and that a person can embody many different ages. At first sight, Welty's text seems to be marked by misogyny and Ageism, yet it invites a re-thinking of Western understanding of age as linear and the questioning of clear age boundaries.

REFERENCES

Baum, Rosalie Murphy. "Work, Contentment, and Identity in Aging Women in Literature." *Aging and Identity: A Humanities Perspective*. Ed. Sara Deats Munson and Lagretta Tallent Lenker. Westport, CT: Praeger, 1999. 89-101. Print.

Beauvoir, Simone de. *The Coming of Age*. New York: WW Norton, 1996. Print.

Cole, Thomas R. *The Journey of Life: A Cultural History of Aging in America*. New York: Cambridge UP, 1993. Print.

Dickens, Charles. *Great Expectations*. London: Penguin Books, 1994. Print.

Faulkner, William. *Intruder in the Dust*. New York: Vintage International, 1991. Print.

Featherstone, Mike, and Andrew Wernick, eds. *Images of Aging: Cultural Representations of Later Life*. London: Routledge, 1995. Print.

Foddy, Bennett. "Enhancing Human Lifespan." *Philosophy Now* 91 (July/August 2012): 9-11. Print.

Fowler, Doreen. "Beyond Oedipus: Lucas Beauchamp, Ned Barnett, and Faulkner's *Intruder in the Dust*." *Modern Fiction Studies* 53.4 (2007): 788-820. Print.

Frey Waxman, Barbara. "Literary Texts and Literary Critics Team Up against Ageism." *A Guide to Humanistic Studies in Aging: What Does It Mean to Grow Old?* Ed. Thomas R. Cole, Ruth E. Ray, and Robert Kastenbaum. Baltimore: Johns Hopkins UP, 2010. 83-104. Print.

Gullette, Margaret Morganroth. *Aged by Culture*. Chicago: U of Chicago P, 2004. Print.

———. *Agewise: Fighting the New Ageism in America*. Chicago: U of Chicago P, 2011. Print.

Harmon, Maryhelen C. "Old Maids and Old Mansions: The Barren Sisters of Hawthorne, Dickens, and Faulkner." *Aging and Identity: A Humanities Perspective*. Ed. Sara Deats Munson and Lagretta Tallent Lenker. Westport, CT: Praeger, 1999. 103-14. Print.

Kristeva, Julia. *The Powers of Horror*. New York: Columbia UP, 1982. Print.

Leder, Drew. *The Absent Body*. Chicago: U of Chicago P, 1990. Print.

Merleau-Ponty, Maurice. *Phenomology of Perception*. London: Routledge Classics, 2002. Print.

"out of the mouths of babes." *Dictionary.com*. The American Heritage ® Dictionary of Idioms by Christine Ammer. Web. 20 Aug. 2012.

Polk, Noel. "Domestic Violence in 'The Purple Hat,' 'Magic,' and 'The Doll'." *Faulkner and Welty and the Southern Tradition*. Jackson, MS: UP of Mississippi. 176-85. Web. 16 Feb. 2011.

Sassoubre, Ticien Marie. "Avoiding Adjudication in Faulkner." *Criticism* 49.2 (Spring 2007): 183-214. Print.

Tulle, Emmanuelle, ed. *Old Age and Agency*. New York: Nova Science, 2004. Print.

Urban Walker, Margaret. *Mother Time: Women, Aging, and Ethics*. Lanham, Rowman & Littlefield, 1999. Print.

Welty, Eudora. "The Purple Hat." *The Collected Stories of Eudora Welty*. New York: Harcourt Brace Jovanovich, 1980. 222-27. Print.

Wyatt-Brown, Anne M. "Resilience and Creativity in Aging: The Realms of Silver." *A Guide to Humanistic Studies in Aging: What Does It Mean to Grow Old?* Ed. Thomas R. Cole, Ruth E. Ray, and Robert Kastenbaum. Baltimore: Johns Hopkins UP, 2010. 57-82. Print.

Scrutinizing the "Medical Glance"

Bodily Decay, Disease and Death in Margaret Atwood's *The Edible Woman*[1]

Marta Cerezo Moreno

In Chapter 17 of Margaret Atwood's first novel, *The Edible Woman* (1969), the third-person narrative voice centers on the reflections of Marian, the protagonist, regarding her fiancé's disturbing vigilant gaze on her: "Lately he had been watching her more and more [. . .] he would focus his eyes on her face, concentrating on her as though if he looked hard enough he would be able to see through her flesh and her skull and into the workings of her brain. She couldn't tell what he was searching for when he looked at her like that. It made her uneasy" (149). Peter is pictured as a physician that inspects Marian's body in detail. After making love, his visual approach is complemented by the feeling of his hand moving "gently over her skin, without passion, almost clinically, as if he could learn by touch whatever it was that had escaped the probing of his eyes" (149). The distressing portrayal of Marian as a patient "on a doctor's examination table" (149) is one of the novel's pivotal medical images as it clearly signifies the sexual politics at work within the relationship between the protagonist and her husband-to-be.

Peter's medical and precise surveillance evokes Michel Foucault's concept of the "medical glance" developed in *The Birth of the Clinic* (1975), first published in French as *Naissance de la Clinique* in 1963. Foucault analyses how discursive formations have structured medical perception in various ways throughout history. That is, he assays how, historically, there have been various "distributions of illness" and different ways in which "one spatializes disease" (Foucault, *Clinic* 3). Foucault's archaeology of medical perception shows how by the end of the eighteenth century there was a mutation in medical discourse. The eighteenth century medical language, "lacking any perceptual base" and

---

1 | The research carried out for the writing of this article has been financed by the Spanish Ministry of Science and Innovation, project no.FFI2009-09242.

speaking to us "in the language of fantasy", transforms itself, by the turn of the century, into a medical language with "a qualitative precision [that] directs our gaze into a world of constant visibility" (x). Foucault's history of the mechanisms of medical perception focuses on the transformation of the clinical gaze and it pays special attention to the development from the medical observing gaze to the medical glance. Whereas the former's correlative is "the immediately visible" (107), the latter reads the deep structures of visibility in order "to discover its secrets" (120). While the gaze "observe[s] what is self-evident" (88) the medical glance "goes beyond what it sees" (121) as it "penetrates into the body [. . .] to perceive what [is] immediately behind the visible surface" (137). In order to plunge "from the manifest to the hidden" (135) the glance is "endowed with a plurisensorial structure" (164) where touch becomes central; "the glance is of the non-verbal order of *contact*" (123). Clinical anatomy turns the body, defined by Foucault as "an opaque mass in which secrets, invisible lesions, and the very mystery of origins lie hidden", into a "tangible space" (123) that is allowed to be thoroughly inspected. The body is now pictured as a text that must be read and interpreted.

The Edible Woman revolves around a two-leveled structure of surface and depth, visibility and invisibility. Marian's body turns into a "tangible space" whose surface and visible elements are subjected to a medical glance that scrutinizes her in order to grasp her deep, hidden psychological entrails and, therefore, control and dominate her subjectivity. Peter's clinical eye portrays him as a gazer embedded within a power relationship in which Marian, the object of his gaze, is opened up in order to be ruled. His medical glance is presented by Atwood as an invasive and violent intrusion within Marian's selfhood. However, the novel makes it evident that Peter's violent trespass is just one of the multiple elements of a social network where power is at work; Peter's medical glance is just one of the axes of the Foucauldian "micro-physics of power" (Foucault, *Discipline* 26). This societal visual constraint works as a power technique that seeks to regulate and manipulate Marian's bodily operations in order to control her mind. This "political anatomy" turns the protagonist into what Foucault describes as a "docile body"; that is, a body "that may be subjected, used, transformed, improved" (136). The effectiveness of relentless surveillance, as a primal patriarchal disciplinary strategy, makes Marian aware of her own visibility to such an extent that she ends up internalizing a male glance that makes her docility complete. Thus, Marian turns into a self-policing subject whose ceaseless self-surveillance is a reflection of her desires to please Peter's expectations and to embody the patriarchal ideal of femininity. As Susan Bordo states, these practices of femininity may lead women to "utter demoralization, debilitation, and death" (91). In *The Edible Woman*, Atwood contends that women's attempts to abide by patriarchal regulations lead them also to bodily disintegration and disease. Many of Marian's bodily gestures, movements, and practices show her body as, first, a locus of social control, and, second, as a text of culture, as a surface on which patriarchal ideological constructions of femininity have been deeply inscribed (Bordo 90-91). Marian's conservative ideas of marriage and motherhood as the assumed role of woman match those bodily behaviors (Atwood 102). However, the novel presents us with a series of images of female bodily decay, decomposition and disease that show how – despite Marian's efforts to comply with patriarchal norms – she progressively becomes fully aware of the degrading effect these male-oriented cultural values have on her identity.

The novel's images of Marian's bodily decomposition and deformity depict the protagonist's body as a textual surface that turns the invisible process of disintegration of Marian's sense of self-control and autonomy into a visible entity. In Chapter 6, Marian describes a dream-like vision of her own bodily dissolution: "Her feet [were] beginning to dissolve, like melting jelly" as "the ends of [her] fingers were turning transparent" (43). In Chapter 17, Marian sees her reflection in a spoon as a sign of physical deformity: "herself upside down, with a huge torso narrowing to a pinhead at the handle end. She tilted the spoon and her forehead swelled, then receded" (146). In Chapter 25, Atwood offers us the ultimate identity-threatening passage of her novel by describing Marian's hallucination of her own bodily distortion, fragmentation, and disintegration. As she prepares for Peter's party, she lies in the bathtub and sees her body reflected back in three silver globes at the base of the two taps and spout. At first she can see "a curiously-sprawling pink thing" and "bulging distorted forms" that she finally identifies as "her own waterlogged body" (218). As she sways herself back and forth, she watches "the way in which the different bright silver parts of her body suddenly bloated or diminished" (218). She now feels her body as "somehow no longer quite her own. All at once she was afraid that she was dissolving, coming apart layer by layer like a piece of cardboard in a gutter puddle" (218). She panics and realizes that, at Peter's party, she will be observed and inspected. His friends will fix their "uncomprehending eyes" on her, and their imminent scrutiny makes her afraid of losing control, of "losing her shape, spreading out, not being able to contain herself any longer" (218).

"I don't like to be stared at" (91), asserts Marian. The protagonist's refusal to be the object of an invasive medical glance, intended to fashion her behavior, is metaphorically presented in the novel by her fear of being captured by Peter's camera. Atwood constantly establishes connections between Peter's interest in cameras and hunting. Marian is described as a perfect visible target in danger to be caught by Peter's photographic lens and weapon (244). As Marian runs away from Peter's party, both the images of the camera and of the weapon merge as one indivisible metaphor of oppression (245). In her escape, Marian finally sees "what lay hidden under [Peter's] surface" (118) and envisions his real violent and coercive nature: "That dark intent marksman with his aiming eye had been there all the time, hidden by the other layers, waiting for her at the dead centre: a homicidal maniac with a lethal weapon in his hands" (246). She finally realizes that her relationship with Peter is leading to her bodily extinction and the consequent death of her selfhood; a death that is initially envisioned through Marian's juxtaposition of the bathtub, where they make love, with a coffin (60).

Peter and Len's conversation about rabbit hunting and their following chase of Marian signal the violent nature of the protagonist's fiancé. In the pivotal dinner scene of Chapter 17, his aggressive nature is highlighted as Marian watches him cut his meat: "How skillfully he did it: no tearing, no ragged ends. And yet it was a violent action, cutting" (150). Peter's fiery manipulation and ingestion of food is a revealing metaphor of his implacable consumption of Marian's identity. Though depicted as Marian's "rescuer from chaos, a provider of stability" (89), Peter treats her as a "stage-prop: silent but solid, a two-dimensional outline" (71) and takes "pride in displaying her" to his friends as she sits "the whole time silent and smiling" (176). Marian's modest lowering of her eyes (89), her "soft flannelly voice" as she tells Peter that she leaves all the "big decisions up to [him]" (90), and her unwilling realization of her fiancé's wish to see her in a nice dress and with her hair styled for the final party, present her body as the incarnation of patriarchal social paradigms of femininity. In a novel structured around food as its central metaphor, Marian's demeanor produces a body that is absorbed, consumed, ingested, and that ultimately epitomizes Atwood's narrative exploration of "symbolic cannibalism" (Introduction) as the regulation of otherness. As Parker states, Atwood probes "the power dynamic of eating and non-eating, she simultaneously confronts the relationship between consumer and consumed. In her fiction, the powerful not only eat, they eat the powerless" (363). The sight of Peter's violent handling and digestion of his meal makes Marian unable to finish hers; meanwhile, "the last of Peter's steak disappear[s] into his mouth" as he "smiles and chews, pleasantly conscious of his own superior capacity" (Atwood 152). This scene triggers Marian's nervous eating disorder, which functions as the leading image of a text in which the act of devouring the other's self is central.

Whereas her eating disorder could be interpreted as a sign of Marian's weakness, her loss of appetite turns her female body into a site of rebellion. Marian's constant attempts to understand the reasons why her body has "cut itself off" (178) persistently entice the reader to appropriate Foucault's concept of the medical glance in order to penetrate Marian's unconscious through the observation of her bodily behavior. Marian's body reveals itself as a site of knowledge that allows us to disclose the intimate relation between the visible, corporeal symptoms of her eating disorder and the invisible, but at the same time substantial, nature of her inner conflict. By refusing to eat, Marian's body, despite her apparent conventional femininity, is protesting against a patriarchal discourse to which the protagonist is not willing to subscribe. Once again, the interplay between surface and depth, visibility and invisibility is at play in a narrative space in which even Marian herself strives to find out what lies behind her own surface by looking in Peter's mirror at her make-up, fingernails, earrings and hairdo before his party begins: "What was it that lay beneath the surface these pieces were floating on, holding them together?" (229).

What lies beneath Marian's visible surface is a woman whose body opposes the ideological construction of women as socially digested entities. Marian's descriptions of motherhood as woman's intellectual and bodily decay, and of female maturity as physically repulsive, display the protagonist's fear of entering a female bodily space that defines woman as the site of revolting and monstrous deformity and disease. For Marian, maternity is synonymous with a lack of mental sharpness and intellectual acuteness that has maternal bodily disfigurement and disease as its correlatives (130). Her friend Clara's pregnant body is compared to a "boa-constrictor that has swallowed a watermelon. Her head with its aureole of pale hair was made to seem smaller and even more fragile by the contrast" (31). Clara's body seems "somehow beyond her, going its own way without reference to any direction of hers" (37). On the phone, she sounds as if she is being "dragged slowly down into the gigantic pumpkin-like growth that was enveloping her body" (114). Finally, monstrosity and maternity are clearly linked by Marian and Clara's speculations about "the mysterious behaviour of [Clara's belly's] contents [. . .] 'Maybe it's got three heads,' and 'Maybe it isn't a baby at all but a kind of parasitic growth, like galls on trees, or elephantiasis of the navel, or a huge bunion [. . .]'" (114). As Rosi Braidotti affirms, within the binary logic of oppositions that structures patriarchal discursive formations, the long-established relationship between femininity and monstrosity in Western thought represents "the negative pole, the pole of pejoration" (64). The woman/monster analogy points to deviance and abnormality.

Marian constantly thinks of Clara as "a perpetual invalid and connect[s] her with meals carried on trays" (Atwood 205). She views maternity as a disability and a disease that does not allow women to be in possession of their lives. Thus, *The Edible Woman* inserts the concept of disease within the negative pole of the phallogocentric binary opposition that equates women and monstrosity. During her visit to Clara at the hospital, the correspondence between woman and disease is made explicit. Marian learns that Clara's pastime is listening to her hospital roommates' conversations about their miscarriages and diseases: "It's a positive gloating about pain. I even find myself producing a few of my own ailments, as though I have to compete" (130). Marian realizes that Clara's hospital room is painted the same color as her office (129). Atwood's narrative link between both spaces is significant since it anticipates the relevant presence of the triple correspondence between female body, deformity, and disease in her description of Marian's office Christmas party, which "seemed to consist largely of the consumption of food and the discussion of ailments and bargains" (162).

During the party, the terms "illness" and "sick" are central in Marian's colleagues' conversations, which are followed by Marian's vision of the deformity
inscribed within the bodies of her fellow office workers. Marian fixes her gaze
on their aging, fat, and mature female bodies "in various stages of growth and
decay" (167). For the protagonist, up till that moment, they had merely been like
"objects viewed as outline and surface only" (167). However, she can now see
their rolls of fat around their bodies "sustained somewhere within by bones,
without by a carapace of clothing and makeup" (167). Initially, she sees them as
detached "creatures": "[. . .] continual flux between the outside and the inside,
taking things in, giving them out, chewing, words, potatochips, burps, grease,
hair, babies, milk, excrement, cookies, vomit, coffee, tomato-juice, blood, tea,
sweat, liquor, tears, and garbage [. . .]" (167). However, she then realizes that she
is "one of them, her body the same, identical" and feels "suffocated by this thick
sargasso-sea of femininity" (167). Marian now sees them not as her colleagues,
but as women immersed within "the vast anonymous ocean of housewives
[. . .]. They could have been wearing housecoats and curlers" (166). For the first
time, Marian examines "the women's bodies with interest, critically, as though
she had never seen them before" (167). The protagonist's inspection of their
bodies is a narrative variant of the Foucauldian medical glance that sees beyond
the surface so as to discover what lies beneath. What Marian finds under her
colleagues' grotesque bodies is her own degrading and decaying future image
as Peter's wife and mother of his children.

Marian sees her colleagues as mirror images that reflect her own body's
deformity as a metaphor of the degrading effects of patriarchal cultural codes
on women. Her feeling of entrapment within a gender ideology that depicts
women as items of social consumption finds certain release in her relationship with Duncan. However, the self-absorbed English graduate also functions
as another mirror image for Marian's anxieties and corresponding bodily extinction. Every time they meet, they constantly stand gazing at each other in
silence (49; 100). When Marian wears his dressing-gown, Duncan finally tells
her, "you look sort of like me in that" (144). Marian's constant inspection of
Duncan's "cadaverously thin" (48) body must be interpreted as the observance
of her own bodily decay. As they both lie on his bed, she studies "the contours
of his skull under the papery skin, wondering how anyone could be that thin
and still remain alive" (144). Duncan's spare body has the "gaunt shape of a
starved animal in time of famine" (171), his "ribs stuck like those of an emaci-
ated figure in a medieval woodcut. The skin stretched over them was nearly co-
lourless, not white but closer to the sallow tone of old linen" (48). She observes
his "thin face, the high stark ridge of his cheekbone, the dark hollow of his eye"
(99) and, after embracing him, she feels his body as if "made of tissue paper or
parchment stretched on a frame of wire coathangers" (100). Duncan's thinness
metaphorically presages the devastating results of Marian's eating disorder on

her body. Their visit to the Mummy Room of the Royal Ontario Museum and their observation of several mummies and a child's skeleton foretell death as Mariam's end if her body's refusal to eat persists. As Duncan passes his hand over the curve of Marian's cheek, he confesses that when he touches someone he "can't concentrate just on the surface" (188): "As long as you only think about the surface I suppose it's all right, and real enough; but once you start thinking about what's inside [. . .]" (188). Through the allusion to Duncan's fascination with the discovery of what lies beneath the surface of human skin, the novel, once more, induces the reader to make use of Foucault's concept of the medical glance so as to see the skeleton, not just literally, as what is beyond our physical surface: "jutting ribs and frail legs and starved shoulder-blades" (188), but also as a deadly physical decrepitude that symbolizes both Duncan's and Marian's inner conflicts.

The leading metaphor of the novel, an edible woman in the symbolic shape of a cake which Marian bakes and ices for Peter is both the ultimate image of bodily dismemberment and also the sign of Marian's recovery. The baked woman is a metaphorical reduplication of Marian as an item of patriarchal consumption. When Peter refuses to eat it after she finally accuses him of "trying to assimilate [her]" (271), she suddenly feels extremely hungry and starts devouring the cake. She re-enters the social symbolic by taking part in the consuming act that her body has been rejecting and, now that she is finally "adjusted" (263), she becomes a healthy member within "the consumer-consumed cycle of society" (Staels 32). However, though she escapes from Peter, Marian has not achieved independence from the degrading effects on her identity process of a patriarchal clinical eye that has made her internalize male-focused cultural conceptions. Before she offers the cake to Peter, she suddenly fears that if he finds it a "monumental silliness" (Atwood 170), she will "accept his version of herself" (271). She finally overcomes such fear. However, though she is capable of expelling Peter from her life, she is not ready to confront the socially constraining phallogocentric medical glance that, at that time and at that place, did not allow women to become successful in both public and private spheres. "I realized Peter was trying to destroy me. So now I'm looking for another job" (277), explains Marian to Duncan over the phone before she invites him for tea. As Atwood herself states, "[M]y heroine's choices remain much the same at the end of the book as they are at the beginning: a career going nowhere, or marriage as an exit from it. But these were the options for a young woman, even a young educated woman, in Canada in the early sixties" (Introduction).

We find the first narrative identification of Marian's body with a cake in Chapter 24. Peter suggests that she might have something done with her hair for his final party, and Marian spends the afternoon at the hairdresser's where "they treated your head like a cake: something to be carefully iced and ornamented" (208). If, as we have already seen, when visiting Clara, Marian makes an explicit connection between the hospital and her office, at the hairdresser's she now feels "as passive as though she was being admitted to a hospital to have an operation" (209). She then identifies the waiting staff with nurses, the chair as the operating table, the hairdresser as the doctor, the towel as a surgical cloth, and the hair care products as bottled medicines. Marian pictures herself as a paralyzed patient, as "a slab of flesh, an object" (209). When baking the cake, she is reproducing this scene, but she is now the surgeon that "operates", gives shape to and decorates the cake-woman (269), described as her own creation, but also as another mirror image that "gaze[s] up at her" (270). Marian points to the suppleness of the cake: "The spongy cake was pliable, easy to mould" (269). The cake-woman is eventually devoured by Marian herself who first starts with the feet, and then neatly "sever[s] the body from the head" (272). Finally, "the remains of the cadaver" (281) are eaten up by Duncan.

As Linda Hutcheon states, "Atwood chooses to hang the narrative upon a solid scaffolding of imagery" (n.p.) whose links are left for us, the readers, to find out. By using Foucault's medical terms, we could conclude that the whole narrative structure of *The Edible Woman* functions itself as a constant medical glance that subtly and gradually assesses Marian's symptoms by plunging into her psychic depths by means of an outstanding manipulation of imagery. Atwood's novel constantly challenges the reader, whereas at the same time it offers the necessary tools, to become a physician in search of the origins of the protagonist's eating disorder, and therefore discover the deep cultural structures at work beneath physical visibility. By applying such critical methods, we can conclude that the interweaving of the final image of the cake-woman with the strands of imagery at work throughout the novel presents female bodily disintegration as the metaphor of a passive, docile, fragmented, decaying and ill female subject that is constantly refashioned not just by the other's patriarchal medical glance but by her own. The only way for women like Marian not to turn into social corpses, and to avoid being finally digested, would be to "take the risk of critically affirming [their] own interests in the symbolic order" (Staels 32). In order to do that, they first have to realize that any act of patriarchal surveillance and control is a learned, cultural, and ideological process that can and must be deconstructed.

REFERENCES

Atwood, Margaret. *The Edible Woman*. London: Virago, 2006. Print.
Bordo, Susan. "The Body and the Reproduction of Femininity." *Writing on the Body. Female Embodiment and Feminist Theory*. Ed. Katie Conboy, Nadia Medina, and Sarah Stanbury. New York: Columbia UP, 1997. 90-112. Print.

Braidotti, Rosi. "Mothers, Monsters, and Machines." *Writing on the Body. Female Embodiment and Feminist Theory.* Ed. Katie Conboy, Nadia Medina, and Sarah Stanbury. New York: Columbia UP, 1997. 59-79. Print.

Foucault, Michel. *The Birth of the Clinic. An Archaeology of Medical Perception.* New York: Vintage Books, 1975. Print.

———. *Discipline and Punish. The Birth of the Prison.* London: Penguin Books, 1991. Print.

Hutcheon, Linda. "Atwood and Laurence: Poet and Novelist." *Studies in Canadian Literature* 3.2 (1978): n.p. Web. 14 April 2013.

Parker, Emma. "You Are What You Eat: The Politics of Eating in the Novels of Margaret Atwood." *Twentieth Century Literature* 41.3 (Fall 1995): 349-68. Print.

Staels, Hilde. *Margaret Atwood's Novels. A Study of Narrative Discourse.* Tübingen: Francke Verlag, 1995. Print.

Wisdom versus Frailty
in Ursula K. Le Guin's *Voices*
and Doris Lessing's "The Reason for It"

Maricel Oró-Piqueras

Doris Lessing (1919) and Ursula K. Le Guin (1929) are contemporary women writers who are well-known for their extended careers. Despite their different backgrounds – Doris Lessing was born in Rhodesia and has lived most of her adult life in London, whereas Ursula K. Le Guin lives in the United States, in Portland – both writers share an acute interest in understanding and analyzing the society around them through their narratives. Both are known for their innovative writing power; both have cleverly presented utopian and science fiction societies in order to analyze, understand and critique present-day society and to propose different perspectives on it. When analyzing the trajectories of Lessing and Le Guin in *A Critical Guide to Twentieth-Century Women Novelists*, Kathleen Wheeler acknowledges the importance of the innovation of their research on form, genre, and theme present in their fiction and highlights how "[t]his 'genre busting' is an example of Le Guin's [and also Lessing's] interest in examining the categories and distinctions which govern our lives, structure our experience and constitute our world" (242).

As acute observers and analyzers of anything around them, it is not surprising to discover that two of their texts written past the year 2000 scrutinize the concept of old age and the multiple cultural connotations it has been related to, embedded in the two dystopian societies they present. Ursula K. Le Guin's *Voices* (2006) and Doris Lessing's short story "The Reason for It" (2003) are set in a place and time unrecognizable for the reader with the common characteristic that their main protagonists live in a land that has been invaded by unwise rulers who have opted to militarize their communities in order to keep both opposition and revolution under control. For the militarized ruling classes present in the texts, traditional knowledge, which used to be transmitted through the figure of an old wise person and storytelling as well as through the reading of books, has been substituted by constant innovation in the military terrain as well as a set of restrictive beliefs that aims to keep active and critical minds under control. One of the leading beliefs in the societies depicted in the novels can be summarized as *anything old is bad* whereas *anything new is good.* It is in that sense that the texts bring to the surface the dichotomy of wisdom versus frailty in relation to old age; since on the one hand, in the new societies, youth and external physical vigor are venerated by dictatorial regimes whereas on the other hand, the old wise men of the communities, physically tired and frail, are the ones who lead the opposition to the intellectual numbing suffered by their communities.

As mentioned earlier, both writers have expressed their interest in understanding the society of their times but also in scrutinizing the concept of *reality* in order to be critical of the established status quo. With regard to Doris Lessing, Gayle Greene characterizes her as always "concerned with getting us to 'step outside what we are'" (8) and stretch our imaginations to conceive of "another order of world altogether. Her fiction is visionary and revisionary in getting us to see that our reality is not the whole of reality and to imagine an elsewhere" (20). Similarly, when Ursula K. Le Guin was asked about the present American economic situation as well as the persistent international conflicts of our times, she answered: "[t]he world is so weird that [. . .] the only way to describe it is by accepting its weirdness - we begin to understand it by accepting the fact that we can't understand it. [. . .] And fantasy and sf are good tools, the best tools, for getting perspective on the big social and political stuff [. . .], and for figuring out what might be changed in our society - for better or worse - and what change might involve [. . .]" (Hogue 2). Their resorting to utopian societies gives them the possibility of stretching their imaginations in order to get to concepts which may be lying just behind the surface of any society but which at the same time constitute the engine that leads such society towards its immediate future. It is in that sense that their focusing on simple stereotyping of the old and young body and relating them to frailty and vigor respectively becomes key to understanding what may be the outcomes of a society which seems only focused on following tendencies and forgets about analyzing and questioning such tendencies.

According to G. Clayes and L. T. Sargent, utopian fiction can be defined as "the imaginative projection, positive or negative, of a society that is substantially different from the one in which the author lives;" and they acknowledge that the primary characteristic of utopia is "its nonexistence combined with topos – a location in time and space – to give verisimilitude" (1). By his part, H.M. Zaki considers that "utopian thought contains a critical component which relates the reader to the author's society. It attacks existing institutions and values, confronts the reigning ideology, estranges readers from their family environs, demonstrates the need for change, and serves as a focal point for social change" (12). These two definitions, that describe utopian texts in a wide sense, can easily be applied to Ursula K. Le Guin's *Voices* and Doris Lessing's "The Reason for It." However, the authors seem to go one step further when they not only set their fictions in an estranged topos, forcing the reader to have a look around and question the existing status quo, but also question the alternatives offered by and available in contemporary society.

The aging body and old age have been the bedrock of negative implications in the history of Western civilization. As Simone de Beauvoir writes in *The Coming of Age*, in Western thought, old age is and has been considered "a kind of shameful secret that is unseemly to mention" (1). For her part, Kathleen Woodward defines old age as one of the discontents of our civilization that has traditionally been represented "in terms of splitting": "Youth, represented by a youthful body, is good; old age, represented by the aging body, is bad" (7).

From the last decades of the twentieth century to the beginning of the twenty-first, a period characterized as the era of technology and information, keeping the body fit has not so much been centered on bodies that have to be part of an industrial workforce as on bodies that require what is known as *body maintenance*, a concept strongly influenced by an economic system increasingly focused on consumerism. Sociologists Mike Featherstone, Mike Hepworth and Bryan S. Turner have studied and theorized the concept of body maintenance and the preservation of health as a way of social control through the body and its close association with consumer culture. Mike Featherstone argues that the term *body maintenance* is an indicator of the "popularity of the machine metaphor for the body," so that "[l]ike cars and other consumer goods, bodies require servicing, regular care and attention to preserve maximum efficiency" (182). As such, the well-kept body not only becomes an object of cult *per se*, but it is also endowed with the meaning of virtue and wisdom in the person who lives within it.[1]

In fact, consumer culture has taken the precious jewel of youth for its own benefit by trying to convince future consumers that the negative qualities attached to an elderly body can be defeated by applying a number of techniques and products. In this sense, consumer culture is another form of social regulation by which the negative stereotypes constructed around old age are redefined from an equivocal perspective that in many cases actually contributes to pervading them. Mike Featherstone and Mike Hepworth reflect on the double-edge of the messages of consumer culture in relation to the aging body and old age and contend that,

---

1 | In Mike Featherstone's own words, "fitness and slimness become associated not only with energy, drive and vitality but worthiness as a person; likewise the body beautiful comes to be taken as a sign of prudence and prescience in health matters" (*Body in Consumer Culture* 183).

as far as body maintenance is concerned, an array of evidence continues to accrue which disproves the necessary decline of mental, sexual and physiological capacities in old age. Chronological age continues to be discredited as an indicator of inevitable age norms and lifestyles and a new breed of body maintenance experts optimistically pre-scribe health foods, vitamins, dieting, fitness techniques and other regimens to control biological age – which is the true index of how a person should feel. (374)

The influence of consumer culture on how the aging body should be cared for and restructured is unquestionable in our present times. The contribution of consumer culture to challenging negative stereotypes related to the aging body is, however, rather questionable since, while it delineates fashionable trends in body image, it indicates at the same time what is socially acceptable and unacceptable. In this sense, the positive aging discourse that is presently ex-tending can be considered equivocal; as Andrew Blaikie points out, it "effec-tively eclipses consideration of illness and decline," whereas "final decay and death takes on a heightened hideousness since these will happen, regardless of whatever cultural, economic, or body capital one might possess" (72)[2]. Thus, in present-day Western society, the aging body has inherited some of the negative values that have been attributed to it from Antiquity, but is now considered a *machine* that can be repaired at any time, with the result that those who show signs of aging on their bodies are seen as untidy and careless, characteristics that apparently match their personalities. On the other hand, those aged people who look young and healthy are those who are praised more, thus creating even more distance in the dichotomy between young and old.

In Le Guin's and Lessing's condensed utopian societies, aggressive capital-ism understood as constant production and consumption above any other val-ues is not openly described as being part of the social organization of the com-munities depicted in the texts. However, the social control exerted by the new ruling leaders is based on control of the external body so that on the one hand, old age is increasingly deprecated and made invisible and on the other hand, the fact of keeping a strong and powerful body becomes a necessary element in order to be accepted within a militarized community. Moreover, knowledge and critical thinking which were transmitted from generation to generation

---

2 | In Ageing and Popular Culture, Andrew Blaikie quotes a report of the "Royal Commission on Population," published in 1949, in which older people are considered to "excel in experience, patience, in wisdom and breadth of view," whereas the young are highlighted by their "energy, enterprise, enthusiasm, the capacity to learn new things, to adapt themselves, to innovate." The report concludes by stating that "[i]t thus seems possible that a society in which the proportion of young people is diminishing will become dangerously unprogressive" (39).

through the old wise men and women in the community are undermined and become increasingly forgotten practices in both utopian societies.

In both texts, Lessing's "The Reason for It" and Le Guin's *Voices*, the narrator is one of the leading characters, a character who has the gift of observing and making conclusions regarding the reality around him or her. "The Reason for It" starts when Twelve, the only old wise man left in the community, remembers the last words his good friend Eleven told him on his death bed: "'While The Twelve have been dying the truth has been dying. When you come to join us no one will be left to tell our story'" (Lessing 133). In this short story, Lessing introduces a community which had been ruled by a wise ruler, Destra, who managed to bring peace, high culture and civilization to their land. In fact, the name *Destra* means *right*. When Destra could envisage her death because of her old age, she decided to teach twelve children from the community in order to ensure that her peaceful and prosperous reign would continue. As the narrator explains, "[s]he was a wonderful teacher. She taught us good behavior, how to make decisions, how to think, how to put the welfare of The Cities before anything else. All this by means of tales and songs. She had tutors to teach us the art of numbers, weights, measurements" (Lessing 141). However, when Destra died and the new ruler, Destra's son DeRod, substituted her, their world went upside down in a few years.

In Le Guin's *Voices*, Memer is the young narrator who leads the reader into her community's turbulent story. As in Lessing's "The Reason for It," the narrator is one of the few people who are aware of the *truth* within her community. However, as in Lessing's story, the truth which leads to the right path is secretly hidden; in this case, it is introduced in the novel as the first remembrance Memer has of her childhood, the so-called secret room: "The first thing I can remember clearly is writing the way into the secret room. [. . .] The light in that room is clear and calm, falling from many small skylights of thick glass in the high ceiling. It's a very long room, with shelves down its wall, and books on the shelves" (Le Guin 2). The hidden treasures in the secret room are books that contain the stories that tell about the history and culture of Memer's community. Those books are hidden in the secret room because the new rulers of the land, the Alds, a saga of warriors who violently invaded the city of Ansul and who keep it under control through military force, forbid the existence of anything related to Ansul's soul – anything that was contained in books. Thus, when the Alds took the city, they destroyed all the books except those that were hidden in Memer's household, which belong to the Waylord, the only old wise man left in the city.

In both utopian societies, knowledge is presented as those stories, both oral and written, that were guarded and transmitted by the wise men and wise women within the community. In Lessing's "The Reason for It," Destra had managed to reconvert her land in a peaceful and prosperous place, through transmitting her fruitful knowledge to younger generations via storytelling. In the case of Le Guin's *Voices*, the city of Ansul was not ruled by a specific person. Instead, the Waylord was the person who would study the books in his library and read the Oracle in order to give advice to his people when they asked for it. Thus, before being invaded by unwise and cruel rulers, in other words, before real events changed the meaning of positive symbols, both societies had flourished due to their centering on teaching and learning, on analyzing and understanding based on storytelling led by those who had the authority of experience. Indeed, it is significant that in both cases it is a person stepping towards old age who is responsible for transmitting that knowledge to younger generations. Contrarily to narratives of aging and old age that have been present in Western societies since the beginning of the Industrial Revolution in which old age became synonymous with lack of productivity and dependence[3], in the utopian societies presented by Lessing and Le Guin the time of prosperity and happiness is clearly related to their old wise leaders and, in fact, once they are substituted by younger ones who lack wisdom and experience, prosperity is only based on external appearance and is thus ephemeral. In fact, in both texts, expressions of ageism towards those who look old and slow are prominent. In Lessing's "The Reason for It," while Twelve is considering the best way to proceed so that neither storytelling nor the history of the Cities is lost, he decides to go for a walk when

[a] gang of seven young men appeared, running up through the trees towards me; they saw me, and then with cries of excitement, as if they had glimpsed a running animal, came towards me. I stopped and faced them. They stopped, a few paces away. Each face was distorted into that sneer which is obligatory now.

'What have we got here?' said the leader. [. . .]

'Look, an old beggar,' said another [. . .]

He snatched my stick away, so that I stumbled and nearly fell, and then used it to lift up the bottom of my robe far enough so they could admire my ancient sex: what they were seeing, what I saw every day in the bath, was something like a bump of dried mushrooms. They pointed and sneered and sniggered. (176)

---

3 | According to Bryan S. Turner, the social position of the aged becomes further diffused when the organization of knowledge is made prominent in the form of "timetables, taxonomies, typologies, registers, examinations and chrestomathies," a schema that allowed "the control of large numbers of bodies within a regimented space" (158).

Not only were these "half-savage" boys ignorant of Twelve's identity and knowledge, they did not respect him for the simple fact that he was an old man. In Le Guin's Voices, the Waylord is also presented as an old and lame man. He had been violently tortured by the Alds as they tried to sabotage the House of the Oracle. When Memer, as a child, used to get into the secret room, she remembers passing "the Waylord's door to come here, but he's sick and lame and stays in his rooms" (Le Guin 2). However, when the people from Ansul rise against the Alds and a group of Alds goes to the House of the Oracle in order to confront the Waylord, Memer explains that "I saw him then. I saw him, for once, as he had been, and as my heart had always known him: a tall, straight, beautiful man, smiling, with fire in his eyes" (Le Guin 259).

Indeed, the Alds, such as the young men in Lessing's "The Reason for It," could not see the wisdom and strength of spirit inside the old wise men they had in front of them. In the case of Le Guin's Voices, the fact that the people of Ansul were invaded by force prevented that a few young people, such as Memer, were blinded by the power of their well-built bodies and militarized looks. In fact, the power of looks is also present in our contemporary society in which the values of strength, power and youth are also enhanced and promised to be kept by consumer culture to the detriment of the natural process which makes a human body become physically old, although not necessarily senile. As Hepworth and Featherstone argue in their book Surviving Middle Age, "[t]he media have played an important role in creating and maintaining this moral climate which challenges the view that the body naturally and inevitably runs down with age" (6). But, instead of accepting this physical process of aging, they explain that "[t]he estimation of our worthiness as a person thus becomes more dependent on the visible signs of the effort we have put into maintaining our face and figure" (6).

In the militarized utopian societies present in the texts, the external appearance of the rulers as well as of those who help to keep the state under control is key for the continuation of their regimes. Thus, knowledge and transmission of knowledge, understood as the history and culture of a community, of the songs and stories that shape it and which are spread by its old representatives, become secondary. They are almost erased from the everyday reality of such communities, since they are not perceived as necessary. The rulers in the militarized utopian societies in "The Reason for It" and Voices do not need their people to understand what is going on around them and thus have critical minds; they need their communities to execute orders and to act according to a standardized behavior. Instead, ageism and an internal fight between generations are enhanced. The military regimes of the new ruling classes based on powerful bodies and bright outfits make the citizens focalize on values such as body maintenance. By changing the value system from knowledge to appearance, both younger and unwise rulers substitute a tradition of promoting study and research transmitted from one generation to the other for the conception that power is neither in knowledge nor in wisdom but in controlling the body and presenting it as symbol of strength and vigor. In that sense, the army becomes the main reference to citizens who intend to become prominent agents within the communities.

In Lessing's "The Reason for It," Twelve explains that their new ruler, DeRod, "had become obsessed with his army" soon after he ascended the throne, and explains, "[i]nstead of an institution that we saw as a useful way of keeping young men out of mischief, and discouraging greedy people who might be tempted by the riches of The Cities, it had become a major part of our economy. It glittered and excelled, it was marched and drilled and exercised out of its wits" (148). However, the most important consequences derived from DeRod's obsession with the army were still to come, since most of the public funds of the community would go to the army to the detriment of education and culture. Twelve remembers how, when these changes were going on, the audience was disappointed with DeRod's military songs. But little by little, as DeRod invaded the cities around their territory, the population got used to these songs and forgot about the others, the ones that talked about their history and culture. Years later, Twelve realizes that with the disappearance of the two buildings that housed the College of Storytellers and Songmakers, "an enquiring habit of mind, how to think, how to make comparisons" (160) had also disappeared with them. The means of transmitting knowledge had been erased and the Twelve, those who had had the responsibility of transmitting it, had been grounded in their houses and discredited by their increasing aging appearance.

In Le Guin's *Voices*, the erasure of knowledge and knowledge transmission is achieved through violence, on a first stage, when the Alds invade Ansul. On a second stage, governmental power and control are kept through a militarized regime in which, in the same way as in Lessing's short story, youth, strength and vigor are praised whereas knowledge and experience are ignored. Thus, it is the function of Galvamand, the House of the Oracle led by the Waylord, to preserve such knowledge through the secret room in which the most important books related to the foundation, history and culture of their people are hidden. However, as the Waylord observes the passing of time and the increasing ignorance that invades his people, he concludes that "[a] generation learns that knowledge is punished and safety lies in ignorance. The next generation doesn't know they're ignorant, because they don't know what knowledge was" (Le Guin 80). In fact, the wise men in both societies, Twelve and the Waylord, decide to choose one or two younger members of their communities in order to teach them the art of reading and storytelling. Twelve does that with two of his grandchildren whereas Memer is the one chosen by the Waylord.

The importance not only of reading and writing, but mainly of storytelling and an ongoing connection between generations is repeated and highlighted in both texts once and again. In fact, both wise leaders, Twelve and the Waylord, consider the loss of storytelling, the beginning of the ending of their cultures. In both texts it is implied that through storytelling not only stories and history are being transmitted, but also the spirituality enclosed in each specific community; in other words, the most intrinsic values and beliefs of a community that differentiate it from another. As Margaret M. Gullette points out when arguing about "The American dream as a Life-course narrative," "[n]arratives may have most power over us when they are most invisible, that is, infinitely repeatable in ordinary life but unnoticed and unanalyzed. The "American Dream" is actually – whatever else it may be – such a narrative. It flourished in the half-lit, semiconscious realm of conversation and writing" (Gullette, *Aged by Culture* 143). In another article entitled "Our Best and Longest Running Story," Gullette underlines the need to acknowledge the importance of "progress narratives," taking "progress" as a subjective category that responds to the culture it is applied to, in order to understand that aging and old age are neither separated from the human condition nor from life itself. In other words, for Gullette, progress narratives become richer as the storyteller of the narrative accumulates experience: "[w]e start from one age class – childhood – and then turn to others. We follow narrative because we understand the fundamental truth: aging is a narrative. We research contexts of story-telling because we know that storytelling never happens in the vacuum of a solitary mind, however self-affirming that mind may be" (*Running Story* 29).

In the utopian communities presented by Lessing and Le Guin, the old body is devaluated and almost demonized, and storytelling as well as knowledge transmission is prohibited altogether. With the progressive disappearance of wisdom and experience represented by a growing distance and a decreasing communication between generations, both texts imply that progress and freedom are also erased from their everyday realities. In Le Guin's *Voices*, Meme is told by her stepmother, Ista, how her city as well as Galvamand, the Waylord's house where every citizen was welcomed, used to be full of life before the Alds invaded them. Ista tells Memer that her city was called "Ansul the Wise and Beautiful" (6) and remembers how Galvamand used to be the witness of people coming and going as well as of different generations living together and sharing time and conversation. As Ista explains, "[t]here were quite a few relatives and old people living in the house. [. . .] The Waylord himself was always travelling up and down the Ansul Coast from town to town to meet with the other Waylords [. . .] 'Oh it was all busy and a-bustle'" (5). At the present moment, Memer moves along "the silent corridors" and "the ruined rooms" as well as "the broken city of ruins, hunger, and fear" (6) that Ansul had become since the

Alds had imposed their regime. She understands that the future awaiting her and her generation is not a bright one.

In Lessing's "The Reason for It", Twelve realizes that once the richness of Destra's education system had been erased and almost forgotten "all kinds of superstitions sprang up, and new gods flourished" (162). Moreover, the new ruler, DeRod, spent most of the resources of The Cities on the army and in showing it to his population. Thus, the streets, the buildings and the gardens had been neglected for a long time. The emergence of all kinds of superstitions were the result of ignorance but also served as a restraining force to possible outbreaks coming from those few aging citizens who remembered the good old days.

By the end of both stories, it is suggested that the interest in knowledge and transmission of knowledge will be recovered little by little with the younger generations led by the wise leaders. After strong earth shakings that take place in Lessing's "The Reason for It," Twelve realizes that some of his contemporaries are "remembering that among the tales from the old part of The Cities are some that speak of earth vomiting, rivers swallowing mountains and changing their courses" (Lessing 188). Twelve sees in this fact the recovering of old tales and, with them, the recovering of the soul and spirit of The Cities. On a similar note, the political and social situation in Le Guin's *Voices* suffers a radical change when the storyteller and culture-loving Caspro and his wife decide to spend a few days in the city. While Caspro manages to lure the Alds' leading classes with his stories, a group of fighters from Ansul see Caspro's approach to the Alds as the best opportunity to reconquer their city. The Alds are finally defeated and Ansul not only becomes a free city but also recovers its religion and culture, its stories and history under the Waylord's auspices.

However, both endings suggest that the threat of savagery can never be erased. In this case, more than focusing on a projection of a better future, both utopian narratives analyzed in this chapter seem to warn about the possible future of a society that is guided by appearance instead of focused on analysis and understanding. It could be argued that both texts respond to a definition of utopia in which the reader is asked to consider possible outcomes of his/her present society more than being presented with a perfect one. In this sense, Hoda M. Zaki refers to Le Guin's novels as going "beyond utopian works in two ways. First, her novels portray utopia dialectically and critically. Utopia is not a static picture of a flawless society, but is an imperfect and evolving community subject to change" (65). The young militarized leaders in Ursula Le Guin's and Lessing's texts provide a biased vision of the values that may sustain a community. In that sense, both texts exhort the reader to stop and consider the values that are leading present-day society. Whereas consumer culture invades us with messages of eternal youth and vigorous and perfect bodies that nourish themselves from advances in technology and science, a growing aging population requires a reconsideration of the challenges that such a demographic revolution actually implies. In that sense, the insistence on body control and maintenance, especially from middle-age onwards, contributes to present the aging process as a problem and, ultimately, to make old age invisible. An aging population should not be treated from the point of view of external appearance which Western culture has equated with loss and decline. Instead, a long life may be read as an accumulation of experience and knowledge which, transmitted to younger generations, represents an invaluable heritage. Indeed, there is a point in which the wise men in the texts merge with the wise writers who produce the texts. Neither Le Guin and Lessing nor the wise old leaders in the communities depicted in the stories show a clear intention to impose their vision over those of their invaders and their people. Whereas Twelve and the Waylord observe from a certain distance how their communities are absorbed by a false sense of power and increasingly restricted views over their realites, Le Guin and Lessing witness the constant changes brought about by consumer culture – a growing ageism in a growing aging society.

REFERENCES

Beauvoir, Simone de. *The Coming of Age*. Trans. Patrick O'Brian. 1970. New York and London: W.W. Norton & Company, 1996. Print.

Blaikie, Andrew. *Ageing and Popular Culture*. Cambridge: Cambridge UP, 1999. Print.

Clayes, Gregory, and Lyman Tower Sargent. *The Utopian Reader*. New York: New York UP, 1999. Print.

Featherstone, Mike. "The Body in Consumer Culture." Eds. Mike Featherstone, Mike Hepworth and Bryan S. Turner. *The Body: Social Process and Cultural Theory*. London: Sage, 1991. 170-96. Print.

–––, Mike Hepworth, and Bryan S. Turner, eds. *The Body. Social Process and Cultural Theory*. London: Sage, 1991. Print.

Greene, Gayle. *Doris Lessing. The Poetics of Change*. The U of Michigan P, 1994. Print.

Gullette, Margaret Morganroth. *Aged by Culture*. The U of Chicago P, 2004. Print.

––– . "Our Best and Longest Running Story: Why is telling progress narratives so necessary, and so difficult?" Eds. Heike Hartung and Roberta Maierhofer. *Narratives of Life: Mediating Age*. Vienna and Berlin: Lit Verlag, 2009. 21-37. Print.

Hepworth, Mike, and Mike Featherstone. *Surviving Middle Age*. Oxford: Basil Blackwell, 1982. Print.

Hogue, Theresa. "Q&A with author Ursula K. Le Guin." *Gazette-Times*. Sept. 12 2008. Web.

Jaggi, Maya. "The magician." *Guardian.co.uk*. Dec. 15 2005. Web.

Le Guin, Ursula. *Voices*. London: Orion Publishing Group, 2006.

Lessing, Doris. "The Reason for It." *The Grandmothers*. London: Harper Perennial, 2003.

Turner, Bryan S. "The Discourse of Diet." Eds. Mike Featherstone, Mike Hepworth, and Bryan S. Turner. *The Body. Social Process and Cultural Theory*. London: Sage, 1991. 157-69. Print.

Wheeler, Kathleen. *A Critical Guide to Twentieth-Century Women Novelists*. Massachussetts: Blackwell Publishers, 1997. Print.

Woodward, Kathleen. *Aging and Its Discontents*. Bloomington and Indianapolis: Indiana UP, 1991. Print.

Zaki, Hoda M. Phoenix Renewed. The Survival and Mutation of Utopian Thought in North American Science Fiction, 1965-1982. Revised edition. The Borgo Press, 1993. Print.

From Cane to Chair

Old Age and Storytelling in Juvenile Literature by Hawthorne, Goodrich, and Mogridge

Eriko Ogihara-Schuck

The decades from 1830 to 1870, according to Thomas R. Cole's *The Journey of Life: A Cultural History of Aging in America* (1992), were marked by an idealization of old age. As part of Romanticism and in response to increasing industrialization, ministers and artists disseminated the idea that each individual had the ability to maintain a perfect, healthy body which is immune to pain until death. They claimed that a good, peaceful old age was attainable for everyone who had a life devoted to hard work, faith, and self-discipline. At the same time, old age marked by decay and suffering was considered the fault of individuals rather than the natural course of living. Diseases experienced in old age were equated to sin that could be eliminated by an individual's pious efforts. Cole concludes that such a splitting of old age into positive and negative experience dismissed the ambiguous aspect of aging as the process of both loss and gain. In this failure to accept a more complex view of aging, he perceives the root of ageism in twentieth-century American society (90-91).

In children's literature, a genre which emerged and flourished simultaneously during the very period that gains Cole's attention, however, old age is represented in a complex and balanced way. In particular, the body of elderly narrators, a phenomenon which was initiated in 1827 in American children's literature with Samuel G. Goodrich's creation of "Peter Parley," does not confirm Cole's observation of the one-sided representation of old age. The following analysis of Peter Parley and subsequent popular grandfather figure narrators who were directly influenced by Peter Parley will demonstrate that the old age discourse was fairly contested from the 1830s to the 1850s. Along with Peter Parley, the British writer George Mogridge's "Old Humphrey" who also became popular in the United States and Nathaniel Hawthorne's Grandfather narrator in *The Whole History of Grandfather's Chair* (1841) engaged with aging as an ambiguous process and proposed the possibility of successful frailty.

GOODRICH'S PETER PARLEY

Samuel G. Goodrich, the nineteenth-century pioneer of American children's literature, was innovative in the use of abundant engravings and language easy to understand for children but his key invention lay in the creation of the elderly, male narrator Peter Parley. Being brought forth when Goodrich was in his mid-thirties, he first appeared in *The Tales of Peter Parley about America* (1827) introducing himself, "Here I am! My name is Peter Parley! I am an old man. I am very gray and lame" (9). Hereafter he continuously appeared in Goodrich's numerous children's books. Although forgotten and being absent in contemporary American minds, in the nineteenth century Parley was very popular, appearing in 116 out of 170 books that Goodrich published, and about seven million copies were sold before the Civil War (Goodrich, *Recollections* 2 543). The series was so successful that it led to the publication of counterfeit Peter Parley books appearing in the hands of multiple authors and publishers on both sides of the Atlantic. Many of the series were translated into numerous languages, including Persian, Portuguese, and Japanese.

The use of a grandfather figure narrator in children's literature was unprecedented. Peter Parley even preceded by half a year the publication on the other side of the Atlantic of the more widely acknowledged author Walter Scott's popular collection of historical tales for children, *Tales of a Grandfather: Being Stories Taken from Scottish History* (1827).[1] However, the idea of an old man being a story-teller/narrator was not particularly innovative. In the realm of early American literature, more than a decade before Peter Parley, Washington Irving used old narrators including Diedrich Knickerbocker in his tales. Rip van Winkle, a prototypical fictional elderly figure in the short story "Rip van Winkle" (1819) narrated by Knickerbocker, was reverenced for his ability to provide "a chronicle of the old times 'before the [Revolutionary War]'" (*Rip van Winkle* 35) after his return from the Catskill Mountains.

Distinct from the former old narrators, however, Parley ages in each subsequent book. After appearing in *The Tales about America* (1827) as "very gray and lame" (9), his physical condition continues to deteriorate. In the introduction to *The Tales of Peter Parley about Africa* (1830), he insinuates a declining health by stating, "If my health is spared long enough, I intend to revise the books I have written" (Preface). At the beginning of the first chapter of *Peter Parley's Tales about Asia* (1830), when he introduces himself, he informs readers that

---

1 | *The Tales of Peter Parley about America*, the first volume of Peter Parley series, was copyrighted on February 24, 1827 (copyright page). The June 1827 issue of *The United States Review and Literary Gazette* includes an advertisement for the book. Scott's *Tales of a Grandfather* was first published on December 15, 1827 in Scotland ("Tales of a Grandfather").

his leg has gotten weaker: "Yes, here I am, alive and well, but I am more lame, than I was last year. I used to get along comfortably, with a cane, but in the winter I slipped down upon the ice, as I was going across Boston Common, and ever since, I have been obliged to go about with a crutch" (5). In *Peter Parley's Farewell* (1839), he announces his preparation for death and thus the end of his series due to his declining physical condition: "My tottering limbs, my failing sight, my deafened ear, forewarn me that my career is drawing to a close" (321). He calls himself "poor old Peter Parley" (322) for whom "[l]ife has ceased to be a source of happiness" (322) and considers that he is too old to continue writing books.

Peter Parley also ages visually. In *The Tales about America* (1827), he starts by looking relatively young.

Fig. 1: *Samuel G. Goodrich, The Tales of Peter Parley about America. 1831, 8.*

His standing posture does not mark old age, no wrinkles are visible, and the color of his hair is hidden by his hat. Although he stands with a cane, the rea-son is not clear without reading the first chapter as his legs are hidden in long trousers. In *Peter Parley's Book of the United States* (1837), he appears further aged, being seated in a chair with white hair as well as a balding head and a white beard.

Fig. 2: Samuel G. Goodrich, Peter Parley's Book of the United States. 1837, title page.

In *Peter Parley's Farewell* (1839), he is again sitting in a chair with a bald head, white hair, and a white beard while additionally wearing glasses, an indication of his declining eyesight.

Fig. 3: Samuel G. Goodrich, Peter Parley's Farewell. 1839, 34.

Peter Parley's physical deterioration largely stems from the author Goodrich's intention; he projected his own physical condition onto the narrator. Goodrich himself had become lame in his twenties after falling from a horse (Michalski). Since the late 1820s when he was writing fourteen hours per day due to the explosive popularity of Peter Parley, he had suffered from weakening eyesight (*Recollections* 2 281). This problem was so serious that he dictated his books and relied on his wife for writing. In the early 1830s, he was also attacked by the symptoms of heart disease (281).

Parley's physical deterioration was further meant to provide a natural end to the publication of the Peter Parley series. In fact, Goodrich wanted to end the series with *Peter Parley's Farewell* in order to stop the publication of counterfeit Parley books. The attempt, however, did not succeed and Goodrich decided to continue using the narrator after *Farewell* and eventually to immortalize him. Peter Parley thus ages only in the first limited number of books in the series. Yet, the aging Parley marked a significant function in the light of nineteenth-century old age discourse. Challenging the move to split old age into good and bad, Parley embodies a complex aging consisting of both loss and gain, growing as a storyteller while physically weakening.

In *The Tales about America*, after introducing himself as "very gray and lame" (9), he continues with, "But I have seen a great many things, and had a great many adventures, and I love to talk about them" (9). Here his old age serves as the sign of abundant knowledge and experience. In *The Tales about Africa*, old age entitles him to write a book with good quality: "I have bestowed upon [the book] such care as an old worn out man may give" (Preface). In *Tales about Asia*, the further deterioration of his legs motivates him to tell more stories: "But if my legs are stiff, my tongue is free; and as I cannot walk as well as formerly, I love to tell stories better than ever" (5). Thus, Peter Parley experiences aging as a complex process of both loss and gain.

Complex aspects of Peter Parley's aging are further articulated by the tools that he relies on due to his physical decline. In the engraving that appears on the first page of *Peter Parley's Method of Telling about Geography to Children* (1830), the chair immediately signifies his weak health.

Unlike the self-portrait hanging on the wall that shows him standing straight with his cane, he is now seated in a chair with a bandaged foot, no longer able to walk well. However, the furniture is traditionally linked to authority and power as well. Considering this aspect, the chair works to empower him in front of his young audience. Likewise, his cane has a similar complex function. While signifying his lame leg, the cane is traditionally a status symbol. In this engraving, it turns into the symbol of his educational authority as he is seen holding it up and using it as an educational tool to discipline children.

Fig. 4: Samuel G. Goodrich, Peter Parley's Method of Telling about Geography to Children. 1830, title page.

Interestingly, among many engravings of Peter Parley it was this engraving epitomizing his two-sided aging that was most vividly imprinted in the readers' memory. A reviewer of *Recollections of a Lifetime*, Goodrich's autobiography, recalls Parley being "a very old man, with white hair, and lame in his foot" shown in the frontispiece as "he was seated in a large arm chair, with a crutch at his side" ("Review" 232). A female reader describes the narrator as being "quite feeble" and gaining "great respect and sympathy" from children, and she recalls herself "gaz[ing] on that [picture of a poor old gentleman sitting in a stuffed chair], between times" (Perry 6). A male adult reader who confesses that "[t]ender sympathy for the old gentleman had filled [his] heart all the way to manhood" remembers in detail the same engraving: "An early boyhood's book lies vividly before me now as then, 'Peter Parley's Tales,' in which hour after hour my youthful soul delighted, with its frontispiece – a long-haired, quaker-hatted, venerable old man, crutch at his side, bandaged foot extended on a chair" (Derby 117).[2]

With the help of this particular engraving, the narrator's old age and disability seemed to become static in the readers' memory. But the fact that existent readers' responses concentrate on this frontispiece suggests that the narrator's tremendous popularity might in part be attributed to his embodiment of aging as a complex process. Bruce A. Harvey argues that the narrator's physical disability with a lame leg was a "mimetic marker that individualized" and "made him a sympathetic figure" (46), but I would further argue that the reader's sympathy was triggered by an ambiguous, two-sided aging. While suffering a physical decline but by taking advantage of his long-living experience, the narrator developed into an excellent storyteller. It was by exemplifying the perception of aging, which was suppressed under a cultural climate idealizing old age that Peter Parley evolved into a popular American figure.

Parley was however not alone being characterized by an ambiguous aging of losing and gaining. The British elderly narrator Old Humphrey, Parley's counterpart who emerged on the other side of the Atlantic and gained popularity on both sides, also enacted such an aging process.

MOGRIDGE'S OLD HUMPHREY

When the British author George Mogridge wrote British versions of Peter Parley books that were published by William Tegg, he gave a twist to the popular figure's aging process. In his *Peter Parley's Tales about Christmas* (1838) published one year prior to Goodrich's *Peter Parley's Farewell*, the elderly narrator had "again been on [his] travels" (1). In *Peter Parley's Tales about Great Britain and Ireland* (1837), the narrator recognizes his old age, "My hair may be a little whiter than it was, and another furrow may be added to my brow" (1) but his lame foot has recovered to the extent that he "can walk without a crutch" (1). In fact he states, "Six thousand miles have I sailed on the salt seas since we talked together" (2). Such a recognition of physical decline as a non-linear process constitutes the complexity of aging that Mogridge pursued in his numerous other writings.[3]

---

2 | I thank Pat Pflieger for consulting many rare Parley books and verifying that all these readers are possibly referring to the frontispiece of *Peter Parley's Method of Telling about Geography*. She also speculates that Parley is actually holding a crutch; it looks too short for a crutch yet Parley sits bandaged and many old-fashioned crutches that she has seen look exactly like it with a cross-piece.

3 | Mogridge's authorship of these two books is confirmed in *Memoirs of Old Humphrey*, 320.

Although absent from the public mind and with no substantial academic study existing, George Mogridge was, along with Goodrich, a prolific writer of children's and juvenile literature in the first half of the nineteenth century. While thriving on Peter Parley books, he wrote numerous tales using male pseudonyms such as "Old Humphrey," "Jeremy Jaunt," "Ephraim Holding," "Uncle Adam," "Uncle Newbury," "Old Alan Gray," and "Grandfather Gilbert." He also wrote under female names such as "Aunt Newbury" and "Aunt Upton," as well as "Grandmama Gilbert," judging that "many young people prefer their grandmothers to their grandfathers" ("Death" 410). Many of these personas were introduced as elderly figures, reflecting Mogridge's belief that the story becomes more convincing and powerful when it comes from the lips of an older rather than a younger narrator (Growser 38).

The most popular among Mogridge's numerous elderly personas was Old Humphrey. Mogridge's tales indeed became popular on both sides of the Atlantic after he started contributing stories under this pseudonym to the British Religious Tract Society's periodical *The Weekly Visitor* in 1833. Until his death in 1854, Mogridge published forty-six articles and books under this name, gaining a large audience especially in Sunday schools. His writings appeared in other British magazines such as *Ragged School Magazine* and *The Family Economist*. In the United States, his tales were printed in various Christian periodicals such as *The Friend*, *The New York Evangelist*, *The Christian Register*, *The Boston Observer*, and *Friends' Review*.

As in the case of Peter Parley, Old Humphrey's old age empowers and entitles him as a storyteller. One major reason for this privilege of old age is that one has accumulated experiences. In the introduction to *Old Humphrey's Observations* (1839), the narrator states that "[i]t is barely possible for any one, with furrows on his brow, to have passed his days without having seen something of a striking kind that another has not seen" (vi) and that his stories can be made "both interesting and instructive" (vi).

Unlike Peter Parley, however, Old Humphrey simultaneously observes the ways in which old age also impairs one's storytelling ability. In fact, before discussing Old Humphrey's appropriateness to be a storyteller due to the abundance of his experiences, he challenges the belief that "wisdom and grey hairs [. . .] go together" (vi) by criticizing it as "a proneness in age" (vi). He describes the way old age impairs the quality of narratives: "While perusing the following pages, they may possibly remind you, that age has its infirmities; and that among them may be reckoned the disposition to talk faster, and to dwell longer, on past occurrences than is agreeable to some hearers" (v). The narrator calls these aspects of his storytelling "errors" (v).

Old Humphrey makes similar observations about old age and its negative impact on storytelling in the collection of tales *Old Humphrey's Addresses* (1841). In the introduction, after calling his writings "poor Addresses" (v), he continues, "A stump of a pen in the infirm hand of an old man, is, to appearance, but a sorry source of advice and comfort" (v). And when his writings get attention, they ironically propel the narrator's physical decline, as his writing "has been made mighty in reproof and in consolation, in strengthening weak hands, and in confirming feeble knees" (v). Consequently, he assimilates himself to "weak instruments" (v).

In spite of all the disadvantages pertaining to his old age and his writings, Old Humphrey continues to justify the significance of his work by claiming that "weak instruments" have often brought about "important purposes" (v). One example is a small amount of money: "A mite is but a small sum, yet when freely given by the poor, it has been reckoned of greater value than the largest amount cast into the treasury" (v). Another example is a shepherd's rope familiar to the Christian audience through the tale of David and Goliath: "A sling in the hand of a stripling shepherd is but a poor weapon of warfare, but when God strengthens the arm that wields it, an embattled, mail-clad giant may be therewith felled to the ground" (v). Using these examples, Old Humphrey suggests that his tales taken alone are worthless but meaning is infused because they are the product of the tremendous effort of a frail old man who has a strong faith in God. Ultimately, he elevates the function of his writings to be religious, aiming to both soothe the readers and spread Christianity:

O that I could pour balm into every wound, and comfort every sorrowful breast! My prayer is, that God in mercy may open every blind eye, unstop every deaf ear, subdue every hard, unbelieving heart, scatter with a flood of heavenly light every cloud of unbelief and doubt, and spread, widely through this jarring world the soothing influence of the gospel of peace! (vi)

For Old Humphrey, aging entails experiences that promote the quality of storytelling, yet there is also physical decline which weakens its quality. In spite of that, however, Old Humphrey's storytelling has a value and significance because of the spirit "with which [the stories] have been written" (vi). According to *Old Humphrey's Walks in London and Its Neighborhood* (1843),[4] Mogridge's storytelling continues because his heart does not age either but remains "cheerful" (iv). In the case of the author Mogridge himself, his non-aging mentality sustained his storytelling: "Nor was his pen less active in this season of bodily infirmity than in times of better health; for his mental power remained in all its freshness and vigour to the last week of his life" (*Memoir* 138). Such an idea of gain *in spite of* old age embodied in both Old Humphrey and the author Mogri-

---

4 | While the book was first published in the United States in 1843, it seems to have been printed in Great Britain a few years earlier, according to *WorldCat*. The exact date is however unknown.

dge differs from Peter Parley's idea of gain *because of* old age. In the case of Parley, not just experience but also physical decline nurtured him as a storyteller by encouraging concentration on storytelling and finding joy in it.

Old Humphrey, however, also scrutinizes the general gains arising from old age accompanied by physical afflictions. In the essay "On a Sprained Ankle" in *Old Humphrey's Friendly Appeals* (1852) which is based on the author Mogridge's personal experiences in his later years, Old Humphrey emphasizes that precious things can be gained from such experiences. When one becomes temporarily disabled, his appreciation is increased for his ordinary state without disabilities. While "being deprived for a season of our bodily faculties" (112), people can become "more thankful to our heavenly Father for them" (113). Another gain is the increase of others' compassion for the disabled: "Another good thing that arises out of affliction is an increased sympathy for all in the like circumstances" (113). Increased self-reflection and faith in God is another gain: "Suitable and solemn reflections, and a clinging to God's holy word, are among the advantages that frequently attend affliction" (116). Thus, the narrator concludes that "there is a sunny side even to a sprained ankle" (118).

The similar gain out of physical afflictions is discussed further beyond Old Humphrey's tales in the story about a grandmother in Mogridge's *Family Walking Sticks* (1864). In the process of narrating a story about his grandmother's walking stick, her attitude toward her physical suffering is considered. While "[a]ffliction renders many people peevish and repining" (29), the situation was different with his grandmother "who was ever of a grateful and hopeful spirit" (29). In her situation, the appreciation of the healthy state increased while experiencing afflictions: "Oh how thankful should the healthy be for the blessings they enjoy! The aching head, the languid frame, the wearisome day, and the long, long, dreary night, are unknown to them" (29). Consequently, his grandmother spiritually grew due to her pains: "My grandmother appeared to be not only chastened, but purified, elevated, and spiritualized by affliction; and then her hope never failed her" (30). A poem is then presented to encapsulate the spiritual growth with hope:

The strength decays, the limbs are tottering now,
Yet sage experience makes the wrinkled brow;
Hope smiles around with influential power,
And gilds with sunshine every future hour. (30)

Counteracting what Thomas R. Cole has described as the mid-nineteenth century widespread tendency to dismiss and negate suffering and pains of old age as an eliminable sin, Old Humphrey thoroughly engaged them in order to highlight the complexity of aging. Namely, he argued that aging is characterized by both loss and gain as one can gain both *in spite of* and *because of* physical afflictions. Along with Peter Parley's, Old Humphrey's concept of old age thus challenged mid-nineteenth century Romantic ministers' and artists' splitting of old age into either positive or negative.

Old Humphrey's use of nature metaphors adds further complexity to the notion of aging as a dialectic process. In the short story "The Woodcutter," that appeared in *Tales in Rhyme, for Boys* (1851), a young boy compares an old woodcutter's body to "the oak / Deck'd with leaves, though its trunk may decline" (11) and considers that the man's cheek "shall be red as a rose" (12). The metaphorical use of a tree and a flower functions to emphasize his life force in terms of physical strength and beauty even in the midst of physical deterioration. A declining oak, like the aging woodcutter, conveys the images of both life and death because trees live and their features do not deteriorate significantly until they fall.

In the same text, nature metaphors also function to complicate aging by conceptualizing it as cyclic. The young boy notes that the old woodcutter's hair is "as white as the snow" (11) and proceeds, "When winter is spread o'er thy time- furrow'd head, / The spring in thy bosom shall bloom" (11). Here, the declining outer appearance is compared to the season which connotes death. The old man's heart is however compared to the seeds of spring blooming flowers lying dormant for the winter waiting for the beginning of a new life. Contesting the idea of aging as a linear process from birth to death, these nature metaphors generate the image of aging as a repetition of birth and death or gain and loss.

Nature metaphors are further used in non-Old Humphrey books by George Mogridge to complicate the perception of aging. In *Ephraim Holding's Homely Hints* (1843), the elderly narrator considers his writings humble due to his old age but imbibes them with a strong life force through comparison with the elements in nature: "If a small seed will produce a large tree, a single feather turn a scale, and a mere spark kindle a conflagration, why should I fear that an old man's words, coming warm from his heart, will be all together worthless?" (1). Seeds and sparks are small and feathers are light, but in the company of outer forces such as water, air, and gravity, they initiate something that is large or create a huge movement. Such implications of the metaphors suggest that, although Ephraim Holding's writings at first glance look insignificant, the narrator expects that in the long run his tales can become meaningful, depending on how readers engage with them.

It is important to note that the aforementioned nature metaphors such as snow, a tree, a rose, seeds, and sparks are all components in nature that are often associated with beauty, joy, and happiness. Other types of nature elements such as iron and stone are used to describe aging as a linear process of physical decline leading to destruction: "Time, that rusts iron and crumbles stone, robs us of our power, and we become almost as weak as infancy" (*Family Walking Sticks* 30).

Mogridge's use of nature metaphors stemmed from a general love of nature. His attachment to nature was so influential that his biographers reiterated nature imagery to describe the author's character traits. His biographer William H. Growser identified Mogridge with "an ever green old age" (38) suggesting he remained full of life until death. The anonymous author of the biography *Memoir of Old Humphrey* published by the Religious Tract Society likewise utilized nature imagery to describe Mogridge's optimistic attitude toward life: "He saw an oasis in every desert, and a glittering star in the darkest sky" (141).

According to the same biography, Mogridge used a nature metaphor to describe physical decline in his old age: at the time when he was suffering from an illness, he was noted for calling himself "as weak as water" (139). The metaphor of "water," however, also has opposite meanings. Water can signify one's weakness because it is fluid and invisible, but it can also be associated with strength and power: water is a basic life-giving force in the world of nature and it can also become destructive, turning into heavy rain and floods. Overall, such a two-sided aspect of nature is what makes nature metaphors effective tools for Mogridge to envisage aging as a complex process that refuses its simple categorization into either positive or negative.

HAWTHORNE'S GRANDFATHER NARRATOR

In *Peter Parley's Universal History on the Basis of Geography* (1837), ghostwritten for Goodrich by Nathaniel Hawthorne together with his sister Elizabeth, the storyteller no more appears standing with a cane but is seated in a chair.

Fig. 5: Samuel G. Goodrich, Peter Parley's Universal History. 1859, 26.

This does not suggest, however, that Peter Parley's health has further declined. In many of the engravings of Parley, there is no noticeable sign of deterioration; he neither wears glasses nor has physical handicaps. Rather, the chair signals his educational authority, making him a pedagogue sitting in front of a map and talking to children who are "curious to hear an old man tell of the older time" (13). The image of old age, associated with a chair but being stripped of physical suffering, occurs again as a central motif in *The Whole History of Grandfather's Chair* (1841) that Hawthorne completed four years after the publication of *Universal History*.

While widely known as the author of *The Scarlet Letter* (1850) and many other short stories such as "Young Goodman Brown" (1835) and "The Gray Champion" (1835), in his early career, Hawthorne was an active writer of children's literature. Starting with "Little Annie's Ramble" (1834), he wrote numerous stories for children, responding to the growth of children's literature into a lucrative, marketable genre. And Hawthorne did not just write stories for children but did pioneering work in this field, incorporating fantasy into juvenile literature in the 1840s when fantasy was dominantly considered inappropriate in writings for children. He thus made an important contribution to the creation of American children's fantasy (Laffrado 11).

The Whole History of Grandfather's Chair, written when Hawthorne was in his mid-thirties, was one of such uses of fantasy. Originally published in three parts as *Grandfather's Chair* (1840), *Famous Old People* (1841), and *Liberty Tree* (1841), it is an American historical narrative told by a grandfather to his four grandchildren and was written under the influence of the Peter Parley series which was often hostile to fantasy and in particular fairy tales.[5] Yet, the historical narrative revolves around a fictitious arm chair in which the narrator is seated, a fictional story about historical figures owning the chair and passing it on one after another, Grandfather being its most recent owner, and a fictional climax, although in the form of Grandfather's dream, in which the chair opens its mouth to talk about what it saw over the course of two hundred years or so.

The Whole History's newness thus lies in the incorporation of fantasy elements into a historical narrative, corresponding to Hawthorne's conception of romance as a "neutral territory, somewhere between the real world and fairyland where the Actual and the Imaginary may meet" (*The Scarlet Letter* 28). In addition, this text made a new attempt in the light of its contemporary old age discourse. Being embedded in the tradition of didactic texts for children which

---

5 | Goodrich's general dislike of fairy tales, the genre which was gaining popularity during his lifetime, was well expressed in his intention to write stories which were "reasonable and trustful" and could "feed the young mind upon things wholesome and pure, instead of things monstrous, false, and pestilent" (*Recollections* 1, 172).

revolved around conversations between an adult and a child, *The Whole History* presented a creative approach to old age.

At first glance, Grandfather in *The Whole History* complies with the mid-nineteenth century discourse of idealized old age. He is an "old and gray-haired" (*Centenary* 9) man in his late sixties (147) and "at that period of life when the veil of mortality is apt to hang heavily over the soul" (51-52). The constant location in a chair and his possession of a cane suggest a physical decline, but Grandfather does not appear inflicted by it. Instead, he embodies a peaceful old age, often illustrated with nature metaphors and imagery. *The Whole History* begins in the summer season focusing on the elderly figure:

Grandfather had been sitting in his old arm-chair all that pleasant afternoon, while the children were pursuing their various sports, far off or near at hand. Sometimes you would have said, "Grandfather is asleep!" but still, even when his eyes were closed, his thoughts were with the young people, playing among the flowers and shrubbery of the garden. (9)

Grandfather reflects on the children peacefully playing in the garden, perhaps recalling earlier days of his life. He feels enlivened when little Alice, his youngest granddaughter, enters like a butterfly: "[H]is heart leaped with joy, whenever little Alice came fluttering, like a butterfly, into the room" (9). Here, the garden and the butterfly are symbols of the life force. This nature imagery contributes to creating the image of a peaceful, if not active, old age.

Nature imagery is further used to describe Grandfather's good old age. He has "a heart that has grown mellow, instead of becoming dry and wilted, with age" (143). The words "dry" and "wilted" remind one of an aging leaf, of little use to the tree, while "mellow" suggests a mature fruit. The metaphor of "sunshine" is used to describe his once vivid imagination: "The old gentleman had once possessed no inconsiderable share of fancy; and, even now, its fading sunshine occasionally glimmered among his more sombre reflections" (205). The imaginative ability has declined due to his old age but arises on occasion shining with an illuminating light.

When the pleasant summer season changes to the harsher winter, Grandfather diverts his attention inward, away from the outside. Protected from the "[d]reary, chill November," "sudden showers of wintry rain," and "gusts of snow," (73) he enjoys sitting in front of the fireplace: "In the twilight of the evening, the fire grew brighter and more cheerful" (74). The wood fire is "a kindly, cheerful, sociable spirit, sympathizing with mankind" (73) and "Grandfather loved [it] far better than a grate of glowing anthracite, or than the dull heat of an invisible furnace" (73). The wood fire is equated to his mental state and a positive attitude in his old age: "And thus, perhaps, there was something in Grandfather's heart, that cheered him most with its warmth and comfort in

the gathering twilight of old age" (74). Such a one-sided use of nature metaphors and imagery in order to elucidate a peaceful old age extensively differs
from George Mogridge's; Mogridge drew upon both the peaceful and harsher
aspects of nature in order to conceptualize aging as a two-fold simultaneous
process of loss and gain, and peace and pain.

But the nature imagery used in association with Grandfather implies both
life and death. Besides the tranquility suggested above, the same images often
subtly allude to Grandfather's approaching end of life. At times his posture suggests death as when his grandchildren are playing in the garden and Grandfather appears to be asleep, not having stood up from his chair for the entire afternoon. His immobility is especially highlighted by a contrast to little Alice who
is fluttering like a "butterfly." The "sunshine" associated with Grandfather's capacity of imagination is fading as is his life. Death is also suggested by the following nature imagery: "[I]t was a striking picture to behold the white-headed
old sire, with this flowery wreath of young people around him" (51). Illustrating
the scene of the four grandchildren sitting around Grandfather listening to his
story, the image of the "flowery wreath" does not simply generate the peaceful
picture of Grandfather, but also alludes to the wreath awarded to the dead.[6]

Such a construction of a peaceful old age as an interplay between life and
death conforms to the idealized old age of the nineteenth century. According to
the historian Thomas R. Cole, the idea of good old age embraced awareness of
approaching death and entry into heaven. This aspect of a good old age is well
articulated in nineteenth-century (eponymous) painter Thomas Cole's series
of four nature paintings titled *The Voyage of Life* (1842). In the fourth painting
"Old Age," the boat's figurehead is broken and the surrounding is dark.

The old man, however, appears calm, suggesting that he is aware of the
approaching end of life and the entry to the next stage, as represented by the
accompanying guardian angel and the light in the sky. His calmness makes a
stark contrast to the male figure in the third painting, "Manhood," where the
younger male figure's situation is depicted in a desperate manner, resonating
with the winter season outside of Grandfather's house.

Old age exemplified by Grandfather through nature imagery is, however,
more complex than the mid-nineteenth century mainstream conceptualiza-
tion. Whereas a good old age, according to Cole, was achieved by an individual's
inward effort during a life of hard work and good health, Grandfather's peaceful old age stems from his outward interest in interaction with the younger
generation. The nature images, as noted earlier, illustrating Grandfather's good
old age are frequently used in reference to his grandchildren. The "butterfly"
which enlivens Grandfather's recollections is associated with Alice; the "sun-

---

6 | Many post-mortem photographs of the nineteenth century picture dead people
decorated with flower wreaths.

shine," in reference to Grandfather's capacity to imagine, arises when another grandchild, Charles, asks for a story in which the oak chair talks; this request stimulates Grandfather's sense of fantasy. The image of a "flowery wreath" also recalls the placing of wreaths in Classical times on the heads of deserving persons and thus well expresses the four grandchildren's interest in listening to Grandfather's tales as well as his joy of storytelling.

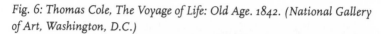

Fig. 6: Thomas Cole, The Voyage of Life: Old Age. 1842. (National Gallery of Art, Washington, D.C.)

Winter's wood fire is a nature image which promotes Grandfather's intimate relationship to his grandchildren. While enabling Grandfather to contemplate the joy of old age, it draws his grandchildren's attention back to the historical tales revolving around his oak chair. When introduced, the children's minds had drifted away from the tales but "now, in the autumnal twilight, illuminated by the flickering blaze of the wood-fire, they looked at the old chair, and thought that it had never before worn such an interesting aspect" (74). Subsequently, one of them, Charles, goes back to Grandfather to ask for further tales.

Similar to these nature images is Grandfather's oak chair. As a product of nature, it carries the function of elucidating the complexity of aging as interplay between life and death and as an interaction with society. While the chair, with its engravings of a lion's head, flowers, and foliage represents life force, it also constantly recalls death because it is made of dead trees. The chair's history is also the history of those who formerly owned it and have now passed away. The chair illuminates the process in which old age is constructed through interaction with the surrounding environment. At the beginning, the reader is informed that the chair "was made of oak, which had grown dark with age, but had been rubbed and polished till it shone as bright as mahogany" (10). Here, aging is compared to the transformation of a baser oak into a more respected mahogany, and this improvement is caused by the work of man.

It is indeed human hands and interest that enable the chair to improve while it simultaneously ages and deteriorates. At one point in the past, the chair "had the misfortune to break its leg" (35) so that it ceased its function as the seat of the governors of Massachusetts. It, however, caught the attention of Captain John Hull who by "carefully examining the maimed chair" and "discover[ing] that its broken leg might be clamped with iron," "made [it] as serviceable as ever" (35). At another point, the chair appeared "somewhat the worse for its long and arduous services" (56) and was "banished as an article of useless lumber" (56). At this point, Sir William Philips entered and took "the good old chair into his private mansion" and "repaired one of its arms, which had been slightly damaged" (56). Later, a new governor found the chair in the Province House and was "struck with its noble and stately aspect, but was of opinion, that age and hard services had made it scarcely fit for courtly company, as when it stood in the Earl of Lincoln's hall" (110). An artist was then employed to "beautify the chair" by "polishing and vanishing," and "gilding the carved work of the elbows, and likewise the oaken flowers of the back" (110). Ultimately, "[t]he lion's head now shone like a veritable lump of gold" (110-11). Personified with a head and legs, the growth of the oak chair suggests that something similar would happen with aging humans when they are supported by society.

Marked by the easy change of appearance through human hands as well as the conflation of life and death, Grandfather's oak chair can be characterized as a grotesque body in the sense of Mikhail Bakhtin. The chair is explicitly grotesque with the "grin[ning]" (10) lion's head and being "strange looking" (10) while suggesting a personified creature, being equipped with a face, arms, and legs. Moreover, it is characterized by its ambiguous quality and its being what Bakhtin calls "a body in the act of becoming" (*Rabelais and His World* 317), a body which is "never finished, never completed; it is continuously built, created, and builds and creates another body" (317). The oak chair is ambiguous because its appearance is fluid and conflates opposing elements such as life and death, and old and new as expressed by Grandfather's lesson about life in general for grandchildren using the chair: "[T]here is almost always an old and time-worn substance, under all the glittering show of new invention" (111). Consequently, this grotesque chair, to use Bakhtin's word, "liberates" (47) the notion of aging from the confinement of mere physical deterioration and decline.

While the chair obtains the liberating function as such due to the presence of human hands, it in turn liberates the human Grandfather from the static notion of old age. As a material which outlives humans and can be passed from generation to generation, it connects them one after another, thereby contextualizing Grandfather's life into the larger context and relativizing his life in relation to the other generations. As a result, while he is an old man who awaits death in contrast to his young grandchildren, he appears to be the youngest in relation to all the previous owners of the chair. The chair then envelopes Grandfather as both old and young, thus destabilizing the binary opposition in which the mid-nineteenth century mainstream notion of old age was grounded.

To summarize, good old age that Hawthorne's *The Whole History of Grandfather's Chair* proposes through the use of nature images is implicated in intergenerational relationships. In contrast to its contemporary mainstream discourse of idealized old age as a solitary, individual experience, peaceful old age embodied by Hawthorne's Grandfather and his oak chair develops out of interaction with other generations. The presence of the younger generation makes Grandfather useful and happy as Grandfather is able to entertain his grandchildren with stories. Likewise, the old oak chair is able to remain functional because younger generations are interested in mending and appropriating it to their needs.

Good old age surfaces also due to the presence of older, deceased generations to which Grandfather brings attention in the process of telling the history of the chair. While Grandfather's approaching death is constantly alluded to, his historical narrative about former generations generates the awareness that death is not the ultimate end of one's life. The narrative reminds us that, even after one dies, he or she continues to live in the mind of later generations as a memory and as a historical legacy. Embracing this idea, the grandchild Laurence is ready for Grandfather's death without fear and lamentation when he states, "We must make haste, or it will have a new history to be told before we finish the old one" (147). Likewise, more than the end of life itself, Grandfather is concerned with finishing the history of the chair before he dies: "[A] year makes no impression on its oaken frame, while it bends the old man nearer and nearer to the earth; so let me go on with my stories, while I may" (147). This statement by Grandfather suggests that the old man will be content when he will be able to finish the story of the most recent owner of his chair before him and will thus be able to connect himself to the array of former generations.

CONCLUSION

In his later works for children, Hawthorne turned towards a younger storyteller. In *A Wonder-Book for Girls and Boys* (1852), a collection of Greek mythological tales published almost a decade after *The Whole History*, a college student by the name of Eustace Bright serves as the narrator. Goodrich and Mogridge, however, continued employing elderly narrators in their tales for children. A few years after the publication of *Peter Parley's Farewell*, Goodrich "gave birth" to another elderly narrator, named Robert Merry, in the children's magazine *Robert Merry's Museum* (1841-1872). While writing numerous tales under the pseudonym Old Humphrey, Mogridge created, as mentioned earlier, many other senior narrators, both men and women, with the belief that stories coming from the mouth of the elderly are more convincing than those told by younger persons. Goodrich's and Mogridge's interest in the use of elderly narrators triggered as well as coincided with its wider popularity in the realm of nineteenth-century children's literature, with the most well-known example being Joel Chandler Harris' "Uncle Remus," an African American fictional narrator of folktales.

Considering these narrators' status as story-tellers for children and an ambiguous, complex aging process represented by Peter Parley, Old Humphrey, and Hawthorne's Grandfather, it may be speculated that other nineteenth-century elderly narrators likewise served as the locus of serious contemplation on the notion of old age and its complexity. In particular, their appearance in children's literature suggests the possibility that, in this genre, the complexity of old age was newly explored and its meaning was contextually conceptualized through the lens of intergenerational relations.

REFERENCES

Primary Sources

Cole, Thomas. *The Voyage of Life: Old Age*. 1842. Oil on canvas. National Gallery of Art, Washington, D.C.

Goodrich, Samuel G. *Peter Parley's Book of the United States, Geographical, Political & Historical*. Boston: Charles J. Hendee, 1837. Print.

——. *Peter Parley's Farewell*. Boston: Geo. A. & J. Curtis, 1839. Print.

——. *Peter Parley's Method of Telling About Geography to Children*. Hartford: H. & F. J. Huntington, 1830. Print.

——. *Peter Parley's Tales about Asia*. 1830. Boston: Gray & Bowen, and Carter & Hendee, 1838. Print.

——. *Peter Parley's Universal History on the Basis of Geography*. 1837. New York: Ivison & Phinney, 1859. Print.

——. *The Tales of Peter Parley about Africa*. 1830. Rev. ed. Philadelphia: Desilver, Thomas, and Co., 1836. Print.

——. *The Tales of Peter Parley about America*. 1827. 5th ed. Boston: Carter, Hendee, & Babcock, and Gray & Bowen, 1831. Print.

Hawthorne, Nathaniel. *The Centenary Edition of the Works of Nathaniel Hawthorne: True Stories from History and Biography*. Ed. William Charvat. Columbus: Ohio State UP, 1972. Print.

———. *The Scarlet Letter*. Ed. Seymour Gross, Sculley Bradley, Richmond Croom Beatty, and E. Hudson Long. New York: W. W. Norton, 1988. Print.

Irving, Washington. *Rip van Winkle and Other Stories*. London: Wordsworth Classics, 2009. PrintMogridge, George. *Ephraim Holding's Homely Hints to Sunday School Teachers*. London: Sunday School Union, 1843. Print.

———. *Family Walking Sticks; or, Prose Portraits of My Relations*. Ed. Mary Mogridge. London: S. W. Partridge, [1864]. Print.

———. *Old Humphrey's Addresses*. 1841. New York: Robert Carter, 1844. Print.

———. *Old Humphrey's Friendly Appeals*. [1852]. London: Religious Tract Society, 1871. Print.

———. *Old Humphrey's Observations*. London: Religious Tract Society, 1839. Print.

———. *Old Humphrey's Walks in London and Its Neighborhood*. London: Religious Tract Society, [1843]. Print.

———. *Peter Parley's Tales about Christmas*. London: Thomas Tegg and Son, 1838. Print.

———. *Peter Parley's Tales about Great Britain and Ireland*. 1837. 4th ed. London: Thomas Tegg, 1845. Print.

———. *Tales in Rhyme, for Boys*. London: Religious Tract Society, [1851]. Print.

Secondary Sources

Bakhtin, Mikhail. *Rabelais and His World*. Trans. Hélène Iswolsky. 1968. Bloomington: Indiana UP, 1984. Print.

Cole, Thomas R. *The Journey of Life: A Cultural History of Aging in America*. Cambridge: Cambridge UP, 1992. Print.

"Death of 'Old Humphrey.'" *New York Observer and Chronicle* 28 Dec. 1854: 410. Print.

Derby, James C. *Fifty Years among Authors, Books and Publishers*. New York: G. W. Carleton & Co., Publishers, 1884: 117. Print.

Goodrich, Samuel G. *Recollections of a Lifetime, or Men and Things I have Seen*. 2 vols. New York and Auburn: Miller, Orton & Co., 1857. Print.

Growser, William H. *Men Worth Imitating*. London: Sunday School Union, 1871. Print.

Harvey, Bruce A. *American Geographics: U. S. National Narratives and the Representation of the Non-European World, 1830 – 1865*. Stanford: Stanford UP, 2001. Print.

Laffrado, Laura. *Hawthorne's Literature for Children*. Athens: U of Georgia P, 1992. Print.

Memoir of Old Humphrey; with Gleanings from His Portfolio, in Prose and Verse. London: Religious Tract Society, 1855. Print.

Michalski, Sally. "Samuel Goodrich Collection." *Elizabeth Nesbitt Collection.* U of Pittsburgh. Web. 14 Apr. 2013.

"New Publications." *The United States Review and Literary Gazette* June 1827: 237. Print.

Perry, Susan T. "Peter Parley." *New York Evangelist* 18 Sept. 1884: 6. Print.

"Review: Recollections of a Life Time." *New York Evangelist* 27 Nov. 1856: 232. Print.

"Tales of a Grandfather." *Walter Scott.* Edinburgh University Library. Web. 8 Sept. 2013.

Contributors

David Barnet is the founding Artistic Director of the GeriActors and Friends and founding Advisory Board Member of the Edmonton Creative Age Festival. In 2011, Professor Barnet (University of Alberta) was awarded the City of Edmonton TELUS Courage to Innovate Award for his contribution to arts and culture through the GeriActors and Friends and the SAGE award for contributions to seniors and the arts. He is a 3M National Teaching Fellow.

Elena Bendien is associated researcher at the Graduate School, the University of Humanistic Studies, Utrecht, the Netherlands. She received her first PhD in linguistics, and her second PhD is in humanities: social gerontology and cultural and social psychology (Utrecht). Elena Bendien's fields of interests are ageing and memory studies, gender and ageing, the meaning of remembering at a later age, existential meaning of space at a later age, identity issues in later life, and new technologies of care.

Elisabeth Boulot is senior lecturer at the Université Paris Est Marne-la-Vallée, France. She is accredited to supervise doctoral studies in American Studies. Her main areas of research are American Politics and Law. Elisabeth Boulot's recent publications include: "Gérer l'héritage des réformes passées et réformer le système de santé américain. Politiques étatiques, proposition des candidats à la présidence." *Héritage(s) dans le monde anglophone. Concepts et réalités.* Ed. Marie-Françoise Alamichel. Paris: L'Harmattan, 2009. 289-307; Ed. Elisabeth Boulot. *Politique, démocratie et culture à l'ère du numérique.* Paris : L'Harmattan, 2011; "Le Social Security Act (1935): loi emblématique du New Deal politique, économique et social des années Roosevelt." *Les années Roosevelt aux Etats-Unis (1932-1945): entre New Deal et 'Home Front.'* Ed. Frédéric Robert. Paris: Ellipses, 2013. 133-44.

Marta Cerezo Moreno is Lecturer of English at the Spanish Distance Learning University (UNED). Her main areas of interest and main publications focus, first, on contemporary English narrative in relation to Gender Studies, Literary

Gerontology and Disability Studies, and, second, on Early modern British Literature, especially Shakespearean drama. She has published articles on works by A.S. Byatt, John Updike and Margaret Atwood and also on Chaucer, Shakespeare, and the tragic hero on the Elizabethan stage. She has published two books about medieval and renaissance literature and criticism. Her current research concerns both the presence of aging and disability in the works of John Banville and the commemorative acts of Shakespeare's Quartercentenary.

Sally Chivers' research interests lie in the intersection between the fields of aging and disability studies. As a humanities scholar, she has contributed to thinking of age as a key element of cultural production. In her 2011 book, *The Silvering Screen*, she examined contemporary film to ask why claims of physical and mental ability are necessary for older actors – and older people more generally – and what those claims say about cultural views of growing old at a time when the global population is aging. Chivers is Associate Professor of English at Trent University in Canada.

Meike Dackweiler is a doctoral candidate in Contemporary German Literary Studies and a member of the research training group "Age(ing): Cultural Concepts and Practical Realizations" of the Heinrich-Heine University (Düsseldorf, Germany). The subject of her doctoral thesis is the concept of romantic love in old age in contemporary German and Anglo-American literature.

Amelia DeFalco is a Banting postdoctoral fellowship recipient researching the ethics of caregiving in contemporary Canadian literature at McMaster University, Canada. She is author of *Uncanny Subjects: Aging in Contemporary Narrative* (Ohio State University Press, 2010) and has published essays on aging, dementia, and the ethics of care in literature and film in journals such as *Contemporary Literature*, *Canadian Literature*, and *Twentieth-Century Literature*.

Jacquie Eales is the research associate working on the Theatre as a Pathway to Healthy Aging Project (University of Alberta), interviewing current and former members of the GeriActors and Friends, implementing the community-based research design, and coordinating activities among the research team, the theatre company, and the partner project Ages and Stages in the UK. She has a longstanding interest in hearing the personal stories of older adults' lives, and understanding how older adults' connections to people and to place play out over their life course.

Ricca Edmondson was born in South Africa and brought up in England, studying philosophy in Lancaster, and the theory of the social sciences in Oxford, receiving her D.Phil. there. She worked as a translator and taught philosophy in Berlin before carrying out research at the Max Planck Institute for Human Development. She is personal professor of political science and sociology at the National University of Ireland, Galway, and is particularly interested in the theory and practice of wisdom.

Eileen Fairhurst, a sociologist, is Professor in Public Health at the University of Salford, England. She has published extensively on the Sociology of Aging. She is a Founding Fellow of the British Society of Gerontology. Her collaboration, with Ricca Edmondson, on contemporary representations of wisdom has been for a number of years.

Janet Fast, Professor of Human Ecology at the University of Alberta, researches family, health and continuing care policy issues. With funding from the Canadian Institutes of Health Research (CIHR), she currently directs a multidisciplinary team investigating the impact of older adults' participation in performer-created intergenerational theatre on their health and well-being. As part of this Theatre as a Pathway to Healthy Aging Project, she is particularly interested in the intergenerational nature of the GeriActors and Friends and how the process of creating stories together breaks down age-related stereotypes.

Rüdiger Kunow is Chair of the American Studies program at Potsdam University, Germany. He is a founding member of the European Network in Aging Studies (ENAS). He also served as director of various international research projects and the European Union research and teaching project "Putting a Human Face on Diversity: The U.S. In/Of Europe." Currently he serves as speaker of the interdisciplinary research project "Cultures in/of Mobility." His major research interests and publications focus on cultural constructions of illness and aging, transnational American Studies and the South Asian diaspora in the U.S. He has recently co-edited with Heike Hartung the first-collection on Age Studies within German American studies.

Ulla Kriebernegg is Assistant Professor at the *Center for Inter-American Studies* (C.IAS) at the University of Graz, Austria. She studied English and American Studies and German Philology at the University of Graz and at University College Dublin, Ireland and holds a master's and a doctoral degree from the University of Graz. Her research and teaching focuses on North American Literature and Cultural Studies, Age/Aging Studies, Inter-American Studies, and Interculturality. Together with Heike Hartung and Roberta Maierhofer, she is editor of the *Aging Studies* book series. She is a member of the steering group for the European Network in Aging Studies (ENAS). Currently, she is working on a monograph entitled *Locating Life: Intersections of Age and Space* in which she analyzes Canadian and US American fictional representations of care-giving institutions.

Patricia Life is an English PhD (A.B.D.) candidate at the University of Ottawa, focusing on Canadian literature and Age Studies. This paper derives from her current research on stories of the nursing home in Canadian literature and the age ideologies, such as the positive-aging and decline-and-progress narratives, that inform them. It stems from a chapter in the thesis "Long-term Caring: Personal Agency, Identity and Late Life in Canadian Literary Narratives."

Beverly Lunsford is Assistant Professor, George Washington University School of Nursing and Director, GW Center for Aging, Health and Humanities. She is Principal Investigator for several grants that provide education for healthcare professionals and students to improve the care of older adults. Dr. Lunsford established the Palliative Care Nurse Practitioner Program at GW in 2009. She has taught a variety of nursing courses, including research, theory, population health, spirituality and health.

Roberta Maierhofer is Professor of American Studies of the University of Graz, Austria, and Adjunct Professor at Binghamton University, New York. Since 2007, she has been directing the *Center for Inter-American Studies* of the University of Graz. Her research focuses on American Literature and Cultural Studies, Gender Studies, Transatlantic Cooperation in Education, Inter-American Studies, and Age/Aging Studies. In her publication, *Salty Old Women: Gender and Aging in American Culture*, she developed a theoretical approach to gender and aging (anocriticism). Together with Heike Hartung and Ulla Kriebernegg, she is editor of the *Aging Studies* book series.

Meiko Makita holds a PhD in sociology and is a research fellow in the Sue Ryder Centre for the Study of Supportive, Palliative and End of Life Care, School of Health Sciences, University of Nottingham. She is currently working on a UK-wide research study exploring end of life care experiences and concerns of older lesbian, gay, bisexual and transgender (LGBT) people. She completed her PhD in sociology at the University of Glasgow in 2012. Her doctoral thesis, entitled 'Ageing experiences of old Mexican women', examines the deeply held cultural values and assumptions about old age and identifies the socio-economic and cultural structures shaping and constraining the lived-experiences of aging amongst old women. Her research interests include aging and gender issues, feminist gerontology, health and social care, aging and religious faith, late in life migration and identity issues, and qualitative research methods.

Leni Marshall, PhD, teaches English at the University of Wisconsin-Stout. Her research focuses on age studies in North American minority and majority literatures and cultures. Advisory Editor for *Age, Culture, Humanities*, she also has served at the leadership level for AGHE, ENAS, GSA, NANAS, NWSA, and MLA. With Valerie Lipscomb, she edited *Staging Age: The Performance of Age in Theatre, Dance, and Film.* Her next book, *Age: Of Bodies, Gender, and Construction*, is forthcoming from SUNY Press.

Ellen Matlok-Ziemann holds an MA degree in Sociology and a PhD in American Literature. Her special interests include History of Science, Feminist Philosophy, and Aging Studies. She is currently working on representations of old women in American literature. Since 2013, she has been working at the Department of Education, Uppsala University, Sweden.

Eriko Ogihara-Schuck is a lecturer of American Studies at TU Dortmund University, Germany. In 2011 she completed her PhD dissertation which is forthcoming in Spring 2014 from McFarland under the title "Miyazaki's Animism Abroad: The Reception of Japanese Religious Themes by American and German Audiences." She is currently working on her post-doc book project on the representation of old age in 19th-century American literature.

Maricel Oró-Piqueras is assistant professor at the Department of English and Linguistics, Universitat de Lleida (Catalunya, Spain). She is also a member of the literature research group Dedal-lit since it started to work on the representation of fictional images of ageing and old age in 2002. In 2007, she finished and defended her PhD thesis which was published by Lap Lambert with the title *Ageing Corporealities in Contemporary English Fiction: Redefining Stereotypes* in 2011.

Barbara Ratzenböck is a research assistant at the *Center for Inter-American Studies* at the University of Graz, Austria where she studied Sociology. Her research interests include Sociology of Literature, Sociology of Knowledge, and Age/Aging Studies.

Julian Wangler is a research assistant of the Allensbach Institute (IfD). He graduated in Media Studies from the University of Bonn. From 2010 to 2012, he was research fellow at the Institute of Media Studies at the University of Tübingen. His main field of interest covers the media representation of certain social minorities and groups, and the reception of media content by different audiences. His dissertation focuses on media representations of old age, their perception and potentials of influence.

Sherryl Wilson is a Senior Lecturer in Media and Cultural Studies at the University of the West of England. Her research area is in television and she has explored both contemporary and historical programmes. Her published work includes material that explores the presentation of selfhood on TV talks shows, the representation of older women in television drama, images of mental illness as social critique. Recent research includes work on a project entitled 'No Such Thing as Society?' (http://www.nosuch-research.co.uk/) that examines shifting notions of the public across a range of broadcast material during the 1980s under the Thatcher governments, and she is an active participant in the Women, Ageing and Media (WAM) research group. (http://insight.glos.ac.uk/researchmainpage/centres/wam/Pages/default.aspx). Sherryl will be commencing research into the social use of second screens while watching television paying particular attention to the ways in which (if) older audiences engage with multi-platform viewing.